D0791150

Does All Begin with Consciousness?

Does All Begin with Consciousness?

(Some theoretical speculations)

Adam Atkin

iUniverse, Inc.
New York Lincoln Shanghai

Does All Begin with Consciousness?
(Some theoretical speculations)

Copyright © 2007 by Adam Atkin

All rights reserved. No part of this book may be used or reproduced by any means, graphic, electronic, or mechanical, including photocopying, recording, taping or by any information storage retrieval system without the written permission of the publisher except in the case of brief quotations embodied in critical articles and reviews.

iUniverse books may be ordered through booksellers or by contacting:

iUniverse
2021 Pine Lake Road, Suite 100
Lincoln, NE 68512
www.iuniverse.com
1-800-Authors (1-800-288-4677)

The views expressed in this work are solely those of the author and do not necessarily reflect the views of the publisher, and the publisher hereby disclaims any responsibility for them.

ISBN-13: 978-0-595-41529-8 (pbk)
ISBN-13: 978-0-595-85877-4 (ebk)
ISBN-10: 0-595-41529-6 (pbk)
ISBN-10: 0-595-85877-5 (ebk)

Printed in the United States of America

In fond memory of my very good friend and fellow-explorer—Jim Newman.

NEURONAL DISCOURSE REVERBERATES, ARGUING ...

Only where
          an inner mesh is reweaving
Itself
Can there be
          Consciousness.

The weave of wondering! There must be
Some kind of
     Wonder. Without surprise—anticipation of crashing—
     All my alertness lapses into
          Snores.

How can the mechanism
          remain open to
Rebirth?
Each instant requires
          Couplings.

Mind's life is not only machine. Every fixed
Rhythm has infinite
     Underbeats. Brain cannot be contained by our images.
     Neuronal fecundity creates generations of creation, in an
          Instant.

Therefore: This plant continually
          generates non-random
Newness!
Nothing else under my life
          Can.

From Atkin, A. (1991). *alarms and mirrors.* NY: Sea Tree Press (p. 162).

> Note: An **arrow** (➔) at the start of a *Table of Contents* heading indicates it is the title of an essay that *had originally been written to stand on its own as a separate piece.*

CONTENTS

ACKNOWLEDGEMENTS

It's certainly impossible to give complete attribution of my sources because they are everywhere and everything I've come from—all I've come *through*.

That said, I to wish to acknowledge, first of all, the *writers* who have especially guided and contributed to my understanding of self, world, and consciousness. I'm sure that much material that has importantly contributed to my understanding was read so long ago, and has since gone through so much digestion and other transformation, that the original sources are forgotten.

So I can mention several people whose writings have moved me and whose thoughts have entered my own—but I know I will unintentionally omit many others. For this I beg the forgiveness of those to whom I have not given due credit.

(1)   First I list a few I studied early and have known for a longer time: K.J.W. Craik; Arthur Koestler; Ulric Neisser; Paul Schilder; Irwin Schrödinger; Vigotsky; Alan Watts; Heinz Werner; Max Werthheimer; Norbert Wiener; Alfred North Whitehead; L.L. Whyte.

(2)   In the last 20-30 years or so I've discovered other highly creative people from whom I've been learning. Here I recall especially: Bernard Baars; Gregory Bateson; David Bohm; J. Bronowski's; K.J.W. Craik; G.M. Edelman; H. Flohr; Erich Jantsch; Arthur Koestler; Thomas Kuhn; E. Laszlo; H.R. Maturana; Ulric Neisser; Jim Newman; Maurice Nicoll; I. Prigogine; Israel Rosenfield; S. Ruddick; Paul Schilder; Irwin Schrödinger; Huston Smith; F. Varela; Manfred Clynes; P. Watzlawick; and Ken Wilber.

(A few names—such as K.J.W. Craik's, Arthur Koestler's, Ulric Neisser's, Paul Schilder's, Irwin Schrödinger's—appear in both lists because early acquaintance was more recently renewed on different terms.)

With many of these I've been pleasantly amazed to find certain of my central lines of creative thinking already set forth, and in some instances my seemingly "independent inventions" had already been expounded with great clarity and convincingness. Further, a few (e.g., Baars, Schrödinger, Smith, Bohm) had supported their insights with surprisingly convincing empirical evidence and scholarly research.

GREATEST, ONGOING APPRECIATIONS

From both my parents I learned to search for deeper understandings of world's and people's ways. Then, at Black Mountain College in the early 50's, I had the good fortune to be taken under the wing of physics professor Natasha Goldowski who encouraged me to gain awareness of many previously unquestioned assumptions—always till then taken to be totally *obvious*—so that I could begin to question them. I thank her deeply for her encouragement and support during those years.

Now, the growing peace of my last 30+ years I owe in very large part to my wise wife, Pearl—bright and forceful, open and generous. We play and fight, struggle to know each other, and to know ourselves. She protects and prods me. Our patience and our playfulness have grown with the years.

Our ways of supporting each other are very different, yet complementary—the fit of differences is beautiful! Differences often lead to pushings and pullings in seemingly conflicting directions. So we are able to wrestle together and thus to strengthen many otherwise little-used abilities. Teaching and learning often comes through these struggles, which—though they sometimes are acutely painful—we mostly enjoy.

We thank each other for our joining and consider ourselves very *fortunate to have found each other!* I am grateful for her compassion, patience, hard work, independent spirit, and for the vast enjoyment of her company. Now I am especially grateful for my chance to begin and pursue this work; her support in this has been one of the many beautiful gifts she has given me. (Most recently she took my "Fig. 1" line-drawing and colored it to make the book's cover.)

/~*~\/~*~\/~*~\/~*~\/~*~\/~*~\/~*~\/~*~\/~*~\/~*~\/~*~\/~*~\/~*~\/~*~\/~*~\/~*\/~

Finally, I wish also to thank Kirk Bromley for his many helpful prepublication editing suggestions.

/~*~\/~*~\/~*~\/~*~\/~*~\/~*~\/~*~\/~*~\/~*~\/~*~\/~*~\/~*~\/~*~\/~*~\/~*~\/~*\/~

===

Preface

On the Title

First, why have I named this book with that question: ***"Does All Begin with Consciousness?"*** The reason follows directly from the book's central thesis: That "consciousness is *creation*" and therefore "consciousness is primary"—may be origin of all. Here's what I mean:

- Assuming that world's structure is ... fundamentally holarchic, my ***continual creation (CC) metatheory of consciousness*** (Atkin 1992)[1] proposes that my holarchic mapping of this world-structure has arisen—is now arising—through self-organizing transformations that are identical with conscious awareness.[2]

- Awareness is the resolution of contradictions, creating greater order. Every kind of order involves relations of *coherence*. The meta-change that is experienced from within as conscious awareness tends, in balance, to increase net coherence and thereby to generate negentropy. Consciousness is likely to be life's most skillful means for negentropy generation. The negentropic changes of life (growth, evolution) reach their zenith of rapidity and complexity in consciousness.[3]

These speculations have excited me with their implications—some of which will be sketched in following sections. They are why the book's title is asking—***"Does All Begin with Consciousness?"***

What's to Follow

Now for more taste of what's to come I'll start at this book's very end. The following are the second and then the last two items of its final summary (of its ***"Main Points in Short"***):

(2) My *ignorance is inevitably vast yet invisible*. The dimensionality of my maps is necessarily limited because human cognitive capacities are limited. But if

---

1   ***Section 2*** is all about this (and see also the Glossary).
2   The book's very first essay (at the beginning of the immediately-following ***Introduction***) gives this as its second point.
3   From the next-to-last essay in ***Section 2***.

(as postulated) there is no upward limit to the dimensionality that would be required to exhaustively map the world's levels of order, then the existence of levels higher than any we can know or imagine is *undeniable*, and human generation of complete predictions is in principle beyond reach. This perspective can reconcile free will with determinism.

...

(9) Cartesian compartmentalization nevertheless intrudes everywhere because it generates, both individually and in society, an *addictive illusion of power*. It goes thus: I achieve some local control—control that may actually be tiny since enormous surrounding regions escape or even negate that control. Yet exactly because in this moment those non-controlled regions are almost entirely excluded from my attention, the tiny region of control that now fills my awareness is experienced as very large—an illusion I love and wish to preserve! Organizations and societies similarly treasure illusions of power.

(10) From an entropic perspective, *violence* is the rising entropy to which all mechanical systems (including unconscious mind) are subject; since the self-organizing change-of-mind that's postulated to be identical with consciousness tends to raise the overall coherence of the mind-world system, thereby lowering entropy, it follows that **to reduce violence, expand consciousness**.

Those paragraphs from the book's end give an idea the sorts of questions and arguments I will delve into—the kinds of complexity I'll be sorting out in ways that will (I hope) be of interest to you readers. Certainly that sorting out has been very important to me. For I feel those concluding points have relevance to the current state of our highly troubled world—though they are not answers, I hope they raise useful questions.

A GLANCE AT MY HISTORY

That's a little about where this book will be going—but how did I come to it?

This book zooms through learnings of my life—a quick scan of a larger perspective. For me it's been a wild ride—always full of surprises!

"What does it all *mean*? What's *really* going on here?" I'm sure every child has asked such questions—many adults keep on asking them. But others stop asking—either they think they've already got the answers, or they are diverted by *more important* tasks, or (most commonly) they are simply bored with the seeming pointlessness of asking the unanswerable.

I certainly never felt I'd found real answers to them, and also never got bored. I did get diverted for some long periods by a variety of seemingly *more important* tasks, but always came back to those bottomless questions—and sometimes even felt for a while that I was making progress with them.

I am very fortunate, I now believe, to have maintained through my adult life something of the strength of my childhood curiosities—fortunate in having kept with some intensity my hunger to *understand,* my desire to make sense of my life, of my existence—while at the same time having begun early to accept the inevitability of tremendous limitations to human understandings.

FIGURING IT OUT

So these writings do not so much propose answers as point to what, for me, were previously unrecognized problems. The further I probe into what I am doing, into what I am trying to do, the more clearly I see that *I know almost nothing* (**Section 1**, below), but that I have found some interesting questions. Some of these highlight the shaky underpinnings of my earlier "knowledge," as I will now try to briefly explain.

Born into a "non-religious" family, from my early years on I was a product of our modern age, convinced that scientific truth was the only *real* truth. Thus, I was a true believer of the new religion, *scientism.* Then in mid-life (practicing meditation and reading more widely) I was surprised to glimpse how this path might have some fundamental limitations—how it could be inevitable that limitless mysteries would always remain and how these might be of greatest importance. So eventually I was repelled by the narrowness and rigidity I perceived among those at the extremes of mechanistic materialism. I increasingly distrusted strictly reductionistic thinking, and positivism began to look suspiciously dogmatic. Thus, I came to see then how wisdom could not come without this *knowing that we do not know*—and knowing the unknowable vastness of our ignorance.

The puzzlement remains. My awareness and suspicion of self-assured ideologies (i.e., of the many "-isms!") has continued to grow—and my awareness of my ignorance (an acute awareness throughout my life) has been guiding me in attempts to *deconstruct* the deterministic worldview that had dominated my earlier attempts at understanding who and where I was.

I. Questions!

But—of particular pertinence to this book—I'm still as mystified as ever by that old question: *Who am I?* And more specifically I'm always asking myself: *How do I think? What is my conscious experience?*

Each of these is a double question. One aspect is general—is the quest for (abstract) explanations; another is specific—a quest for (concrete) descriptions and distinctions. I've been wanting to find both so I can better comprehend my own thought and experience—can know better "*what's going on here.*"

These questions are peculiarly difficult because of their intimately reflexive nature. *That which asks is simultaneously being asked about.* Nevertheless, highly tentative answers, arising more out of "intuition" than linear logic, will be suggested (*Sections 2* and *3* of this book). They are not answers in the usual sense but rather are really further development of questions—they are directions in which to look and ideas about how to look. For the further I probe into what I am here and now doing—and into what I am trying to do—the more clearly I see that I know almost nothing, but that I have indeed found some very interesting questions! Some of these call into question my earlier "knowledge."

Further, I've become more hopeful that I could eventually make some unifying *sense* out of the myriad contradictory messages always being given out by the "experts"—the "authorities." Certainly for most of my life I did well in keeping them conveniently compartmentalized (as our culture teaches) so their clashes should not disturb me too much. Yet their clashes did often disturb me—disturbance that has provided a main impetus for these writings.

II. Beginnings

Relatively early on in my education, as I got deeper into the study and practice of science I wanted more understanding of the variables and their units of measure that I was always dealing with. For a long while they were simply accepted as *unquestioned* building blocks of thought. But I hoped for some grasp of the most fundamental ways in which they could be defined.

Eventually something began to come—it was when (rather long ago, under my first teacher of love-with-understanding, Natasha Goldowski) I read the physicist Percy Bridgman (Bridgman 1927, 1950) and learned about *operational definitions* and *dimensional analysis* of variables. What revelations!

And much later, just in the past few years, as I've been developing my view of the *holarchic* structure of ourselves in our world (Koestler 1978; Wilber 1997)[4], I have begun to see the deep relevance of ideas about dimensional analysis for this multi-level conceptual system.

Further, in looking at relations between different kinds of knowledge and different realms of experience, I've been taken by the pertinence of Ken Wilber's ideas on the four quadrants of knowledge (Wilber 1983, 1997) and on the principles by which these very different kinds of *knowing* can each be given strong validation. I see how his ways of expounding those understandings relate quite naturally to what I had long before been excited about immediately after I'd been introduced to Percy Bridgman's (1927, 1950) thoughts about *operational definitions*. For the manner in which Ken Wilber validates the truths of his four (very separate yet intimately connected) realms is exactly through specifying the manner by which they are all to be defined *operationally*.

Thus I've attempted to gain some clearer intellectual understanding of the human predicament—of my personal predicament here in this strange life, this strange world! That *knowing of the mind* has come hard with only a small result so far. But there's also a *knowing of the heart* which is even more mysterious to me, and in which my beginning is even more modest.

Beyond yet including both of those is that pervasive, ubiquitous *knowing* that permeates life yet may easily be kept so inappropriately apart from those other kinds of *knowing*—the knowing of my own *being* and of other *beings*. Who am I? Who are you? And how, actually, are we (or are we not) in connection with each other?

GROWING UP

My father was a psychoanalyst, and this intensified at an early age my curiosity about the nature of relationship, the workings of people's intentions and motivations—and later my desire to better understand the structure and dynamics of their minds and emotions. I wanted to understand where I was and how to guide myself. My mother was an artist—a painter; my early and sustained wonderments about vision came partly from her.

Also, for a while in adolescence I experienced depression (during and after their divorce) and afterwards noticed tremendous shifts in the clarity, vividness, vitality of my perceptions as my mood lifted.

---

4   Discussed below, in **Section 1** "Closed and Open Worldviews"; also (in **Summing Up** section near end of book) in "➔ Being, Doing, Knowing—A Theoretical Perspective on Consciousness".

From my two parents I imbided highly conflicting worldviews, seeking with some small success to accommodate them both within myself. Consequently in early adolescence I became very interested in perceptual mechanisms and how they were modulated with shifts in level of *arousal*. I became interested also in spatial *orientation*—in how living organisms navigated and kept track of where they were and what was around them.

For nearly two years (1958-1959) I worked as laboratory assistant to Manfred Clynes helping with evoked potential and autonomic response (pupil reflex) studies of the series that eventually led to development of his sentic cycler methodology for evoked emotional responses (Clynes 1969).

Ultimately I became a neurophysiologist, trying to learn something about the brain's control over movement as it related to the perception by a moving organism of a stable world. I set up a laboratory in the neurology department of a medical center to study such phenomena in patients with CNS/brain pathology and was co-principal investigator of the research program.

I. Getting Into It

After I got into that laboratory research my behavioral studies on human *orienting* behavior (Atkin 1967, 1969) yielded patterns of motion that could not be accounted for by any of the then-studied theories of motor control. I was led to postulate that the human sensori-motor apparatus must control movement (specifically movements of the head and eyes) by *first* "executing" the movement in *simulation*—that is, by shifting, slightly in advance of the real movement, an inner model. This inner model was assumed to include all the essential dynamics that the directing neural systems had to take into account to execute the desired movement with precision and with the desired result. (For eye movements, this meant an inner model not only of the surrounding environment but also of the eye-head dynamic system that included musculoskeletal mechanics: specifically, contraction properties of muscles as well as the eye's elastic and viscous resistances to rotation, etc.)

This dynamic inner model of self-and-world is my "virtual reality"—and the implication of this, of course, is that this virtual reality is my only reality. Soon, I applied such ideas to other brain functions: not only to other aspects of how an organism maintained orientation in space during exploratory behavior and locomotion, but also to the essential dynamics of language, speech comprehension, and reading.

And especially, I have in many ways been fascinated by *time*—not merely the particulars of a certain shifting in position and orientation but the rhythms and velocities of the shift. These, it seemed to me, were not being adequately studied.

For the situations we constructed and controlled in the laboratory were simplified and repeatable, but those which we experience in life are much more complex—each instance unique, at least in details. Thus the temporal profile of the living organism's action must be correspondingly unique.

But unique how? What is the brain's inner logic by which this unique action is accomplished? What are the various kinds of temporal framework for the brain's informational transactions? The inner life is abuzz with a million simultaneous conversations—what are they talking about? How is some requisite synchrony ensured? I tried to find ways to study such questions.

Then I was introduced to the practice and theory of meditation—first "transcendental meditation" (TM) and soon after Zen Buddhism. Meditation not only helped me to cope with the stress I was sometimes under but also stirred a desire to broaden and deepen my *consciousness* while bringing glimpses of alternative perspectives on the brain's workings. Again (as since childhood) the biggest questions were the most ordinary. (Certainly, many *seekers* went through such changes in the '60s and '70s!)

II. Beliefs and Explorations

And that's how it is now as I sit in thought, writing. I'm wanting to grasp the biology of my present-moment awareness—to get more clear about my place and process here in each moment. Isn't this an excitement of the most intimate kind of biology possible? For again, the observed phenomena are identical with the observer—a kind of reflexive complexity that has come more and more into the awareness of scientists of many specialties (notably quantum physics). What now is actually going on with this observer—with the conscious being who is here observing?

In mid-century, according to the worldview that I'd maintained for most of my life, such questions were almost improper! They were not an acceptable field of investigation. Since I was raised and trained a modern science-intoxicated rationalist, I'd accepted this faith (of reductionism and logical positivism) enthusiastically—and was guided by it in my studies and my rejections.

Nevertheless more recently others have also become more interested in enlarging worldviews. Two forces especially—the "cognitive revolution" and the siren-song of "artificial intelligence"—have been driving a renewed scientific and philosophical interest in the foundations of consciousness. Mechanisms of mind are receiving increasing attention.

So finally I started to look at ways in which these inner processes could *work* and at some wider implications of alternative approaches to them. Also, in my concern with sources of (and possible remedies for) human violence on many scales, I began to glimpse connections with another, seemingly separate twenti-eth-century endemic urban problem—that of "substance abuse" or "addiction." What underlies addictions? There are, I begin to see, factors that cannot be dealt with by biochemists or pharmacologists, and that probably are not reducible in a helpful way to patterns mediated by neurotransmitters and neuromodulators, etc. (not, at least, in the way that this has usually been attempted). For it's clear how this is a far wider phenomenon than it's seemed—how we've *all* been deeply indoctrinated with automatic attention-strategies that narrow our consciousness in *addictive* ways.

I am still fascinated by these puzzles. I want to know *where* and *what* and *who* I am. What is my consciousness? What is under my control? And who is the *"I"* I'm asking about? I know I have no secure, rigorous answers. But at least I am devel-oping a vocabulary of stories and images for thinking through the questions.

HOW (AND WHY) AM I DOING IT?

For the past couple of decades since my retirement from laboratory research and diagnostic testing I've been studying these questions as best I could, both by reading and by writing. Most of my writings have been essays—usually about 5 or 10 pages long but some up to 30 or 40. This work now of attempting to organize these materials into larger sequences—to give them, together, some "unity"—tells me that though I have written quite a lot and have published scientific papers, I have never before attempted anything like this and therefore am a complete ama-teur at it.

Nevertheless I've lately been making real efforts to attain some readable larger structure. One movement in this task that sustains my interest in it is a kind of "time-weaving." As I recall the sources of various thoughts in these essays, I find that I am knitting together themes from many different phases of my life—that I am going back to early questions and confronting them with later learnings. I am recalling some early insights that had been jotted down and then forgotten in the rush of current demands for performance. This is very interesting and encourages me that I am writing up a kind of summary of my whole life's development. I feel now that finally I've achieved some continuity and unification—have gotten my materials together into an organization which feels appropriate to me. A first glimpse of this can be had by going to the summary of "**Book-Structure**" at the end of the just-following *Introduction*.

INTRODUCTION

As mentioned in the preface, this book is essentially an anthology of my previous writings.[1] Central pieces in it are longer essays—presentations at the Tucson conferences "Toward a Science of Consciousness"[2]—which expounded and discussed theoretical speculations regarding consciousness as part of an overall worldview. They were speculative theorizing at a high level of abstraction, dealing with issues of psycho-philosophy and meta-psychology that have been closest to my heart.

Now look back at the *Table of Contents:*

- Note that these conference presentations and other earlier essays are marked by an **arrow** (➔) preceding their titles. Each such essay can be read as a separate piece, though I have, of course, done my best to put each within the flow of the whole book. The essays have generally been left in their original form, though there has been some editing here and there for brevity and clarity.

- Also, because my terminology may sometimes be tricky to a new reader of these essays—since several terms are either my inventions or are old terms which I've been using in special and somewhat unconventional ways—I advise the reader to please take a look at the *Glossary* at the back of the book and then to refer to it again frequently and freely.

The progression goes from foundational issues (**Section 1**) to presentation of my metatheory of consciousness (**Section 2**) to consideration of some of its implications and consequences (**Section 3** and **Summing up**). Further, **Sections 1-3** also consider relations of the author's theoretical position to those of several other scholars, theorists, philosophers—including Searle, Dennett, Churchland, Chalmers, Baars, Skinner, Tani.

Basically, the main arguments and explanations are implications of what are assumed to be two fundamental features of our world: (1) That *our world is thoroughly holarchic in structure*; and (2) that *most (if not all) structure is subject to self-organizing transformation*. Given that these are at bottom consistent with contemporary scientific knowledge and methodology—as I believe they are—then what's being presented should likewise be acceptable within that worldview.

---

1   They are given here almost exactly as originally written. Here and there some editing has been done to improve clarity and/or readability (and the uniformity of terminologies), but with no important changes in the structure of presentation or in the ideas presented.

2   Atkin 1994, 1996, 1998.

The main themes and intentions of this book were concisely set out in an essay written in 2005:

→ Consciousness, Holarchy, Negentropy— Three attributes of ONE Transcendent Ongoing Event?

Can I begin to *tie **everything** together?* I've opened myself to a *metatheoretical* stance by which "Consciousness, Holarchy, Negentropy" determine all we know (and, I believe, can ever know). It affirms the hypothesis—long discarded by conventional Western Science—that **consciousness is primary, is the origin of all** (at least, of **all** my understanding). Of course, in a consciousness book that's how I begin—with consciousness. *But maybe, too, that's how **all** begins!* For the root assumption is that *consciousness is ongoing emergent self-organization* (Atkin 1992).[3] Then:

1) Evolving deterministic structure can be mapped as a sequence of ever-more-inclusive levels—a "holarchy" of "holons" (Koestler 1978; Wilber 1997) rising as an endless progression (see essay below in *Sect. 1*, "→The Restriction of Ignorance").

2) Assuming that world's structure is thus fundamentally holarchic, my **continual creation (CC) metatheory of consciousness** (Atkin 1992)[4] proposes that my holarchic mapping of this world-structure has arisen—is now arising—through self-organizing transformations that are identical with conscious awareness.

3) This thrust of CC metatheory is consistent with other major consciousness theories—especially the Global Workspace model of Bernard Baars (1988, 1997). *Both* theories postulate that "consciousness always involves adaptation, [implying] ... an intimate connection between conscious experience and all kinds of adaptive processes, including comprehension, learning, and problem solving" (Baars 1988, p. 213).[5]

---

3 This is the essay "→On Consciousness: What is the Role of Emergence?" near the beginning of *Section 2*. On the same themes see also in that section the essays "→Conscious Beyond Mechanism" (Atkin 1994) and "→Reflections on Order and Disorder."

4 *Section 2* is all about this (and see also the Glossary).

5 *Section 3* essay (below) "→The Primacy of Self-Organizing Structural Transformation" compares Baars' (1988) GW theory with CC metatheory.

I hope our current paradigms are open to those understandings. Though deterministic science is focused upon stable systems of lawfulness, there is increasing attention to the self-organizing generation of more complex systems with new and higher systems of lawfulness. If such creation is identical with sentience, then indeed sentience will be everywhere, intertwined with the better-recognized *mechanisms* of matter—sentience will be the origin of *new* mechanism, emerging as mechanistic matter *evolves*.[4]

Such sentience will have many levels, but human sentience is all we know directly.

4) CC metatheory proposes that in our consciousness (and that of other higher animals) the main inner structure that is thus re-organizing itself is the organism's dynamic (predictive) internal model of itself-in-its-world (Atkin 1992; Craik 1943; Kawato, Furukawa, and Suzuki 1987)—an evolving virtual machine (Dennett 1991; Sloman & Chrisley 2003) that is the ongoing product of the brain's neural networks (Edelman 1989; Flohr 1991; Hebb 1949; Kawato, Furukawa, and Suzuki 1987). This dynamic map—to be labeled the organism's ***"Anticipating self-world model"* or A[sw]**[G]—anticipates the organism's actions and predictively generates controlling feedback (*"virtual* feedback") which is derived from SIMULATION *of the activity and effects of the organism's own action systems.*

The A[sw] model's predictions are continually tested, its structure then modifying itself to compensate for discrepancies so as to make subsequent predictions more accurate. These ongoing accommodative changes in the organism's Anticipating self-world model generate its conscious awareness (Atkin 1992).[6]

5) The causal efficacy of consciousness can thus be understood anew, as can the relations of conscious to unconscious process—and that *"hard"* problem of recent consciousness discussions simply evaporates![7]

G   See this entry in *Glossary*.

6   This is the second essay in *Section 2* (but other essays of *Section 2* and *Section 3* are also pertinent.)

7   Chalmers' "hard" problem dealt with at the beginning of *Section 3* in the essay "→ Finding the Beginning: Consciousness Precedes Theories" was there introduced as follows: "Chalmers (1995)…suggests 'that a theory of consciousness should take experience as fundamental,' saying: 'We know that a theory of consciousness *requires the **addition** of something* fundamental to our ontology, as everything in physical theory is compatible with the absence of consciousness' (p. 14—emphasis added)."

Consequently, Chalmers' (1995) somewhat dualistic solution to the *"hard"* problem becomes superfluous.

6) Further, since the meta-change that now is consciousness tends, in balance, to increase world's net coherence, thereby *generating negentropy*, it follows that at upper regions of system complexity, consciousness may be entropy's principle sink—life's most skillful means for negentropy generation.

7) Violence is a manifestation of decaying order—of the rise in entropy to which all mechanical systems are subject. Unconscious mind—a vast network of automatisms—cannot escape such degradation.

8) Counter-movement, generating higher and more integrated levels of order, entails the transformation of that network. Since (by CC metatheory) this negentropy-generating emergence of new structure *is consciousness*, it follows that **to reduce violence, increase consciousness**.

What needs to be recognized is that Cartesian compartmentalization nevertheless intrudes everywhere because it generates, both individually and in society, an *addictive illusion of power*. We are all victims of conditioned cognitive strategies that fragment our consciousness. We close off our queries by *willful* neglect of contextual questions, thus simplifying our awareness. We thereby gain both security and dreams of power. That is, we enlarge our apparent power through inattention to all that shows its smallness and ineffectiveness (the *addictive illusion of power*).

But some understanding of this can begin to open our consciousness. (Big surprise then is total uniqueness everywhere![8]) May it be that (over long human history) many varied threads of logical reasoning and intuitive insight have led to pointers toward this single direction—the direction of *unbounded holarchic progression?* It seems that an amazing variety of religious and spiritual teachings have this intention.

\:/\|/\:/\|/\:/\|/\:/\|/\:/\|/\:/\|/\:/\|/\:/\|/\:/\|/\:/\|/\:/\|/\:/

---

8   As may be experienced with expansion of consciousness (e.g. deep meditation)—and it's an implication of CC metatheory that "every conscious moment is the creation of a new and unique structure of lawfulness" (see essay "➔ Retrospect on 'Path'" at start of *Section 2*)

\|/oOo\|/oOo\|/oOo\|/oOo\|/oOo\|/oOo\|/oOo\|/oOo\|/oOo\|/oOo\|/oOo\|/

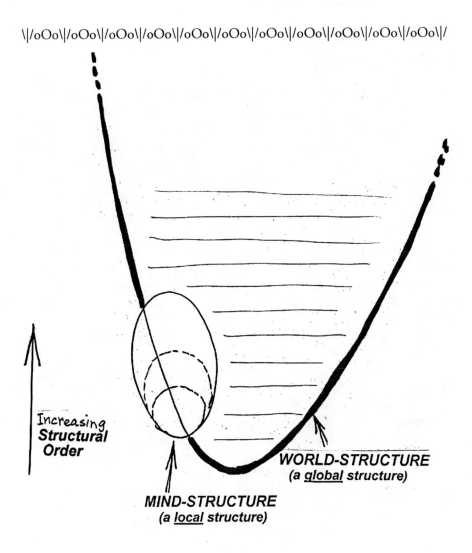

FIGURE 1. *World-Structure and Mind-Structure*
(An Unimaginable 'Size' Disparity):

Please see next page for full caption to this figure.

FIGURE 1. MIND-STRUCTURE AND WORLD-STRUCTURE (AN UNIMAGINABLE "SIZE" DISPARITY):

Since there is no evidence of any limit to the upwards progression of world's structural levels, for parsimony we will not make the unwarranted assumption that this is a closed series. Rather, the Fundamental Holarchic Assumption of a conceptually **open** world is indicated in the diagram by the parabola labeled "*WORLD-STRUCTURE*." It opens upwards, growing larger and larger without limit …

In contrast, the **structure**^{G} of **mind**^{G} is presumed to be finite (though of course enormously complex). It is therefore represented here by a **closed** outline—the ellipse labeled "*MIND-STRUCTURE*." The presumption is that this mind-structure is a virtual machine that is *simulating* region(s) of world-structure. But the central point here is that the simulation is necessarily **partial**. For if mind-structure is closed, it can simulate no more than a part (a relatively tiny part!) of an open, unending world-structure. Specifically, the assertion is that mind-structure entrains only some of the lower (though not the lowest) levels of world-structure.[9] (Further, inevitably some of mind-structure will actually correspond to nothing in world-structure; such regions are represented by parts of the oval completely outside of the parabola.)

As discussed in the text the effective expanse of a mind is often made still smaller.[10] This can happen in various ways—the two ways discussed are (a) **segmenting**^{G} *strategies of attention* and (b) *worldview* **closure**.^{G} In these ways the size (and thus predictive power) of any particular mind-structure can be still further contracted beneath its very modest "optimum." Such contractions are represented in the diagram by the smaller dotted ellipses within the larger one.

<< Drawing by A. Atkin. >>

\|/oOo\|/oOo\|/oOo\|/oOo\|/oOo\|/oOo\|/oOo\|/oOo\|/oOo\|/oOo\|/oOo\|/

G   See this entry in **Glossary**.

9   Since *world*-structure is presumed to be one single whole system that is of vast extent, and (still more crucial) is of *unlimited dimensionality*, we can designate world-structure as **global** structure. While the *mind*-structure that here concerns us is that of one particular, 'individual' mind of a single organism who is one of many; therefore we can consider a particular mind-structure to be **local**. (See "Local vs. Global" in **Glossary**.)

10   See **Section 1** essay "➔The Restriction of Ignorance: Inverting the Principle of Parsimony" especially subsection III ("Open or Closed")—and see also the last part of the last essay in **Section 2**, "➔Reflections on Order and Disorder."

G   See this entry in **Glossary**.

\:/\|/\:/\|/\:/\|/\:/\|/\:/\|/\:/\|/\:/\|/\:/\|/\:/\|/\:/\|/\:/\|/\:/\|/\:/\|/\:/

>>Book-Structure

The sequence of book-sections proceeds thus:

Section 1 opens up certain fundamental worldview issues as underpinnings for the consciousness presentations to follow; first discusssing implications of our world's totally-holarchic, open-ended substructure, then explaining why we should use the Principle of Parsimony not only conventionally but also to banish needless and overly broad *simplifications*—and how this has relevance to limitations of reductionist science.

Section 2 explores evocative questions about consciousness from a monist perspective, pointing towards observables that are not object-like and kinds of change that are non-mechanical. This leads toward understanding consciousness as *meta-change* identical to creation. The essays (i) propose that what's re-organizing itself is the organism's *dynamic (predictive) internal model* of itself-in-its-world; (ii) examine reasons why this "continual creation" (CC) metatheory of consciousness has generally not been "self-evident;" then (iii) elaborate the means by which conscious re-organizing is postulated to work; (iv) begin to discuss implications (especially for *the evolution of mind* and for *entropy-levels in life-systems*) of this view of consciousness; and (v) end with neurophysiological speculations.

Section 3 begins with discussion of the consciousness *"hard"* problem in relation to CC metatheory; then shows how that metatheory relates to two other theories of consciousness; and finishes by presenting some of the metatheory's social and ethical implications.

Finally the **Summing Up** section does just that, ending with these main points that had been made in preceding sections:

> World's basic structure is best mapped holarchically^G in a way that yields downward causation as tautological necessity.

> If (as postulated) there is no upward limit to the dimensionality that would be required to exhaustively map the world's levels of order then (since human cognitive capacities are limited) the existence of levels higher than any we can know or imagine is *undeniable*—so that my *ignorance is vast yet invisible*.

> My *mind* is a holarchic system of dynamic *maps* that *anticipate* my actions and their consequences, predicting aspects of world structure that relate to my perceptions, actions, intentions. Mind's overall struc-

ture is determined in large part by its belief system, that is shaped largely by systems of *presuppositions*.

CC metatheory postulates that consciousness is the reconstruction of these anticipatory maps, thereby continually increasing the dynamic, predictive coherence of the mapping system with the mapped system and producing higher levels of order—thus *consciousness is creating syntropy*.

My *freedom* arises from those self-organizing transformations that (by CC metatheory) **are** my consciousness, and is further amplified when (through downward causation) my choice is determined from a higher level than the ordinary compulsions that are predictively modeled by my unconscious anticipatory automatisms.

Though mind's overall structure is determined in large part by its belief system shaped largely by systems of *presuppositions*, yet unconscious mind's many substructures or *context hierarchies* (Baars 1988) are almost entirely inaccessible to our awareness—which knows nearly nothing, explicitly, about our systems of presuppositions.

The *open* person (or culture) is parsimonious of *simplifications* and *maximizes* attention to *context* (Hall 1976); therefore those people form the group of "context-maximizers." The *closed* person (or culture) is parsimonious of *complications*—thus tending towards many locally-attending simplifications—and *minimizes* attention to *context*; such people can be thought of as forming the group of "context-minimizers."

But such local simplifications lessen the unity of overall cognitive structure. And disunified cognitive structure perpetuates the very disunified attention-strategies by which such mind-architecture arises and is sustained.

Cartesian compartmentalization nevertheless intrudes everywhere because it generates, both individually and in society, an *addictive illusion of power*. Local control can *seem* large because non-controlled regions are almost entirely excluded from awareness—organizations and societies treasure resulting illusions of power.

From an entropic perspective, *violence* is the rising entropy to which all mechanical systems (including unconscious mind) are subject; since consciousness tends to lower entropy, it follows that **to reduce violence, expand consciousness**.

>>NOTE TO READERS

Now a few words to readers with special areas of interest. Although I hope you may gain from reading the whole book, certainly it might be good to go first to that section which speaks most directly to your deepest concerns. For pertinent information, thoughts and insights concerning:

- A larger framework for viewing scientific and other theoretical structures, with possibilities and arguments for paradigm-shifts—go first to **Section 1**.

- Consciousness theories, mental development, brain-mind questions—go first to **Section 2** (but see paragraphs below).

- Causes and cures for social and environmental destructiveness, ways of conflict resolution—go to later essays of **Section 3** and of the **Summing Up** section.

Note however that if you are particularly interested in consciousness theories, mental development and/or brain-mind questions, then before you jump over **Section 1** you might consider this: Reading **Section 1** *first* can prepare the way for **Section 2** by explaining the need for openness to theoretical paths *beyond* the usual mechanistic assumptions of our conventional *scientism*. (But if you're already open to such paths then you can go straight to **Section 2**.)

Note also that essays in Sections 2 and 3 suggest available and/or potential sources of support for the proposed consciousness theory, the "CC metatheory."[11]

---

11 See especially the subsection "Directions for Further Work" of the last essay in **Section 2**, "➜Reflections on Order and Disorder"; and note also that close parallels with Baars' (1998) theory of consciousness (discussed in **Section 3** essay "➜The Primacy of Self-Organizing Structural Transformation") imply that much of the empirical support he's found for his theory also supports the CC metatheory.

/~*~\/~*~\/~*~\/~*~\/~*~\/~*~\/~*~\/~*~\/~*~\/~*~\/~*~\/~*~\/~*~\/~*~\/~*~\/

>>PREVIEW OF SECTION 1 (CLOSED AND OPEN WORLDVIEWS)

The first section opens with a short essay written in 1998, entitled "➔Thoughts on The Progression of Paradigms." Different *paradigms* seem to lead us into quite contrasting views (maps) of our world and ourselves, but the differences may not be as deep and total as they seem. Each may convey valuable truths in what it *asserts*—making, however, some errors of overgeneralization in what it *denies*. (This goes for *scientism*, which has made negative assertions that its approved methods of testing cannot test.)

A paradigm's positive assertions are those which raise the level of order (increase negentropy) of the map it is generating, while the negative assertions lower them.

Second (immediately after a brief piece with several defining quotations from Koestler [1967] on "The Way the Idea of 'Levels' is Being Used") is a short essay written in 2005, entitled "➔Minimalist Basis for Expanding Understanding." It presents the fundamental insight—on our world's totally-holarchic, open-ended substructure—that undergirds most of what's discussed in the following essays.

Third is an essay (put together in 2005-06 for this book) entitled "➔On Free Will, Holarchic Structure and Downward Causation."[12] It presents an alternative to the contemporary deterministic view of human behavior (and that of most of the psychiatric world) which makes free choice (free will) an illusion, denying the reality of personal responsibility. The perspective presented here says that yes, we are mechanisms; but takes exception to the claim of the completeness of this view, denying we can know that we are *nothing but* mechanisms. The relation of free will to downward causation is explained, then something is clarified about the nature of downward causation, and a differentiation between two kinds of downward causation is proposed. Finally, it's noted how *non-algorithmic causality* may be understood as a manifestation of downward causality.

The fourth essay (written 1994)—entitled "➔The Restriction of Ignorance: Inverting the Principle of Parsimony (with comment on Searle)"—presents another but related insight pertinent to how knowledge is gained and evaluated. It is an alternative view on the Principle of Parsimony (also called "Occam's Razor"),

---

12 It incorporates some material taken from later essays in this book—e.g., from "➔Being, Doing, Knowing" in **Summing Up** section. (And it forms part of a longer essay entitled "➔Freedom and Responsibility," to be published elsewhere.)

a methodological principle of philosophy commonly used to banish "needless" *complexity*—to restrict the introduction of explanatory hypotheses beyond strict necessity. It is here suggested that this same Principle should also be used to banish needless and overly broad *simplifications*. For a theory can be likened to a map, and any *closed-minded* hypothesis that implies the complete correctness and adequacy of a map (or of a method for generating maps) everywhere outside of those regions in which its correctness and adequacy either have been tested or can now be tested is to be discarded by the criterion of parsimony.

The fifth essay (written in 1997) is entitled "→**Some Thoughts on Reductionism, Mechanism, and Determinism, re Searle, Dennett, and Churchland**." We think that now—using our proven methods of empirical research—we're moving towards explaining everything. But if I assume that the complexity of my cognitive models *completely* represents the complexity of that which is modeled, I will necessarily be unaware of most of the ways in which my cognitive models "fall short." In the alternative, open worldview, the organizational levels of our most elaborate, precise, and creative thoughts form just a very tiny region of a vast spectrum of still-unknown organizational levels—a *limitless* expanse of infinite extension.

Finally, the sixth and last essay in this first section (written in 1991) is entitled simply "→**Closing and Opening**," and it concerns not only the meanings I'd found for "closure" as a shorthand way to describe all kinds of intellectual fundamentalisms, but also my discovery that I'd been discovering "post-modernism" as I learned and embraced "non-closure."

/~*~\/~*~\/~*~\/~*~\/~*~\/~*~\/~*~\/~*~\/~*~\/~*~\/~*~\/~*~\/~*~\/~*~\/~*~\/

Section 1: Closed and Open Worldviews

Well now, what about the prevalence of disagreement and conflict everywhere? Is that about belief in "… isms" and irrational negations? How exactly can broader attention and greater openness bring us toward resolutions? Concerning this question, here first is a previously unpublished paper, completed in 1998:

→ *Thoughts on*
The Progression of Paradigms
I. A Wonderfully Broad Hypothesis

In looking over writings on the history of ideas about consciousness, I have tried to see some sequence of developing, evolving answers to a very few old and fundamental questions—and have been, I'm afraid, singularly unsuccessful! But an interesting idea has occurred to me, and I've been playing with it for a while. (Of course, when I see it from the perspective of tight arguments, I must admit that it's not very clear, that it's really a "way out" conjecture—but I'll present it anyway, in hopes it will be interesting). Here it is:

A. Affirming and Denying (Additions and Subtractions)

One of my favorite thoughts about disparate theories, specialized ideologies, and conflicting paradigms is that almost all of them are *right* in some way(s). I've been trying to see and put together disparate perspectives in that way for a long time. More recently, I've come to the following notion: That in fact the proponents of those warring perspectives are all saying valuable truths in what they *assert* positively and specifically (concretely) about our being, the world and our relations to it, but they are making errors primarily in what they each *deny*—more specifically, in their denials of the truths pointed to by the other paradigms.

So, in short, the idea is to look for both the *positive* and the *negative* assertions in each point of view—where by "positive" I mean suggestions of truth-value, of validity, of connectedness, interrelatedness and cooperativity; and by "negative" I mean claims (usually directed at *other* viewpoints) of falsity and invalidity, of opposition or independence, of disconnectedness.

The idea, then, is that a *positive* assertion simply says that something occurs or has occurred, but it is a claim without boundaries—what happens outside of

12

the region of which it speaks is wide open. Nothing is said, one way or the other, about those regions beyond that referred to in the assertion; only, something *positive* is asserted about occurrences *within* that region. And that is all.

In that way a positive assertion expands the image of the *real*—its extent, its duration, its dimensionality. It makes new connections. In contrast, a *negative* assertion denies the possibility or existence or truth of some possible (implied) positive assertion. It constricts the image of the *real*—lessens its dimensionality.

Therefore a key idea here is that the meanings of such overconfident terms/ ideas as "always," "never," "totally separate," "completely independent," "absolute," "unchanging," and so forth must incorporate something fundamentally *negative*. The assertion *"never!"* is of course purely negative; within the realm about which the assertion is made the 'x' happening does not occur—and further, any (imaginable) region in which it would occur has had its existence denied. It is non-existent, *unreal*.

B. These Components of Other Common Generalizations

But some assertions may consist of both a positive and a negative claim in combination. "Always" (opposite, of course, of "never") asserts not only that events of type x *are* to be found within region Z (the positive, affirming assertion), but that parts of region Z that do not contain event x *do not exist* (the doubly-negative, denying assertion).

Assertions that the situation (or some larger system—the total universe, the *absolute*) is *"unchanging,"* then, can be understood as simply expansions or generalizations of "always" and "never"; everything in the situation which is "unchanging" is *always* there, and every possible occurrence in the situation which could bring change is *never* there. Thus if saying "never" negates the kind of event to which it refers, the "unchanging" attribution then broadens this negation to include every event that may constitute *change*.

But what about claims frequently made that objects or phenomena of category A and those of category B are "separate," "unrelated," "independent?" Aren't there patterns of denial similar to those above (to those just described for "unchanging") in the assertions of "absolute" disconnection and difference which seem to be implied by such claims? Here the restricted, locally-negative assertion that similarities, relations or interconnections between A and B are not to be found within some particular region of observation is accompanied by the unrestricted, globally-negative assertion that any other imaginable regions of observation within which such similarities, relations or interconnections would occur are regions which don't exist—which have no reality.

This kind of examination may then help us to see such negating patterns more clearly in the evolution of philosophies of mind and consciousness. Let's start with the confidence, in Neo-Platonist philosophy and Descartes, of a *fundamental split* between mind and body. Now, it's clear that there are positive assertions about consciousness in the recognition of the reality and great value of certain of its components—of "rational mind"—and in recognition also that this crucial aspect of our reality is not limited to and cannot (in any simple, direct and immediate way) be accounted for by the structures and workings of "material body"—especially as these were held to be totally *mechanistic*; that is, deterministically explainable by the principles and laws of machines.

Certainly, those positive assertions were valuable contributions to our understanding. But then, it seems, there was a hunger for further simplification, and this was gained by adding a confidently overextended *denial*. For the key negative assertion was to see this "going beyond" (of *mind* and *awareness* going beyond *body*, beyond *matter*) as complete disconnection, as independence.

II. Can "Scientism" Hold?

Then we have Newtonian physics and the "clockwork universe." Yes, certainly Newton's laws portrayed a beautiful *clockwork* aspect of how things work in those regions of our perception and comprehension that had been explored by the celestial observers. Describing this clockwork precision, and attributing it to those well-observed aspects of our universe, was a *positive* assertion—and apparently quite true as far as it went in the positive direction, within its range of applicability. It was a wonderful accomplishment of human thought-powers—of Cartesian "systematic doubting"—analyzing or reducing a problem to resolvable parts and intuiting wonderfully simple logical, mathematical relationships between them.

A. Negative Assertions Far Beyond the Evidence (Beyond Any Possible Evidence)

But the *negative* assertion implicit in the "clockwork universe" worldview was that ultimately there would be *nothing* that could not be explained in similar ways, by totally deterministic mechanical laws. That is, the implicit negative assertion was that the (potential) region that would be beyond the bounds of the explicit positive assertion was necessarily *non-existent*. Its existence was very confidently denied, though there could be no evidence that would scientifically back up such denial.

To see how this went, let's now take a quick look at a specific example that relates to our current epidemic of "scientism." Consider the following common presupposition:

"For every phenomena of interest there is (or will be) an adequate mathematical representation (AMR)."

But notice! This assertion really has *two* components:

Positive assertion: A wide range of phenomena have (or potentially can have) an AMR.

Negative assertion: *All* phenomena (potentially) have an AMR. That is, there *are no* phenomena of interest that cannot and will not eventually have an AMR—they do not (and will never) exist.

This, clearly, is the common "nothing-but" syndrome. Those who have found an answer to some problem that has dominated their efforts for a long while seem to love, when they have finally arrived at a solution that satisfies them, to believe that this solution is, potentially, the answer to *every* other problem! It happens over and over again. To illustrate:

Has explanation E_1 seemed to account for the phenomena of problem P_1? Well good! Then quite obviously it will also account for all phenomena P_n of a wonderfully extended field of happenings—they are all "***nothing but***" E_1.

And then, for some broader kinds of theories, such as classical physics, and more recently quantum mechanics, it may be very tempting to conclude that there is nothing but P_n, and that this all-encompassing P_n is therefore *nothing but* the consequences of that beautiful theory, E_1.

So again, "nothing but" means that *all* regions outside those of the (often highly beautiful and valuable) *positive* assertion have been completely *denied* the possibility of existence.

And usually such an arbitrary "nothing but" is assumed to be an end-point—a *final* conclusion that is obviously true forever and will never be transcended! The originators of each new worldview seem to assume, automatically and thus unconsciously, that the changes that they are struggling first to unfold for themselves and then to persuasively bring to others are somehow a new *end-state* of human cognitive development, and should totally replace the old one. Now that idea is fine—but what seems to commonly accompany it is a lack of any recognition that this transition is simply a fore-runner of an endless progression of possible future transitions, so that it is just as tentative, temporary, limited, and eventually replaceable as what came before.

Thus all of these past and contemporary "isms"—*idealism, rationalism, empiricism, scientism*, etc.—have wrought wonderful *simplifications* of ourselves and our place in this world we inhabit and/or construct.[1] This simplification has been accomplished, in large part, through banishment—or at least vast contraction to near-insignificance—of our recognition and awareness of that which we are not yet able to express or explain.

Now, here is where we can see how negative assertions may not be out-and-out false, but only *highly overgeneralized*. For certainly it's true that there is a very great deal that—though now seeming beyond explanation—will nevertheless be ultimately explainable through application of reductionistic methods via the derivation of appropriate mechanical laws. Thus regions of ultimate ("forever!") inexplicability—where there might be such—will undoubtedly be far smaller than our now-known region of present-moment inexplicability. But to totally deny the existence of regions of mechanistically unexplainable phenomena—rather than merely contracting them—cannot be supported by any conceivable kind of evidence.

So our present paradigm seems to put materialist science in the role of a fundamentalist religion. Within this paradigm it is the denial that there are any sorts of phenomena or meaningful problems that may forever escape this totally materialist approach that constituted the empiricist's arrogant dogma. (One present-day facet of that dogma may be seen in the confidence of some that a deterministic "theory of everything" is bound to be found sooner or later—the messianic end-game of the religion of "*nothing but!*")

Is this scientism not basically a constriction of vision, of cognitive structure, and therefore of contents of consciousness, of the sort that generates lots of "unnecessary" conflict? Certainly the conflicts will appear *unnecessary* from the vantage of some higher being who can see the much larger picture—but from the ground-level of each participant they are of course inevitable, generated by the characteristics of the level of development that each one as attained up to that point.

B. Affirmation Opens—Negation Closes

Of course, our whole language structure (*a la* Wittgenstein) and our systems of objectification and categorization also come crucially into how this process of positive and negative assertions works at each stage in the evolution of our ideas.

---

1   See the following essay, entitled "➜The Restriction of Ignorance: Inverting the Principle of Parsimony".

What follows is a speculative reflection upon the differences which particular ways of categorizing have made.

My tentative hypothesis concerning the most fundamental effects of such affirming and denying is this:

- The affirming components of a paradigmatic characterization effectively *raise* its dimensionality.

- While the denying components are those which tend to *lower* its dimensionality.

In the nature of how life flows, I both affirm and deny. Sometimes I enter into peace and joy—immersed in affirming, I relax and awaken. My vision opens out, as from a high place. But then, it easily and quickly constricts again as, captured and constricted by negating, I lock myself into tiny focal identifications thus losing consciousness of nearly everything! It's a grand sleep—filled with intense but tiny excitements.

The key question then, is:

Are the presuppositions—the fundamental assertions—that are the foundation of my worldview *reducing* the dimensionality of the map (of the image of the *real*) or are they *increasing* it?

But further, there will be many theory-generating assertions that do neither— call these neutral and "corrective." So there are actually three sorts of theoretical assertions. Thus we can also ask:

Does the assertion *make* or *break* or *shift* connections? And in so doing, does it thereby raise the complexity of the total system, lower it (i.e., simplify the system), or do neither?

We may, then, call these three large categories of theoretical supposition **(1)** assertions which *complicate*, **(2)** those which *simplify*, and **(3)** those which only *modify* our map of the total system.

==<<((([]||[]))>>==(((\[^]/\\[^]))==<<((([^]|_|[^]))>>==(((\[^]/\\[^]))==<<((([]||[]))>>==

~~THE WAY THE IDEA OF "LEVELS" IS BEING USED

Next, note that the paradigm being presented gives the idea of "levels" a central role. What I mean can be sketched using Koestler's (1967) "*open hierarchical systems*" idea.

1.2 The organism is to be regarded as a multi-leveled hierarchy of semi-autonomous sub-wholes, branching into sub-wholes of a lower order, and so on. Sub-wholes on any level of the hierarchy are referred to as *holons*....

1.4 Biological holons are self-regulating open systems which display both the autonomous properties of wholes and the dependent properties of parts. This dichotomy is present on every level of every type of hierarchic organization, and is referred to as the *Janus Effect* or Janus principle.

1.5 More generally, the term 'holon' may be applied to any stable biological or social sub-whole which displays rule-governed behaviour and/or structural Gestalt-constancy. Thus organelles and homologous organs are evolutionary holons; morphogenetic fields are ontogenetic holons; the ethologist's 'fixed action-patterns' and the sub-routines of acquired skills are behavioural holons; phonemes, morphemes, words, phrases are linguistic holons; individuals, families, tribes, nations are social holons.

(Koestler 1967, p. 341)

6.1 Hierarchies can be regarded as 'vertically' arborising structures whose branches interlock with those of other hierarchies at a multiplicity of levels and form 'horizontal' networks; arborisation and reticulation are complementary principles in the architecture of organisms and societies.

(Koestler 1967, p. 345)

8. Holons on successively higher levels of the hierarchy show increasingly complex, more flexible and less predictable patterns of activity, while on successive lower levels we find increasingly mechanized, stereotyped and predictable patterns.

(Koestler 1967, p. 346.)

==<<((([]||[]))>>==((([^]/\[^])) ==<<((([^]|_|[^]))>>==((([^]/\[^]))==<<((([]||[]))>>==

And now: What do we want to know? And what *can* we know? The following 2005 essay is my most recent attempt to encapsulate (as concisely as I can) my present widest view of directions and possibilities for human knowing.

→ *Minimalist Basis for Expanding Understanding*

It's become clear to me that all I know and experience fits within a **holarchic**[G] world-model—a vertical cascade of levels, each encompassing all those beneath it (Koestler 1967,1978; Wilber 1997). Certainly, I know of no empirical observations or data that indicate any difficulties with this general characterization of world's deep structure[G]. To therefore assume its general validity is a simple yet possibly momentous affirmation:

> This assumption—that all I know and experience actually does fit into a holarchic world-model—I will call my *Fundamental Holarchic Assumption*, or *FHA*.

Certainly, the FHA brings a new simplicity to my outlook, framing a world of overwhelmingly vast, endless complexity in a wonderfully **simple** way! But take care: I am habitually, unconsciously addicted to *other* kinds of "simplification" which—though they seem equally generalized and useful—are not so supportable.[2]

First, I'm simplifying nearly everything, nearly always, by *focusing* my attention—thereby shutting out almost everything! That mindless constricting of awareness (unknowing neglect of context) is my life-long pattern. It's how I've been well trained to deal with life's complexities. This addictive pattern is based largely in unvoiced, implicit assumptions about what's *unquestionable*, what's to be questioned—and especially, about what **is** and what **is not** *relevant* to my questions.

Second, I am continually making *judgments* which I treat as certainties—as given Knowings—with no recognition at all of the many *assumptions* upon which each is based and so without recognition also of the myriad uncertainties underly-

---

G   As previously noted, this symbol after a technical term means it may be looked up in the **Glossary** at the end of the book.

G   Again, see **Glossary**.

2   For more on habits of simplifying, see also the following essay ("→ The Restriction of Ignorance").

ing each of those assumptions. When I'm so judging, a mind-boggling range of all kinds of ignorance is constantly locked out from my consciousness.

But to challenge this lockout can I attain some awareness of it *while I'm doing it?* Then, at the very least, I may thereby begin to gain a little awareness that right in this present moment (as in every moment!) there are vast realms which are pertinent to my moment-to-moment existence and actions yet necessarily remain beyond my recognition and even slightest comprehension.

Doing that can point the way toward a major shift! For now I begin to see how my addictive world-constricting must implicitly be based in unconscious assumptions about the fundamental *nature* of my world. I believe that the most general of those world-constricting assumptions either implies or directly asserts that the upward procession of my world's holarchic levels has a *top* level—a highest level. However, I further believe that it is logically impossible to find evidence for such an assertion, and therefore that the assumption is always invalid.

> So the contrary assumption of *toplessness* is more reasonable and sup-
> portable. This assumption of *no end to the rising cascade of holarchic
> levels* I'll call my *No-End Assumption* or *NEA*.

Yet in practice I'm forgetting my *NEA* all the time. Can I more often remember it—and therefore more often remember to actually let go of those arbitrary, scientifically-unsupportable limitations that (for the sake of seeming gains in "simplicity'[3]) I'm always tempted to place upon my *Fundamental Holarchic Assumption,* my FHA? With that remembering (when I occasionally do) the parsimonious NEA keeps everything *open* as a limitless expanse of infinite extension.

Opening consciousness to this limitlessness generates higher and more integrated levels of inner order—a negentropy-generating *emergence* of new structure within unconscious mind's network of automatisms. When I can actually let go of the restrictive processes by which I'm constantly (in effect) denying the generality of FHA, I thereby achieve, momentarily, a truer and deeper simplicity.

All quite paradoxical—that my search for simplicity is best resolved through thoroughgoing acknowledgement of unlimited complexity! Yet there's also something else of deep significance which follows from my holarchic world-model: It generally turns out that paradoxes and contradictions which trouble me while my thought remains on its present level will disappear when I can open myself to a level above.

So just keep opening, keep going up—and all is healed. Even the *simple* story of existence's unlimited *complexity*. And further, note how seemingly-insoluble

---

3   As mentioned in the previous note, this is an issue dealt with at greater length in the
     following essay.

conflicts can disappear: Things which at one level are observed *(obviously!)* to be totally disconnected from each other—disconnected by seemingly irreconcilable splits—will be seen at a higher level to be parts of some larger whole.

The essence of the foregoing ramble can be summarized as follows:

1. All of my intricate, many-leveled universe can be *holarchically* described in terms of a nested sequence of levels with each level inclusive of all the levels beneath. That's my *Fundamental Holarchic Assumption (FHA)*.

2. There's no empirical basis for assuming any termination to the upwards progression of levels—thus, *toplessness* is a second reasonable null hypothesis proceeding directly from FHA. It's the *No-End Assumption (NEA)*.

3. These together imply a fundamental unity—a kind of *oneness* of all existence—because whenever, at any level, some division, contradiction, or paradox is apparent, there will always be a higher level at which a healing, a resolution can take place. Then every contradiction can be healed by going up to a higher level.

Some of this understanding goes way back. It seems that varied threads of logical reasoning and intuitive insight have pointed in the direction of *unbounded holarchic progression through expanded consciousness.* Haven't the deepest religious, spiritual, and alternative-health teachings pointed this way? Consider this empirically-justifiable looking, based in the intuited absence of empirical justification for ceasing upwards enlargement: Won't it project further to seek Ultimate Unknowingness? Can it not, then, be called *"spirituality," "mysticism," "God"*—or (Buddhist) *"emptiness?"* (Total amazement is essential!)

```
)>>==<<((([]||[]))>>==(((([^]/\[^]))==<<((([^]|_|[^]))>>==<<((([]||[]))>>==<<(
```

But what are we *now* doing? What about our assumptions concerning our freedom of choice, our "free will" in our movements and actions of all sorts? Here are several parts taken from another recent (2005–06) essay.

→ ON FREE WILL, HOLARCHIC STRUCTURE AND DOWNWARD CAUSATION

I. Logic or Illogic of Scientism

The modern temper is generally eager to deny the reality of personal responsibility by treating us all as externally programmed *mechanisms* that behave in ways that are (at least in principle) completely predictable. Thus we do what we want and/or what we can, but what we *want* to do and *can* do are entirely determined by prior conditions; so we are said to have no real free choice and therefore no real responsibility for our actions. The medical model of "mental illness" that is now promulgated by biopsychiatry says exactly that: All is determined by genes, viruses, "chemical imbalances" and other factors that are beyond our voluntary control, so we can in no way be responsible for our various "mental disturbances" or for the pain-producing behaviors that they bring about.

I am grateful for the meaningful scientific knowledge incorporated in the positive assertions of the medical/biopsychiatric model but I question specifically (and strongly) its claim to *completeness*.[4] In contrast with this paradigm's exclusively deterministic frame of belief, I argue for the reality and the significance of my *experienced* abilities to make considered *choices*. I therefore assert that there is something more beyond the mechanical.[5]

Here now is my *anthropic counter-argument*. My confidence that I have (or do) *free will* rests not only upon the evidence of my direct experience nor upon my alternative *metatheory* (see **Section 2**) but also upon a rather simple yet usually neglected point of logic. In effect, the argument that results in a denial of free will (i.e., of *freedom* of *choice*) cuts off its own head. For the very fact that we assume the *meaningfulness* of our discussions of this free-will question means that we are implicitly assuming the reality of free will—of the validity of freely rational choice-making, of considered *judgments* based on the *truth*-value of arguments.

4   Regarding such claims, see especially the preceding first essay in **Section 1**, "→Thoughts on the Progression of Paradigms."

5   First see immediately following subsections of this essay for a few introductory specifics on CC metatheory; then see essays of **Section 2**.

Of course the proponents of this denial of free will present it as the conclusion of their "irrefutable" rational argument, but in this instance the conclusion of their argument reflects back upon the argument itself—upon both its purpose and its process—and invalidates it. In fact, it is a conclusion that effectively undercuts the persuasiveness of *any* argument.

The case I am making here for the reality of free will has something in common with the argument for the "anthropic principle"[6] in that it eliminates the counter position by demonstrating its absurdity—that is, by showing how it unavoidably generates a contradiction. Certainly, any disinterested consideration of the respective truth-values of competing arguments requires that we be able to *reflectively compare* and *critically evaluate* their conflicting truth-claims, and this in turn implicitly assumes some capacity for non-random yet unfettered *choice* founded upon *deliberative judgment*. It seems to be quite generally understood that the element of freedom—and therefore of unpredictability—is the indispensable basis for valid deliberative judgments. The very fact that we assume the *meaningfulness* of our discussions of this question, presenting our arguments along with our evaluations of alternative arguments as if their truth or falsity is a meaningful and decidable question that *matters*, means that we are implicitly assuming the reality of free will—of freely rational choice-making.

For if free will were not real, then our cogitations and judgments about this question could only be the completely determined reactions of mechanism to impinging conditions[7] with perhaps some role also for random fluctuations. If all is determined then *choice* simply does not happen. Or alternatively, it might be considered that some kind of a "choosing" action does take place but is either random or is totally fettered—and in either case is unfree.[8] In that event each individual's belief-system—and any argument made for it—would be simply a function of external conditions and prior conditioning, and thus would be of interest primarily for what it might reveal about that person's mechanisms.[9] But then (either way) we would necessarily lose our respect for their validity as considered *judgments* of the *truth-value* of those arguments. They could no longer be persuasive.

---

6   It is also reminiscent of the idea: "if the brain was so simple that we could understand it, we would be so simple that we couldn't"—Lyall Watson (quoted by Hooper & Teresi, 1986, p. 21).

7   And in the even more up-to-date *computer* metaphor, the automatic running off of a complex, pre-existing *program*.

8   Therefore in terms of what we ordinarily understand about the freely deliberative character of 'choosing,' it should perhaps be termed "pseudo-choice"!

9   Such an argument has been given before as a critical weakness of dogmatic behaviorism.

Certainly, this assumption of freely critical judgment must apply to all who are judging the persuasiveness of arguments—including therefore *listener* as well as *speaker*. For the persuasiveness of any argument inherently rests upon assumptions that not only the arguer but also we as evaluators of the argument presented to us have some capacity for deliberative judgment grounded in unfettered choice.

In summary, the whole idea of contending arguments rests upon the assumption of deliberative judgment, which in turn implicitly assumes the reality of a capacity for unfettered choice—assumes, that is, the reality of *free will*.

II. Who Says We Are Nothing But Mechanisms?

Can studying my brain's structure ever bring me to an understanding of my freedom? Certainly, if we know the structure of a system, we can determine how it will behave.[10] And my common sense tells me that to the extent that its actions are predictable it is not free. Brain scientists commonly assume that *every* aspect of human behavior and experience—even our conviction of our free will—can ultimately be accounted for by more complete knowledge of brain's dynamic structure. That is what they *choose* to believe! Yet to the extent that we can successfully analyze the "mechanisms" of this act of choosing in terms of abstractions specifying causal linkages, it is fettered, determined, unfree.

Therefore again we achieve a contradiction: By finding the mechanism of a free *act* we prove that it is *not* a free act! Perhaps this means that free will does not exist. But there are other ways in which we can escape this dilemma. With two of them we do it by modifying the exclusive appeal to mechanism, adding something else as well. One way to thus escape is by *dualism*; another however is by a *transformational monism* that has been referred to as the **continual creation (CC) metatheory of consciousness** (Atkin 1992, 1994).[11] In essence it says this:

> If consciousness and choice are *transformation* of structure, they can be inherently beyond prediction—and thus free.

III. How Free?

There's another fundamental aspect of the free will question. It has seemed natural to assume that a dominance by causal constraints means an absence of free

---

10 This will be true by definition—for we are defining a system's *structure* as the laws of its behavior (see **Glossary** entry for "structure."

11 See especially two essays in **Section 2** ("➜On consciousness: What is the Role of Emergence" and "➜Conscious Beyond Mechanism"); and the first essay in **Summing Up** ("➜Being, Doing, Knowing")—see also "CC metatheory" in the **Glossary**.

will. That in fact is what the mechanistic worldview is all about. But here is an entirely different perspective, within which free will and causality are *not antithetical*. My understanding now is that I act with greater freedom when I know and adaptively conform to *higher* causal constraints—so to become *freer* I open my *awareness* to *higher* orders of causality.

A. Constraints of Choice[12]

There seem to be two fundamental aspects to my experience of "freedom," the first being the *non-algorithmic causation* that (by CC metatheory[G] to be dealt with further in **Section 2**) is inseparable from consciousness, and the second (just mentioned) having to do with *downward causation*. Both involve an intuited absence of certain constraints.

The first aspect of my experience of "freedom" is about kinds of constraint that are *not* controlling my choice because the determinants are "non-algorithmic"[13]—that is, cannot be fully characterized by rules or specifiable principles of procedure. I label it *non-algorithmic free will* (FW_{na}). *Choosing* is the non-algorithmic component in volitional actions—it is the accommodative restructuring that generates conscious awareness through the non-algorithmic transformation or creation of algorithmic structure. Thus (as will be developed at greater length later[14]) free will is directly a consequence of and is inseparable from consciousness.

Secondly (very different yet also tremendously important) there's downwardly caused freedom, which I will label "FW_{dd}" for *downwardly-directed* choice. I can feel free of lower-order constraints on my decision by knowing it was *not* forced from *below* since its determinants originated in the whole that constitutes a higher level of structure, thus the choice was downwardly, not upwardly caused. This free will is free from the perspective of this presently-inhabited *action level* in relation to lower levels of order, in that it is not reductionistically determined by phenomena at or causal links from those lower levels. So it's not acausal but rather is determined from higher structural levels—the higher and more globally inclusive the

---

12 This subsection is a contracted version of subsection "What are the Constraints of Choice?"—in the first "➔ Being, Doing, Knowing" essay of the last (**Summing Up**) section.

G This symbol after a technical term means it may be looked up in the **Glossary** at the end of the book.

13 See subsection later in this essay called "Downward Causation and Non-Algorithmic Causality."

14 Especially in two essays of **Section 2** ("➔ On consciousness: What is the Role of Emergence" and "➔ Conscious Beyond Mechanism") and then in the first essay of the **Summing Up** section ("➔ Being, Doing, Knowing").

determinants of my choice the greater its freedom. To wisely make choices that more fully anticipate consequences I attempt to enlarge the span of my consciousness, and thereby to attain greater freedom—the wiser choice is the freer choice.

This monist way of understanding FW differs from the purely reductionistic way. It's more like the dualistic way in that it refers to control of action from above rather than (only) from below. But for the dualist the controlling region is absolutely separated from the controlled region by an ontological chasm, while in the proposed monist answer the controlling regions are continuous with—though above and inclusive of—the controlled choice-region.

B. Freedom Real But Very Tiny

Certainly, understood this way my freedom is very small because my knowledge of higher levels of order is so limited. And I'm quite sure that this is a logical necessity, because:

> If I understand our Kosmos holarchically then my most reasonable, parsimonious hypothesis is to assume *no limit* to the upward progression of its levels of order.

> But it seems to me that it is also my most reasonable, parsimonious hypothesis to assume that a human mind's capacities for comprehension—though it may be potentially larger than we can now even imagine—cannot be thus unlimited.

Taken together these two assumptions imply that though my understanding of my universe—and my consequent freedom of choice within it—is very real and highly significant, it nevertheless must remain very tiny.

C. Experiential Support

However *tiny* our freedom may be, this causal explanation for its *reality* has experiential support. After all, we all know that the most careful and profoundly deliberated choices have, in effect, the most constraints. What is here asserted is that an essential portion of these will be constraints that cannot be adequately accounted for reductionistically.

How can freedom relate to downward-directed constraints? Certainly, we feel that we are maximally using our freedom when we make deeply considered choices. And in retrospect we understand that for us it was more of a choice, not less—a more deeply free choice—than was a choice we made impulsively, with little or no deliberation, on some other occasion. That very word—"deliberate"—which characterizes a higher kind of choice, thus perhaps a *deeper* freedom, means a "careful and thorough consideration." When I deliberate, I examine the situation and the possible consequences of my alternative actions from as many "sides" as I can, widening my perspective to the best of my ability. And this ordinarily means that my process of choice is to a large extent positioned within some of the "higher" levels of order that are invoked by such words as *morality, justice, fairness, love, compassion, friendship, brotherhood/sisterhood*, etc.

Certainly, when I relate my own concerns and actions with those of another person, I am thereby widening my perspective. I wonder now: Is a true "I-You" relationship (Buber 1970) going a long way (if not all the way) in the direction of opening myself to the highest levels of order I'm capable of reaching—of even briefly touching? Might it not therefore be the deepest freedom I ever attain?

Those higher levels of order will have been learned by individual brains. Then, when an individual brain is choosing with its focus of attention at those higher levels, important causal connections are operating from those levels downward. And any retrospective analysis of the resulting choice will need to study the kinds of higher-order lawfulness that have developed within that particular brain.

Of course, investigations of how the higher-level causal systems were conditioned by social expectations, of how they are in large part products of prevalent "memes," may be revealing. But the "up-and-down" determinist holds that these paths of upward causation cannot tell the whole story. As Newman (JCS-Online 12/27/95) notes, "consciousness is … a meta-cognitive process." I suggest that this applies to conscious *choosing* (as real choosing requires and is inseparable from consciousness).

Certainly this attribution of *free will* (FW) to downward causation has been done before (e.g., Sperry 1985; Lemkow 1994). For example, Roger Sperry expressed it well:

> A person does indeed determine with his own mind what he is going to do and often from among a large series of alternative possibilities.
>
> This does not mean, however, that there are cerebral operations that occur without antecedent cause. Man is not free from the higher forces in his own decision-making machinery. In particular, our model does not free a person from the combined effects of his own thoughts, his own impulses, his own reasoning, feeling, beliefs, ideals, and hopes, nor does it free him from his inherited makeup or his lifetime memories. All these and more, including unconscious desires, exert their due causal influence upon any mental decision, and the combined resultant determines an inevitable but nevertheless self-determined, highly special, and highly personal outcome.…

... If one were assigned the task of trying to design and build the perfect freewill model, consider the possibility that the aim might be not so much to free the machinery from causal contact as the opposite; that is, to try to incorporate into the model the potential value of universal or unlimited causal contact. In other words, contact with all related information in proper proportion—past, present, and future.

At any rate, it is clear that the human brain has come a long way in evolution in exactly this direction, when you consider the amount and the kind of causal factors that this multidimensional, intracranial vortex draws into itself, scans, and brings to bear in turning out one of its "free choice" decisions. Potentially included, through memory, are the events and wisdom of most of a human lifetime. Potentially included, also, with a visit to the library, is the accumulated knowledge of all recorded history. And we can add, thanks to reason and logic, much of the predictive value extractable from all these data as well as creative insights newly conceived.

(Sperry 1985, pp. 40-41)

In contrast, the act of violence—the criminal or "evil" action—is either impulsive—has had little deliberation and thus is hardly an act of choice—or else is founded in higher-order cognitive structures that are severely at odds with the corresponding structures of those who consider the actions criminal or evil. Often it may be demonstrable that those higher-order structures that give rise to criminal/evil choices are internally contradictory or are severely at odds with broadly consensual, testable views of reality.

Furthermore, such *aberrant* structures are almost always sustained by a suppression of questioning. The persistent questioner becomes a "heretic," to be vigorously dealt with. In contrast, an important part of the choice-process that is most profoundly free is a readiness to question every presupposition upon which a given analysis of the situation rests—a readiness which is ordinarily totally absent from choice-processes leading to acts generally acknowledged to be "evil."

What we've been speaking of could now be summed up by saying:

"The larger the consciousness, the freer its choices."

This position—though perhaps a kind of determinism—is neither "soft" nor "hard" determinism. It purports to give a more adequate and accurate definition of *free will*. Does it thereby define away the freedom of free will? I don't believe so—I believe it deepens rather than destroys its meaning.

IV. Higher Meanings and Healing Connections

Freedom and truth are intimately related—there cannot be one without the other. In another essay[15] I said the following about freedom and truth:

- Freedom is the healing of connections. Truth is generated by connecting whole systems into greater wholes, lies are generated shattering systems (understandings) into fragments. Truth comes only from truth (and lies from lies).

- Freedom generates truth, and truth generates freedom. They are inseparable ...

Now with a holarchic worldview, that truth must include higher and higher levels. Here's what I've concluded:

- Upward causation is imprisoning, binding, *unfree*. But downward causation is the nature and source of freedom; free will is *following necessities from above*—the higher, the freer.

Recall that a main postulate in the foregoing parts of this essay was that freedom—free will—is inseparable from downward causation. Reductionist systems of explanation are marvelously effective in bringing new order into many areas of mystery and confusion. Is their power limited? They have place *only* for upward causation, not downward causation, yet it seems obvious that downward causation must also be very real and very important. So now in the next section I will tell what I've deduced concerning the actual nature of one of two types of downward causation—the one that in a later essay I've named "tautological downward causation."[16]

V. Downward Details—The Structure-Causality Identity Postulate

Let's examine more closely the existence and importance of downward causation (DC). I believe I can better understand the workings of downward causation in a holarchically-structured system if I now clarify what I mean by (1) different levels of phenomena, and (2) downward causation from one level to a level beneath. To start this desired clarification I make use of the notion of *coherence*. The key idea is this:

---

15 Still unpublished (though possibly to be published in the near future).

16 That's in the **Section 3** essay "➔More on Downward Causation and Free Will"— where I distinguish this kind of downward causation from "meta downward causation."

- An (n+1) structural level refers to systems of coherence between structures of level (n). These systems of coherence are cooperative dynamic interrelations of those n-level structures. Thus (n+1) structure is a particular way in which "things" at level (n) "work together." So downward causation from the n+1 level—whereby (n+1)-level structures have causal effects upon (n)-level structures—is implicit in the very existence of that (n+1) level. That's because these downward causal effects are the coherence of interactions at level (n)—the very coherencies that define the (n+1) structure.

Thus understood, downward causation becomes a kind of tautology, for it simply says in two different ways that "an (n)-level coherence exists." The first time it calls this (n)-level coherence an (n+1)-level structure, and the second time it calls this (n)-level coherence the "downward causation that this (n+1)-level structure exerts upon (n)-level structure." Note that the (n)-level coherence is **not** an *effect* of the (n+1)-level structure; rather, it *is* that (n+1)-level structure.

In short:

An (n+1)-level structure is *identical* with dynamic coherencies at level (n), and these dynamic coherencies are *identical* with "downward causation" from level (n+1) onto level (n). Therefore the *(n+1)-level structure of (n)-level components is identical with "downward causation" from level (n+1) onto level (n).*

A good name for this understanding would be the *"Structure-Causality Identity Postulate."*

VI. Anthropic View on Endurance and Continuity

Look now at the temporal dimension—at the idea of continuation, of endurance. This is generally implicit in the notion of "structure."[17] Only those relationships, those coherencies that continue to manifest over time are likely to be labeled "structure."

Consider how this applies to levels: An (n+1) structure—since it is this particular coherence—endures only so long as this coherence endures. A kind of "anthropic principle" seems again to be involved here: If we *observe* (n+1)-level structure—i.e., if the (n+1) level *endures*—that can only mean that the (n)-level coherence which is its downward ordering/coordinative "effect on" structure at level (n) is continuing.

---

17 See "structure" in *Glossary*.

It can all be summed up in ten words: ***The stable existence of structure is identical with downward causation.*** A version of the "anthropic principle" is in this way relevant to the most comprehensive principles of our total worldview.

Consider one representative of such a comprehensive system. I have been impressed in re-reading Arthur Koestler with the power of his concept of "a system-theoretical model of Self-regulating Open Hierarchic Order, or SOHO for short" (Koestler 1978, p. 289) as a super-ordinate conceptual system into which it should be possible to fit all our smaller understandings of ourselves and our world.

Now I begin to believe that this "SOHO" structure of the universe—with its central idea of "a polarity between the self-assertive and the integrative tendency of holons on every level" (Koestler 1978, p. 302)—can be seen as an anthropic necessity.

Here are first the *macro-level* and then the *micro-level* of that anthropic necessity:

- Most broadly world's SOHO structure is exactly that way because (1) otherwise we would not exist as we are in this world—now able to know this SOHO world. That may be called *the macro-level of anthropic necessity.*

- But (2) there is also a *micro-level:* At each step in the evolution of structure, though many kinds of coherence may emerge, most kinds will be transient (and/or not amenable to the further emergence from them of more complex coherencies). However, the particular kinds of coherence that have the structural stability required to maintain some constancy or identity (and also have the potential to self-organize even more complex kinds of coherence) are the kinds of coherence that endure and thus have become the world-structure we now observe. That's *the micro-level of anthropic necessity.*

So, like conscious awareness, downward causation is not *an element to be added* to our conceptual system; rather, it is a *fundamental root* of that system. This is because downward causation, being *identical* with every level of structure except the lowest, is *implicit in the very existence of our world's total structure*—and also in that of any conceptual system suitable to describe (map) our world in so large a way.

```
)>>==<<((([]||[]))>>==((([^]/\[^]))==<<((([^]|_|[^]))>>==<<((([]||[]))>>==<<(
```

And now an essay written in 1994 which presents another but related insight pertinent to how knowledge is gained and evaluated. It is an alternative view on the Principle of Parsimony (also called "Occam's Razor"), a methodological principle of philosophy commonly used to banish "needless" *complexity* by forbidding the introduction of explanatory hypotheses beyond strict necessity. It is here suggested that this same Principle should also be used to banish needless and overly broad *simplifications*. (Searle knew about that, yet made the simplification-mistake himself.) In conclusion, open-mindedness is compared with closed-mindedness and it's shown how the latter violates parsimony.

➜ THE RESTRICTION OF IGNORANCE:
INVERTING THE PRINCIPLE OF PARSIMONY
(WITH COMMENT ON SEARLE)

I. A New Look at "Occam's Razor"

Worldviews are shifting. We seem to be moving toward a new paradigm, larger and more inclusive than those of the *modern* age of scientism, logical positivism, and materialistic reductionism. Defects and inadequacies of those old "modern" theoretical formulations become more and more apparent—especially through recent research on neural networks, fractals, chaos theory, dissipative systems, and the probing, rigorous work of such philosophers, mathematicians and scientists as Bateson, Bohm, Bronowski, Gödel, and Prigogine. This shift to a "postmodern" perspective has been well depicted by several contemporary writers, including Wilber (1983), Berman (1984), Smith (1989), and Anderson (1990).

What gave the *modern* worldview its long-held power? One pivotal support for the modern stance has been a methodological principle of philosophy, the Principle of Parsimony, also called "Occam's Razor."

A. How It Is Now Used

There is no dispute about the usefulness of the Principle of Parsimony's usual mode of application, which is aimed at avoiding needless complexities. Additions of *particular* hypotheses (based on the claim that some particular entity, relationship, or process is involved as a component of some causal explanation) may be ruled out by Occam's Razor if there is insufficient supporting evidence. Here's an example:

Do I have a theory of a certain class of phenomena, by which I can explain adequately almost all happenings—all except those occurring under certain exceptional conditions? And then, do I propose some other peculiar state of matter, never before observed, to account for those peculiar phenomena? What if I have no other basis for that proposal, and cannot give any means for obtaining any evidence?

Then it may legitimately be said that it is "not parsimonious" to complicate our universe with such an absurdity for which there is no evidence—if any alternative explanation that does not entail the additional assumption can be found.

(Weber 1990, pp. 105-106)

Used thus (as it often is), the Principle of Parsimony or Occam's Razor is a helpful and appropriate criterion for the acceptance of an offered theory. Its purpose is to rule out needless and baseless *complications*. Advocates of our modern simplifying worldviews—e.g., of *positivism, scientism, materialism*—have in fact used this "normal" application of the Principle as a major weapon in their war against the discomforting (and in their view illegitimate) diversity and complications of the explanatory projects pursued under older paradigms.

(Armstrong 1981, p. 43)

Yet there is, perhaps, a particular *unreliability* that has been unnoticed till now. I've come to see that the Principle of Parsimony has disregarded implications. Therefore I will examine and advocate a seeming inversion of the usual way in which it is applied. Not that the old way is *wrong*, but that there is also another way, with implications sometimes opposite to those usually drawn from this Principle.

B. Violation by Simplification

Though the Principle of Parsimony is commonly used to banish "needless" *complexity*—complexity consequent to the multiplication of hypotheses beyond strict necessity—this same Principle can be seen, when one looks from a different and perhaps unfamiliar angle, to be applicable also to the banishment of needless and overly broad *simplifications*. Some of the simplifications to be thus banished have likewise been accomplished by multiplying hypotheses beyond strict necessity; most often this has been done through the imposition of a single unfalsifiable hypothesis that makes assertions that are needlessly broad and absolute.

It is here maintained that not only, e.g., anthropomorphisms, but also such exclusionary "isms" as reductionism and materialism—varieties of "nothing but …" hypotheses—can and should be ruled out by Occam's Razor, for these latter are hypotheses that assert unfalsifiable claims to a kind of total knowledge.

Why "unfalsifiable"? Because to whatever might be said to be unexplainable in the terms of the theory in question, the proponent can always reply: "Well, we have not worked that out yet … but we will! Ultimately, *our* theory will provide the explanation."

Wilber (1983) neatly clarifies the logical defect implicit in scientism's belief system. He notes that:

> [If] the positivist simply said, "We will limit ourselves to the study of relative knowledge," then that would be quite acceptable. But he goes beyond and says, "Only relative knowledge is valid." And that is an *absolute* statement: it says, "It is absolutely true that there is no absolute truth."
>
> (Wilber 1983, p. 28.)

> In a similar vein the scientician does not merely say, "The empiric proof is the best method of gaining facts in the sense realm," but goes on to say, "Only those propositions that can be empirically verified are true." Unfortunately, *that* proposition itself cannot be empirically verified. There is no empirical proof that empirical proof alone is real.
>
> (Wilber 1983, p. 29)

Consider the possible illegitimacy of such tempting simplifications from the point of view (using Alfred Korzybski's [1941] pregnant metaphor) that a *theory* is a *map* of a certain territory. If the theory concerns some class of phenomena in our observable world, then the *territory* (target) of the theory is our observable world. The simplifications we are discussing reduce the conceptually recognized territory to a size not much larger than that of some particular map—the map that is presented as the only relevant theory.

But let's consider this more closely. Is this territory in some sense *necessarily* larger than the set of observations that we have already made—the set that provides the basis (the *data*) for our mapping (our theory)? Certainly, it is larger—generally far larger. The first reason concerns the way a theory is tested. The territory is larger than any existent set of observations precisely because the theory makes *predictions* (mappings which extend beyond that already known range of observations), and the test of a theory is whether or not its predictions will be confirmed.

Thus, this whole standard method for *confirmation* of a theory (i.e., of a map or mapping principle) rests upon the assumption that the territory is larger than all the already-tested parts of the map—that is, than the presently-available set of observations. It is here maintained, however, that it is also far larger than any *possible* set of observations. But how much larger?

Consider that if the territory were actually of infinite extent, then, of necessity, no matter how much time and resources were available for theory confirmation, it would be possible to test the adequacy and precision of its mapping only over some finite portion of this infinite territory.

And here, now, is the key point concerning this application of Occam's Razor to theory *simplifications*. It concerns the likelihood, just referred to, that the map's territory is infinite in extent. It is held that acceptance of this is not really a positive proposition but rather is the *lack* of one. It is the lack of an assumption that the map's territory is *bounded*. For though the territory could possibly be bounded, in general there can be no proof or demonstration of its ultimate boundedness. The *map*, certainly, is finite and bounded; therefore the part of the map's *territory* that demonstrably corresponds to the map must likewise be finite and bounded. But is there infinitely more territory extending *beyond* the bounds of our map? The assertion that *there is not* is arbitrary and beyond proof or falsification.

Before going further a clarification is necessary concerning just what is here meant by the "sizes" of a territory and of its map. I must emphasize that (in the way the *map* and *territory* metaphor is being used here) it's not the map's or territory's size in the ordinary sense of extension that are being referred to but rather their *dimensionality*. Otherwise it might seem that there is an effective objection to the argument that is being developed. After all, even though any specific map is itself limited in extent, it would seem that the possible productions from a given mapping principle can expand without limit.

That is, while any map that has been or can be shown explicitly—drawn, or given in diagrams, tables, figures, etc.—must remain finite in extent, due to the finitude of available time and available resources for its production, the *range of implications of a particular mapping principle*—of a method or algorithmic procedure for generating further extensions of the map—seems unlimited. And this goes also for the extension of the mapped territory; though what at any particular time has already been explicitly mapped may remain finite in extent, what is implicit in mapping algorithms (the mathematical formulae of the theory) for future map-generation is not. Thus future expansions and extensions of a map can indeed continue without end. The map's further elaboration, in terms of kinds of phenomena and fields of data that can be accounted for using the variables of the theory, can grow endlessly.

But none of this alters our understanding expressed just before these last considerations, that any particular map we can generate is finite and bounded, and that therefore the part of the map's *territory* that demonstrably corresponds to the map must likewise be finite and bounded. Yet *we cannot know that there is not infinitely more territory extending **beyond** the bounds of our map.* Of that I'm increasingly sure.

For every map—and all our thought and conceptual systems—is limited in dimensionality as a consequence of our finite cognitive capacities. Even the theory with the widest and seemingly infinite ramifications must be specified in terms of relationships between some finite set of variables (or of *kinds* of variables). In that sense, the dimensionality of every theory is held to be finite. But what basis can we have for assuming that the *territory's* dimensionality is limited in the same way—or in any way? Certainly, we might exclude certain combinations of dimensional specifications on the basis of internal contradictions. Yet what basis can we have for asserting that this does not leave infinite other combinations of dimensional specifications for which no such problems can be found?

So it is in that sense that I here assert that any ultimate limitation of the territory is a *positive* assumption. I will repeat this crucial step of the argument for emphasis:

> Any assertion of finitude or ultimate limitation of extent, dimensions, or levels of complexity of the full, **global** territory that any significant theory is attempting to map **locally** must rest upon some non-provable and unfalsifiable assumption, whether or not the making of such an assumption is recognized by the proponents of such limitation.[18]

Is such a non-provable, unfalsifiable assumption to be invalidated on the basis that it is a violation of the Principle of Parsimony? I believe so! My argument, therefore, is that if boundedness is nevertheless assumed, it is an assumption that is a matter of *faith*, not of observation or coherent reason. More specifically:

> Every absolute, totalizing explanatory assertion that claims to be the only high-road to complete knowledge, thus the *exclusive* basis for achieving "truth" or "understanding," violates the Principle of Parsimony ("Occam's Razor").

In terms of the *mapping* metaphor, any hypothesis which asserts the general correctness and adequacy of a map (or of a method for generating maps) *everywhere* outside of those regions in which its correctness and adequacy either have

---

18 See "Local vs. Global" in **Glossary.**

been tested, or can now be tested, is to be discarded by the criterion of parsimony.

C. Yet Why So Invisible?

But now, even if the validity of this argument is accepted, a puzzling discrepancy with my experience remains. For if in fact such absolute generalizations are so *irrational*, then why are they so commonly at the base of dominant paradigms?

The reason, I believe, is the automatic way in which this assumption about the territory disappears from view and cannot be seen from within the paradigm it supports—only from outside of it. As suggested above, such totalizing assumptions implicitly assert some kind of unfalsifiable *boundedness* of the territory that is the target of the theory. These assumptions of territorial boundedness are equivalent to an *exclusion from notice, meaning, and consciousness of all that lies beyond the boundary*.

In fact, to the extent that such exclusion is complete, awareness of the boundary itself will be lost. After all, one might ask: "If there is *nothing* beyond it, there is not really a *boundary*, is there? For as there is nothing on the other side, it *separates nothing* from us!" Thus, the assumption that the territory is bounded quickly drops out of awareness and becomes invisible to the one who makes it (though it is sometimes still apparent to the outside observer).

In short, these exclusions are ways by which we *simplify* our set of theories by suppressing our recognition of their necessary incompleteness. Such simplification, I hold, is generally illegitimate and often destructive. Ordinarily, its function is to preserve the presently dominant paradigm—that is, to maintain the *status quo*. In effect, representatives of the dominant paradigm are saying (often vehemently): "The way *we* do it, or at least are trying to do it, is the *only* way to do it!" It is a closed-minded perspective.

But as already implied, this is hard even to discuss, far harder to correct. For before an excluding assumption can be dropped (if it will be), it has to be recognized. Yet it is inevitable that non-recognition is the usual condition. That is, the closedness of a closed-minded perspective tends to be invisible—therefore ineffable—from within and is only detected from the outside.

Thomas Kuhn (1970) has said some of this:

> [Normal science] seems an attempt to force nature into the preformed and relatively inflexible box that the paradigm supplies. No part of the aim of normal science is to call forth new sorts of phenomena; indeed those that will not fit the box are often not seen at all. Nor do scientists normally aim to invent new theories, and they are often intolerant of those invented by others. Instead, normal-scientific research is directed

to the articulation of those phenomena and theories that the paradigm already supplies.

Perhaps these are defects. The areas investigated by normal science are, of course, minuscule; the enterprise now under discussion has drastically restricted vision.

(Kuhn 1970, p. 24)

[One] of the things a scientific community acquires with a paradigm is a criterion for choosing problems that, while the paradigm is taken for granted, can be assumed to have solutions. To a great extent these are the only problems that the community will admit as scientific or encourage its members to undertake.

(Kuhn 1970, p. 37)

That is, Kuhn is describing active *exclusion* of that which does not fit the paradigm. But it's exclusion which mostly is not deliberate, because totally without deliberation. What is excluded and the act of excluding—both remain totally beneath awareness.

II. Reductionist Habits

A. Thoughts on Reading Searle

An instance of this difficulty occurs in a book by John Searle (1992) in which he uncovers the internal contradictions and other serious faults in many reigning philosophic "isms"—e.g., materialism, monism, dualism. Nevertheless, he contradicts himself by falling into one of the materialist fallacies that he so penetratingly uncovers and criticizes everywhere else.

Searle understands that one underpinning of modern materialism (understood to include an exhaustive *reductionism* as a key assumption) is the assumption that "Every fact in the universe is in principle knowable and understandable by human investigators" (p. 11). He emphasizes that this is an error:

It is inconsistent with what we in fact know about the universe and our place in it to suppose that everything is knowable by us.... Of course, methodologically we have to act as if we could understand everything, because there is no way of knowing what we can't: to know the limits of knowledge, we would have to know both sides of the limit. So potential omniscience is acceptable as a heuristic device, but it would be self-deception to suppose it a fact.

(Searle 1992, pp. 23-24)

Yet Searle seems to make this very error himself. Not at first: By rejecting the factuality of omniscience he seems implicitly to recognize the relevance of the Principle of Parsimony (Occam's Razor) to unwarranted simplifications—though he does not actually invoke it. But then he in effect violates it. (It is so hard to clean out these ingrained habits of thought!)

For Searle places himself in the impossible stance of omniscience when he speaks repeatedly as if his own alternative to conventional materialism rests upon an *indisputable fact,* which he expresses as a kind of *absolute*: This is his eliminative, unqualified assertion that consciousness is *nothing but* the consequence of processes in the brain. He says "we know for sure that inside our skulls there is a brain, sometimes it is conscious, and brain processes *cause consciousness in all its forms*" (p. 247—my emphasis).

That thought certainly reflects our modern understanding. But though it's a generalization that now seems to rest upon our observations and experience, perhaps it need not be asserted as an absolute. For if our knowledge is limited, how can we be so sure that our consciousness is *nothing but* our brain processes?[19] After all, Searle emphatically asserts that "omniscience is acceptable as a heuristic device, but it would be self-deception to suppose it a fact" (p. 24). So he is acutely aware (at least some of the time) of the *limits* of our experience.

Nevertheless, his blanket assertion about consciousness and brain seems to indicate that this awareness sometimes slips away! I take exception to his confident display of omniscience and would like to remind him that though we may not now have the experience upon which to base exceptions or qualifications, we cannot with such absolute assurance rule out the possibility that such experience may at some time become available. And though I have never, to my best recollection, had such experiences myself and therefore am quite willing to agree to a version of Searle's pronouncement (a version less narrow and absolute than his), throughout human history there certainly have been innumerable experiential reports that seem to demand a profound revision of it (e.g., Smith 1989; Wilber 1983).

Further, there can be objection to Searle's over-certain generalization based not only on the inevitable limitations of our experience, but also on special features of how that experience may be interpreted. Even when there is no hint of dualism in one's ontogenetic assumptions, it may be possible to come to an understand-

---

19 Hodgson (1995) is also critical of Searle's reductionistic stance—though he employs a different line of argument.

ing that does not locate consciousness *only* in brain processes. For example, from the rigorously objective, empirical, "third-person" perspective that is the goal of cybernetic (control systems) theory, there can be some doubt that consciousness should be entirely restricted to the brain in the way that Searle repeatedly states. Rather, consciousness involves brain in complex interaction with the larger systems in which it is embedded and from which it is separable only through abstract simplification. Bateson's (1972) understanding of mind as network of internal and external feedback loops suggests this larger understanding. Altmanspacher (1995) also expresses such an insight and discusses its implications. So we might ascribe mind—and therefore, presumably, consciousness—to a system which includes the brain as necessary but *not sufficient*, for it also includes some contextual aspects of the organism of which the brain is a part as well as some contextual aspects of the environment of which the organism is a part.[20]

So it is possible that our direct experience may be consistent with a view that widens the biological context and physical matrix of consciousness more than Searle does. Perhaps, in fact, the wider context is more consistent with our experience than Searle's absolute generalization which limits it to "brain" *only*. In sum, given the foregoing reasons to affirm Searle's depiction of the impossibility of omniscience, his dictum on consciousness must be rejected on grounds of parsimony.

B. The End of Science

And now we'll glance at one other way to demonstrate the illusoriness of reductionist absolutes. The argument from the incommensurability of a finite map and a territory presumed to be infinite is not the only basis for asserting that no map or procedure of mapping can reasonably be presumed to be the last and final map or procedure. There is another reason, perhaps still stronger:

> It could be said that all theoretical science is the attempt to uncover an ultimate and comprehensive set of axioms from which all the phenomena of the world could be shown to follow. But the theorems of Gödel and Tarski in particular make it evident that this ideal is hopeless. They show that every axiomatic system of any mathematical richness is subject to severe limitations, which cannot be foreseen and yet which cannot be circumvented. An axiomatic system cannot be made to generate a description of the world which matches it fully, point for point: at some points there will be holes which cannot be filled in by deduction, and at other points two opposite deductions may turn up.... Finally,

---

20   This theme has been further developed recently by Manzotti (2006).

Tarski's theorem demonstrates conclusively that there cannot be a universal description of Nature in a single, closed, consistent language.

I hold, therefore, that the logical theorems reach decisively into the systemization of empirical science. It follows that the laws of Nature cannot be formulated as an axiomatic, deductive, formal and unambiguous system which is also complete....

It follows, not merely in practice but in principle, that every scientific system must be enlarged from time to time by the addition of new axioms, which cannot, however, be foreseen nor proved to be free from contradictions.... The step by which a new axiom is added is a free play of the mind which cannot be supported by any logical procedure.

(Bronowski 1966)

Why, in the face of such rigorous demonstrations of the impossibility of omniscience, do highly intelligent and ingenious scientists persist in their pursuit of a "theory of everything"—a final and *complete* theory from which all natural phenomena can be deduced and which will therefore herald the end of our ongoing quest for understanding? This has already been proven to be logically impossible, has it not? And yet this seemingly delusional project goes on! Certainly better theories that are larger and more inclusive may come out of that pursuit. But to believe that any can be *final* seems inherently illogical. And is not this *assumption of closure*—of a final limit to which we are drawing ever closer—not to be rejected also on the basis of the Principle of Parsimony?

III. Open or Closed?

I hope that it's become clear that my focus upon Occam's Razor is more than a philosophical quibble. Rather, I believe that what I've described is symptomatic of a profoundly dangerous inversion of our perspective and therefore of our priorities.

Consider the following: What I've said about Occam's Razor is highly relevant to a distinction between two fundamental worldview perspectives—the *open* and the *closed*. Just as there are two applications of Occam's Razor, two kinds of parsimony—*complication-parsimony* (the conventional kind) and *simplification-parsimony* (the unfamiliar kind expounded here)—correspondingly there are two overall cognitive strategies that a person may use to construct her world and her relations to it. The closed person is implicitly concerned with supporting complication-parsimony above all; the open person, on the other hand, is implicitly much more concerned with supporting simplification-parsimony. I will now attempt to spell out what I mean by that.

A. Identification and Reflection

People can be dichotomized according to many characteristics. The most obvious is sex: male and female. Other ways of dichotomizing require some more or less arbitrary division of a continuous variable: young and old; healthy and sick; rich and poor.

My primary interest right now, however, is in another variable—also continuous—that has to do with *worldview* and *habitual cognitive strategies*, and that can give rise to a dichotomy based upon the organizational principles that different minds follow. This is the commonplace distinction between **closed-mindedness** and **open-mindedness**. It is a matter of a general approach to all kinds of issues— and especially to the question of implicit assumptions about limits to possible knowledge. It is a distinction between two fundamental worldview perspectives that underlies myriad other cognitive distinctions.

To start with, ordinarily we can hardly conceive *how* we have constructed our world.[21] It's not merely that while we are doing it we don't know *that's* what we are doing. The fruit of this grand project is likewise nearly invisible to us, and we can hardly imagine anything of what we have done. It's an immeasurably deep ignorance! (That deepest ignorance is, for me, the basis of the *illusory* character of our world that Buddhists speak of.)

So our habitual certainty of direct, unquestionable apprehension is our most fundamental and ubiquitous illusion. Even if we were to assume that our perceptions and knowledge are *accurate* (which of course would be a highly dubious assumption!), we must acknowledge that they are *selective*. What we perceive, what we know, can necessarily be no more than small fragments of far larger sets of *possible* perceivings and knowings.

But now I begin to understand how our relation to *reality* is still more indirect: Because we habitually misconstrue the nature of our *perceiving, understanding, knowing.* Actually in those inner actions we are always constructing a map—while remaining unaware that *the map is not the territory.* And even when we begin to recognize this distinction, for most of us (at least most of the time) it is an abstract idea with little or no experiential content. Nevertheless, while a *closed* worldview results from ignorance and/or denial of this distinction, an *open* worldview must be based upon recognizing and remembering it. (However, even if we can't do that

---

21 E.g., see in **Section 2** the 1995 essay "➔About the Invisibility of Constant Change."

recognition and remembering explicitly, we must at least somehow do it implicitly). It goes like this:

- To *know* that there necessarily is far more beyond my knowledge than I know—that in the world beyond my present knowledge there are forms of organization that are so different from all the forms I know that I can have no inkling of them—is to remain open to every possibility. This is what I mean by "open mind": for a person with open mind is aware that her experience is limited by her inner map, which is *not the territory*, and inevitably can refer only to a tiny portion of it.

- A person with a "closed mind" lacks this awareness. The closed worldview seems to deny the map-territory distinction entirely[22] and will hardly even entertain the idea of it. The link of knowings to the real is assumed to be far more direct—yet the closed mind, thus limited, is not seeing *itself*. It is directed outward, seeing *the world* in its own image, its idiosyncratically-constructed image or map, but cannot conceive that this world is its own home-made fabrication. It is convinced that what is perceived is just **what is**—and perhaps, is **all** that is. Not only is *awareness* of its own constructive role lacking, so is any *belief* that such a strange notion could possibly have any personal relevance. "Are these perceptions my idiosyncratic constructions? Of course not! What I know, what I experience, what I perceive is *the way it is*—is **reality!**"

So, to sum up, when our mind is closed our key disability is that we are not fully distinguishing our map from the territory. That is, *the closed worldview identifies the map with the world.*

And again, in taking this stance the closed mind does something more—it implicitly denies most of its ignorance. It does this automatically by *assuming limits to possible knowledge*—that is, *limits on what there is that needs to be known.*[23] For the closed mind does not conceive of the unimaginable. If I *know* that my knowledge includes all possible kinds of knowing that have any possible relevance to the "real world," and therefore that any other kind of knowing, should it happen to impinge upon me, is *irrelevant* and *unreal*, then my mind is closed.

This confusion concerns not only the contents but also the dimensions of our world and our awareness. As mentioned before, both our map and the territory are describable in terms of specific sets of dimensions. But in the closed worldview

---

22 Or if admitting it as an isolated idea in the abstract, still remaining totally oblivious to any possible generalized present-moment application of this distinction.

23 That is, what is asserted here is that *any* closed worldview grossly violates the Principle of Parsimony ("Occam's Razor").

the dimensions of our *map* are identified with dimensions of the **whole** *territory* that it maps, though the former set must necessarily be infinitely smaller than the latter. It is an infinite distortion with broad implications.

- A consequence of the foregoing arguments is that *closed-mindedness* is *irrational*, for it is a violation of the Principle of Parsimony.

All the dogmatically fundamentalist positions (including atheism) violate the criterion of parsimony in this way while agnostic and ecumenical positions do not. Thus, *scientism* and *materialism* might well be considered to be secular fundamentalisms which exemplify the closed-minded alternative.

B. How to Construct a Worldview

Further, it is my understanding that the origins of these two diametrically opposed approaches to the construction of a system of knowledge are deeply *developmental*—that open-minded and closed-minded perspectives evolve through histories of contrasting cognitive strategies.

Perhaps it goes like this:

- Both the open-minded and the closed-minded start with the vast manifold of immediate impressions—direct communications from the vast and mostly unknown world. A person of either group moves, acts, and observes. Then, every observation the person makes of repeated relationships and stable configurations brings some new *apprehension of order* into that person's theory of the world.

- But perceptions of the *matrix* within which this discovered order is embedded differ between the two groups. The first group's awareness is almost entirely restricted to the *already-discovered order*, while the second group's awareness encompasses far more, including much of the matrix also, even though the order of the matrix has not yet been discovered.

In effect, those in the first group perceive a decoded message immersed in a barely perceptible sea of *noise*, while those in the second perceive the decoded message immersed in a wonderfully variegated, fascinating sea of *messages*, which though still undecoded are nevertheless assumed to be meaningful. (That is, the second group retains its wonderment and sense of mystery, while the first does not.)

- So, the *closed* person (or culture) *minimizes* attention to context (Hall 1976) and is parsimonious of *complications*; such people can be thought of as forming the group of "context-minimizers." The *open* person (or culture) *maxi-*

mizes attention to context and is parsimonious of *simplifications;* therefore those people form the group of "context-maximizers."

- The first group of "context-minimizers" we might for convenience label the "*null-context*" group. They would dwell most comfortably in abstract thought and tend toward analytical, sequential, *left-brain* configurations of awareness. In contrast, the second group of "context-maximizers" we might for convenience label the "*plenum-context*" group, tending toward more concrete thinking (Ruddick 1989) and toward holistic, inclusively-simultaneous *right-brain* configurations of awareness.

When the first, *null-context* group then begins to build a theory founded upon a set of axioms, the founding set of axioms is totally abstract with no supporting context of incipient order. The set of axioms of the theory thus starts out as a null set and gradually expands to become more and more elaborated.

In contrast, the other approach—that of the *plenum-context* group—implicitly starts with an open, infinite set, comprising every possible axiomatic basis, known and unknown. Thus, in effect it starts with acknowledgment of the *plenum*—of the set of all possible theories of the world—both the finite closed set of those theories now conceivable and the infinite open set of those theories not yet conceivable. Experience shows that a few of these conceivable theories are immediately useful, and some others seem inconsistent with experience. But experience is local, progressive, and limited—can only have relevance to a finite subset of the infinite open set of possible theories.

- So, the first and presently more usual *null-context* approach starts with the empty set and must test and justify every *addition* by Occam's Razor to arrive at the *null set + n*. The other *plenum-context* approach, here advocated, starts with the plenum (an open, infinite set) and must test and justify every *subtraction* with Occam's Razor. The "null-context investigator" keeps it simple by not accepting unnecessary inclusions; the "plenum-context investigator" keeps it simple by not accepting unnecessary exclusions.

- Finally, when a null-context investigator is faced by a worldview propounded by a plenum-context investigator, the null-context investigator automatically begins to totally reject and push out of sight whole vast categories of possible theories—in effect, to strip the plenum down, as rapidly as possible, to approximate the familiar *null set + n*.

Here the close connection of these contrasting applications of the Principle of Parsimony (Occam's Razor) with the contrast between "closed-mindedness" and "open-mindedness" again becomes apparent. For the contrast between the *null-*

context group and the *plenum-context* group[24] is another aspect of the fundamental contrast between closed and open worldviews.

C. Staying Closed

Closure, though powerful, is also fragile. The danger of undermining is always present. The best protection is some variety of *denial* that can be mediated by an automatic emotional reaction evoking an aversive response. Anything that is out of place in the accepted scheme must arouse abhorrence; then it is rapidly and definitively rejected.

Such rejection and denial are often accomplished through procedures of *justification*. The disturbing intrusion is labeled as bad, stupid, subversive, delusional, imaginary, *quackery*, fantastic, anachronistic, primitive, or some other pejorative label that justifies devaluing and ignoring it. (Certainly such aversive responses are often quite explicit!) Justification is a rampant defense of closed-minded people, and sometimes arises in the reactions of the more open when they "lose balance" under the assault of some difficult challenge. The purpose of justification is to maintain (or restore) closure. Justification is commonly linked with anxiety and anger/resentment—from *fear that the closed system will crumble*. Justification is a most effective way to shut out disturbing incursions of unwanted thoughts.

That is one defense—closing the door and then denying that any door exists. That defense is needed if a door should ever show itself, even briefly. But there is a second defense that is far more effective because it ensures that doors will never appear. It does this by narrowing consciousness. This denial is unheralded, beneath awareness; the intrusive material is simply unperceived or quickly forgotten.

The closed person maintains this perspective through *addiction to abstract modes of thought* while the open person preferentially makes use of *concrete* thought (Ruddick 1989), treating abstraction as an occasional tool with its restrictive assumptions always recognized. Closed thought, however, cannot be in touch with such recognition for it undermines closure.

These constrictions are not always obvious; although closed people are prone to assertions of certitude that an open person would generally find unreasonable, the closed person may also sometimes acknowledge a particular, local ignorance. In this way, confusion of map with territory may be camouflaged so that (by projection) the more open listener may suffer the illusion that the acknowledgment of ignorance is an open door to a limitless universe and thus to a limitless progression to still-unsuspected views. But when such admissions of ignorance are examined closely, it may be found that this openness to possibilities is severely

---

24　Do people really fall so neatly into one or the other of these two postulated cognitive styles? That's a question for empirical investigations.

constricted with only certain categories of possibility admissible. For the closed mind any recognized unknown must have strong resemblances to the known.

In contrast, the *open* worldview recognizes (i) that the dimensionality of our *map* is necessarily limited and must be finite; but (ii) that there is no way in which limits can be placed upon the dimensionality of the mapped *territory* and no possible empirical basis for assumptions of its finitude.

In short, corresponding to the two kinds of parsimony—*complication-parsimony* (the conventional kind) and *simplification-parsimony* (the unfamiliar kind expounded here)—are two cognitive strategies: The *closed* person *minimizes* attention to context and is parsimonious of *complications*; the *open* person *maximizes* attention to context and is parsimonious of *simplifications*. But (unfortunately!) the closedness of a closed-minded perspective tends to be invisible—therefore ineffable—from within and is only detected from the outside.

\|/\:/\|/\:/\|/\:/\|/\:/\|/\:/\|/\:/\|/\:/\|/\:/\|/\:/\|/\:/\|/\:/\|/

Now, more on what I've come to understand is a crucial insight for our coming to know better *how* we know:

~~MAP AND TERRITORY

As already gone into a bit in the previous essay, a concept which has become centrally important in my thinking is that of a dynamic relation between *map* and *territory*. That is now an integral part of my understanding of mind and consciousness (see **Section 2**, below).[25] I believe that all our perceptions—both of ourselves and of the world *out there*—are mediated by mapping processes.[26] Further, for clarity of understanding it is important to remember (as Korzybski has emphasized) that *the map is not the territory.*

> The map is not the territory; the map doesn't cover all of the territory; and the map is self-reflexive (it becomes part of the territory).
>
> (Korzybski 1941)

So the distinction of *map* from *territory* plays an important role in my present understanding. Following is a previously unpublished paper (completed in 1997) which looks further at implications of that distinction and then gives preliminary glimpses of the theory of consciousness I will present more fully in the following sections **(Sections 2** and **3)**:

→ SOME THOUGHTS ON REDUCTIONISM, MECHANISM, AND DETERMINISM, RE SEARLE, DENNETT, AND CHURCHLAND

I. A Large Universe

A. Neatness and Mess

Reductionisms make our world so neat! Without them, in contrast, the world remains distressingly messy. So the temptation is great. We want to believe that we know exactly how it all works—if not in every specific detail then at least "in principle." That belief gives us some confidence and security; confidence that we

---

25 See also the essay "→Being, Doing, Knowing—A Theoretical Perspective on Consciousness," presented in the **Summing Up** section near end of this book.

26 I gather that my outlook is therefore a form of *constructivism*.

have some control over our destinies, and the security of "knowing what we have to watch out for."

And when we begin effectively to actually figure "how something works" (i.e., to delineate its *mechanisms*), we want to feel that we are thereby approaching the end of our quest. For this we have *science,* the perceptual-cognitive-manipulative-procedural tool that actually works! Magic has been superseded by *empiricism.* We have learned how to coax *nature* to speak to us and to reveal her secrets. Here are recent words of an eminent psychologist:

> Brain processes cause consciousness but the consciousness they cause is not some extra substance or entity. It is just a higher level feature of the whole system. The two crucial relationships between consciousness and the brain, then, can be summarized as follows: lower level neuronal processes in the brain cause consciousness and consciousness is simply a higher level feature of the system that is made up of the lower level neuronal elements.
>
> (Searle 1993, p. 6.)

> Many people who object to my solution (or dissolution) of the mind-body problem object on the grounds that we have no idea how neuro-biological processes could cause conscious phenomena. But that does not seem to me a conceptual or logical problem. That is an empirical/theoretical issue for the biological sciences. The problem is to figure out exactly how the system works to produce consciousness, and since we know that in fact it does produce consciousness, we have good reason to suppose that there are specific neurobiological mechanisms by way of which it works.
>
> (Searle 1993, p. 7.)

There we have a contemporary consciousness researcher's confidence that the **mechanisms** of consciousness will be found since "consciousness ... is *just* a higher level feature of the whole system" (emphasis added); more specifically, "conscious-ness is **simply** a higher level feature of the system that is made up of the lower level neuronal elements" (Searle 1993, p. 6; emphasis added). So, the relation of consciousness to its lower-order substrate is a simple and unambiguous one! Consequently, there seems no doubt that neurobiological research techniques will be adequate to find the responsible neural mechanisms: "The problem is to figure out exactly how the system works to produce consciousness, and since we know that in fact it does produce consciousness, we have good reason to suppose that there are specific neurobiological mechanisms by way of which it works" (Searle

1993, p. 7). The implication is that consciousness is **nothing but** the action of neural mechanisms—and certainly, we already *know* how to investigate neural mechanisms.

So we're bound to get there. Great! Yet, in truth, how close are we? Certainly, we are "progressing"; what we know through the methods of science is increasingly complex, subtle, and powerful. Its significance and impact seem enormous! But is this more than a comforting illusion? Our goal, we think, is the asymptote of *full* understanding—of being able to comprehend and predict everything about our world and our place in it. We acknowledge, sometimes, that this is a goal we can never quite reach. But we see ourselves (collectively if not individually) as coming closer and closer to it. We see the gap becoming narrower and narrower.

Yet that too may be an illusion. The systems we can account for, explain and sometimes predict are still relatively simple. At this moment in history our knowledge is adequate only to a certain maximal level of complexity. That has been true in every past moment and (I'm now increasingly certain) inevitably will continue to be true at every moment in the future. We strive to raise that level and with some success. But our comforting conviction of an asymptote which we are approaching is based upon an implicit *assumption*.

The assumption is that there is an upper limit to the world's complexity. This assumption is implicit in the faith that scientific theories of finite complexity can adequately describe—can precisely and fully map—the world. Yet *why should there be* an upper limit to the world's complexity?

B. Limiting the Knowable

Certainly, it seems that our science points implicitly toward an upper limit— that our successful theories have till now not had to rise above some limiting level of complexity. This seems to be an upper limit that we know of through our own experience. But in actuality, this limit does not tell us about the *world's* complexity; it tells us about the levels of complexity that *we can begin to comprehend*. What relation might that *cognitive* limit have to the possible elaboration of higher and higher levels of complexity in the *structure of the universe*? On that we have no information.

Yet take the assertions of typical reductionists. They imply that all that is worth knowing about life, mind, and spirit can be derived (at least "in principle"!) from our knowledge on those levels that the reductionist believes s/he already well understands. Thus, we have some precise understanding of the motions of particles—at least, of one particle at a time. Even when two particles are interacting, we can account for their motions with amazing precision. Of course, the "three-body problem"[27] can become intractable. Yet we can believe that it is just a matter of improved computers and simulation programs, and these more complex dynamics will also yield.

Further, with probabilistic techniques we can already handle the dances of large numbers of units that may no longer be identified as individuals. This too permits precise explanations and predictions—and we thus get chemistry and thermodynamics. Now apply those understandings to living organisms or to their organs, tissues, cells, and further disrupted fragments. Structures and compositions are cataloged so that myriad more complex relationships can be mapped. Biochemistry, pharmacology, biophysics, and physiology are born.

We have thereby learned a lot about living organisms and think that this mapping will eventually comprehend the whole territory of life. We go more and more deeply within our own bodies, hoping to approach the end of our explorations. Similarly, going outward toward the furthest reaches of the universe, our comprehension comes to include more and more of the galactic, astral and planetary relationships we observe. We can account for the evolutions of different types of heavenly bodies and predict their further evolutions.

So now, we think, we begin to have the basis for explaining nearly everything! It's just a matter of *more work* (undoubtedly, *much* more work!) *using the same proven methods.* Ultimately *all* will be reduced to these levels that we most thoroughly (and satisfyingly) comprehend—to physics (with its various branches such as biophysics and astrophysics); to chemistry (physical chemistry, biochemistry, etc.); and to the mathematical theories that structure those empirical fields of knowledge.

II. A Larger Universe

That's one picture—one that is prevalent in modern technological societies. It may be characterized as a *closed* worldview. It has a highly satisfying arrogance! But another is at least conceivable. And not merely conceivable; I find it increasingly *plausible.* This alternative includes nearly all the elements that make up the closed reductionist perspective but gives them very different places in the whole.

A. Complexity: Spectrum and Perspective

In the alternative picture—which may be characterized as an *open* worldview—the organizational levels of our most elaborate, precise, and creative thoughts form just a very tiny region of a vast spectrum of unknown organizational levels. An analogy is the relation between the total electromagnetic spectrum and the visible

---

27 How three particles can simultaneously interact.

spectrum. The frequency band of the radiation we can use for sight is a minute segment of a vast range of radiant energies.

If the world does in fact open out toward so vast a spectrum of complexities, mostly unseen, then the narrow-band picture is inadequate in unrecognized ways. For it is taking a *tiny part* to be the *whole*—thereby greatly distorting the actual situation through a kind of perceptual foreshortening.[28]

Consider: We see only that which our perceptual-cognitive systems are adequate to map—and if we fail to distinguish the map from the territory, that which lies beyond their mapping capabilities has no existence for us, no *reality*. That holds especially for understandings concerning levels of organization, levels of *complexity*.[29] If I insufficiently distinguish the map from the territory, and therefore assume that the complexity of my cognitive models completely represents the complexity of that which is modeled, I will necessarily be unaware of most of the ways in which my cognitive models *fall short*.

How much of the relevant fields of phenomena are being totally neglected? Are some pertinent phenomena incapable of representation within the terms of this model because they lie on a higher level of complexity? If my worldview is closed, I will hardly recognize such questions. After all, I am convinced, reality is of course "nothing but" that which is portrayed by my cognitive model.

Thus, I hardly see anything extending beyond the territory that my models (a) can already adequately map or (b) can be envisioned as mapping in the future with some now-conceivable kinds of modifications. Thus, that which does not fit within my schemes very nearly ceases to exist for me. Consequently, if somehow I catch some hints that there is an expanse of the "unknown" that stretches out beyond my immediate view, I will tend to view it as being relatively limited and small.

That's the reductionist view. It is almost entirely closed to non-reducible levels of organization. And whatever it does see of those more complex phenomena, it believes to be reducible to "nothing but" the level at which it is competent.

---

28 That last notion brings in still another kind of image, having to do with perspectives and how we sense distances. World complexities to which my cognitive models are adequate can be thought of as lying close at hand, while those that because of their far higher complexity are beyond the capabilities of my present cognitive models are far away. Thus, this imaging of the situation has to do with "near" and "far".

29 Such cognitive constriction in the "hard" sciences may be supported by the immediate usefulness of some beautifully-simplified concepts. May it be that even the concept of "information," as it is presently formulated as a binary, quantized variable, is only the simplest end of a continuum that rises in complexity to more and more subtle ways of being informed—of being *spoken to*. Our languages have evolved to convey some of these ways at levels that the present "information" concept cannot reach.

The alternative view emphatically remembers that *the map is **not** the territory*, and since there is no basis for constricting the *territory* of "unknown" realities, the parsimonious hypothesis[30] therefore keeps it *open* as a limitless expanse of infinite extension. In contrast, the "nothing but" assumptions of the closed reductionist worldview quietly shrink those vast distances to very short perceived segments—to steps that the confident reductionist *knows* will sooner or later be efficiently taken. That contraction of perceived distances is what I mean by "foreshortening."

An analogous distinction between map and territory occurs when three-dimensional space is represented in two dimensions by a "picture." The picture may be highly convincing. We may think we are looking at the actual scene that it depicts. The *representation* of depth is wonderful.

Here (gazing "into" a photo) we may implicitly say to ourselves: "Of course the map (this photo) is not the territory—for this is only a *picture*." But look at some parallels with other map-territory relations of which we are less aware: In the picture, how much depth is actually present? (Of course none as it's two-dimensional.) How much depth is represented? (Nearly all—is it not?) And how much is indicated of that which lies beyond the depths that are depicted? The *infinite* distance (in a certain direction) is represented by an infinitely small region—the "*vanishing* point." Thus in the picture the illimitable is perceived as a sort of limit. It is paradoxical—one of the many paradoxes of compressed thought. Now, in the case of the two-dimensional picture, our interpretive processes tell us that the vanishing point actually has the meaning of an infinite outward extension beyond the picture-plane. However, we have not yet learned to make the analogous kind of interpretive jump when attempting to perceive the infinite depths of the real world's complexity—the levels beyond levels of structural complexity that our *open-minded null hypothesis* must allow for.

Such constriction of awareness is typical not only of our perceptions but of all our thinking; we are acutely aware of the figure but tend to forget about the ground. Our attention is taken over by the *near*, and the *distant* is forgotten. Thus, our conscious world tends to be "foreshortened" through an almost unavoidable *neglect of context.*

And the foreshortening may be enormous! In the closed reductionist scheme the unknown is in some essential way finite. It has limits—limits at least in a vertical sense if not horizontally. That is, the levels of organization that our conceptual systems now deal with are believed to very nearly exhaust those that are possible and significant. But what if this finitude is illusory—is wishful thinking? Then the foreshortening of our vision has been infinite!

---

30 This we may call the ***open**-minded null hypothesis*—in effect, it combines into one the two null hypotheses, Pnh and NEnh, of the previous essay.

Early cosmologies were, it seems plausible to me, derived through the same natural (at the time inescapable) foreshortening. Consider an old picture:

- The sun, moon, and starry heavens as lights carried in concentric "crystal spheres" turning about the earth not too far above the clouds.

Now, this seems highly naive, primitive, quaint; evidence that mind of that time was not operating at a very rational or effective level. Those were of course just ancient superstitions, totally at variance with reality!

But reconsider: Based upon visual experience with the naked eye, there was no way to infer the vast distances which we now perceive as "obvious." The foreshortened model incorporated what was actually *seen* at that time, in a not unreasonable way. (Though, amazingly, some early natural philosophers did postulate an extended, more open universe that comes remarkably close to the contemporary picture!) Since those times it took great extensions of observational and interpretive techniques to move toward our present model of a vast, possibly infinite universe. Perhaps the outer limits of reality's complexity is just as far beyond our present reductionist conceptions—that are based upon presently understood levels of organization—as the distances from us of furthest nebulae exceed the assumed heights of the starry crystal spheres!

Of course, the advocate of the usual *closed* reductionist scheme acknowledges that our present conceptual systems may need to be expanded and modified to encompass additional aspects of reality—but only within unacknowledged limits which actually are far narrower than the advocate recognizes. For that reductionist naturally assumes that these expansions and modifications will lie (mostly if not entirely) within those "manageable" levels of organization—those finite and familiar levels of complexity—with which our present thinking struggles. There may be a suspicion of some unseen level of organization that bounds those with which we are familiar. But for the most part the conceptual space is flat—it lacks a vertical dimension of levels extending far beyond those we already know best. (In effect, it restricts itself to a few convenient "crystal spheres.")

The alternative *open* conception acknowledges a very deep vertical dimension and makes a fundamental distinction between (a) the complexity of our world (complexity still largely unknown, perhaps unknowable) and (b) the complexity of our understandings of our world. This recognition of difference in ranges of complexity is a crucial step toward recognizing that the map is not the territory.

The idea of fractal dimensions may be useful here, at least metaphorically. In the just sketched *open* conception of the relation between our own limited understanding and the illimitable *real*, the fractal depth of the map can never approach the fractal depth of the territory. The former is relatively shallow, finite; the latter, in the absence of any empirical basis for limiting it, must reasonably be assumed to be infinite (until there is evidence to the contrary).

• In summary, then, we can think of the reductionist paradigm as a gross simplification that is based upon a distortion of scales. It is my suspicion that the reductionist has a tremendously foreshortened perspective, seeing the small part of the scale that is *now* understood as comprising *nearly all* of it. ("There's *just a little bit more* to go!")

However, the reality may be very different.

B. Onion Layers

Here's another image (an image in which the usually upwards direction of the greatest unknown is now taken instead as *downwards*) to clarify the usual *invisibility* of that ubiquitous distortion. If progress in understanding is like peeling the layers of an onion so that one cannot even begin to detect, much less *characterize*, the next layer until one is nearly finished with the current layer, then it is no wonder that I know nothing of other layers. For the only onion layers I've ever touched (so far) are the ones I've already eaten and the one I'm eating now.

Here it is the hierarchy of levels of organization that is being likened to the layers of the onion. The world hierarchy that corresponds to contemporary scientific knowledge starts with the very simple—single particles moving in fields—and extends up through thermodynamics and chemistry toward levels of complexity that are beyond our present comprehension—organism, biota, cosmos. As noted, the scientifically understood region is experienced as vast, and the gap that separates it from the levels of complexity that it does not yet adequately encompass is seen as rapidly narrowing and soon to disappear.

It is this "*narrow and narrowing gap*" that I postulate is an illusion of foreshortening; the gap may be infinite, and unbridgeable by our present conceptual approaches. The gap *seems* small simply because most of it is invisible to our present conceptual apparatus.

• So here we are! The complexity—the dimensionality—of our maps is necessarily limited because human cognitive capacities are limited. Yet (it is hypothesized) there is no upward limit to the dimensionality that would be required to exhaustively map all the world's levels of order—these must (for lack of any contrary evidence) be presumed to be infinite (without end).

- Therefore, if this is true, then the existence of levels of order higher than any we can know or even conceive of is undeniable, and the human generation of complete predictions is in principle beyond our reach.

==<<((([]||[]))>>==((([^]/\[^])) ==<<((([^]|_|[^]))>>==((([^]/\[^]))==<<((([]||[]))>>==

That was a 1997 essay—but I'd come to some of that opening by 1991, when I'd written the following:

→ CLOSING AND OPENING

My first use of the "closure" notion is to characterize my whole belief system (my *worldview*). A closed belief system is the faith—an absolute, unquestioning conviction—that some specialized conceptual system can ultimately be adequate for the complete description and understanding of the world.[31] Therefore every reductionist scheme of knowledge is "closed" in the way I mean. Familiar examples are various species of fundamentalism: convictions that all knowledge is implicit in the Bible, or in the Koran, or in quantum physics.[32] A knowledge system is closed if it includes the belief that confirmation of its adequacy or "correctness" means that other, competing knowledge systems that apply other sets of concepts to the same field, are necessarily thereby wrong and deficient. The closed mind automatically assumes a monopoly on truth: "If I understand this situation accurately and correctly, and you understand it differently, then *your* understanding *must* be *wrong*." The pre-modern absolutist said "I have access to the only and full truth." The modern absolutist says "I have access to the means for ascertaining the only and full truth." The post-modernist will say only something like "I have partial access to maps of partial 'truths' I have constructed, and have partial access to means for constructing more such partial maps. (Your maps may be equally valid) …"

Does my worldview rest upon an *assumption of "closure,"* or does it not? If it does, then I subscribe to a "fundamentalism." That is, there is a single absolute truth, that is either (i) already known (e.g., the religious fundamentalisms, with all truth available in their scriptures), or is (ii) ultimately determinable by known means (e.g., scientism, with assured and privileged access to procedures for verification). Thus "closure" may refer either (i) to a fundamentalism of known *answers*, of already possessed knowledge, of truth "in the bag"; or (ii) to a fundamentalism of known *questions*, of already possessed methods and procedures. The first (i) may be labeled "closure around answers" (the unquestioned possession of absolute *answers*); the second (ii), "closure around questions" (the unquestioned possession of absolute *questions*).

---

31 The tragic dangers of the total reliance of military defense specialists upon a closed conceptual system is made dramatically apparent in Cohn's paper (Cohn 1990) on the constriction of awareness induced through learning a specialized technical language.

32 And any fully deterministic position is "closed" (e.g., determinism based in classical physics) but a system need not be fully deterministic to be closed (e.g., a fundamentalist conviction based in quantum physics).

The scientism I unquestioningly accepted for most of my life was a faith of the second type. That is, my conception of *reality* was intended to be a closed system, with some conceivable (though of course still unreached) terminus of "knowability." I implicitly assumed that, at least in principle, *reality* can some day (with sufficient dedication to the task) be fully known and completely understood?[33]—or can, at least, be fully known and understood except for details.

Those pesky "unresolved details" assured plenty of work for the foreseeable future! Here, there were two main possibilities: Unresolved details might form a contracting sequence, asymptotically approaching zero-ignorance. Or, in a more open version of scientism (a version I favored), the unresolved details might be ever-refreshed as the accessible world become larger through technological advances—and therefore the sequences of details yet to be resolved might not be contracting. But in imagination all these *unknowns* were nevertheless qualitatively familiar questions, and their solutions would serve to continually upgrade the resolution of the single absolute image of "the real."

Those are larger meanings given to the term "closure." But "closures" can occur in a smaller theater: Even without the assumption that some unified conceptual system will ultimately be adequate for describing and explaining the whole of reality, the notion of "closure" is applicable to our thought about any more limited conceptual system that we may be using at a given moment. Here the "closure" notion refers to an unquestioning assumption[34] of the internal consistency and completeness of that conceptual system. That is, it is assumed to be a *logically closed* system. "Closure" in this sense has been sought for grand or tiny theories everywhere—and was assumed to be nearly everywhere attainable—before Gödel's demonstration of its logical impossibility for any except the simplest conceptual system.

I lately learn that this meta-knowledge can be spoken of with other words. Since coming to these views by some combination of osmosis from the culture I am embedded in, combined with my own intuitions and deductions, I now learn that the stance that I am calling "open"—i.e., that of "non-closure"—is exactly the burgeoning *post-modern* stance.[35] (So, like M. Jourdain's discovery[36] that he had, unknowingly, been speaking "prose," I discover that I have unknowingly been discovering and expounding "post-modernism"!)

---

33 Of course, an assumption of the ultimate attainability of complete knowledge may also acknowledge that this completion must take a very long time...

34 Grounded at first in partially tested faith, but aiming toward eventual logical demonstration ("proof").

35 Anderson 1990.

36 In Molière's *Le Bourgeois Gentilhomme*.

==<<((([]||[]))>>==((([^]/\[^])) ==<<((([^]|_|[^])))>>==((([^]/\[^]))==<<((([]||[]))>>==

>>PREVIEW OF SECTION 2 (KNOWING CONSCIOUSNESS):

Abbreviations:

CC—*continual creation*

A[sw]—*Anticipating self-world model*

After a few introductory paragraphs (entitled "Seeing Through the Opening"), the first essay entitled "➔**Retrospect on the Path**" sketches my cognitive route to the metatheory of consciousness that will be expounded in the rest of this section—explaining how at the start I'd gotten nowhere because (as I saw in hindight) my *scientism* mindset had turned off the tools of perception and thought required for productive movement into that territory. I just couldn't really see my quarry! However I shifted and began to see something new—the rest explains how and what.

Next comes my essay developing the same theme, published in 1992[37], entitled "➔**On Consciousness: What is the Role of Emergence?**" It proposes that *consciousness is ongoing emergent change, the continuing creation of unprecedented pattern.* In short, "consciousness is creation"—continual creation. It is the continual birth of meaning. That relatively unfamiliar notion about consciousness is developed further. It is proposed that the inner structure that is thus re-organizing itself is the organism's dynamic (predictive) internal model of itself-in-its-world—an *evolving virtual machine* that is the ongoing product of the brain's neural networks. This perspective on brain-mind puzzles, which can be related to certain recent explorations in science and technology, is not on the same explanatory level as most other brain-mind theories but entails the inclusion of a *meta*-level.

Third is "➔**Further Thoughts on Foregoing Essay (Atkin 1992),**" is a brief amplification of ideas in the preceding essay (ideas concerning: *Sperry's prescience; consciousness as information; causal efficacy of consciousness; the key lack in previous theorizing*). It especially examines ways in which our CC metatheory can be related to other theories of consciousness. The first subsection (*"A. Hunt for Mechanisms"*) considers questions about "mechanism" citing researchers who argue for the insufficiency of mechanistic explanations. Following subsections show how the insufficiency may have to do with *levels* of explanation, suggesting that we expand the

---

37   in *References* see Atkin (1992).

theoretical structures of current "normal science" in order to move toward a meta-level. The assertion is that something is left out by attempts at mechanistic explanation, and that this "something" is only rediscovered by a paradigm expansion to include as theoretically legitimate the self-organizational capacities of dissipative systems. Comments are then made about a current approach that suffers less than most from this insufficiency—Gerald Edelman's *Theory of Neuronal Group Selection* (Edelman & Mountcastle 1978; Edelman 1989). It concludes with a proposal of a related way to understand the workings of language and speech.

The fourth essay (developing the consciousness theme of the preceding essays) is a shortened version of the paper written in 1994 and presented at the 1st conference "*Toward a Science of Consciousness*" (Tucson, Arizona). Entitled "➔ **Conscious Beyond Mechanism (Shifting a Paradigm)**," it begins by noting that neuroscience has been seeking *mechanisms* of consciousness but suggests that there may be none, then goes on to explain again the *continual creation (CC) metatheory of consciousness,*[G] proposing (as just told in the previous essays) that the inner structure that is thus re-organizing itself is the organism's dynamic (predictive) internal model of itself-in-its-world. This dynamic map—to be labeled the organism's *anticipating* self-world *model* or A[sw][G]—anticipates the organism's actions and predictively generates controlling feedback ("virtual feedback"[G]) which is derived from *simulation of the activity and effects of the organism's own action systems.*

The model's predictions are continually being tested, and the model readjusts, modifying its structure to compensate for discrepancies. That is, it "accommodates,"[G] and these ongoing accommodative changes—as well as other modifications to resolve internal A[sw] inconsistencies—generate conscious awareness (Atkin 1992). In this way *downward causation* and the causal efficacy of consciousness can be understood anew, as can the relations of conscious to unconscious process.

Lastly, some epistemological implications are presented relating CC prototheory[G] to constructivism and noting why it is so difficult to comprehend the nature and depth of our experiencing.

This is followed by a short 2006 addition to the previous essay entitled "➔ **Addendum: Amazing Complexity and Vivid Creativeness of Visual Awareness.**" It asks—How can CC metatheory account for the tremendous complexities I see every moment in the world around me? That great dynamic complexity of light-patterning is entering my eye, activating ocular sensors and visual-system neurons, therefore driving the ongoing accommodative updating of my A[sw]. And since A[sw] is defined as a proactively *anticipating* self-world model, added levels of dynamic complexity arise because A[sw] must in every moment be *predicting* all the sensory feedback being generated through this moment's motor actions. So, while this big picture fits what I know about visual perception, I'm sure that the subtle, highly-dynamic complexity of my ever-changing, continuously-evolving A[sw] is in its full details beyond my comprehension—just as the full story of brain's dynamic interconnectivity must be.

The next essay (written in 1995) is entitled "➔**About the Invisibility of Constant Change.**" According to CC metatheory, mind structure is always changing since consciousness is the *revision* of structure. But then we would think that this "nature" of consciousness could not for so long have escaped notice by most "experts"—if constant mind-change really doesn't stop. This essay looks into why the process of ongoing change that's postulated to underlie awareness nevertheless remains mostly *hidden* from us (so that its role in consciousness has not before now been accepted by everyone as *obvious*).

The more stable our environment, and the more repetitive our actions within that stable environment, the less change is demanded of our mind-structure. Then our consciousness remains narrow, restricted, shallow—and this promotes stability of mind-structure. Accommodation will be largely cyclical, continually converging towards and recreating a relatively stereotyped mind-structure that is adaptively adequate within the stable ecology. In short—this and other sketched-out reasons may explain why some consciousness explanation like CC metatheory, though anticipated in part or whole by others, has not been long and widely accepted as *obvious*.

The essay ends with suggestions on empirical evidence for CC metatheory.

The penultimate essay in this section (written in 1994, entitled "➔**Reflections on Order and Disorder: Is Consciousness Inherently Negentropic?**") explores some further implications of the role consciousness is presumed to play in structural evolution. If consciousness itself is creation—is the evolution of new structure—this brings the creative evolution of living beings from biological centrality to a still more central point in my own life, as it becomes the actuality of my experiencing in this present moment. For the world's infinite complexity demands that my inner world undergo continual reorganization in order to remain predictively adequate to the larger world. The meta-change that is thus experienced from within as conscious awareness tends, in balance, to increase net coherence and thereby to generate two components of negentropy: consciousness-mediated environment-organism cooperative negentropy, which concerns the organism-environment system; and consciousness-mediated intra-organismic negentropy, which concerns the *inner mental life*. Thus understood, consciousness is a main generator of negentropy, and at the upper regions of system complexity it may be entropy's principle sink—life's most skillful means for negentropy generation. Implications of these speculations for social and personal *effectiveness* are then examined.

The section ends with an essay from 1991 on "➔ **Earlier Neurophysiological Speculations**"—which is just that. It asks questions that had been of interest to the author about some fundamental neurophysiological principles that may underlie unconscious mind and consciousness, and suggests directions in which to look concerning synaptic arrangements and neuronal organization.

/~*~\/~*~\/~*~\/~*~\/~*~\/~*~\/~*~\/~*~\/~*~\/~*~\/~*~\/~*~\/~*~\/~*~\/~*~\/~*~\/

SECTION 2: KNOWING CONSCIOUSNESS

~~SEEING THROUGH THE OPENING

Here I briefly introduce my new theme—the main theme concerned with the nature, functions, and implications of *consciousness*—that will be developed in greater depth in the rest of this section, and then further expanded in various ways in the book's later sections. The essays will be dealing with questions such as:

- What IS consciousness?
- HOW might it WORK?
- How can we understand the inseparability of World State and Mind State?

/~*~\/~*~\/~*~\/~*~\/~*~\/~*~\/~*~\/~*~\/~*~\/~*~\/~*~\/~*~\/~*~\/~*~\/~*~\/~*~\/

I begin with a previously-unpublished paper (begun years before, completed in 1995) about my route towards a new view of those questions, then sketching my first glances at an alternative metatheory of consciousness—based in old understandings, therefore anticipated in works by others, but here put together and developed in ways not (so far as the author knows) done before.

➔ RETROSPECT ON "PATH"

I. What has Come Into View

Questioning—and Finding

The particular conception of mind which I will now present was the fruit of a growing curiosity about the "nature" of my own awareness. I had been asking questions about the fabric of my experience—the fiber of which it is constituted, where and how it grew, its intimate weave, and how it is woven. I started with the questions:

- Who and what am I, moment to moment?
- How is it that I am aware?

From there I moved on to these:

- Can I find the sources and meanings of consciousness?
- Can I know the workings and purposes of my own consciousness?

And I also wondered: In what way(s) can I work towards greater clarity and unity of awareness? For most of what I was hunting was terribly elusive—seemed vague, clouded, …

It was only later that I began to understand why. I began to understand that it was because all my powers were honed to deal almost exclusively with *objects*—with human objects certainly, but most especially with machine-objects. Yet these questions now pointed towards matters that were not object-like—toward kinds of change that were non-mechanical. Thus my tools of perception and thought seemed to have nothing to get hold of. All that I was asking about—though perhaps in full view—was hidden from eyes trained to detect totally different sorts of patternings.

For a long while, therefore, it seemed that such questions had no answers, and that in asking them I was "chasing rainbows"—looking for that which had no verifiable reality. Was I merely trying to see meaningful form in the accidental shapes of passing clouds—looking for pattern in what was inherently chaotic, accidental, and therefore meaningless?

As I continued to pay attention not only to the *object*-contents of my moment-to-moment stream of experience, but also to its *texture* and to the vortices and pulsations of its *flow*, I began to see this flow more clearly. It was *very interesting!* (But was it really "flow?" Or was it a disjointed yet rhythmical cascade of contrasting yet associatively-linked baubles?) I was in a fascinating but incomprehensible faery-land watching beautiful stories that seemed, however, still to make no *sense!* I wanted to understand something here, but was stymied.

Thus (as just sketched) I began eventually to suspect that the trouble was that I was unequipped for this adventure. I began to see how the explanatory methods and categories available to me could do little or nothing with most of what I was observing—how these practiced methods and categories were restricted with respect to the materials they could assimilate. For they required enduring objects and repeatable patterns of change.

Yet becoming more patient, I began to see *something*—always changing (yet not repeating). I could catch tiny flashes of mind's workings—without "enduring objects" and "repeatable patterns." My simplistic conceptual notions about consciousness, therefore, seemed hardly to relate to my increasingly differentiated direct experience.

In puzzling about this, I came to an idea that immediately rang true for me, as it gave me ways to begin to understand much that had till then been incomprehensible. With it, I could begin to grasp what I was observing as I watched the passing parade of my own awareness. The nameless now had a name—and I began to see how to *make sense* of connections that in my earlier reflections I could hardly even perceive and keep hold of.

The revelatory notion was that consciousness *is*, in fact, exactly as elusive to our habitual analytical thinking as I had experienced it to be, for it is *inherently and fundamentally irregular*. Here's what I saw:

- Of the complex patterns of adaptive change always going on within us, *consciousness* has exactly to do with all in my adaptive responses that is *non-reproducible* and *non-predictable*.

- I continually reconstruct myself, and my consciousness is identical with the ongoing generation of whatever in my self-transforming structure is *fundamentally new*.

That is, consciousness is **birth of meaning**. Consciousness has to do with the generation of new information—in contrast with predictable process, which generates no significant new information. Thus:

- Consciousness is identical with creation. The organism's adaptational patterns continually reorganize themselves, so that the laws of their operation are undergoing unforeseeable alterations; the field of my awareness is identical with the field of this fundamental reorganizing.

This was certainly a startling switch! I had completely misconstrued the nature of my quarry. I was looking for the Cheshire Cat and had been frustrated when all I could glimpse was its smile. *But* then I realized that the smile was in fact what I was after! That is, "consciousness" was not previously-existent information nor the *carrier* of that information—rather it was *newly-emerging information* at the moment of its generation, or was the *system-transformation* by which it was emerging.

Questioning Again

I had come to this hypothesis by a route of negations—of exclusions. I had examined the available hypotheses on "consciousness"—those I knew of—and had come to find them all unsatisfactory or unconvincing. Here's what I ultimately **eliminated**—as I was driven to conclude that:

Consciousness was *not* "a *state*" and therefore was not to be correlated with particular "brain states."

Consciousness was *not* ascribable to the operation of some specialized mechanism or brain subsystem, could not be localized to some particular brain centers or patterns of neuronal firings.

At first I was confused, finding that everything "sensible" was excluded. But then I realized that something important was, after all, left over. And I discovered a **clue to the remainder:**

Consciousness was rather to be thought of in entirely different terms, those of a kind of "meta-change"[1] foreign to my previous thinking about brain and consciousness.

That was what was left—it seemed the only viable remaining direction in which to look. Because it seemed a direction of great promise, I proceeded to look more carefully where it pointed, to work out some of its implications.

But this notion immediately faced me with objections. Though it seemed to fit wonderfully with much of my experience, with some it seemed not to fit: For is not much of my awareness stereotyped—seeing and feeling *again* just what I have seen and felt a million times before? Where then is the "fundamental newness"? I could meet this problem in two ways:

First, it was clear that though separate details of my experience might seem identical with past experience, the total configuration would always be unprecedented—certainly, the larger the field of the comparison, the lower the possibility of exact repetition.[2]

Second, when clearly there was very little new in either my situation or in my response to it, the *depth* of my awareness might be correspondingly thin.

---

1   This identity hypothesis, asserting that "consciousness-*is*-creation," can be seen as a vast extension—a generalized equivalent—of a (subsequently verified) insight from sensory deprivation research that sustained visual sensation depends upon a *changing* sensory input.

2   Thus, a direct implication of the "consciousness-*is*-creation" hypothesis was that stereotypy was necessarily beneath consciousness, and that boredom (or "stimulus hunger") must therefore have to do with expectations for particular kinds of novelty.

This last implication led me to look more closely at the notion that *consciousness could vary in depth*. It seemed that such variation could be analogous to differences in depth of *meaning*. But most interesting of all, I came to see how change in *depth* of awareness would itself inevitably remain beyond awareness. The reason for this prevailing invisibility of depth can be seen by considering a simple tautology: I am not aware of that of which is outside my awareness; and being aware only of that of which I am aware, I have no context or frame against which to measure variation in the expanse of my awareness.[3] Thus I could hardly be aware of the depth of my consciousness.

Nevertheless, now I'll attempt to look at the place I've come to. Giving primacy in a theory of consciousness to the creative challenge of novelty has important consequences for the implications of the theory.

II. What's the Difference?

What difference will it make if it should turn out that this "continual creation" (CC) hypothesis is, in fact, an accurate way to describe consciousness? It will make a lot of difference to me. For if every conscious moment is the creation of a new and unique structure of lawfulness, which self-organizes to lessen the world's disorder, then I know how consciousness *cannot* be understood. That is:

(1) I have the underpinnings for a new *philosophy of neuroscience*—one which makes clear that conventionally-deterministic science will never succeed in discovering the "mechanisms of consciousness," for there are none.

But I also know how consciousness *can* be understood—and this understanding will have implications in many areas of psychology:

(2) I have a straight-forward, clear and unambiguous understanding of just how the conscious regions of my mind differ from those much more extensive regions which remain beneath my awareness;

(3) thus I have a basis for a new framework in which to unfold some deeper groundings for dynamic psychology.

---

3   This cause for an inherent limitation of self-observation (thus, of mind's self-understanding) has also been noted by Jaynes (1976). Buddhists say: "The eye cannot see itself".

Most immediately, however, my own self-appreciation—and my appreciation of others—is directly affected, for I now know that:

(4) I am truly creative in every conscious moment—creative at least in small disjoint ways, and sometimes (not very often!) in a more unified and larger way;

(5) and since this ongoing creativeness is the gift of every conscious being, I have a new and more profound basis for honoring every conscious being.

But the single implication that—when I remember it—can most penetrate and transform every moment of my awareness is this:

(6) Right now, and in every moment, *I am constructing myself.* This understanding requires me to take responsibility for who I am, and for all that I understand and do not understand.

For I have spent my life constructing my limitations and my flexibilities. At present, I am constructing the form which my mind takes, thereby affecting the whole course of its future evolution, by the way I regulate the breadth, depth, and distribution of my awareness in *this* moment.

Part of my present mind^G is the strategies which I have organized for this regulation—and how I use these strategies is to some degree subject to my deliberate (conscious) control. These are *strategies of attention.* Thus my active choices of the strategies of attention by which I now, in each present moment, regulate the form that my awareness is taking will direct the course and outcomes of my mind's evolution.

Consequently the history of all my past moments of consciousness must be exactly responsible for my mind's present structure. Thus:

(7) My awareness now is largely determined by who I am; but who I am is the product of the history of my past moments of awareness.

So, as I thereby reveal to myself how I have become who I am, I see a complex dynamic interpenetration of freedom and constraint:

(8) Who I am and the present pattern of my awareness is vastly constrained by that whole past history of awareness; yet because every moment of awareness is creative, and unpredictably new, the course of my mind's evolution is not only continually constrained by its structural history, but also, is wide open to conscious choices which permit continual and free shifts in the direction of its evolution.

G For more on this (and other) special, technical terms, see **Glossary**.

This is a vast increase in my awareness of *responsibility*. Much that had before been assumed to be an accident of environmental impacts and genetic regulations is now brought into the arena of my deliberate choosing. And of course, once I gain this awareness of what I can choose, and of the consequences of choice, I begin to expand my real responsibility to much larger dimensions still. For before I could appeal to my ignorance: I didn't know the effects of my strategies of attention, and of the deliberate control I could exert to modify those strategies. But now, once I have begun to be aware of the deep consequences of these strategies, and therefore to understand the implications of my real though limited conscious control over their moment-by-moment implementation, then my responsibility for exerting or not exerting this control—and for how I exert it—expands correspondingly.

In the same way, the responsibility of those who educate, inform and entertain is amplified, since they exert their talents and energies to affect and shape many moments of their audience's attention, and thus are instrumental in channeling, at least to some degree, the way many attentive minds are evolving, and what they will evolve to.

What Next?

This proposed way to understand my consciousness brings the creative evolution of this living being to a still more central point in my understanding of my life—as it becomes the actuality of my awareness in this moment. I bring the world within myself, but the world's infinite complexity demands that this inner world undergo continual reorganization to remain adequate to the larger world. My brain, more complex perhaps than any other replicated subsystem of the universe, is the main organ of this ongoing evolution.[4]

I have for a while been examining implications of what I've called the "consciousness is creation" (or CC) hypothesis[5]—this view of consciousness places a main locus of unacknowledged self-organizing transformation so close to me that I can now see it's the fount of my experience in each moment. It is the very source of my awareness, with which it is identical. It is an idea that has been put forth before, in various forms. But it seems not yet to have been taken seriously

---

4   As has been proposed, in a somewhat different way, in Edelman's theory of "neuronal group selection" (Edelman & Mountcastle 1978; Edelman 1987, 1989).

5   See "***Continual creation (CC) metatheory***" in ***Glossary***; see also following papers in this section, especially essays "➜On consciousness: What is the Role of Emergence" and "➜Conscious Beyond Mechanism" (Atkin 1994).

or developed to any extent. That is something I am interested in instigating … if I can!

First, however, note that this theoretical proposal concerning consciousness is entirely dependent upon the correctness of an assumption concerning possible sorts of emergence—the assumption that some *emergence of higher-level structure takes place through self-organizing transformations which give rise to genuinely new structures that could not have been fully predicted from any knowledge of the lower level structures from which they arose.* There are some philosophers of mind and consciousness who totally deny the possibility for such emergent changes of structure to genuinely new structure. See for example Strawson (2006) and Seager (2006).

Seager (2006; p. 25) says that the possibility for such "ontological emergence" is inconsistent with what he refers to as the "Scientific Picture of the World" (p. 25) or SPW. Certainly my past insights and intuitions regarding consciousness have implicitly assumed that this grandly simplifying implication of SWP is in error.[6]

Strawson (2006) notes that a recent conception of emergence in relation to consciousness goes thus: "Experiential phenomena are *emergent* phenomena. Consciousness properties, experience properties, are emergent properties of wholly and utterly non-conscious, non-experiential phenomena" (p. 12). Now certainly this is consistent with my proposal. Yet Strawson then says that he thinks this "conception of emergence" is "incoherent" and goes to great lengths to deny its theoretical value. He gives examples to support his argument—but it's my view that he nevertheless does not effectively undercut my emergence-consciousness connection because his supportive examples and his arguments are extremely *simple*[7]—giving no recognition whatsoever to the tremendous, open-ended complexity of systems in which such consciousness-generating emergence is postulated to occur.

And so I will proceed now on the assumption that "scientism" and SWP are themselves in error when they negate of the possibility for "ontological emergence"—and that it is in fact occurring all the time as main basis for consciousness.

So following now is a sequence of papers on this alternative metatheory of consciousness. Each of the five essays in this section will explain it

---

6   Essays of **Section 1** present reasons for taking exception to scientism and to the SWP.

7   See essay in **Section 1** (especially "➔ The Restriction of Ignorance: Inverting the Principle of Parsimony)" which points out the unreasonableness of such excessively simplistic lines of argument.

more deeply, going over much of the same ground—yet in sufficiently different ways, that I've felt justified in keeping them all.

I start with the paper that was my first presentation to a larger audience of this perspective on consciousness. It's *Atkin (1992)*—the first previously published piece included in this volume (from *Medical Hypotheses*, **38**, pp. 311-314).[8]

→ ON CONSCIOUSNESS: WHAT IS THE ROLE OF EMERGENCE?

Abstract: Can *consciousness* be understood as the ongoing active *creation* of information (of meaning)? *"Emergence"*, the central concept in this hypothesis, plays an essentially different role in it than in theories previously proposed.

Introduction

What is the place of consciousness in neuroscience? How can we argue for causal efficacy of mind? The purpose of this memorandum is to suggest that interesting ways to conceive of consciousness have not been exhausted. Carefully considered answers have been given by Sperry (1980, 1991) and others (Baars 1988, MacKay 1982, Pribram 1976). Here is a significantly different alternative.

Three related but separate hypotheses concerning consciousness will be presented: The first, a characterization of its source and "nature"—of what is *happening* in the most general terms; the second a more restricted proposal concerning a particular way in which these happenings might be *organized;* and the third a suggestion concerning a possible "*matrix*" or material basis, instantiating the first two proposals. Following these three sections is a brief discussion relating the primary hypothesis to proposals of others.

The hypotheses are on three different levels; each successive level is more specific and concrete than the one before. The validity of the first does not depend upon the correctness of those that follow—each is to be evaluated independently of the other two.

8　The only alteration from the original published version (other than minor ones in citation formatting and punctuation) is that the abbreviation for "Self/World model" has been changed to what I've been using in more recent writings—changed from "sW-m" to "A[sw]."

I. Essential Nature

First, here's the central thought, which can provide a new frame for discussion: I propose that "consciousness" be viewed not as the *ground, matrix,* or *carrier* of information, but as *the emergent information itself* at the moment of its generation. My *consciousness* is emergent, self-organizing change, which continues to generate new information through the ongoing inner *transformation of my structure*—its continuing dissolution and re-creation. In short: Consciousness *is* ongoing emergent change, the continuing creation of unprecedented pattern. It is the continual "birth of meaning." The organism's adaptational patterns continually reorganize themselves, so that *the laws of their operation are undergoing unforeseeable alterations.*

Here, by "alteration of laws" I do not refer to laws of physics and chemistry, but to higher-order laws characterizing the function of complex systems—e.g., their sets of behaviorally descriptive *transfer functions.*

During each conscious moment, the lawfully-behaving brain-body system is transformed into another, again lawfully-behaving, but now by altered high-level laws. I posit that such *transformation* is the essence of real *learning*—and that it *is* both consciousness and freedom. If this is so, consciousness inherently defies prediction—which it must, to the extent it is linked to freedom.

II. Functional Organization

The second proposal is that the "structure" being reorganized (*transformed*) to generate consciousness is the organism's self-constructed model (its dynamic "map") of itself-in-its-world. This mapping structure can be termed the "Anticipating self-world model" (A[sw]). The business of my A[sw] is *prediction*, and my awareness is the continual self-remodeling by which it carries out its business.

The notion that through our experience we generate maps or "models" (or "schemata") to guide our subsequent behavior, and that this has relevance to phenomenal experience, is not new (Yates 1985, Craik 1943, Neisser 1976, Klopf 1982, Tart 1986). What was missing from those previous discussions, however, was any suggestion that it is the **changing** of the map or model (or schema) that is crucial for consciousness. That, however, is central to this proposal. Also central to it is the idea that most of the updating is actively **predictive:**

> When the organism is active, its modification of its internal model *anticipates* (rather than passively follows) its actions.

Thus the organism's A[sw] updating process is identical with its action-regulating process: This is control by *virtual feedback* which is derived not from sense-organs, but from the *virtual world* of the A[sw]—derived, that is, from the predictive behavior of the internal model, which effectively implements **anticipatory simulation** *of the organism's own action systems.*

In this way time-lags in the control loop are reduced or eliminated. This strategy of control—proposed by the author during his eye movement research (Atkin 1969) to account for certain types of movement control with no detectable time lags—has more recently been demonstrated in an engineering system where time lags would otherwise cause serious problems (Kawato, Furukawa & Suzuki 1987).

Here, however, to account for the full breadth of conscious experience, the concept originally elaborated for motor behavior is generalized to one that now includes the over-all organization of behavior and mentation. Thus the A[sw] is an active mapping not only of sensory-motor behavior but also of cognitive and emotional realms.

The second proposal, therefore, is that the A[sw], through its activity, modifies its own structure, and that this transforming constitutes ongoing consciousness.

III. Structural Matrix

The third proposal is that the biological matrix of consciousness is self-organizing pattern-detection by *neural networks.*

Self-evolution appears to be a unique and essential capability of neural networks. Adaptive self-reorganization by neural networks has been demonstrated in many computer simulation experiments, which have already shown self-organizing abilities that not long ago had seemed beyond the capabilities of any machine (Rumelhart et al. 1986, Caudill & Butler 1990). For a neural network learns patterns: Given transducers for interacting with a "world," it incorporates that world's patterns—generates a "world-model." It can actively accommodate to its environment by reworking its own dynamic patterns of response to more precisely "*assimilate* the world".

What is proposed here is that self-organizing changes by the brain's neural networks may be the substantial *stuff* of consciousness—that is, that self-restructuring *accommodation* by my neural networks is identical with my awareness.

IV. Similarities and Differences

These ideas seem generally consonant with those now being elaborated about *dissipative structures* (Prigogine & Stengers 1984) and *self-organizing systems* (Maturana & Varela 1988)—though there may be discrepancies (Kaplan &

Kaplan 1991) concerning flow of information. It is, however, a consonance of broad ideational framework—of "paradigm."

Looking for more specific insights concerning consciousness, I have found just four authors (so far) whose writings imply similar directions of thought about consciousness—Karl Pribram, Jean Piaget, D. M. MacKay, and Roger Sperry.

Pribram (1976) said: "[To] the extent that our experiences fail to correlate, to the extent that our actions are uncontrolled by habit, to that extent they are voluntary and we are conscious" (p. 306); and Piaget et al. (1976) spoke about "cognizance as a compensation for lack of adaptation by the mechanism of regulations" (p. 333). MacKay (1982) said that he "would describe ... conscious agency as embodied in ... the special re-entrant pattern of cerebral information flow that continually and actively revises its own programme, and so becomes its own arbiter" (p. 293). These remarks seem to imply that consciousness is meta-change—that it is not structure or mechanism but rather structural *change* and *modification* of mechanism that is fundamental for the development of consciousness. But none say anything directly about "emergence" or "emergent change" (though it may be implicit).

A position that focuses upon "emergence" and is generally close to my position is that of Roger Sperry (1980, 1991). We both assert that consciousness is not reducible simply to patterns of neuronal excitation that can be fully specified at the neuronal level, but is an emergent phenomenon that can only be fully described and understood on its own level. Yet there is a fundamental difference, which concerns just *how* consciousness is related to emergence.

For Sperry (1980, 1991), a new level of phenomena *has emerged*—the *mental* level. Mental phenomena are forces, movements, and interactions on that level— which, in relation to the level of neurons and their interactions, is a meta-level. That is, emergence is *prior to* consciousness.

So here's the differentiating question: Is the emergence of the meta-level a *prior condition* for consciousness, so that once this level has emerged, it from then on provides the *locus* for the phenomena of consciousness? Or is this emergence of meta-level structuring *coincident with* consciousness, so that cessation of ongoing *emergence* means cessation of ongoing *consciousness*?

My proposal, in contrast with Sperry's, is that consciousness relates to emergence in the second way: i.e., that emergent change is what those substrate neural systems are doing *continually*, and that it is this self-transformation that *is* our consciousness.

These are distinctly different ways to relate consciousness to emergence. And as a consequence of this radical difference, there is a divergence in understanding about *causation*. A "mental content" is not simply a manifestation of an existing system of causation (—a system that *has emerged*), but is the **coming into being** of a particular **new** system of causation (—a system that *is emerging*). The lawful interplay of neurons continues, but the system of *laws* (e.g., "transfer functions") that most completely describes (or *governs*) this interplay is continually altering.

Compared to the "downward causation" of an emergent determinism, it is a "*meta*-causation." Notice the different order of control: If another, changed causal system is emerging continually—then we have not simply one durable *emergent determinism*, but the continual emergence from it, in each conscious moment, of a *new* emergent determinism. That, I have postulated, is where "*freedom*" enters.

V. Conclusion

1. *Consciousness*—as ongoing **emergent** change—has to do with the *de novo* generation of new information, and thereby *escapes prediction* (in contrast with predictable process, which generates no significant new information). That is how *freedom* ("free will") is inseparable from *consciousness*.

2. The *structure* that is self-organizing and self-reorganizing is a model of the organism-within-its-world (an "Anticipating self-world model" or *A[sw]*), which maintains its adaptive correspondence by continuing anticipatory adjustment.

3. The *substance* that structures and restructures itself is the brain's neural networks.

Thus if the basic correctness of all three hypotheses were to be assumed, the explanation of consciousness could go like this: The organism's neural networks continually form, maneuver, and reorganize *models* that anticipate its changing relations to its world. The *active re-structuring* needed to maintain an adaptive anticipatory match (plus—sometimes—other, non-adaptive restructuring) *creates information* and is the exact correlate of *consciousness*.

/~*~\/~*~\/~*~\/~*~\/~*~\/~*~\/~*~\/~*~\/~*~\/~*~\/~*~\/~*~\/~*~\/~*~\/~*~\/

That's the end of the published paper (Atkin 1992)—except for the citations which are included in the full reference list at the back after the **Glossary**.

Following however is amplification (written not long afterwards) of ideas in that preceding publication. It begins:

→ FURTHER THOUGHTS ON FOREGOING ESSAY (ON ATKIN 1992)

I. Emergence, Causality and Consciousness

There are analogies with differing viewpoints on other kinds of creation. Might the contrast between these consciousness models resemble the contrast between the "big bang" and the "continual creation" models in contemporary cosmology? Or, from older belief systems, the contrast between the God who (transcendent) creates the lawful universe which thereafter runs on under those unchanging laws, and the God who (immanent) is continually involved in creating and maintaining his universe, intervening at every moment in its lawfulness?

But here's another image:

> We might compare the emergence of *mind* from a cell-aggregate to the development of a lawful system of government by a human horde, so that mind's "downward causation" (Sperry 1980) could correspond to the active governance of the country.

> But is *consciousness* to be identified with the implementing activities of the administration and its administrative agencies, governing the land under its established system of laws? (That would be like Sperry's "emergent determinism" option: **Prior**, *transcendent* emergence, then **lingering** *clockwork*.)

> Or rather, is consciousness to be identified with the restructuring activities of legislature and court system, continually reinterpreting, revising, and reforming that system of laws? (That would be like the "transformative learning" option: **Coincident**, *immanent* emergence as **ongoing creation**.)

Those are very different ways to relate consciousness to emergence; and as a consequence of this radical difference, there is a divergence in understanding about *causation*.

But what now about causality and consciousness? Sperry (1980) is particularly concerned with the "causal efficacy" of consciousness:

Of all the questions one can ask about conscious experience, there is none for which the answer has more profound and far-ranging implications than the question of whether or not consciousness is causal.

(Sperry 1980, p. 205)

He emphasizes "downward causation" in explaining his "concept of mind as a causal functional emergent." He says:

It is the idea, in brief, that conscious phenomena as emergent functional properties of brain processing exert an active control role as causal determinants in shaping the flow patterns of cerebral excitation. Once generated from neural events, the higher order mental patterns and programs have their own subjective qualities and progress, operate and interact by their own causal laws and principles which are different from and cannot be reduced to those of neurophysiology ...

(Sperry 1980, p. 201)

But if, as I have suggested, consciousness is identical with transformative learning, then the situation is significantly different. A "mental content" is not simply a manifestation of an existing system of causation (a system that *has emerged*), but rather is a *coming into being* of a particular *new* system of causation (a system that *is emerging*). The lawful interplay of neurons continues, but the system of laws that most completely describes (or "governs") this interplay is continually altering.

It follows that the relation of consciousness to causality will be somewhat different from that proposed by Sperry. If "consciousness is transformational learning" (the "continual creation" hypothesis), this means that the system's causal network is changing *continually* wherever there is consciousness. My *awareness in this present moment* means that my structure (more specifically in the suggested exemplification of the general CC idea, the structure of the "virtual machine" that constitutes my "Anticipating self-world model") is *now* transforming itself, and a *new* causal network is *now* emerging out of the old. Since the self-organizing shift of causation is from moment to moment modifying attainable outcomes, this self-organizing shift may be considered to have "causal efficacy." And if this shift *is* "mental content," then "mental content" is "real and causal in [its] own right, as subjectively experienced" (Sperry 1980, p. 204). But the causal efficacy and "reality" are attained in a way that differs significantly from that of Sperry's theory.

Perhaps, in fact, one might go a step further and say that the "continual creation" idea implies a markedly stronger kind of *causal efficacy* for consciousness than previous theories. For saying that consciousness is identical to the *restructur-*

ing of causal links ascribes to it a deeper, far more consequential control over the organism's actions than saying that consciousness *activates* causal links. Compared to the "downward causation" of an emergent determinism, it is a "*meta*-causation." Notice the different order of control: If another, changed causal system is emerging continually, then we have not simply one durable emergent determinism but the continual emergence from it, in each conscious moment, of a *new* emergent determinism. That, it was postulated, is where *freedom* enters.[9]

II. Consciousness as Information

A. Processed or Created?

Now consider the informational theory of consciousness proposed by John Battista (1977, 1978). It seems to differ from our CC metatheory in somewhat the same way that Sperry's theory does. (Thus the comments in the foregoing discussion will apply to Battista's theory if we simply substitute "information" for "emergent" property or mechanism.) And so the pertinent questions are these: Has the *emergent* (Sperry's theory) or the *information* (Battista's theory) **been** created at some **past** time (and is now there serving our consciousness)? Or is it *being created now*, continually, so long as we are conscious?

Battista labels his theory "informational holism" and in it "defines consciousness as information" (Battista 1978, p. 75). He says:

> The different forms of consciousness refer to different hierarchical levels of information. Events are conscious at a particular level of consciousness when they contain the threshold amount of information for that level. If they do not they will be unconscious.
>
> (Battista 1978, p. 75)

On the surface his theory presents a relatively static view of consciousness as compared with the proto-theory proposed here. He says "consciousness is information" (Battista 1978, p. 82); CC metatheory says "consciousness is *creation* of information" (Atkin 1992).

This seeming discrepancy between consciousness as "*presence of sufficient information*" and consciousness as "*emergence of new* information" might, how-

---

9 See above in essay at beginning of this section (***Section 2***) in the essay "➔On consciousness: What is the Role of Emergence" (subsection II). See also in the next section (***Section 3***), the last subsection of the essay "➔Worlds Without Ground," as well as paragraphs in the middle of the 1ˢᵗ essay of the final ***Summing Up*** section, "➔Being, Doing, Knowing."

ever, be bridged if he broadened his definition of "information." As presented, his theory is based in the "information" concept used in communication technology: "[T]he conventional, mathematically elaborated information theory founded by Claude Shannon and Warren Weaver [in 1949] is primarily geared to equilibrium and the stabilization of structures" (Jantsch 1980, p. 51). But Battista's theory could be modified toward one that would be very close to our proposed CC metatheory by shifting its concept of information to the "pragmatic information" described by Jantsch (1980, pp. 11 & 51-52) and referred to in the next section. This concept of information is more appropriate to self-organizing systems as it centrally involves not only *confirmation* but also *novelty*.

B. Out of the Void: "Nothingness" as Source

Can some more secure underpinning be found for the CC idea set forth above and previously (Atkin 1992)[10]—that consciousness is the ***de novo*** *creation of information?* Certainly, work on "self-organizing systems" (Jantsch 1980; Prigogine & Stengers 1984) supports the idea that such creation, though not easily apparent to us, is everywhere important, most of all in living systems.[11] It gains further plausibility whenever it is conceded that predetermination by "mechanism" must have exceptions so that the possibility of "choice" (and therefore of "freedom") is admitted—as may be the case if adaptive problems are not always soluble, even in principle, by rules of procedure that can be specified in advance. Penrose (1989) has asserted this (see below), as has Baars (1988); and Calvin (1989) seems to have skirted an explicit avowal while implying it.

Possibilities of "freedom," and therefore of real "choice" that can generate new information, are implied by some contemporary theories of consciousness. One is the theory of Baars (1988). He writes of the unpredictable resolution of problems that are "*under*determined" because they lie in a "domain that is novel, degraded, or ambiguous" (Baars 1988, pp. 92-93). A global confluence of information may lead to a resolution beyond the capability of any of the system's preexisting "expert" mechanisms.

This is at least partially compatible with ideas put forth here. For in our "continual creation" (CC) hypothesis the conscious situation is exactly this: The system is self-organizing, is performing a non-predictable change in structure, to accommodate to the situation in which it finds itself at the moment. This change

---

10 See preceding essay.

11 Signs of movement toward a paradigm that is supportive of this possibility are to be found now in many places, including such other writings as these: Bateson 1979; Battista 1977; Bohm 1983; Bronowski 1966; Laughlin et al. 1990; Laszlo 1987; Maturana & Varela 1988; Pribram 1976, 1986; Schrödinger 1958.

is *under*determined—the change that occurs is *not* the uniquely possible consequence of that situation. Thus, in our CC metatheory, it is a *choice* and implies some freedom.

For "choice" means development of altered, novel structure—its form being only partially determined by what came before. To the extent that the structural change was *underdetermined*, new information has "arisen of itself" in this particular actualization of one out of an unknowable multiplicity of potentialities.

So assume, then:

- Choice has been made, and here is something new. When *this* particularization is queried by situations other than that which evoked it, it exhibits its specific and unique implications. The generation of these implications is the generation of its newborn information.

How can this de novo generation of information—rather than "information processing"—be a central implication of CC metatheory? Conventional information theory does not have a place for such creation of information, but the "information" concept can be opened up:

> The principle of order through fluctuation which underlies all coherent evolution also requires a new information theory which is based on the complementarity of novelty and confirmation in pragmatic (i.e. effective) information. The kind of information theory which has become so useful in communication technology holds only for information which consists almost totally of confirmation. In the domain of self-organizing systems, information is also capable of organizing itself; new knowledge arises.
>
> (Jantsch 1980, p. 11)

When the concept of "information" is so broadened, it becomes more relevant to newer understandings of dissipative, self-organizing systems. As Jantsch (1980) says: "In the domain of dissipative self-organization, and especially life, information is not transferred in one-way processes, but is exchanged in circular processes and is born new" (p. 51).

"Born new!" Is it really genesis from *nothing?* Look again: Certainly that which arises in consciousness is born of "*no thing*"—for information is not "things," it is *patternings*. When this is well remembered, the creation out of nothing takes a different cast—as the universe of discourse has now shifted from that of most older, reductionist theories about "mechanisms."

For mechanisms are "things" put together out of "things." Their information content is locked into the rigidities of their "thingness." Mechanically, information can be processed or lost but not created *de novo*. But within an organismic, holistic conceptual framework, the conservatism that characterizes matter and things need no longer rule. New structure can arise, and can come from no "thing."

And exactly this may be the nervous system's ultimate specialization—as Jantsch (1980) suggested. He said that "groups of neurons lead to a phenomenon which may be identified as the self-organization of information" (p. 160), and "mind is self-organization dynamics proper" (p. 162).

This view of consciousness, combining our CC metatheory with the idea of "pro-active A[sw] updating," provides a new way to think about some perennial questions of behavioral determinism versus personal freedom. It speaks especially to the following four questions:

(1) What is the *causal effectiveness* of consciousness?

(2) What is the connection of *personal freedom* to consciousness?

(3) How, therefore, can we understand the nature and "reality" of the personal freedom that we experience?

(4) In what ways must free choice be limited by behavioral determinism?

These questions will not be pursued here, but this paper lays some groundwork for their further discussion in future writings.

III. Sufficiency of the Mechanical?

A. Hunt for Mechanisms

When I recall the proposals on "consciousness and the brain" that have been published in the past three or four years, I am amazed by their apparent lack of any common framework. The variation in approach—in conceptual structure, in method and range of exploration, and in central questions asked—is tremendous! Each author seems to speak a unique language, yet each presents ideas that may help in a search for clearer comprehension.

For example, Dennett's interesting theory of consciousness is plausible and it may be at least partially consistent with these CC ideas. But we differ, it seems, in the role that his "virtual machine" concept is given in consciousness. Dennett says "consciousness is a virtual machine" (p. 218-19)—i.e., that it **is** this machine's structure.[12] He acknowledges that *revising* processes are a ubiquitous characteristic of consciousness (he says: "Information entering the nervous system is under

---

12 Strawson (2006) notes that Dennett is "so in thrall to the fundamental intuition of dualism, the intuition that the experiential and the physical are utterly and irreconcilably different" (p. 5) that he is prepared to deny the existence of experience.

continuous 'editorial revision'"—Dennett 1991, p. 111), but he does not make the revising central as it is in our CC metatheory.

Another theory (mentioned in the preceding section) that is closer in some features to the ideas I've sketched has been constructed by Bernard Baars (1988). He suggests that "conscious experience involves a *global workspace*, a central information exchange that allows many different specialized processors to interact" (Baars 1988, p. 43).

This is in some ways like the picture I have worked out by another route.[13] Certainly, it implies the same kinds of relations between consciousness and unconscious automatisms, which he refers to as "processors":

> This [global workspace] is very useful in dealing with a novel problem, one that does not have a known algorithm for its solution. Information from many knowledge sources may be combined to reach a solution.
>
> (Baars 1988, p. 89)

> The main use of a [global workspace] system is to solve problems that any single expert cannot solve by itself—problems whose solutions are *under*determined. Human beings encounter such problems in any domain that is novel, degraded, or ambiguous.... The global workspace architecture is designed precisely to allow resolution of ambiguity by unpredictable knowledge sources.
>
> (Baars 1988, pp. 92-93)

Since his "global workspace" is the field of consciousness, he associates consciousness with a kind of freedom—or at least with unpredictability. Thus, I wonder whether my CC metatheory is largely consistent with his theory; that is, whether CC metatheory presents in fact a deep property of the "global workspace," a property that is hinted at here and there in his theory, but nowhere made explicit.

Yet the difference between the theories may be considerable. For although Baars' automatisms have a network relationship to each other, this is conceived to be a *communication* network, not a self-structuring, pattern detecting network. And if "conscious experience involves a *global workspace*" which is essentially a *communication* network, does this not imply that consciousness is the *communications* that it carries—i.e., that consciousness is the messages produced by automatized "processors"? If so, where is learning? And what, therefore, might undergo "transformation"? (For further discussion of similarities and differences between these theory-perspectives, see essay in *Section 3* below, "➔The Primacy of Self-Organizing Structural Transformation: Can Consciousness Theories Converge?")

---

13 E.g., see the beginning of this essay.

In seeming contrast with this decentralized "global workspace" idea, Johnson-Laird (1988) has suggested that consciousness resides in the centralizing operation of an ultimate-level executive, supervisory and evaluative system. He says: "Simple consciousness—the bare awareness of events such as pain—may owe its origin to the emergence of a high-level monitor from the web of parallel processes. This 'operating system' at the top of the hierarchy sets goals for lower level processors and monitors their performance. Since it is at the top, its instructions can specify a goal in explicitly symbolic terms ..." (Johnson-Laird 1988, p. 356).

Certainly it is plausible that some top-level "operating system" is intimately involved in regulating the brain's operations, including transformative modifications. But if so, this may still offer only a little clarity about the shape and extent of consciousness. For such a monitor might play a crucial role in consciousness, yet consciousness could include much more than the operation of the "operating system." Our CC metatheory implies that operations of the monitor would be beneath consciousness so long as it was "operating" but not self-transforming, not undergoing emergence of new or changed structure.

B. Can Choice be a Mechanism?

Calvin's approach (Calvin 1990) is again quite different. His concerns about *consciousness* have to do with its construction through the act of looking and planning ahead—"We create the world we see."

> Consciousness is a term we seem to apply to choosing between alternative scenarios for what we might do next.
>
> (Calvin 1990, p. 18)

These invocations of creation and choice seem consonant with the CC hypothesis. And he also at one point makes brief reference to the "world model" notion (1990, p. 261), quoting Craik (1943). But there are difficulties. The relation of consciousness to freedom and restructuring remains ambiguous in Calvin's presentation—for though in one sentence he assigns consciousness to the *act of choosing* between alternative scenarios (p. 18), in another he assigns consciousness to *that which is chosen* ("The best candidate becomes what 'one is conscious of'"—p. 332).

Penrose (1989)—like Calvin (and also like Baars 1988; Calvin 1989; Dreyfus & Dreyfus 1986; and Edelman 1989)—concludes that the "von Neumann machine" (serial computer) provides an unsatisfactory metaphor for the workings of consciousness, and that consciousness cannot be mechanical. He suggests that "the hallmark of consciousness is a non-algorithmic forming of judgments" (Penrose 1989, p. 413), implying that though unconscious actions are programmed by predetermined rules of procedure, conscious actions are not. (This of course is precisely consistent with the CC metatheory presented here.)

In summary, Penrose has marshaled many arguments "to support [the] view that there must indeed be something essential that is missing from any purely computational picture" (Penrose 1989, p. 447), which is just about the same conclusion that was arrived at from a quite different angle by Dreyfus and Dreyfus (1986) in their study of the efforts of artificial intelligence workers. But Penrose does not even hint at what this "something special" might be.

Thus these authors (Calvin 1990; Penrose 1989; and also Dreyfus & Dreyfus 1986), though somewhat vague in specifying what consciousness "is," come close to CC metatheory in assertions about what it is *not*.[14]

IV. Pulling it Together

A. Has Something Been Left Out? If So, What?

Certainly, then, what each of those thinkers portrays as his "explanation of consciousness" may be accurate as far as it goes. But each theory (excepting Penrose 1989) seems to carry the implication that *its* viewpoint is the place from which to comprehend the whole picture. I am reminded of the behavioristic learning theories. They were certainly reasonable summaries of certain phenomena observed under special conditions and examined with statistical techniques. But many orders of complex phenomena—of relationships depending upon higher and less linear forms of intelligence—were hidden in their statistical summaries. Thus, the error was that of generalization.

Today, in present theories of consciousness, what might still be left out? The CC notion suggests one possible answer to this question—an answer that could, if supported, alter our views in fundamental ways. Now I'm sure that even if CC metatheory adds something of real value to our understanding of consciousness, it too cannot be "the whole picture"—to my understanding, no theory of anything will ever be a the whole picture (that is, I'm convinced that a closed and final "theory of everything" is an impossibility).[15]

In any case, whatever might be lacking in present theories of consciousness, those authors cited above and others too (e.g.: Jaynes 1976; Klopf 1982; Minsky

---

14   Also Ulrich Neisser who wrote (1976, p. 104): "A better conception of consciousness, which has been suggested many times in the history of psychology, would recognize it as an aspect of activity rather than as an independently definable mechanism."

15   Regarding this see ***Section 1*** essays—especially "➔Thoughts on the Progression of Paradigms" and "➔The Restriction of Ignorance."

1988) have each related consciousness to a substratum that seems appropriate, and that may have at least metaphorical usefulness. Here's the gist of their proposals:

The organism's consciousness *is* *its analog or model of the world* (Jaynes 1976; Klopf 1982).

The organism's consciousness *is* *information that surpasses a threshold level* (Battista 1982).

The organism's consciousness *is* information that enters the nervous system and is under continuous "editorial revision" (Dennett 1991, pp. 111-113).

The organism's consciousness *is a* *"virtual machine"* (Dennett 1991, p. 218-19).

The organism's consciousness *is* the pandemonium of communications between processors within a "global workspace" (Baars 1988).

The organism's consciousness *is* *the functioning of its "operating system"* (Johnson-Laird 1988).

The organism's consciousness *is* the scenario it chooses for what it might do next (Calvin 1990).

The organism's consciousness *is* *the activities of agencies that manage its memories* (Minsky 1988, p. 151).

Each theory as given seems to provide useful material for thinking about consciousness, but in my view each can come even closer to the *truth* about consciousness through a certain kind of modification. Just as I did in relation to Sperry—comparing his idea of consciousness as *an emergent* with my idea of consciousness as *the action of emerging*—I suggest modifying each of these other proposals in a similar way to yield an altered version that I believe will be more accurate.

Specifically, in each case I will ask whether it is possible to relate consciousness not directly to the kind of structure, process or change that was proposed, but rather to some ongoing transformative *restructuring* of that structure, process or change. And when the original theoretician had proposed that consciousness was a result or correlate of some ongoing change-process, this means transforming the postulated change to a *meta*-change (Watzlawick et al. 1974). Here's the kind of shift in perspective that I'm suggesting:

I propose that we might identify consciousness

— not with an analog or model of the world, or its shifting configurations (Jaynes 1976; Klopf 1982) but rather with the world-model's **restructuring and transformation**.

— not with existent information (Battista 1982) or its processing (Dennett 1991) but rather with the ***creation of new*** information.

— not with a "virtual machine" or its machinations (Dennett 1991) but rather with the ongoing ***revision of its design***, the ***transformation*** of its mechanisms.

— not with the communicative actions taking place within a "global work-space" (Baars 1988) but rather with the ***restructuring*** *of rules governing* the patterns of intercommunication within it.

— not with the functioning of an "operating system" (Johnson-Laird 1988) but rather with ***transforming*** *the rules* by which it operates.

— not with the chosen scenario for what to do next (Calvin 1990) but rather with ***transforming*** (or choosing[16]) the scenario.

— not with the activities of agencies that manage memories (Minsky 1988) but rather with ***modifying*** *and* ***restructuring*** the management rules.

I'm not yet sure that any of these conceptual alterations (or several of them somehow combined!) can lead toward a viable theory of consciousness. The first three are versions of the CC proposal (Atkin 1992), and the rest—except, per-haps, for the last—also make considerable sense within that framework.

But the goal of this exercise has not been to construct a synthesis of their theo-ries or of the suggested meta-variants of their theories. It has been, rather, to show that CC metatheory is an alternative that is not on the same explanatory level as those other theories since it demands the introduction into the discussion of a *meta-level.*

B. Beyond Mechanism

Thus, CC metatheory may lead to kinds of understanding that are necessarily neglected by lower-level theories. If CC metatheory does prove to correspond more fully with "reality" than preceding attempts at understanding, that will be because it includes the previously invisible but crucial meta-level correspondence.

This inclusion must in turn lead to the development of an explanatory con-ceptual framework that is not confined to mechanism. Bunge (1977, 1980), Edelman (1989), Jantsch (1980), Rosenfield (1992) and Sperry (1980, 1991) have gone some way toward this, and at some points their arguments seem almost to touch the position I've taken. On the other hand, some mind-theo-rists still cling to a positivistic stance from which a non-mechanical explanation

---

16   As Calvin (1990) also suggested—see above.

seems nonsensical. Dennett (1991), for example, repeatedly asserts that *all* must be explained mechanically. Nevertheless, he succeeds in opening many of the old deterministic conceptual constructions about mind and brain to probings that, though still reductionist in aim, include previously unrecognized and unacknowledged levels of complexity.

Modern science wants to simplify. Theories of mechanism, based in Cartesian strategies of abstraction, purposefully minimize complexities. This is done through skillful neglect of *history* and *context*—a maneuver that begins and ends with the idea of the "machine." Now it seems that the *machine* idea, though necessary, *may not be sufficient* for our understanding of mind-in-world. The central question is whether some crucial component of structural change that may be associated with the self-organizing potentialities of living systems might not until recently have been overlooked. Inclusion of "something more" entails an inversion of perspective, moving *history* and *context* from the periphery to the center.

Possibly the closest parallel, over all, to the present proposal is Edelman's *Theory of Neuronal Group Selection* or "TNGS" (Edelman & Mountcastle 1978; Edelman 1989). As I try to comprehend his theory of consciousness, I detect an encouraging convergence of understandings.

Edelman postulates a "world-model" (though it seems not to be given an executive role in the anticipatory control of actions through virtual feedback, as it is in the CC metatheory). He says that "consciousness is considered to be a form of associative recollection with updating, based on present reentrant input, that continually confirms or alters a 'world model' or 'self theory' by means of parallel motor or sensory outputs" (Edelman & Mountcastle 1978, p. 95). Though the vocabularies and conceptual backgrounds of our two proposals differ considerably, there are nevertheless major areas of overlap. The most crucial overlaps may be (i) in ideas of the historical emergence of unpredictable change, and (ii) in the notion that consciousness has something specifically to do with world-model updating.

But there are also significant differences. First, Edelman (1989) speaks of consciousness arising out of "ongoing categorical comparison" involving "a special kind of memory" that, in relation "to the satisfaction of physiologically determined needs, ... is brought up to date by the perceptual categorizations that emerge from ongoing present experience" (p. 93). Thus, in Edelman's theory *categorization* is the fundamental perceptual action that underlies all possibility for consciousness; whereas in our CC metatheory, categorization is just one perceptual mechanism among many, which, though entering pervasively into consciousness, is not absolutely essential for experiencing it. Second, it seems that he most frequently identifies consciousness with processes of "matching" or "comparison" rather than with accommodative updating—that is, with *computation* rather than with *structural transformation*. And third, perhaps the most fundamental distinction is in locating the essential basis for the "free will" of conscious organisms. Edelman's theory seems to predicate an escape from "bottom-up determinism" on the process of *selection* within populations with sufficient variance, while our CC metatheory locates this same escape not there but in the events by which variability is *generated* (whether or not selection ensues).

The two proposals, therefore, may complement each other. Certainly, Edelman's "extended TNGS" (Edelman 1989) greatly exceeds the current version of our CC metatheory in its neurophysiologic specificity. But CC metatheory shows that an understanding of consciousness similar in many respects to Edelman's might be built upon a base that has no obvious connection to "neural Darwinism." Certainly, Darwinian selection might be formative of preconscious perceptual automatisms, but I question whether it has a major, direct role in consciousness.

The CC metatheory may therefore point towards a way to define a simpler conceptual framework that is nevertheless adequate in principle to clarify the relation of neurophysiologic processes to the realities of our experience. This conceptual framework will largely overlap, I expect, with the understanding of self-organizing systems expounded by Erich Jantsch. Jantsch (1980), in the following noteworthy sentence, comes close to the central theme of the thoughts I've presented: "Mind and matter are complementary aspects in the same self-organization dynamics, mind as dissipative and matter as conservative principle" (p. 211).[17]

Does this mean that "mind" (conscious mind) is everywhere and is not limited to primate brains (or even to living organisms)? In a way it may. But note that just as "emergence" may include kinds of change that differ enormously in complexity, continuity and coherence, the qualities of "mind" at different levels may be vastly (perhaps incommensurably) different, thus justifying our acceptance of a "privileged" status for human consciousness.

C. The Crucial Difference

What place can our *experience* of consciousness find in our *scientific* understandings? That is the central concern of this paper. The first question that should confront a neuroscience theory of consciousness is: How do those brain processes and activities that correspond with our aware *experiencing* differ from those that we do not *experience* and that remain beneath our awareness? That is, what's the difference in brain *states* and *actions* (and/or *systems*) between conscious and unconscious cognition? Ideas on consciousness have, for the most part, implied that the difference is one of some kind of "localization"—that our consciousness is

---

17 Here I'm assuming that Jantsch (1980) is using the term "mind" a little differently from my use (see **Glossary**)—assuming that in his use it signifies what I term "*conscious* mind."

the operation of some particular system or the activity of some special interactive configuration of systems. Explicitly or by implication, such systems have generally been considered deterministic varieties of "mechanism." If they are discussed in terms of "information," then information is *processed* by them.

In contrast, CC metatheory asserts that consciousness corresponds exactly with what is *not* mechanism, and therefore that consciousness is not the *processing* but rather the *creation* of information. Of course, we know that *mechanisms* and *information processing* abound in the workings of the nervous system, but for the most part they act entirely without our awareness. Under CC metatheory, "consciousness" means that extant mechanism is undergoing some fundamental alteration of structure, and therefore that either it is processing information in a fundamentally new way or processing new and previously non-existent information—or both. That is, consciousness is *creation*.

But to even consider this idea it may be necessary first to enlarge and open one's conceptual system. Otherwise, the idea may literally be *unthinkable*—be without meaningful content. CC metatheory cannot make sense without a meaningful notion of "creation" as the arising of new structure—or as the transformation of old structure, characterized by its functional laws of behavior, to a changed structure characterized by new and altered functional laws of behavior.

Therefore I can understand why, in asking for comments on CC metatheory, often I have had little or no response—because what I was attempting to convey lay almost entirely outside the reader's/hearer's frames of reference. The *possibility of something fundamentally new* must be realized before this idea about consciousness can make any sense. For this, the thrust of certain recent developments in scientific theorizing should be taken seriously—*neural networks, fractals, chaos theory, dissipative systems, Gödel's theorem*, etc. Then the implications of these new developments for the brain sciences can become a crucial question.

They are part of an essential paradigm shift—the expansion of our worldview to include the ongoing, unforeseeable evolution of fundamentally new complexities by self-organizing systems. CC metatheory frames questions that are meaningful within this expanded paradigm.

V. What's Next?

That's the idea—I'm anxious to see what will come of it! So far, attention has mainly gone to the working out of these ideas and to making them clearer. The plausibility of the resulting proto-theory has been a matter more of intuition than of explicit argument. The many kinds of phenomena and conscious experience that need to be "fitted" by any adequate explanatory construction have been implicitly in mind, but till now have hardly been confronted directly.

Nevertheless it is felt that this conceptual structure does in fact fit well not only with my own introspective observations but also with phenomena from many areas of psychology, both Western and Eastern. The foregoing thoughts are being presented therefore not as "answers" but as a stimulus to further discussion and observation.

The result, so far, of this speculative inquiry is the three nested hypotheses, independent yet augmenting each other, that were presented in the first sections of the just preceding 1992 paper—which then concluded:

> [If] the basic correctness of all three hypotheses were to be assumed, the "explanation" of consciousness could go like this: The organism's neural networks continually form, maneuver, and reorganize *models* that anticipate its changing relations to its world. The *active re-structuring* needed to maintain an adaptive anticipatory match (plus—sometimes—other, non-adaptive restructuring) *creates information* and is the exact correlate of *consciousness*.
>
> (Atkin 1992, p. 313)[18]

Notice that I have not yet said anything about "imagination" and its products. For *assimilative* activity and *accommodative* alteration of one's A[sw] can be unlinked from the *actual* performance of actions and therefore from ongoing comparisons with their *actual* consequences. This "life of the imagination," elaborated through play and art of all kinds, is an essential underpinning of human language—an enormously important regulator and extender of consciousness (e.g., see Sokolowski 1992) that is not even touched upon in this or the foregoing essay.[19] It must however be remembered that my direct awareness of my world and of my actions in and upon it—as has been described (in this and the preceding essays) in terms of *accommodative transformation*—is postulated to be responsible for the birth and much of the development of my dynamic Anticipating self-world model and thus is the necessary foundation for those higher (and freer) functions that occupy so much of human mental life (and that are amply exercised in writing and reading this essay).

::<<<\/\/\/\/\/\/\|||=|||=|||\/\/\/\/\/\/\|||=|||=|||\/\/\/\/\/\/\|||=|||=|||\/\/\/\/\/\/\/\>>>::

---

18 This is the ending paragraph of **Section 2**'s 2nd essay "➔On consciousness: What is the Role of Emergence."

19 This will however be dealt with (in a preliminary way) both in the next essay ("➔Conscious Beyond Mechanism") and in the last essay in this section ("➔Reflections on Order and Disorder: Is Consciousness Inherently Negentropic?").

VI. Mind and Language

How do language and speech fit into my prototheory? I haven't come very far with this but here's a preliminary suggestion of one possible direction.

If our non-language mentation, understanding, and relation between ourselves and our world can be mediated by a dynamically predictive model (which I have labeled "A[sw]"), then might our linguistic mentation, understanding, and relation between ourselves and our world also be mediated by another dynamically predictive model that is in some ways tightly linked with my A[sw] yet has a somewhat different origin from the latter, as well as a distinct structure? Call this, tentatively, my "self/*Linguistic*-world model" or "spoken-*Language* model"—abbreviated "sL-m." Presumably, my A[sw] is an earlier creation than my sL-m, both in terms of species evolution and of my individual development.

What I postulate, then, is that spoken or heard language comes about through interactions between two quite differently structured yet in certain ways parallel world-models: One pre-and sub-linguistic and the other linguistic. Linguists (such as Chomsky) have been working on generative structures underlying language production and comprehension. Those researches may tell something about how my postulated "sL-m" might work. I will attempt now to develop and sketch some thoughts about this.

The structure of a language—its grammar/syntax—is distinct from its semantics. My dynamically predictive language model ("self/Linguistic-world model" or sL-m) will govern my construction and comprehension of grammatically appropriate phrases, sentences and larger units of communication (its grammar/syntax), while the significance of these communications will depend upon the semantics of the word-components of these language units, and this will arise through *linkages* between my language model and my (non-language) A[sw]. Therefore in some way, it is postulated, my A[sw] both drives and is driven by that later development, my sL-m.

I generate or comprehend language, then, with assimilative activity of my dynamically predictive language model—my "sL-m." But as my sL-m is highly interconnected with my A[sw] by its bi-directional semantic links, this sL-m assimilative activity drives and is driven by simultaneous assimilative activity of my A[sw]. When I am generating language, there is a main flow of action from my A[sw] to my sL-m; when I am comprehending language, the main flow of action is in the other direction.

How could all this go? Consider first what might be going on when I speak:

• Before that, when I am neither speaking nor responding to speech, I am nevertheless perceiving-thinking-feeling-acting, though perhaps largely if not entirely non-verbally, and thus some parts of my A[sw] are illuminated by my "attention" which, in effect, softens the structure of regions of my A[sw] so that it can recongeal in new forms.

- But does the momentary resolution of stress reveal another stress, and point toward a direction of further resolution that will be aided by a verbal communication with another being? Then the resulting decision to speak increases the salience of semantic linkages that implicitly connect the actively accommodating regions of my A[sw] with relevant regions of my sL-m, my "language-constructor."

- The ongoing accommodation of A[sw] is now more tightly linked with my sL-m and may thereby require some action on the part of the linked portions of my sL-m (this is experienced as the urge to formulate words that will express the non-verbally-felt intended meaning) with the result that the latter's assimilative motion generates acts of speech. These acts, as they progress, in turn impinge back upon my A[sw], modulating its accommodative adjustments, and in that way the meaning of my words is apprehended in my consciousness.

When, on the other hand, I listen to the speech of another, my sL-m automatically mimics what is heard, silently generating the same stream of language. My comprehension is only as good as this dynamic mimicry, which constructs what I hear. This construction is constantly compared to the sensory inflow that guides it. The construction activities also raise the salience of relevant semantic links with my A[sw]. The rest is substantially identical with what occurs when I speak and comprehend ("hear") what I am saying. That is, the assimilative motions of my sL-m (now following rather than generating speech) impinge back upon my A[sw] via the semantic linkages between sL-m and A[sw], modulating my A[sw]'s accommodative adjustments—and in that way, the meaning of the words I'm hearing is apprehended in my consciousness.

We see, then, that according to this (hypothetical) scheme both speaking and comprehending heard speech start with the activation of the proposed "self/ Linguistic-world model" or sL-m, my "language-constructor." Only the means of this activation differs: For *speaking*, my sL-m is activated and guided via semantic linkages by accommodative activities of my A[sw]; for *comprehension of heard speech*, on the other hand, it is activated and guided (via phonologic mechanisms) by the stream of heard speech, which it reconstructs by anticipatory imitation. The rest is the same in the two cases: The active sL-m modulates, via semantic linkages, the ongoing accommodative activity of my A[sw] and thus influences my stream of consciousness.

That's one possible conformation—two distinct dynamic models, one non-verbal and the other verbal, connected by semantic strands but still with distinctly different structures. Another conformation would be a single structure with verbal and non-verbal ways of moving. I have no substantial basis—at least not yet—for choosing one picture over the other, nor am I sure that they are necessarily different in how language and comprehension functions would work. Clearly, this needs further exploration.

::<<<\/\/\/\/\/\/\/\|||=|||=|||\/\/\/\/\/\/\/\|||=|||=|||\/\/\/\/\/\/\/\|||=|||=|||\/\/\/\/\/\/\/\>>>::

And now an essay written in 1994, developing the consciousness theme of the preceding essays—it's a shortened version of the my presentation at the first "Toward a Science of Consciousness" conference in Tucson, AZ:

→ CONSCIOUS BEYOND MECHANISM (SHIFTING A PARADIGM)

I. Mind Change—An Ontology of Consciousness

Just *how* are we conscious? To answer this question, neuroscientists have been seeking *mechanisms* of consciousness (e.g., Churchland 1986; Dennett 1991). However, in this essay it will be suggested that there are none—that neuroscientists who have been looking for them have not used appropriate conceptual tools to study relations of consciousness to brain.

This paper begins with a shift of explanatory paradigm, develops an explanation for conscious *behavior*, broadens this explanation to include mental content unlinked from actually executed ongoing overt behavior, and ends by examining the theory's epistemological implications.

Most past theories rested on assumptions that our consciousness has to do with the operation of some special mechanism—a "virtual machine" (Dennett 1991), an "operating system" (Johnson-Laird 1988), "memory managing agencies" (Minsky 1986), a "global workspace" (Baars 1988). But while nearly every brain mechanism may in some way be involved in consciousness, this does not mean that any—or any combination—is a *mechanism of consciousness.*

My own intuitions in this realm began more than 20 years ago. Could it be that, of the complex patterns of adaptive change always going on within us, *consciousness* has exactly to do with all in my adaptive, exploratory responses that is *non-reproducible* and *non-predictable*? This was subsequently expressed in terms of *emergence*: "*Consciousness* **is** *ongoing emergent change, the continuing creation of unprecedented pattern*" (Atkin 1992, p. 311). The central idea is this: While both unconscious and conscious actions are the play of mechanisms, consciousness enters when the activated mechanisms are at that moment undergoing essential structural modifications which are altering their laws of operation. It is a notion of consciousness that for brevity has been labeled the "continual creation" (CC) hypothesis.[20]

II. Prediction and Correction

It is next proposed[21] that the inner *structure* that is thus reorganizing itself is the organism's dynamic (predictive) internal model of itself-in-its-world[22]—an evolving virtual machine (Dennett 1991) that is the ongoing product of the brain's neural networks.[23] This dynamic map has been labeled "**Anticipating self-world model**" (abbreviated "A[sw]'). My A[sw] is a map or model of my *world*, of my *place within my world*, and of *dynamic regularities* of our actions and interactions—and (by CC metatheory) it is changing in *structure* whenever and wherever I am conscious, for my A[sw] needs to be continually *updated*.

The notion that through our experience we generate *maps* or *models* (or "schemata") to guide our subsequent behavior, and that they have relevance to phenomenal experience, is not new. It will suffice to mention here that Craik (1943) spelled out a theory with many similar features more than 50 years ago, as had Bartlett (1932) eleven years earlier (and more recently Combs 1994).

So it's an old idea here linked to consciousness in a special way:

> Based upon studies of motor function (e.g., Atkin 1969), it is proposed that the Anticipating self-world model (A[sw]) *anticipates* the organism's actions and predictively generates controlling feedback ("virtual feedback"), which is derived from SIMULATION *of the activity and effects of the organism's own action systems*
>
> (Atkin 1992)[24]

---

20 This alternative to the search for mechanisms was anticipated nearly a century ago by William James (1905), and more recently by D. M. MacKay (1982), Jean Piaget (1976), and Karl Pribram (1976)—still more recently also by Hans Flohr (1991), Israel Rosenfield (1992), and Allan Combs (1994). (There have been other anticipations of this idea about consciousness—but for reasons of brevity they will be cited elsewhere.)

21 As said also in the previous essay—because both papers had gone through much of the same conceptual development.

22 Atkin 1992; Craik 1943; Kawato, Furukawa, and Suzuki 1987.

23 Edelman 1989; Flohr 1991; Hebb 1949; Kawato, Furukawa, and Suzuki 1987.

24 This is a preceding essay, the second essay in **Section 2**, "➔ On consciousness: What is the Role of Emergence."

This pro-active control-mode has adaptive advantages. Regulation of movements by virtual feedback can increase the rapidity and flexibility of complex yet precise actions since a feedback control strategy is retained, yet the feedback time-lags that would be inescapable with control through external feedback loops are effectively eliminated.

And here I come to two more terms used to specify ways in which the postulated A[sw] *updates* continually to maintain its correspondences with the territory that it maps: These are the Piagetian terms "assimilation" and "accommodation." In *assimilative* updating (or simply, *assimilation*) the "virtual machine" performs actions of which it is capable with its *present* structure, so that its *configuration* changes in accord with the dynamic virtual-machine laws that define it and without change in those laws. Since the function of the model is predictive (see below), this *change of configuration without change of structure* will occur when the model's actions continue to "fit" (Glaserfeld 1984) the organism's situation accurately.

But whenever during wakefulness the continuing assimilative prediction is imperfect (as is usual), then fit can be improved by *modifications of anticipating A[sw] structure*[25]—modification, that is, of the *virtual-machine laws* governing the ongoing changes in A[sw] configuration. This structure-changing component might be termed *"accommodative* updating" (or simply *accommodation*).[26] CC metatheory, then, would imply that consciousness has to do with accommodation.

Thoughts

The above described source of accommodative adjustment—what will now be termed **external incoherence**, which is discrepancy between predicted (virtual) and actual (sensory) feedback from the outer world—was a concept derived through studies of how animals move and the means by which they adaptively regulate their movements. But what of *thoughts* and *feelings* that may be linked very loosely or not at all with immediate awareness of motor actions? To account for these we need another kind of incoherence—what I call **internal incoher-**

---

25 Here "**structure**" (see *Glossary*) is used in the following sense: The "set of rules or functions which relate the variables of a system to one another" and provides "information about the particular way a system is organized…is known as the structure of the system" (Battista 1977, p. 67). "[The] elements of a structure are subordinated to laws, and it is in terms of these laws that the structure *qua* whole or system is defined." (Piaget 1970, p. 7.) Since structure, then, has to do with *predictable pattern of change*, consciousness is thereby identified with *change* in this pattern of change; that is, with *meta-change* (Watzlawick et al. 1974).

26 This usage of "accommodation" (and "assimilation") is generally consistent with Piaget's (and see *Glossary*).

ence. It originates from inevitable internal inconsistencies between the assimilative actions of different A[sw] subsystems.[27]

Both types of discrepancy—both *external* and *internal* incoherence—will evoke accommodation and thus give rise to contents of consciousness. The externally-evoked accommodations, evoked by action, are accommodations that modify A[sw] in directions that lessen discrepancies between the predicted and externally-generated sensory feedback; in contrast, the internally-referenced accommodations evoked by internal incoherencies which are intrinsic to the A[sw], are the accommodations of stimulus-independent *thought*.

So **consciousness** means the virtual machine[28] is redesigning itself (1) to accommodate its dynamic structure more fully and accurately to the organism's interactions with its world and (2) to resolve its internal inconsistencies. Presumably, these ongoing accommodations are my *experience* of every conscious moment. My present Anticipating self-world model (A[sw]) would be a complex construction (or virtual machine) that has in this way been evolving over my whole life. I have constructed my reality by being conscious, and am keeping it current now through the accommodations that are my consciousness in the present moment.

III. Further Questions

A. Causal Efficacy

Here the question of the causal efficacy of consciousness needs to be examined (Atkin 1992). The continual creation idea implies a markedly stronger kind of causal efficacy for consciousness than previous theories. In saying that consciousness is identical to the **restructuring** of causal links, CC metatheory ascribes to consciousness a deeper, far more consequential control over the organism's actions than theories (such as Sperry's [1980]) that say consciousness **activates** causal links. Compared to the "downward causation" of that kind of emergent determinism, it is a **meta**-causation.

---

27 Subsystems which might correspond to Minsky's (1986) idea of "agents"—or perhaps more precisely, what he calls "agencies" (pp. 23, 25).

28 What kind of neural substrate could be matrix of *continual creation*? The proposed assimilative and accommodative activities of an A[sw] may be mediated by *neural networks* (Caudill and Butler 1990; Edelman 1989; Hebb 1949; Kawato, Furukawa, and Suzuki 1987; Rumelhart 1986). Hans Flohr (1991) notes the "activity-dependent self-organization of neural nets" (p. 251), and then proposes the "speculative hypothesis claiming that the occurrence of phenomenal states depends critically on the presence of [these self-organization] processes" (p. 251). This of course merits further discussion, which it will receive elsewhere.

B. Freedom

Notice the different order of control: If a new, changed causal system is emerging continually, then we have not simply one durable emergent determinism but the continual emergence from it in each conscious moment of a ***new*** emergent determinism.

- That, it was postulated, is where *freedom* enters.[29] Accommodation means that the virtual machine laws change, modifying ongoing assimilative actions, so that they take particular courses rather than others.

- *Choice*, then, is this ceaseless redirection of a system's assimilative actions. It is here suggested that exactly this is the root of free will—these modifications in A[sw]'s structure ***are*** *choosings*, going on during all of consciousness.

C. Supervenience and Downward Causation

Note the relevance of CC metatheory to questions raised by Sperry and others (e.g., Sperry 1991; Szentágothai 1984) concerning "supervenience" and "downward causation." Using CC metatheory, I assume that my A[sw] is structured as a many-layered hierarchy (something like Minsky's [1986] postulated "society of agents")—a hierarchical network of a great many subsystems, many of which may seem to function with partial autonomy, but which are nevertheless closely linked together. A great many of these subsystems are active assimilatively much of the time, but assimilation remains beneath awareness.

The linkings of active and accommodating (conscious) subsystems with the active and non-accommodating (unconscious) subsystems that surround them are two-way. Therefore, not only do unconscious processes constrain conscious choices (as will be discussed further in the next subsection), but reciprocally, conscious choices are at every moment profoundly modulating the directions of the ongoing unconscious processes in which they are embedded. Thus the accommodative changes that effect conscious choosings may be said to "supervene" over the assimilative activities both of the accommodating subsystems and also of non-accommodating subsystems to which they are linked. Such causal influences of consciousness upon "lower-order" unconscious mechanism is *downward causation* in action. It seems therefore that downward causation may be easier to comprehend as a direct implication of CC metatheory than it has been when consciousness was explained as a "past-tense" emergent—as it was by Sperry (1980).

---

29   E. g., see preceding essay "➔On consciousness: What is the Role of Emergence" (see its subsections *II* and *V*).

D. Conscious and Unconscious Mind

Comprehension of the relation of conscious to unconscious mind, so emphasized in dynamic psychology, may also thereby be made easier. Certainly, conscious actions occur within the far larger context of ongoing unconscious activity. The awareness I am now experiencing is therefore presumed to be the accommodative change in structure of only certain subsystems within my more widely active A[sw]. If the ongoing assimilative activities of these conscious (accommodating) subsystems are embedded in and tightly linked to the assimilative activities of larger unconscious (non-accommodating) systems,[30] then it may be those more inclusive but unconscious systems that are the ultimate sources of my *initiatives, motivations, drives* and *purposes*.

- In this way I begin to better understand the near invisibility of all the paradigms that govern my every thought and action—not only the paradigms of my science, but those of my habitual movement styles and those governing my interests and aversions, my language habits and my social relationships.

- These dynamic patternings must be the dynamic patternings of ongoing assimilative actions of my A[sw], most of which go on with little or no accommodation and so without awareness, yet which constrain my choices by driving and guiding the assimilative actions of the more restricted A[sw] regions that do accommodate as they move and thus move with awareness.

- Therefore myriad unconscious constraints always surround the choices which accompany my awareness—constraints not only invisible but also durable, as they don't change so long as they do not enter my awareness.

Here, then, is a more explicit portrayal of the two directions of causality—simultaneously upwards and downwards—that Sperry (1991) has spoken of: The *downwards* effect (sketched at the start of this section) showed accommodative choice modulating assimilation mechanisms; the *upwards* effect (just noted) showed assimilation mechanisms constraining accommodative freedom.

E. Ontologic Implications

So that's an attempt to better describe what consciousness *is*. That is, up to this point the discussion has concerned the *ontology* of consciousness.

---

30 Quite similar to the relationship which Baars (1988) postulates between conscious "global workspace" and surrounding "context hierarchies" (see **Section 3** essay "➔The Primacy of Self-Organizing Structural Transformation: Can Consciousness Theories Converge?").

The crucial ontologic contention was that in consciousness something new is continually being created—that consciousness *is* the ongoing evolution of a self-world model (A[sw]). The current repertoire of this structure's assimilative actions has arisen through its past history of accommodative change—through the history of its *conscious* events. Its current consciousness is the accommodative evolution that is happening right now.

F. Epistemologic Implications

This way of understanding consciousness—when combined with recognition of the practical necessity that a map or model of a complex system be partial and simplified—has epistemologic implications. We will ask what CC metatheory can tell us about our knowledge of ourselves and our world—our knowledge of and relation to "reality." We find it generates an *epistemology* that is essentially different from that which underlies the modern reductionistic worldview.

Our simulation-system or "model" (our A[sw]) is a dynamic map of all those aspects of the world that we know and interact with. It is this map-of-our-world that is actually *all* that we directly know of the world. Since the map is smaller and simpler than the territory, predictive excursions *outside* of the mapped region must depend upon extrapolations of dubious validity.

Certainly, it seems very like a constructivist view in which the world "outside" is hypothetical—we only know our map, which we have constructed. But the CC epistemology is not quite this; if my *awareness* corresponds to the ongoing accommodative *alteration* of my model's structure, then I do not even know the map—what I alone know is ways in which, at each moment, the map does not "fit." I know the momentary departures from homology—the map's imperfections.

That will be our third-person understanding of consciousness, viewed from the outside. But now, see this from the inside: The implication for my first-person experience is that it is this continual requirement for accommodation which is always *pointing toward the real*. So, in this epistemology, conscious experience is exactly "the 'real' world manifest[ing] itself ... there where our constructions break down" (Glaserfeld 1984, p. 39). Thus, we come to a conception of the real in which every moment of our highly complex experience does in some way point towards that which is its corrective from without and beyond—and which we experience as "reality."

Yet that which points is not the target. So again, to remember this, I remind myself of the crucial importance of always remembering to distinguish the map from the territory. I make this distinction and recognize that *I have constructed my map*. But how do I know anything beyond it? In principle, the boundaries of my map can tell me nothing about any ultimate boundaries of the territory. My most parsimonious assumption, therefore, is that the territory is unbounded, so that my consciousness must be continually pointing toward a reality far wider than any of our necessarily limited maps.

• In summary, then, what I know is always and everywhere pointing at that which is beyond my map; thus, what I know is exactly and completely *not* my map (my A[sw]), but rather a *pointing* out toward near parts of boundless territory *beyond* it.

This radical incompleteness of our mappings applies not only to our mappings of our world but also to our mappings of our own structure. That is, our self-knowledge must remain partial and forever unfinished. Consequently, of all the regions of our experience that we may have difficulty in comprehending, the most difficult may be to comprehend the nature and depth of that experiencing itself—not therefore just what that experiencing intends, but the principles by which it arises, and the very fact of our experiencing.

IV. Summation

Thus *two nested hypotheses*,[31] independent yet augmenting each other, have been presented:

(1) The **continual creation** (CC) hypothesis,[32] stipulating that consciousness is ongoing, emergent change whereby structure is transforming itself (generating new information).

(2) The **pro-active world-model updating** hypothesis, stipulating that the self-transforming structure is a model of organism-in-world (called an **Anticipating self-world model** or A[sw])[G] that predictively assimilates the organism's actions and their context, responding to **external** incoherence by accommodatively modifying its structure to maintain accuracy.

---

31 Intimations of one or both of these hypotheses were noted in ideas of Allan Combs (1994), Hans Flohr (1991), and Walter Freeman (1990).

32 Also called the *"Continual creation (CC) **metatheory**"* (see this term in **Glossary**).

G This symbol after a technical term means it may be looked up in the **Glossary** at the end of the book.

Then followed exposition of how these hypotheses can clarify certain other aspects of consciousness:

(3) To explain *thinking* it is proposed that awareness unlinked from motor actions is the result of **internal** incoherencies (inevitable internal inconsistencies between the assimilative actions of different A[sw] subsystems); these evoke accommodative readjustment that accounts for thoughts.

(4) The strong *causal efficacy* of consciousness is clear when consciousness is understood to be the restructuring of causal links. This is a deeper, far more consequential control over the organism's actions than saying that consciousness *activates* causal links (compared to which it is a "*meta*-causation").

(5) *Choice* is the ceaseless accommodative redirection of a system's assimilative actions, going on during all of consciousness—this is the root of *free will*.

(6) *Downward causation*^{G} is the causal influence of consciousness upon *lower-order* unconscious mechanism. Conscious choices are at every moment profoundly modulating the directions of the ongoing unconscious processes in which they are embedded. This is *downward causation* in action.[33]

(7) The crucial **ontological** contention is that consciousness *is* the ongoing evolution of a self-world model (A[sw]); thus the current repertoire of this structure's assimilative actions has arisen through its past history of accommodative change.

(8) Given that our simulation-system or "model" (our A[sw]) is a dynamic map of all those aspects of the world that we know and interact with, the crucial **epistemological** contention is that I do not even know the map—what I alone know is ways in which, at each moment, the map does not "fit." What I know is always and everywhere pointing at that which is beyond my map. Therefore, if my *awareness* corresponds to the ongoing accommodative *alteration* of my model's structure, then what I know is exactly and completely *not* my map (my A[sw]) but rather a pointing out toward near parts of boundless territory beyond it.

::<<<\/\/\/\/\/\/\/\|||=|||=|||\/\/\/\/\/\/\/\|||=|||=|||\/\/\/\/\/\/\/\|||=|||=|||\/\/\/\/\/\/\/\/\>>>::

---

33 Actually, it is just one type of downward causation—there are others.

Here now is a short 2006 follow-up to the foregoing essay:

→ ADDENDUM: AMAZING COMPLEXITY AND VIVID CREATIVENESS OF VISUAL AWARENESS

A few words now about the mystery of sensory perception. I'll focus on my visual experience—its high complexity, perfect artistry! How does mind do it, bringing it into such brilliant awareness? Can my CC metatheory possibly account for the startling beauties I see every moment in the world around me? I do see that no other theory of consciousness and perception that I know of can better account for my experiencing; certainly the other relatively simple theories (simple because highly abstract and finite) seem inadequate to deal with how I'm now *seeing* the miraculous (unlimited!) complexity of the "real" world. Is CC metatheory more adequate?

Here, look! We're walking about in this great city, glancing at big buildings everywhere. And sharing these street-sidewalks with many fascinating-looking people. We're all passing each other by—I step, step, step vigorously, guiding my movements to avoid collision with any other pedestrian. And I *see* it all!

Do I not, simultaneously, model it all, within, proactively—am not I making each step within (with my internal A[sw]) just *before* I actually make the move? If (as I speculate in formulating and discussing my CC metatheory) my conscious experiencing is identical with the ongoing accommodative updating of my A[sw], must that not mean that my *visual awareness* is too? How can a virtual machine-model (an A[sw]) create such experiencing? How can the updating action generate so much constantly-shifting complexity?

Certainly, as perceptual theorists going way back have seen clearly, a tremendous and dynamic complexity of patterning enters the eye and is activating ocular sensors and visual-system neurons. If this is a major part of what is continually driving the ongoing accommodative updating of my A[sw], then of course A[sw] must incorporate all that dynamic complexity—and keep continually incorporating it.

I glimpse now that my mystification may have a simple cause—a seeming clash of complexity-levels. My simple-minded tendency is to assume that something that I've described in a pretty simple way (my A[sw]) must itself be correspondingly simple. Of course that's not true! I'm sure that the subtle, highly-dynamic complexity of my ever-changing, continuously-evolving A[sw] is beyond my comprehension—just as the full story of brain's dynamic interconnectivity must be.

So consider now just those tiny sectors of my A[sw] that are now undergoing accommodative change to bring me visual awareness. I must assume they are (by their ongoing accommodation) attaining and staying in most intimate correspondence with the complexly dynamic patterning of light-rays entering my eye at each moment. But that's not the whole story; since A[sw] is defined as a proactively *anticipating* self-world model, there are many added levels of dynamic complexity to be assumed—coming from the requirement that A[sw] must in every moment be predicting all the sensory feedback being generated through this moment's motor actions. Therefore, what's really going on with A[sw] accommodative updating must be of even greater mind-boggling complexity than had been just inferred above when only the dynamic complexities of the visual *input* were being addressed.

So I'll repeat one sentence from the foregoing, knowing that what I described then was only a small part of the total picture. I said:

> I'm sure that the subtle, highly-dynamic complexity of my ever-changing, continuously-evolving A[sw] is beyond my comprehension—just as the full story of brain's dynamic interconnectivity must be.

But if I've now included additional, highly-important dynamic facets of what's going on (as I believe I have), by returning my attention to include the centrality in my metatheory of A[sw]'s *anticipatory* function, then indeed my mind certainly is far more boggled than it was before (when it had only the dynamic complexity of retinal *stimuli* to contend with).

Noe & O'Regan wrote about this—about "seeing as a dance"—thus:

> … seeing is a skill-based activity of environmental exploration. Visual experience is not something that happens *in* us. It is something we *do*. Seeing, on this view, is comparable to dancing with a partner. Just as dancing consists in a delicate interaction between *two* partners, so seeing, we argue, depends on patterns of interaction between the perceiver and the environment. There is no doubt that neural activity is necessary to enable one's skillful participation in a dance, but it is unlikely this neural activity is sufficient to give rise to the dancing. After all, the dance, with its weight changes, moments of disequilibria and rebounds, depends on the actions and reactions of the partner (not to mention the nonbrain body). For exactly similar reasons, we argue, neural activity is not sufficient to produce visual experience. Seeing does not consist in the activation of neural structures (even though it causally depends upon such activation). A further consequence of this approach to seeing and visual experience—seeing is something we do, not something that

takes place inside us—is that it allows us to develop a new framework for thinking about the *qualitative character of experience*. One of the chief advantages of this new framework, we argue, is that it enables us to overcome the famous problem of the explanatory gap (Levine 1983).

(Noe & O'Regan 2002)

So I've been resolving my puzzlement—beginning to see now more clearly (in "mind's eye") how my CC metatheory can indeed begin to account for the amazing beauties (and tremendous complexities) I see every moment in the world around me.

::<<<\/\/\/\/\/\/\|||=|||=|||\/\/\/\/\/\|||=|||=|||\/\/\/\/\/\|||=|||=|||\/\/\/\/\/\/\>>>::

Here now is another essay (written in 1995) on closely related themes. It will discuss why the process of ongoing change that's postulated to underlie awareness remains mostly *hidden* from us (so that its role in consciousness has not before now been accepted by everyone as *obvious*).

→ ABOUT THE INVISIBILITY OF CONSTANT CHANGE

We're sure that all is always changing. But then, sometimes we're not so sure. Certainly, stabilities and constancies are much easier to understand. It's therefore hoped that this note will complement and counterbalance our first explanations of CC metatheory.[G] They have told how the fundamental character of consciousness is the restructuring of the system within which it arises—and therefore that consciousness cannot repeat. Now we try to see why this continual change so frequently remains hidden from us.

After all, if in fact my consciousness is always changing my mind, we would think then that it would be more obvious to me—that this "nature" of consciousness could not for so long have escaped my notice because constant mind-change doesn't stop. But maybe I didn't see it because, relative to the whole, the change was so small! Mostly the field of my consciousness remains so constricted that it changes just very tiny parts of a very extended and complex A[sw].

So perhaps that's why so many of those who've be most concerned to understand what consciousness "is" have not seen it the way I'm now proposing—have not taken this explanation to be *self-evident*. First, maybe in general ordinary mind-changes are—as just noted—so constricted, so relatively tiny, that we can't reflexively notice their effects. And maybe also much of that usual lack of recognition of what's presumed to be happening all the time is because our consciousness is almost entirely unreflexive. (Is that why occasional large mind-changes stand out for us as very special?)

Yet another reason that mind-flux remains beneath our awareness is that we *want* it that way. Though as noted my mind is continually (according to CC metatheory) being transformed by my awareness, that mind-change is ordinarily not sufficiently obvious to overcome our long-held and deeply-embedded cognitive preferences—our mechanistic prejudices of recently and currently prevalent scientism. For modern science wants to simplify. Theories of mechanism, based in Cartesian strategies of abstraction, purposefully minimize complexities. This is done through skillful neglect of history and context—a maneuver that begins and ends with the idea of the "machine."

Now we are seeing that the machine idea, though necessary, may not be sufficient for our understanding of mind-in-world. In that direction the central question that led to CC metatheory was whether some crucial component of structural change—a component associated with the self-organizing potentialities of living systems—might not until recently have been overlooked. But inclusion of "something more" entailed an inversion of perspective, moving *history* and *context* from the periphery to the center.

In ways that in some important respects anticipate the cognitive architecture of CC metatheory, Baars (1988) has done this as well. In his cognitive theory of consciousness, as in CC metatheory, consciousness is constantly instrumental in effecting the ongoing evolution of mind's structure:

> Conscious events help to create new contexts and to evoke old ones. *Conscious events, when receiving systems adapt to them, can serve to create a new context....* Once adaptation has occurred, the new context may help shape future conscious events without itself being conscious.
> (Baars 1988, p. 198, Figure 5.2—emphasis added)

As already noted many times, according to CC metatheory mind structure is always changing, for consciousness is proposed to be identical with the revision of its own substructure. But here (as noted at the start of this essay), certainly the ways in which we habitually constrict the field of our consciousness has large effects upon the extent of any changes in mind. That is, to the extent that our consciousness remains narrow, restricted, shallow—to just that extent mind-structure may in fact be almost entirely unchanging, thus far more enduring than not.

That is one reason why our belief that our experience is largely repetitive and stereotyped is not altogether incorrect. To go over now-familiar ground again, it's like this:

> The **matrix** of consciousness is a vast structure of almost entirely **unconscious** mind. It is a web of automatisms—of "agents" (Minsky 1986) that are hierarchically interlinked into agencies and super-agencies[34]— which as already noted may *in toto* be called our "mind-structure." These are all "mechanisms," and their assimilative actions are inherently deterministic—are predictable and in that sense repetitive.

34　The general picture also corresponds closely to the cognitive architecture which underlies Baars' (1988) theory of consciousness, of nested 'contexts' composed of hierarchies of modular 'processors.'

Consciousness restructures this deterministic causal web. Our conscious experiencing is the ongoing modification of automatisms and/or of the links that interconnect them. That is, consciousness revises our mind-structure—or in a different terminology it is *the accommodative changing of our "Anticipating self-world model" (A[sw])*.[35]

But this dynamic web-matrix (our deterministic mind-structure) is so vast and deep, and our consciousness is ordinarily so constricted and shallow, that our mind-structure is being only slightly modified in most conscious moments.

Thus, although the structure that is accommodating in this moment of consciousness cannot, in general, be the same as the structure that was accommodating in a previous moment of consciousness, the difference can be so small that the present can be experienced as very nearly identical to the past.

Furthermore, though this situation is the consequence of the smallness of our conscious awareness, we are inherently incapable of perceiving that smallness exactly because it is also that same small awareness which must (reflectively) do the perceiving.

To repeat this briefly, in spite of the inherently transformative nature of consciousness, mind-structure may be enduring because mind-structure is (usually) very large while consciousness is (usually very small.

However, under some circumstances the visibility of change can be reduced even further, for the just-described basis for mental stereotypy can be potentiated by stabilities in our adaptive situation. Doing what are essentially the same actions in the same places, over and over, will tend to stabilize mind-structure.

The more stable our environment, and the more repetitive our actions within that stable environment, the less change is demanded of our mind-structure. Then (because of these reduced adaptive demands) our consciousness may tend to remain even smaller, and the structural changes that it brings about may, like our repetitive actions, be in many ways cyclical.

That is, if the environment—the immediate sensory ecology (in the Gibsonian sense) including its relations to the organism—is stable and/or repetitive, then accommodative change will tend to converge toward some "steady state." It is the ubiquitous generality of such convergence and consequent dynamic stereotypy that may justify our tendency toward static characterizations of consciousness. (After all, much that is written about it speaks about "*states* of consciousness.")

Briefly put, this gives us the following picture:

---

35   See previous essay, and also **Glossary**.

Stable environment (+ repetition of the organism's patterns of action within it) promotes stability of mind-structure. Accommodation will be largely cyclical, continually converging towards and recreating a relatively stereotyped mind-structure that is adaptively adequate within the stable ecology.

Summarizing, then, one reason that we don't see much change is that whatever change takes place is far overshadowed by mind-structure's vast regions of relative stability.

But there's another reason also—another manifestation of the reflexive "Catch 22": We are inherently incapable of perceiving the possibility for a mind-structure that differs greatly from our present mind-structure exactly because it is the present-moment awareness through which the alternative possibilities must be perceived. Necessarily, therefore, the present substructure has largely lost its capacity for perceiving—for knowing or even knowing *about*—the structures it once had but has no longer. How it is now is confidently known as "the only way it can be."[36]

This last reason for our frequent lack of awareness of even the most crucial kinds of mind-change was clearly presented by Baars:

> Any developmental process must involve choice-points between different potential paths.... At the moment of choice, we may be quite conscious of the alternatives; once having chosen, we enter a new context that is created by the choice, and within which the original choice is often not even defined.... Thus we often cannot make previous choice-points conscious once we have entered the new context created by those choice-points.
>
> (Baars 1988, p. 173)

==((([^]/\[^]))==<<((([^]|_|[^]))>>==((([^]/\[^]))==

In short—all these reasons together may explain why some consciousness explanation resembling CC metatheory has *not* been long and widely accepted as *obvious* (though—as cited in several places—this general theoretical approach has been anticipated in part or whole by others).

Further, it's worth mentioning here that close parallels between CC metatheory and Baars' (1988) empirically-supported GW consciousness theory are shown later (see **Section 3** essay "➔The Primacy of Self-Organizing Structural Transformation")—in fact they might be very nearly equivalent

---

36   See Kuhn (1970) on 'incommensurabilities of paradigms.'

in basic structure. If these theoretical comparisons are indeed valid then CC metatheory may actually have considerable empirical support—since (i) much of the experimental research data that Baars cites in support of his GW theory should equally support main ideas of CC metatheory; and (ii) the neurophysiological correlates that he and Jim Newman have inferred for GW theory (e.g., Baars & Newman 1994; Newman, Baars & Cho 1997; Baars, Newman & Taylor 1998) should serve also as underpinnings for CC metatheory.

Finally, note that the next essay ("➔ Reflections on Order and Disorder") ends with proposals for ways to further experimentally test CC metatheory.

/~*~\/~*~\/~*~\/~*~\/~*~\/~*~\/~*~\/~*~\/~*~\/~*~\/~*~\/~*~\/~*~\/~*~\/~*~\/~*~\/

::<<<\/\/\/\/\/\/\/\|||=|||=|||\/\/\/\/\/\/\/\|||=|||=|||\/\/\/\/\/\/\/\|||=|||=|||\/\/\/\/\/\/\/\>>>::

\|/oOo\|/oOo\|/oOo\|/oOo\|/oOo\|/oOo\|/oOo\|/oOo\|/oOo\|/oOo\|/oOo\|/

And now as the last essay in this section I present one written in 1994, looking into implications of CC metatheory for the continual evolving of new, more and more encompassing levels of order in our universe:

➜ REFLECTIONS ON ORDER AND DISORDER: IS CONSCIOUSNESS INHERENTLY NEGENTROPIC?

I. How My World Begins to Open

Completing the Triangle—A Third Force in Science

Modern science—at least until very recently—has recognized two main explanatory principles, each capable of pervading all thought and each projecting a different worldview and set of attitudes about life. Both have their recent roots in the explanatory triumphs of modern physics—and for a while have co-existed, in a somewhat muddled, unclear mixture. The first is classical Newtonian physics, giving rise to the image of the clockwork universe, running a course that in principle is taken as *totally predictable* from complete knowledge of its initial state. The second—first thermodynamics and then quantum physics—seems opposite to this, allowing no such detailed prediction of precise events, but specification only of *probabilities*. (As we know, Einstein was uncomfortable with this idea of fundamental randomness.)

The world ruled by predictable mechanism runs on without fundamental change. In fact its laws and descriptions are symmetrical with respect to time—its phenomena are reversible; they work the same way whether time runs from past toward future or from future toward past. Thus there is no way, from a description of the unfolding of the phenomena of this reversible world, to tell the direction of time's arrow.

The alternative world (are they the only two possible?) gives time its unambiguous direction—that in which entropy (disorder) is always increasing. This world moves inexorably toward chaos. The clockwork is corroding—is continually and inevitably wearing out.

In combination, these descriptors give us a dismal picture of our universe and our place in it. Microdeterminism, whether by "clockwork" or by "dice," rules all, and "free will" is therefore illusory. Life and mind are merely trivial accidents, transient and only momentarily interesting. So why try to save the world?

But now a third kind of fundamental principle is being uncovered by creditable scientists and is gaining some scientific respectability. First, Gödel proved the impossibility of a complete and universal explanatory system, thus opening previously closed minds. Chaos theory and fractal mathematics showed other kinds of limitations and insufficiencies in the old ideas. And explorations of non-linear open systems and of neural networks reveal situations in which order is increasing rather than running down.[37]

This third realm of physical theory may complete a picture that has thereby become much more interesting! If so, it has "completed" it in away that renders it forever open and unfinished. This idea leaves me with many questions. Here is a first set:

Are processes of the third kind ubiquitous? Is self-organizing (anti-entropic) change a component in most change, though it has usually been invisible to us? Has it been invisible because absent—or because we don't know how to see it?

World's Principal Locus of Complexification

If the complexification door is everywhere more open than has been assumed,[38] then much of great significance that is happening now within and around us may be invisible to us just because of the *inherent limitations of our perceptual and cognitive apparatus*. This general point has certainly been made many times before.[39]

The hypothesis I have recently been developing[40] places a main locus of this heretofore unacknowledged complexification so close to me (and to you and to everyone) that it is the fount of my experience in each moment—it is the very source of my consciousness, with which it is identical. I once named this the "consciousness is creation (CC) hypothesis," but now (for short) call it the **CC metatheory**.[41] (As already noted it is an idea that has been put forth before in various forms, but that seems not yet to have been taken seriously or developed to any extent.)

If consciousness itself is creation—is the evolution of new structure—this brings the creative evolution of the living being from biological centrality to a

---

37 Do these "self-organizing systems" comprise a category of phenomena that contradict accepted necessities of thermodynamics? This seems the case—at least locally in closed systems.

38 As is now being demonstrated in some of the newest science—e.g., see Bronowski 1966, Jantsch 1980, Lazlo 1987, Prigogine & Stengers 1984.

39 E.g., by Wittgenstein, by Buddhists—and most recently by Ken Wilber (1997).

40 See the previous essays in this section.

41 More fully call it "*Continual creation (CC) metatheory*" (see **Glossary**)—also see Atkin 1992 (it's the second essay in this section, entitled "➔On consciousness: What is the Role of Emergence") and Atkin 1994 (the fourth essay in this section, entitled "➔Conscious Beyond Mechanism").

still more central point in my life, as it becomes the actuality of my awareness in this moment. I bring the world within myself, but the world's infinite complexity demands that this inner world undergo continual reorganization to remain adequate to the larger world.[42]

My consciousness, then, may directly derive from the adaptational needs posed by the wide open character of the world's levels of organization. Should we open our conceptual systems to the idea of a universal spectrum of complexity, extending upwards without any known or even inferable limit? Perhaps in this upward direction ultimate limitations are in principle unknowable and beyond inference. Certainly, the Principle of Parsimony[43] mandates that we not *assume* an upper limit for which we have no evidence whatsoever—except perhaps by generalizing from our own limitations!

Yet it is exactly our overwhelming evidence concerning *our own limitations* that we do unthinkingly generalize. We are automatic *dualizers*; our perceptions and cognitions are built upon *divisions*. Only *difference* is perceptible and thinkable (Bateson 1972). We separate and compare, split and objectify. Thus, we ourselves know only *limits* and *boundaries*—separations that we take, usually, as absolute. Since this is what we can sense and think of, this becomes for us the ultimate nature of the real. Yet that, I am coming to see, is our grand illusion.

In what follows I will attempt to point up some possible implications of these thoughts, which are descriptive of my ongoing personal paradigm shift.

II. Order, Linkage, and Mind

A. On Coherence

The idea of a fundamental discrepancy of ontological levels is present in theories (such as Roger Sperry's[44]) that treat mind as an "emergent." That is, they assert that the relation of brain to mind is that of system to *meta*system—the metasystem having emerged at some time in the past from the system over which it now exerts *supervenient* control (Sperry 1980). CC metatheory, however, introduces something new into this level-discrepancy, for it implies that the relation of brain processes to conscious mind is that of *change* to *meta-change* (Watzlawick et al. 1974)—that the lawfulness of unconscious mind is stable but that of conscious

---

42　Thus brains, more complex perhaps than any other replicated subsystems of the universe, are the main organs of this ongoing evolution. For example, see Edelman's "Neural Darwinism" (Edelman 1987).

43　See above, next-to-last essay of **Section 1:** "➔ The Restriction of Ignorance: Inverting the Principle of Parsimony."

44　E.g., Sperry 1980.

mind is not, for the emergence of new lawfulness is *happening now* in every conscious moment. It is therefore a fundamentally less static kind of emergence theory that has the potential to introduce something new into brain-mind discussions.

However, to appreciate this possibility, one must be prepared to open one's own mind to a larger picture—to push back one's mental horizon by cognitively rising, in thought strategies, to the meta-level that can encompass such ideas.[45]

Here is one way to do this. It is, perhaps, all a matter of *order* and of *levels* of order. The order which is here of most concern is not static order—not the order of still pictures, of stable patterns, no matter how elaborate. It is, rather, the order of *transformation* of dynamic systems. What needs to be fully recognized is (1) that *all is changing,* and (2) that all independence between different systems of local change is partial and transient—that is, that *all is interconnected.* For every local change (happening "right here") influences and is influenced by every other local change (everywhere else).

Yet it seems obvious that some interconnections are far stronger and more intimate than others. Certainly, all is not equally or similarly interconnected. Some connections are excruciatingly tight, others diaphanously loose. And these differences—differences of almost unimaginable magnitude—give us our ordinary, everyday world of seemingly *separate* "objects," *independent* forces, and mechanically specifiable causal systems.

If "everything is connected with everything," how is it that this is so hidden? It is exactly because much of my acting and thinking depends upon *assumptions* of separation, of independence, of discrete and limited linkages. My world of objects—and all "objective" knowledge—is built upon such assumptions, which I rarely question.

Can I bring these conflicting worldviews—that of my common experience of *objective separability* and that of an idealized theory of *world-unity*[46]—together? That is, can all be intimately interconnected, thus constituting a single unified system, even though it certainly doesn't look that way to me? How can I understand the conflict of such holistic theory with much of my direct experience other than by postulating that the theory is simply wrong?

Perhaps this can be done by means of a particular concept of order, which can be labeled "coherence." *Coherence* is, in my understanding, a particular component of negentropy. It has to do with *alignments* and *synchronies.* In turn, "alignment" has to do with *spatial* coordination—especially with coordination of *directions*;

---

45 Reasons why this expansion has progressed rather slowly were discussed in the preceding essay.

46 A concept that has a very long history, as it is a fundamental idea of what has been called the "perennial philosophy" (Huxley 1944), or the "primordial tradition" (Smith 1989).

and "synchrony" has to do with *temporal* coordination—especially with coordination of *rhythms*.

Take two parts of a system—two subsystems. Are they tightly or loosely linked to each other? Does some change—say, a movement—of one have a great effect upon the other? Or is there little or no apparent effect? Certainly, sometimes the latter will be observed. But must it be interpreted as absence of linkages? Perhaps it could be accounted for by incoherence of the component linkages of sub-part to sub-part, even though the individual strengths of these component linkages has not been diminished.

Consider the many parts of each subsystem; each may be linked to all the parts of the other subsystem. When one subsystem changes its configuration, its parts will move, and this will affect the second subsystem. If all these component effects are coherent, the second subsystem will be strongly influenced, as the coherent influences will augment each other; but to the extent that they are incoherent they will oppose rather than augment each other, so that the resultant influence will be lessened.

This seems a reductionistic argument. But it is a reductionism that attempts to explain how a whole, basically unified and unfragmented system can nevertheless behave as if fragmented. Thus it is a reductionistic argument in support of a holistic viewpoint.

B. Self-Organization

Self-organizing systems are systems that transform their own structure[G]—their structure changes itself driven by its own internal dynamics. What I will postulate is that self-organization is primarily the development of increased (and changed) *coherence* of connections. "Structure" describes this coherence of connections— structures are particular *configurations* of coherence.

What kinds of systems do this self-organizing? They are everywhere! They are non-linear systems, far from equilibrium—*dissipative* systems (Prigogine & Stengers 1984). They eat available energy, and in degrading it, at the same time generate new kinds of *order*—generate *negentropy*.

Can we say anything more about this? Contemporary science focuses almost exclusively upon the study of "mechanisms" (the operation of extant structures)— the life sciences upon the *mechanisms* of living systems; the psychological sciences upon *mechanisms* of brain and mind.[47] Only with the recent birth of irreversible thermodynamics and open systems theory has this begun to change.[48] It seems entirely plausible, therefore, that almost nothing of what we as scientists have

---

G   See **Glossary**.
47   E.g., Chalmers 1995.
48   E.g., see Jantsch 1980, Prigogine & Stengers 1984.

been studying until now could be the postulated generator(s) of negentropy; for the entropy of *mechanisms* (viewed as closed systems) can only go *up*. But open systems—dissipative (self-organizing) systems—have possibilities for local entropy *reduction*.

Thus, if these notions are correct, *dissipative (organismic) aspects of complex systems (locally) decrease entropy while mechanical aspects increase it*. That is, entropy rises through mechanism, lowers through organism. (A neat simplification! But still very tentative.)

III. Consciousness as Negentropy-Generator

Now, back to the problem of consciousness. What's the crux of the answer suggested here? It's about *change*—the claim that *consciousness signals meta-change*; that the difference between activity that is and activity that is not accompanied by conscious awareness is the difference between change that is and change that is not accompanied by meta-change. Structural alterations that *modify the laws of the system* are the meta-change that—when they are done by brain—are experienced from within as conscious awareness.

These ideas have interesting implications concerning *consciousness and entropy*. By our hypothesis, awareness is the resolution of contradictions, creating greater order. Every kind of order involves relations of *coherence*. The meta-change that is experienced from within as conscious awareness tends, in balance, to increase net coherence and thereby to generate negentropy. That means change toward greater harmony and unity of dynamic interactions, since "coherence" signifies *correlated motions*—going together, in synchrony. The idea, in short, is that *awareness is inherently anti-entropy*.

A. Further Questions

Do the foregoing speculations, if well founded, mean that negentropy is actually *identical* with consciousness? An interesting generalization—but probably a gross oversimplification. First, the *overall* entropy level need not go down in a conscious mind, for the unconscious regions of mind—generally far more extensive than the conscious regions—may be undergoing degenerations and fractionations of structures that greatly outweigh the declines of entropy in the conscious regions.

And second, while our hypothesis implies that all consciousness brings greater order, not all increase of order may be accompanied by consciousness. Rather, though all life generates negentropy (this is the essence of both of the evolution of new forms, and of the growth of each individual organism), I'm quite sure that not all of this generation is conscious.

However, consciousness is likely to be life's most skillful means for negentropy generation. Life (growth, evolution) is negentropic, with time-scales of significant entropy-reduction that range from millennia down, perhaps, to seconds. The negentropic changes of our *awareness* are generally much faster. Nevertheless, the latter is truly part of the former; the negentropic changes of life (growth, evolution) may well reach their zenith of rapidity and complexity in consciousness. For I postulate that *consciousness is the specialized negentropy-generator*.

We have two components of environment-organism entropy that may be reduced by consciousness: (i) That of the total system,[49] involving *A[sw] relations to the rest of the system*, where A[sw] mismatch to organism-environment interactions is reduced; and (ii) that *internal to the structure of the A[sw]*, where mismatch between different components or subsystems of the A[sw] is ameliorated. The first might be characterized as consciousness-mediated *environment-organism cooperative negentropy*; it concerns aspects of the organism-environment system that have been discussed by systems theorists such as Gregory Bateson (1972). The second might be characterized as consciousness-mediated *intra-organismic negentropy* and is closer to the concerns of depth psychologists such as the Freudians.

B. A Possible Version of "The Big Picture"

This proposed opening up of biological-psychological theory to organismic negentropy generators *does not negate anything of contemporary science other than its conventional and unquestioning negations*. Further, that *disillusioning* contribution of the enlarged paradigm is the implication of its *positive* contribution—that of a hopefully more adequate theory of consciousness. Nor is the latter *against* mechanistic explanatory schemes; rather, it *adds to them*.

The conclusion is that the mechanistic, deterministic systems of lawfulness are necessary *parts* of any large explanatory scheme but are *not sufficient*. Consciousness is the great generator of negentropy. (Can it be that consciousness

---

49 Note that the system in question is not the organism considered in isolation, but is the much larger system of which the organism is only a small part. It is intuitively obvious (though it remains to be proved) that the entropy of an environment-organism system will be lower, the better the match between the organism's A[sw] assimilations and the actual organism-environment interactions. The disorder of this combined system will increase with the mismatch between the A[sw]'s predictions and the actual occurrences. All effective accommodative change in A[sw] structure reduces this mismatch, and should therefore lower the entropy of the environment-organism system. (Note that this may go at least some way in the direction of "Radical Externalism"—e.g., see Honderich 2006.)

is a black hole into which entropy falls? Is it possible that at the upper regions of system complexity it can be entropy's principle sink?)

But at the same time that consciousness is generating order, mechanisms are falling apart. Disorder, separation and differentiation tear apart the unity of the whole system. These are the unconscious entropy-generating processes that, in minds, entrain flaws and predictive unreliability in A[sw]'s structure. Yet (as said before), in the regions of attention and awareness, conscious accommodation is resolving flaws and generating negentropy, unifying and integrating the system.

I will summarize what has so far been said:

1. If consciousness itself is creation—is the evolution of new structure—this brings the creative evolution of the living being from biological centrality to a still more central point in my life, as it becomes the actuality of my awareness in this moment. I bring the world within myself, but the world's infinite complexity demands that this inner world undergo continual reorganization to remain adequate to the larger world. My consciousness, then, may directly derive from the open-ended adaptational needs posed by the wide open character of the world's levels of organization.

2. Awareness is the resolution of contradictions, creating greater order. Every kind of order involves relations of *coherence*. The meta-change that is experienced from within as conscious awareness tends, in balance, to increase net coherence and thereby to generate negentropy. Consciousness is likely to be life's most skillful means for negentropy generation. The negentropic changes of life (growth, evolution) reach their zenith of rapidity and complexity in consciousness.

3. We have two negentropy components: Consciousness-mediated *environment-organism cooperative negentropy*, which concerns the organism-environment system; and consciousness-mediated *intra-organismic negentropy*, which concerns the "inner mental life." Thus understood, consciousness is the great generator of negentropy, and at the upper regions of system complexity it may be entropy's principle sink.

IV. Power and Glory—Where Are We Today?

Next, some of the implications of these speculations for social and personal *effectiveness* will be examined.

Increasing entropy degrades the unity of the conscious system. The higher the entropy of the system, the more fragmented, localized and constricted the negentropy-generating events. Nearly all of us have entrained, and effectively preserve, rather high levels of internal disorder—all kinds of unresolved conflicts, graspings, and incoherent cognitive subsystems. This means that our consciousness is itself fragmented and constricted and therefore only of small effect as consumer of entropy. For generation of negentropy by a fragmented, constricted consciousness can only be sporadic and local, so that the net entropy level, if it declines at all, does not go down very fast or very far. Therefore consciousness, as (possibly) the world's principal anti-mechanical process (or "event" in Heschel's [1955] terminology), can have only very gradual and limited efficacy in opposing this self-reinforcing generation of entropy.

A case can be made (though it will not be here[50]) for the generalization that a closed worldview is less integrative and more preservative of entropy than an open worldview. Thus progression toward greater unity, greater wholeness of mind, will proceed through a progressive opening of the whole being's stance, including an opening up of its worldview.

Furthermore, as already hinted, entropy rises and falls not only within individual, isolated minds, but within cultures and civilizations. The individual and social levels strongly affect each other here, as they do in many other ways. Divisions *between* people generate divisions *within* people and vice versa. These mechanical generators of entropy are, therefore, mutually reinforcing.

In a society—in the whole world—all kinds of order and disorder can be described and accounted for in terms of *power relationships*. Who can exert control over what and/or whom? What kind and degree of control? And what gets "out of control"? (With regard to these kinds of questions, some preliminary link with entropy concepts will be attempted a little later.[51])

A. Varieties and Degrees of Power

For a start, look at the accomplishments of our modern technology. They have given us tremendous powers as compared with those that we had in previous ages, have they not?

Yet concerning our contemporary conceit about the conquests of modern science—especially about its glories in achieving vast new powers—how much power have we achieved after all? What are the actual magnitudes of our "new powers"? And what is their significance? Might our confident estimations actually be very wide of the mark? I will suggest that what has been achieved has been tremendously magnified in our sight by a redistribution of our attention (and that

---

50　However, see *point B.(3)* in subsection "III. Violence and Power" of last **Section 3** essay "➔Attention and Violence: How Each Moment of Consciousness Matters" and also similarly-named subsection "*II. Violence and Power*" of last essay in **Summing Up** section, "➔Can that Big Picture Help with Mind and Violence?"

51　And see the just-preceding footnote.

we put that perceptual magnification over on ourselves with the kinds of skillful attention-manipulating strategies used in theaters by magicians and other tricksters). This maneuver extensively but invisibly restructures the frame of reference within which we evaluate our powers.

The strategy can become apparent if we introduce the idea of an essential distinction between **global power** and **local power**. Global power is conceived of as the power to alter the total configuration and outcomes of a complex system, where the applied regulation controls a broad range of variables that concern the total system; local power, in contrast, is power to alter some limited segment of the total system, controlling only certain variables with no direct concern for outcomes affecting all the remaining, uncontrolled variables. The latter are *external* to the controlled subset of variables and thus are labeled "externalities." (Global power may be impressive, while local power usually is exceedingly small.)

Certainly, through the expansion of our science and technology we have achieved some highly significant *local* powers, but this has been largely at the expense of any advance in our *global* powers. In fact, there seem to have been serious regressions in our global powers.

Thus, are we now really significantly more powerful than we were? I maintain that our increased power is restricted to certain very narrow arenas—so narrow that they may hardly show in the big picture. But we can no longer see the big picture (we see it hardly ever and with great difficulty—it is vague: "a dream ...").

We have developed (as Bateson [1972] says of our medical advances) many startling tricks and easily become obsessed by them. But we have lost sight of the larger costs of these tricks. Actually, their benefits lie within only an extremely narrow segment of the full range of possible ways in which human well-being might be augmented; but we experience this segment as very large—as encompassing nearly all that matters.

B. The Importance of Openness

How can we increase the wisdom of our anticipatory actions? Our world is full of unanticipated "side effects." Our vision has been so constricted that we are frequently taken completely by surprise by deeper and longer-range effects of our well-intentioned "curative" actions. Of course, every technological and medical advance has risks. But often there will be many effects that lie completely outside of the world-models that the innovators and entrepreneurs are using to guide their perceptions, anticipations and actions.

My point is that a closed worldview greatly increases the chances of disaster by promoting inattention to phenomena other than those mapped and emphasized by the set of models that comprise that worldview; while an open worldview broadens attentiveness and increases the likelihood that "peculiar," extraordinary phenomena will be noticed and unfamiliar lines of anticipation will be attempted.

Thus, openness or closedness of worldview is likely to be accompanied by openness or closedness of attentiveness, with profound consequences for what can be noticed. If this is so (and I believe it is!), then the consequences of this difference in worldview may be, at least in the long run, quite world-shaking. Notice that most of the recently-expanding ecological observations and environmental concerns have been associated with more open viewpoints.

So our hope for avoiding disasters lies as much in opening our minds as it does in developing more techniques for avoiding already recognized dangers. Without open minds we will not notice the dangers that we do not already know about until, perhaps, it is too late to escape them. Mind-opening means explicit attention to the places at which our models of reality are no longer fully adequate to represent reality and need to be revised or extended. By my CC metatheory that active process of revision and extension *is* consciousness.

Yet our world is increasingly being run by "experts." The narrowing down of the academic mind has been remarked upon before; as one advances in academic pursuits, it has been said, one "learns more and more about less and less!" Certainly, this has often seemed the process. Specialized fields of study split into subspecialties, and practitioners increasingly sharpen their increasingly narrow, restricted skills. The academic mind wants to be sharp as a razor! This sharpness divides and subdivides. It achieves a kind of sharply focused clarity for the tiniest details. By increasingly precise definitions of terms, by separating categories and subcategories, by holding larger conditions constant so that they can be neglected, it gains great control over a very narrow region. But the larger picture practically disappears from view. It is not the subject of interest!

To sustain and develop this narrowing process, an intelligent being must rely not only upon "common sense" insights about what matters and what can be neglected in considering a given problem, but also upon traditions (sometimes dogma) concerning what is *relevant*. Thus decisions about what can be neglected are for the most part automatic—hardly considered. They are generally taken as *obvious*.

Yet, when made society-wide, automatically accepted decisions about *relevance* are of the most crucial importance! They are directly responsible for vast areas of blindness in the society, and in each individual. For they freeze into our minds, which natively are sensitive and flexible, vast regions of insensitivity and hard unyieldingness—of inability to respond to the real conditions.

C. Power and Knowledge (The Triumph of Blade)

The realms of my deliberate power cannot be larger than my world of experience, and ordinarily are far smaller. Yet by contracting my world of experience, I can keep it closer in extent to my field of experienced power—so that the *relative* magnitude of the latter is large. Since in this way I can restrict the span of my experienced powerlessness, I thus have strong motivation to contract my world of experience!

The arrogantly negating assertions of positivism and scientism, then, can be understood as products of this motivation.

Smith (1989) portrays our "Promethean Motivation"—how science and our whole contemporary culture is focused on *control*. He argues

> first, that the exceptional power-to-control that modern science has made possible has made us reach out insistently ... for ever-increasing control;
>
> second, that this outreach has forged a new epistemology wherein knowledge that facilitates control and the devices for getting at such knowledge are honored to the neglect of their alternatives;
>
> and third, that this utilitarian epistemology has constricted our view of the way things are, including what it means to be fully human ...
>
> (Smith 1989, p. 104)

But what we do not realize—though we are beginning to suspect it now, sometimes—is that such control as we have attained, though marvelous, is also largely illusory. That is, it is *local*, and *temporary*. Perhaps, even acknowledging the impressive *conquests* of science and technology, we have hardly more control now than we had before—hardly more control in any large sense. Seen thus in a large frame, our "control" is both pitiful and horrifying.

What we have is an implicit calculus of trade-offs—one that is almost entirely beneath our awareness. It is a Faustian bargain: In order to get more "control" we let more and more go out of control. We "make productive use of natural resources" forgetting the resulting destruction of ecosystems. We "select organisms we want to use and neglect or eliminate those we don't" at the cost of tremendous reductions in the diversity of life-forms—about which, however, we remain unconcerned, hardly noticing.

We get more of what we want, by wanting less and less. Certainly there are strong motivations—speed and complexity are related reciprocally; the simpler a mechanism, the more rapidly it can complete its cycle of movements. So, to speed up, simplify!

Sword has triumphed. Cut away that which interferes—whatever blocks rapid progression to the goal. That is the nature of *decision*—cut away the unwanted. (True *choice* is entirely different.) Decide upon the goal, and then destroy every obstacle.

Certainly, this *simplification strategy* has worked wonders! But seen in reference to frames larger than those used to construct them, these wonders are distressingly tiny.

> The achievements of this thrust toward truth——I am thinking of the noetic achievement of pure science quite as much as the pragmatic achievements of technology—have been so dazzling that they have blinded us to the fact that they are products of an exceedingly restricted kind of knowing.
>
> (Smith 1989, p. 84.)

How can we picture all this in terms of the entropy speculations that were sketched out earlier? Certainly, it can make a big picture that is very dramatic. For now we can see a system that has emphasized local power at the expense of investment in the development of global power—as a great *mechanism,* a mostly closed system that is hardly evolving as a whole, but rather is mostly *devolving,* its overall entropy swinging upwards in spite of a few dissipative subregions that self-organize and generate negentropy. Because these restricted pockets of less mechanical, non-degrading local evolution have little effect upon the overall rise in disorder. So—as already noted using the local/global dichotomy—*local* power may be impressive, while *global* power is exceedingly small.

Certainly, it seems obvious that something like this holds for societies and political-technological systems. I believe that it holds just as well for individuals, and not only in the larger patterns of their lives (which it does!), but also in their moment-to-moment cognitions and actions.

V. How Consciousness Might Create Order

Let's try to see a little more precisely how consciousness generates negentropy (or synonymously—generates "*syntropy*"[52]). Consider the order and disorder of a *mapping* relationship: The more accurately predictive the map, the higher the level of order of the map-territory system. Conversely, defects in predictiveness are elements of disorder—of entropy.

Next consider an organism and its environment (both natural and social environment)—they may respectively be called an "inside" and an "outside":

---

52   Term for negentropy of Szent-Gyoergyi 1974. See **Glossary** entry for "syntropy."

1. Part of the "inside" is a *map* of the total inside-outside system, which is the *territory* of the map.

2. It is a *predictive* map—its function is to anticipate the future states and movements of the inside-outside system. It thereby "assimilates" them.

It is then proposed that:

3. Predictive *discrepancies* (i.e., assimilative incoherencies) are to be considered components of systemic *entropy* so that an increase in discrepancies is an increase in entropy.

If entropy can be defined to include this type of disorder, then since CC metatheory specifies that consciousness is the *accommodative* response to predictive discrepancies,[53] it further predicts that *consciousness creates syntropy* because the end result of accommodative responses is the overall reduction of the predictive discrepancies that evoke them.

This relates entropy to *incoherence*, which (as noted before) is another way of speaking about disorder. Let the map be an *inner virtual machine* defined by the virtual-machine laws that specify its behavior. Discrepant predictiveness is equivalent to defects in the coherence between map-dynamics and territory-dynamics. So that's what I'm talking about when I say that "consciousness is *negentropic*" (i.e., generates *syntropy*). Consciousness is *repair of incoherencies between map and territory* by modifying the mapping process.

A. Two Concepts of Predictive Mapping

Here I must make a choice. There are two ways in which the predictive mapping relationship can be conceptualized. One is that the behavior of the *inner virtual machine* is predictive of (i.e., is anticipatorily isomorphic with) the behavior of a larger *outer virtual machine* in which it is embedded; the other is that the *inner virtual machine* predicts the patterns of future inputs that it will receive from all the systems that surround it and within which it is embedded. Most of these inputs will be sensory inflows together with reafferent neural information from motor and motivational systems. That is, the *inner virtual machine* generates *virtual feedback* in anticipation of the actual feedback against which it will be checked.

Thus, in this second way, nothing need be assumed about the source of those inputs against which the predictions of the *inner virtual machine* are tested—our concept involves those testing inputs themselves and does not attempt to infer

---

53 E.g., see **Glossary** entries for "Assimilation and accommodation," and "Virtual feedback."

their source. The first way—more of a *realist* position—does make that inference, taking the source (as noted above) to be the encompassing *outer virtual machine* (a way to envision "the real world").

In either case, the function of consciousness is to modify the virtual-machine laws[54] of the *inner virtual machine* in ways that will lessen the incoherence between its predictions and what actually occurs. (In the first concept this will be the incoherence between the behavioral predictions of the *inner virtual machine* and the actual behavior of the larger *outer virtual machine* in which it is embedded; in the second concept this will be the incoherence between the patterns of *feedback* that the *inner virtual machine* predicts and those that are actually received.)

But whichever way we conceptualize the inner virtual machine's predictive function, the function of consciousness is to modify its virtual machine laws in ways that will lessen the incoherence between its predictions and what actually occurs. This resolution of inner-outer incoherence is mind's most intimate and significant response to what is actually occurring. We may consider such responsiveness the most fundamental meaning of mind's *receptivity*.

B. Characterizing and Naming Mind's Predictive Map

Thus consciousness is the immediate fruit of mind's receptivity. It is a receptivity that depends upon some pre-existing receptive structure. This has been called the *anticipating* "Self-world model" or "A[sw]."[55] Inflows to the "A[sw] constructor" initiate and guide the creation and revision of A[sw]. (This is the "participatory response" to the unexpected [Pribram & Melges 1969]).

C. Known and Unknown

The pre-existing receptive structure—the A[sw]—is tuned to receive experiences that do not differ too widely from those that constructed it, for only then does A[sw] have means to generate predictions. Thus, what it is most easily responsive to can be called "the *known*." Here the incoherencies that generate consciousness are of modest magnitude.

Certainly, one needs to be receptive to the "known," but it is just as necessary to be receptive to the "*unknown*" for it is always impinging as if from everywhere. Thus, not all accommodative updating of A[sw] will respond to discrepancy between assimilative prediction and actual response; some (perhaps much) will

---

54 The laws defining the behavior of the virtual machine.

55 See the very first essay in book, "➜Consciousness, Holarchy, Negentropy" at the beginning of the **Introduction**; and also the ***Glossary***.

respond to inflows that A[sw] was largely or entirely unable to anticipate. What happens then when there cannot be prediction? I believe it works as follows:

These would be two distinguishable varieties of incoherence—that with the *known* and that with the *unknown*. In the first instance (with the *known*) we have incoherence between configurations that are at approximately the same level of specificity and detail, though some of the specifications and details of the prediction differ from the corresponding specifications and details in the actual occurrence. In the second (with the *unknown*) the incoherence derives from the lacks of specificity and detail in the predictive mapping configuration; the *unknown* occurrence delivers specificity and detail that had not been anticipated at all. Therefore in the first instance (the *known*) there is accommodative *revision* of assimilatory mechanisms. In contrast in the second instance (the *unknown*) there is creation of *new* assimilatory mechanisms. (This distinction is crucial for it is important to include both kinds of "continual creation" (CC) in our model of consciousness.)

Thus, incoherence is reduced either by *fixing something old* or by *creating something new*. Both result in a more ordered relationship between parts of the larger system, thus in a higher level of order of the system as a whole. Both result in lessened disorder, lessened randomness—and in this sense can be said to have generated negentropy (or syntropy).

In summary, the dynamic, predictive coherence of the mapping system with the mapped system is a high level of order, which might be specified in terms of a measure like *syntropy*. Thus consciousness, in continually creating the capacity to sustain this coherence, is thereby in effect creating *syntropy*.

VI. Directions for Further Work

A. Another Question About Levels

Now look more closely at the idea of negentropy-generation in a complex multi-level causal network such as mind-brain. What happens as a system becomes more unified—as its overall level of *coherence* goes up? Can we infer that this might work changes not only at the level of the whole system—the level at which we find increased unity and greater overall coherence—but also at levels beneath? Consider a system composed of many subsystems, perhaps of many "modules." If such a system self-organizes—e.g., *accommodates*, thereby raising its overall level of coherence—are there changes that are effective not just at the level of the larger system but also at the level of the modules?

After I had been asking this question for a couple of days, several ways to image such effects began to occur to me—but until the evening that I wrote the following paragraph none seemed significant or appropriate. Then I began to see just how negentropic changes in the network's organization could be effective not just at the level of the larger system but also at the level of the modules.

Let's say that the system is a neural network (*nNW*), and the modules are the *elements* (neurons) that are highly interconnected to constitute this network. Then may it not be that *as the nNW self-organizes and rises in overall coherence, there will simultaneously be an increase in its level of effective **connectivity*** (and also, possibly, in its level of overall *activity*)? This can be spelled out by sketching the properties of two neural networks that have had contrasting kinds of histories of accommodative evolution: The first, a history of mostly *global* accommodations; and the second a history of mostly *local* accommodations:

(1)   The most effective modular interconnections of the nNW that has been undergoing global accommodations will eventually tie it into a very dense unitary web that tends to generate actions and anticipations as a single whole system. That is, the assimilative actions and anticipations generated by any one module will thus be modifying and modulating the assimilative actions and anticipations that are simultaneously being generated by all the other modules. This will be in effect a very high-connectivity system.

(2)   In contrast, the most effective modular interconnections of the nNW that has been undergoing highly segmented (sequential) and therefore local accommodations will eventually tie it rather into a hierarchy of loosely linked but largely independent subsystems that tend to generate actions and anticipations in succession using algorithmic strategies. That is, the assimilative actions and anticipations generated by any one module will thus be modifying and modulating the assimilative actions and anticipations of only a few other modules—those beneath it in the particular modular hierarchy of which it is part. Consequently the effective connectivity of this segmentally-accommodating system will be markedly lower than that of the aforementioned globally-accommodating system.

The foregoing differentiation of two diverging styles of mind-architecture points back toward my previous reflections[56] on the importance of the inclusiveness of thought-strategies and especially on the implications of this inclusiveness for the persistence or solution of many nagging problems of individuals and societies.

---

56   This theme is discussed not only in this essay, but also in others—see especially: In **Section 1** "➔The Restriction of Ignorance;" in **Section 3** "➔Attention and Violence;" and (in the "**Summing Up**" section) the essay "➔Can that big picture Help with Mind and Violence?"

B. Testing the Connectivity-Consciousness Connection

And the foregoing differentiation of two diverging styles of mind-architecture having contrasting sorts of connectivity also leads to contrasting expectations for *spread of activation effects*. Any test of the outwards-spread of modulating effects from activity in a particular module will show far more widespread effects in a system of the first sort (one with relatively high connectivity) than it will in a system of the second sort (one with relatively low connectivity).

And further, the inferred difference in overall levels of effective connectivity will manifest itself not only globally at the level of the total system, but also more locally when smaller regions are examined. This suggests an approach to empirical tests of CC metatheory—i.e., of its portrayal of present-moment consciousness as the active emerging of mind's structure, and further of its historical implications that the moment-to-moment patterning of consciousness is cumulatively a potent determinant of the eventual architecture of that evolved structure.

One help for testing this would be some way to differentiate experimental subjects with regard to their habitual patterns of attention-spread. Say we have such a technique and use it to assemble one group of individuals with habits of narrowly-focal attention and another group of individuals who tend toward more global, usually widely-spread attention. Could some way then be used to see if the groups differed with respect to spread of activation from a particular brain-focus out through the rest of the brain?[57]

If we had a way to do this we could then try a research strategy such as the following:

(i)— Sample attention-strategies of potential experimental subjects in order to set up groups of subjects with highly contrasting strategies, thereby assembling otherwise comparable samples of high-segmenting and low-segmenting people.[G]

(ii)— Then if precise methods can be devised for perturbing the assimilative activity of one local A[sw] module at a time and then testing immediate effects of this perturbation upon a sample of other modules, we may be able to infer each subject's overall pattern of inter-modular connectivity.

Even if we get only as far as this second phase and can arrive at estimates of the overall pattern of inter-modular connectivity of each subject, we will thereby have

---

57 Since I've been away from these kinds of experimentation for so many years, I'm not now in a position to propose anything more about a possible experimental design.

G For the specific way in which this term "segmenting" is being used, see also the **Glossary** (at end of book).

gotten data pertinent to a first and most basic implication of CC metatheory— that *the moment-to-moment patterning of consciousness is a potent determinant of the eventual architecture of mind's evolved structure.*

Of course, there will remain uncertainty with regard to cause-effect directionality; even if we find that inclusive attention-strategies are correlated with cognitive unity, we will not know whether the habit of inclusive attention builds a more unified cognitive structure (as the hypothesis of interest here maintains); or whether, conversely, individuals who have for whatever reason a more unified cognitive structure will also for this reason tend toward habits of inclusive attention.

That is, has attention style been effective in developing brain interconnectivity, or has brain interconnectivity been responsible for attention-style? My considered answered to this will be "Yes!"—both! For CC metatheory also implies that the relationship is thoroughly two-way.

Certainly, a disunified, fragmented cognitive structure tends to perpetuate the fragmented, disunified strategies of attention which (it was hypothesized) are the ways in which this kind of mind-architecture originally comes into being.

C. Testing the Entropy-Consciousness Connection

Also, once we have assembled those two attention-style samples, it may be highly relevant to return to the theme of consciousness as generator of negentropy. For it seems entirely plausible that differences in entropy will correspond to the differences in connectivity; that given the very different overall levels of connectivity that we have inferred for the two systems, based upon the differences in their developmental histories, it will be possible to determine correspondingly different estimates of "systemic entropy." To do this, of course, some method for computing such an estimate will need to be devised. If this can be done, then we may have the basis for an empirical test of the hypothesis that *consciousness functions as a negentropy-generator*. That is:

(iii)—   If we can then find a precise way to rigorously derive an estimate of the overall *entropy* level of each subject's inferred dynamic modular architectures, we can see whether the two samples of subjects, presumed to differ substantially in their life-long attentional strategies and therefore in their histories of conscious construction of mind (of A[sw]), also differ correspondingly in present estimated levels of mind-structure entropy.

This could give us empirical data on attention-strategy and negentropy generation. If that data supports the conjectures of a correlation between them, then we may have data supporting the speculation that—since conscious accommodation resolves flaws and generates negentropy, unifying and integrating the system—consciousness may be a specialized negentropy-generator, i.e. that ***awareness is inherently anti-entropy***.[58]

One caveat worth repeating here is what was just said about bi-directionality of the causal relationship between connectivity and spread of activation: Though disunified strategies of attention will give rise to a disunified, fragmented cognitive structure, conversely the latter tend to perpetuate the fragmented, disunified strategies of attention that caused it.

As discussed elsewhere[59], it is exactly this circle of reciprocal causations (the familiar "Catch 22") that makes any movement toward a more unified mental structure so slow and difficult; the fragmented mental structure does not provide the means for the necessary strategy of attention, and so movement must be by small steps—e.g., a slight expansion of attention may begin to heal some local mental disparities, which in turn may facilitate some slight further expansion of attention.

To find out whether, in fact, awareness not only depends upon structure but also builds structure, a prospective design may be used. One way to go will be to experimentally manipulate awareness, and then find out whether or not this has over time any cumulative effects upon structure.

We might do this by adding another dimension to the experimental design sketched above, making it a 2 x 2 design:

(iv)— We can randomly divide each sample of subjects in two, then give one of the halves mindfulness training and/or other exercises designed to influence their habitual strategy of awareness, making it more inclusive and global, and give the other half another exercise thought to be ineffective in this direction. (We might or might not use a cross-over design, later on switching the trainings used with each subgroup.)

\|/oOo\|/oOo\|/oOo\|/oOo\|/oOo\|/oOo\|/

In short, for the steps I've just suggested the following tools and procedures will be needed:

---

58 This was first suggested in the 6th of the numbered proposals of the book's first essay (at start of its ***Introduction***)—"➔Consciousness, Holarchy, Negentropy"—then again mentioned earlier in this essay, at the start of the previous *Subsection V.* "How Consciousness Might Create Order."

59 E.g., see essay earlier in this section entitled "➔About the Invisibility of Constant Change."

- Specific experimental procedures by which the habitual attentional strategy of a given subject can be objectively evaluated;

- precise methods for perturbing the assimilative activity of one local A[sw] module at a time and then testing immediate effects of this perturbation upon a sample of other modules in order to then infer the overall pattern of inter-modular connectivity of each subject;

- some way to rigorously derive an estimate of the overall entropy level of each subject's inferred dynamic modular architectures; and

- possibilities for a double-blind cross-over experimental design using a treatment designed to affect attention-strategy with some subjects and a placebo treatment with the others.

D. Corroborations from Other Sorts of Consciousness Studies

I believe there are other sources of support for these hypotheses and for the implications concerning CC metatheory that have been drawn from them.[60] These will be data on the direct experience of many who have studied their own consciousness and worked at modifying (widening) their attention strategies using many special techniques developed in various cultures over millennia. Also pertinent are results of previous studies on the cognitive effects of meditation training and practice—or in the realm of psychotherapy research, studies of the effects of learning "focusing" or other techniques for opening and deepening awareness. Varela et al. (1991)[61] portray the basis and depth of some of these understandings and advocate their closer linkage with the knowledge that has been gained in Western psychology and brain sciences. These various sources may yield data on consciousness that should not be ignored.

Therefore from this perspective I believe that the kind of objective, direct experimental testing that was discussed in the previous subsection should be supplemented by an examination of the knowledge about consciousness that is crystallized in ancient and still living traditions. Here, Buddhist psychology of various schools may be particularly pertinent. I find a remarkable consistency between the observations made in those traditions and the hypotheses I have been discussing. Fruitful research might arise through closely examining ways in which CC

---

60 As discussed in several of my essays—in this book in **Section 3**, under "Relations to 2 Other Theories," and in the essay "➔Worlds without ground: Comments on *The embodied mind:* Varela et al. 1991."

61 See essay "➔Worlds Without Ground" in next section (**Section 3**).

metatheory and its implications might be supported—and may have been anticipated—by the understandings of those traditions.[62]

==<<((([]||[]))>>==(([^]/\[^]))==<<((([^]|_|[^]))>>==(([^]/\[^]))==<<((([]||[]))>>==

---

62 And also various other kinds of 'spiritual' teaching, including Kabbalistic, the
Gurdjieff and Taoist teachings—and the undying *perennial philosophy* as described by
Huston Smith (1976) and others.

The following questions were formulated in 1992-92. Though considerably more is now known in some of these areas, these thoughts are included with the hope that they retain some pertinence and interest.

→ EARLIER NEUROPHYSIOLOGICAL SPECULATIONS

As (formerly) a neurophysiologist with strong interests in questions concerning consciousness, an overall question of great interest to me has been the following:

- How might synaptic function and especially *synaptogenesis* be associated with consciousness?

In some earlier writings (not included here) I had raised the question: "Is our neural network (nNW) stratified with an 'entering,' exploratory layer of the most active accommodative evolution?"

To enter further now into the speculations that this question suggests, I want first to ask for more information on "neuro-ontology"—the *progression of synaptic transformations in our inner connectivity.* Here are two first questions:

- What over the organism's life-span is the temporal progression of its synaptic "birth" and "death?"

- Is synaptognesis *continual* everywhere in the cortex? What are its temporal-spatial *distributions?*

The *developmental* aspects of these questions are of particularly great interest. I'd love to know more about the following:

- Over the "life-span" of each synapse, how do its activities and its properties *change?* Are synapses most "plastic" when young (like whole organisms, tissues, etc.)?

- If so, might it be that the cellular regions most associated with *consciousness* are the regions of *synaptogenesis* and of *early synaptic maturation* ("infant→adolescent synapses")?

I believe it may turn out that these questions have relevance to how synaptic development and functioning relates to consciousness.

Now here are some further exploratory notions and questions concerning that first question asking "How might synaptic function and especially *synaptogenesis* be associated with consciousness?"—also some speculations on functional architecture:

I. "Conscious" and "Unconscious"

A. Closed (Hierarchic) and Open (Network):

First, here is a hypothesis about a structural distinction between conscious events and unconscious processes:

- The general structure of *non-conscious* psychobiologic process is **hierarchical**; but the structure of *consciousness* is that of a **network**.

- A corollary is that *unchanging* organization of life-*process* is **hierarchical**; while the *transforming* organization of life-*event* is **network**.

That's how it may be at a highly abstract level. But can this be translated into a system of conceptualization that talks of concrete material systems—that considers the organization and function of *brain*?[63] In that realm conscious and unconscious processes are intimately intermingled happenings within the same unitary system. They are totally different ways of changing, going on together, spatially and temporally inseparable yet totally different in kind. (Are these *orthogonal components* of change?)

Can both types of change take place together ("inside the same substance")? And if so, can the former (*unconscious*) type of change be understood as involving the system's **hierarchical** structure of linkages, while the latter (*conscious*) type of change involves the system's **network** structure of linkages? Can one system contain both kinds of structure, simultaneously, coextensively? Can we conceptualize structure that is *simultaneously* hierarchical and network? And if so, can hierarchical and network actions proceed together, inseparable yet totally *different*?[64]

---

63   Karl Pribram's epistemological stance of "constructional realism" maintains that mind-brain dualism is best understood as a "duality...of conceptual procedures, not...any basic duality in nature." "Commencing with...ordinary experiences, two modes of conceptualization have developed. One mode operates downnward in a hierarchy of systems, analyzing experiences into components and establishing hierarchical and cause-effect relationships between these components. The other operates upward toward other organisms to attain consensual validation of experiences by comparing and sharing them....Thus two mirror images...are constructed from experience. One we call material, and the other mental." (Pribram 1986, p. 511.)

64   The principles of brain architecture that have been studied and expounded by Vernon Mountcastle and others may offer the beginning of an answer: "Distributed systems are...composed of large numbers of modular elements linked together in echeloned parallel and serial arrangements....An important feature of such distributed systems...is that the complex function controlled or executed by the system is not localized in any one of its parts. The function is a property of the dynamic activity within the system: it resides in the system as such." (Mountcastle 1978, p. 40.)

If these questions can be answered affirmatively, then my hypothesis (at the start of this subsection) about *unconscious* **hierarchical** processes and *conscious* **network** events implies that the brain is a system which is **simultaneously** *both* hierarchy and network. Here I recall Pagels' remark that "most real systems are mixtures of hierarchies and networks" (Pagels 1988, p. 50). My hypothesis, however, assumes not a *mixture* of these two kinds of organizations but rather (perhaps) a *compound*—the two fused to generate something different from either and having possibilities absent from either alone.

B. Automatized or Deliberate (Fast or Deep)

The organism restructures itself in many ways (not all of them obviously "adaptive"). The two ways that have recurred in these writings are: (i) the transformative learnings hypothesized to be *consciousness*; but also (ii) automatization of repetitive portions of these learnings, hypothesized to give more rapid performance but to remain *unconscious*.

Clearly, the *operation* of an automatization is (by definition) stereotyped and therefore highly predictable. In general "automatic" has an implication of *rapidity*; it's "*quick* and *efficient* but *stereotyped*." Automatizations are highly predictable; they are **conditionings**—the stuff of which behaviorism (a preeminently *predictive* theory) was constructed.[65]

In contrast the original idea of *structural alterations* that corresponded to **consciousness** concerned "brain *events*," where "event" (Heschel 1955) referred to usually-slower emergence of *new* structure that was *unique*, and that could not be predicted from what preceded. Deliberation may be deeper but tends also to be slower; with originality and creativity (decision-making, choice) it will all usually need to take longer (though it may be more efficient in the long run). The student (the "learner") may need lots of time!

In short, of these subsystems the relatively rapid operation of those which are most simple and rigid in structure (the "automatisms") enters least into "consciousness." But conditioning—or *automatization*—is not a *transformative event*; and therefore the slower "transformative event" (or "transformative learning") remains exclusively the order of change underlying consciousness.

---

65   For other pertinent observations see comparisons of CC metatheory with Baars' GW theory in essay "➔The Primacy of Self-Organizing Structural Transformation" (*Section 3*).

II. Contrasting but Complementary Optimizations?

Now here's a neuronal speculation: What if hierarchical and network systems coexisted by constituting two partially separable though highly overlapping subsets of synapses—the *hierarchical* subset we'll call "H-synapses" and the *network* subset we'll call "N-synapses"—with H-synapses being those on or closer to neuronal cell bodies, and N-synapses being those further away (dendritic, and especially further out on dendrites)? This speculation comes to me from the following considerations:

1. Hierarchical, automatized actions are specialized for rapidity and efficiency of action, though often at the expense of flexibility—of adaptability to altered circumstances and demands—as compared to conscious actions. They would therefore be expected to involve a relatively smaller number of more secure and rapid links.

2. Conscious awareness and action may be slower than unconscious, automatic action and reaction—not only, as previously conjectured, because additional neuronal levels and longer loops are involved, but also because slow dendritic modulations of neuronal excitability mediated by myriad dendritic inputs, individually low-level though powerful in aggregate, are of major importance. These dendritically-mediated modulations might *select* the particular hierarchical automatisms that were operative at a given moment. If so, the kind of selection postulated by Edelman (1978, 1987) might give rise to situation-specific neuronal groups, serving as neuronal substrata for hierarchical activity patterns, where the situation was determined by the postulated network of dendritic N-synapses.

It would follow, then, that the *operation of the hierarchies* would not be conscious, but that the actions of *selecting the particular hierarchies to be activated* would be conscious. The plausibility of this suggestion can be tested, in a preliminary way, by examining what is known of relations between conscious processes—"voluntary" movement, decision and choice processes, etc.—and slow cortical waves associated with discriminatory decisions, and some of the slow motor prepotentials seemingly associated with deliberate movements.

The transforming aspects of brain actions (related to Heschel's "events") may be termed "organic" (or "holistic"—Dreyfus & Dreyfus 1986), in contrast with "mechanical." Fully "organic"/"holistic" actions *simultaneously* involve *all* the interrelations of the whole, and are therefore less predictable than "mechanical" actions.

In contrast, "mechanical" actions are of much lower dimensionality, and therefore are simpler to predict, simpler to understand than "organic"/"holistic" actions.

To the extent that hierarchical systems are sequential and "mechanical" they also are simpler to predict, simpler to understand than "organic" actions.

The "organic"/"holistic" or "event" aspects of brain function seem to conform to the "network" paradigm. Therefore, if we are to push prediction as far as possible, then the dimensionality of predictive laws must be extremely high. A[sw] updating is conceived of as "organic"/"holistic"—as parallel actions of a large and complex whole. If this is appropriate, then if any *laws* which might predict or at least describe A[sw] updating are possible, their dimensionality must be extremely high.

III. Brain's Connectivity (Fractal Brain?)

Consider more closely the brain's general pattern of connectivity. While it has astronomical numbers of connections, most of these are short-range. Thus, it certainly does not fit the relatively simple nNW idea of a set of interconnected nodes (neurons) in which every node (neuron) makes a direct connection with every other. Among engineering systems, the similarity is a bit closer with multi-layer systems. But no engineering systems begin to approximate brain's architecture if, as I suspect, brain's nNW architecture is fractal-like. Note the following:

- Most of brain's connectivity is cortical; the various cortices are highly cellular, with great density of relatively short-range interconnections; the interior, in contrast, though containing highly cellular and highly interconnected "nuclei," is largely "white matter" composed of long-range tracts interconnecting distant cortices and nuclei.

- Cortices may be largely organized as local "column" structures (Edelman & Mountcastle 1978). These seem to be the outcomes of local nNW's self-organizing activities. The neurons within each column are highly interconnected.

Is each column, therefore, a local nNW that interacts, via its inputs and outputs, with other local nNW's both near (profusely) and far (more sparingly)?[66] And may these interlinked local nNW's then form a higher-level nNW, of which they are the higher-order nodes? If so, how does the short-range connectivity within each local nNW (column or nucleus) compare with the long-range connectivity of such a proposed higher-level nNW?

---

66 Each column might be considered a nNW "holon" (Koestler 1967).

IV. Alternation of Levels

Of course, much of the brain's long-distance intercommunication seems to be concerned with hierarchically organized functions. This suggests—in combination with the above thought about networks as nodes of super-ordinate networks—that nNW units (such as columns, or larger units) can be elements in hierarchical structures.

In fact, hierarchic and network structural principles have been combined in some recent nNW simulations, in particular that by Kawato et al (1987) that was closely patterned after knowledge of the neural organization of the primate motor system. Their report (1987) was entitled "A Hierarchical Neural Network Model for Control and Learning of Voluntary Movement," and its nNW portions generate and update models of musculo-skeletal dynamics. Their system is, in fact, a seemingly well thought-out embodiment of the "Anticipating self-world model (A[sw])"[G] principles I have sketched (in several essays earlier in this section), and is reported to function effectively.

But the "layering" of levels may go the other way as well: Why not hierarchically-structured elements interconnected to form a super-ordinate network? Certainly, networks are "served" by input and output systems that are hierarchically organized. Are there also hierarchical structures *within* networks: Do networks develop hierarchical, "mechanical" specializations? That this occurs is suggested by the great adaptive importance of "automatization"; we observe in many circumstances that well-practiced actions drop from awareness and become automatic. How does this happen? And what is its significance for our consciousness and our freedom?

In other words, nNW development may lead to differentiation of semi-autonomous units that are interconnected either into higher-order networks or into hierarchical structures. And conversely, stable local neuronal structures with hierarchical internal organization can serve as elements either of larger hierarchies or of networks.

Thus hierarchy structure and nNW structure can be combined through location at different levels of the system. But must a system function, at a particular level, *either* in a hierarchical manner *or* in a network manner? I have a nagging intuition that there is some way that hierarchy and nNW patterns of action can be intimately combined at the *same* level of a system.

Near the beginning of the first subsection of this essay—after asking "can hierarchical and network actions proceed together, *inseparable* yet totally *different?*"—I said: "My hypothesis, however, assumes not a *mixture* of these two kinds of orga-

---

G   See **Glossary**.

nizations but rather (perhaps) a **compound**—*the two fused to generate something different from either and having possibilities absent from either alone.*"

I'd like to believe that somehow this "fusion" can be made possible by the synaptic distributions postulated in the second subsection above *(II. "Contrasting but Complementary Optimizations?")*. There I'd said I wondered "if hierarchical and network systems coexisted by constituting two partially separable though highly overlapping subsets of synapses—the *hierarchical* subset we'll call 'H-synapses' and the *network* subset we'll call 'N-synapses'—with H-synapses being those on or closer to neuronal cell bodies, and N-synapses being those further away (dendritic, and especially further out on dendrites)." Right now, that's my closing speculation! Perhaps *that* **is** the "way that hierarchy and nNW patterns of action can be intimately combined at the *same* level of a system."

==<<((([]||[]))>>==(((\[^]/\[^]))==<<((([^]|_|[^]))>>==(((\[^]/\[^]))==<<((([]||[]))>>==

==<<(([]||[]))>>==((([^]/\[^]))==<<((([^]|_|[^]))>>==((([^]/\[^]))==<<(([]||[]))>>==

>>Preview of Section 3 (Implications & Reconciliations):

The first essay in this section—on *"the 'hard' problem"*—was written in 1997 and is entitled "➔ **Finding the Beginning: Consciousness Precedes Theories.**" In seeking a deeper understanding of Chalmers' *"hard"* problem (Chalmers 1995) the following points are developed:

(1) *Consciousness* is not a foreign ingredient to be added into our objective theorizing but rather is our theorizing's indispensable matrix, prior to all our understanding.

(2) Theories derived specifically with the aim of explaining *correlations* between consciousness and cognitive function are relatively untroubled by the *"hard"* problem.

(3) Given the vast, dynamic, unconscious substructure of all our experiencing, *experiencing* is aroused by *unexpectedness*—when predictions of our automatic mechanisms are not confirmed.

(4) Then resolution of the *"hard"* problem is achieved by a "bridging principle" that states: *Consciousness is the creation and revision of automatizations.*

This metatheory further predicts that:

(5) Our experiencing is unrepeatable.

(6) The stable presuppositions that are responsible for the hardness of the *"hard"* problem will usually remain invisible.

This is followed by an *Addendum on Relations to Alternative Perspectives,* and then "➔ More on Downward Causation and Free Will. "

Section 3's next subsection (entitled "-Relations to 2 Other Theories") compares other theories of consciousness to CC metatheory.

It begins with an essay (written in 1995) entitled "➔ **Worlds Without Ground,**" which argues that the *ungrounded* psychology of *enaction* propounded by Varela et al. (1991) is remarkably consistent with CC metatheory of consciousness (set forth in *Section 2,* just preceding). Though the former abjures realism and representationalism while the latter is described in terms that seem stuck in those philosophies, closer examination suggests that these inconsistencies are only apparent—that rather than abandoning the terminologies of this grounded modern worldview, CC metatheory uses them as a bridge to an ungrounded postmodern worldview. Both the enactive paradigm and the CC worldview increase our awareness of the constricting and rigidifying consequences of over-reliance on abstract thought.

In the next essay (written in 1999 and entitled "➔The Primacy of Self-Organizing Structural Transformation: Can Consciousness Theories Converge?") two theories of consciousness are again compared and contrasted: Bernard Baars' "global workspace" (GW) theory and "continual creation" (CC) metatheory^G. It is concluded that there are fundamental similarities, as both theories are based in the notion that consciousness arises out of a complex, dynamic and hierarchically-structured matrix of unconscious automatisms, and both theories postulate that "consciousness always involves adaptation" (as phrased by Baars; Baars 1988, p. 213).

But there are also differences: Baars suggests that "conscious experience involves a global workspace, a central information exchange that allows many different specialized processors to interact" (Baars 1988, p. 43), and that what we are consciously experiencing is the communicative interaction of these "processor" experts within the "global workspace" (GW). In CC metatheory vastly complex dynamic interactions between processors are also going on all the time, but mostly *unconsciously*—and consciousness arises not simply out of their intercommunication as the GW architecture suggests but rather out of the accommodative (adaptive) restructuring both of individual active modules and of their automatized patterns of interaction. Further, though in both theories there is an intimate connection between consciousness and internal consistency, in GW theory it's a *condition* for consciousness, while in CC metatheory it's a *consequence* of consciousness. But the main difference between theories may be in language rather than meaning.

Immediately following this essay will come another (much shorter) on a report of a related neural-network modeling experiment published in 1998, entitled "➔A Dynamical Systems Perspective (Jun Tani)" briefly describing seeming similarities of that work to CC metatheory of this book.

The concluding part of *Section 3*, on "Social and Ethical Implications," consists of an essay presented in 1996 entitled "➔Attention and Violence: How Each Moment of Consciousness Matters." It delves into social and ethical effects of attention-strategies, asking: With violence everywhere, threatening our futures, might clearer understanding of consciousness help our survival? It is contended that it could by unfolding heretofore neglected consequences of different strategies of attending.

Violence is a manifestation of decaying order—of the rise in entropy to which all mechanical systems are subject. Unconscious mind—a vast network of automatisms—cannot escape such degradation. Counter-movement, generating higher and more integrated levels of order, entails the transformation of that network, creating different automatisms. It follows that to reduce violence, increase consciousness.

However, what needs to be recognized is that Cartesian compartmentalization nevertheless intrudes everywhere because it generates, both individually and in society, an *addictive illusion of power*. It goes thus: I achieve some local control—control that may actually be tiny since enormous surrounding regions escape or even negate that control. Yet exactly because in this moment those non-controlled regions are almost entirely excluded from my attention, the tiny region of control that now fills my awareness is experienced as very large—an illusion I love and wish to preserve! Organizations and societies similarly treasure illusions of power.

Such seduction exacts a price; the system is disordered by unanticipated destructions. *Unattended* consequences are *unintended* consequences.

/~*~\/~*~\/~*~\/~*~\/~*~\/~*~\/~*~\/~*~\/~*~\/~*~\/~*~\/~*~\/~*~\/~*~\/~*~\/~*~\/

SECTION 3: IMPLICATIONS & RECONCILIATIONS

~~ON THE "HARD" PROBLEM—JUST HOW IS IT HARD?

I ask:

> Is the famous *"hard"* problem a consequence of some crucial *forgettings* that are central to our still-reigning *scientism*? Baars (2003) speaks of dissociations central to Skinner's Behaviorist worldview, and how these have continued to infect psychological, scientific and Western philosophical thought. Does their healing dissolve that *"hard"* problem?

> The following essay is a response (which I wrote in 1997) to the article by David Chalmers (1995): "Facing Up to the Problem of Consciousness," *Journal of Consciousness Studies*, 2(3), pp. 200-219.

→ FINDING THE BEGINNING: CONSCIOUSNESS PRECEDES THEORIES

I. Origins

Chalmers (1995) in presenting his *"hard"* problem suggests "that a theory of consciousness should take experience as fundamental," saying: "We know that a theory of consciousness *requires the **addition** of something* fundamental to our ontology, as everything in physical theory is compatible with the absence of consciousness" (p. 14—emphasis added).

However, here's another frame of reference within which the *"hard"* problem has a different appearance. This alternative perspective was implicit in previous discussions[1] but will here be presented more sharply. I wish to remind us that conscious experience is not an "extra ingredient" and thus cannot be a *new, additional* fundamental entity or property since it is the matrix of our knowledge and thus is prior to all our explanations.

---

1   See the previous section, **Section 2**.

The Primacy of Experiencing:

The question can be put thus: *Is most of the "hard" problem's difficulty a conse-quence of the paradigm within which we generate the problem?* I will suggest that it is, and further that its difficulty can be transformed by shifting to another larger and more inclusive explanatory paradigm. More specifically, the insight as far as I have developed it is that the hardness of our "hard" problem comes from *the unquestioned primacy of the **objective** in our habitual subject-object dualism.*

We have generated the hardness by our habitual separation of observer and observed (so that our discourse must be *either* in one realm *or* the other), together with the primacy which we then give to the observed—to the *objective*. The con-sequence is our demand that an intellectually satisfying explanation must *reduce* the observer to the observed—that it must explain the subjective in terms of the objective; or if this fails, that it can only *add* some new and foreign element to the objectively observable.

This subject-object dualism is a secondary cognitive accomplishment, though we almost always assume it to be primary—assume it to be a necessary prerequi-site of all rational thought. Certainly, it is useful. It is a cognitive disconnection that seems to vastly simplify our conceptual worldview, but that simplification has a price. For once this simplifying separation dominates our thought processes, it effectively hides the *ubiquitous primacy of experience*—that is, *of subjectivity.* Then *subjective experience*—looked at "objectively"—becomes an "other," a kind of external, foreign phenomenon that cannot be fitted into the objective world (which is now unquestioningly—and erroneously—assumed to be primary). That is our presently dominant paradigm.

- But this perspective is a constriction of consciousness—a vast inversion in which abstraction has become primary, concrete experience secondary.[2]

- The reality is the reverse. For though abstraction becomes a powerful tool for cognitive probing (*vide* mathematics), our concrete experiencing is our only entrance into *reality* and is the necessary source of nearly all our mental structure—including our capacities for abstraction and other secondary cog-nitive techniques (e.g., see Piaget 1952). The vast and original unity of our concrete experiencing is our only entrance into all that we know.

---

2   In a later essay in this section ("➔Worlds Without Ground") I called attention to this by noting how the complexity of our concrete experiencing may be incommen-surate with the vast simplifications that inhere in the abstractions out of which scien-tific theories must be constructed. The contrast between abstract and concrete modes of thinking—and the contemporary dominance of the former—has been discussed by Ruddick (1989, pp. 93-95).

What a revelation! Taking conscious experiencing to be a "fundamental property" of the world is no longer some *additional* assumption that we are introducing into our world-picture, thereby making it more complex. Therefore it is not a surplus complexity to be, perhaps, banished on the basis of parsimony. Rather, it is our first and last reality, coming before all else—and certainly is prior to all the abstract cognizing by which we construct a theory of consciousness. How, then, can there be a *"hard"* problem which is only to be resolved by the introduction of this *additional* element in our conceptual system, an additional element that perhaps unavoidably *complicates* it? On the contrary, that *experiencing* was there first—and therefore *experiencing* is the fundamental "element" which *is to be added to*. That is, the immediate and irreducible fact of our *experiencing* is the original simplicity, onto which all other aspects of our theorizing are added.

What is being said here is quite distinct from empiricism. Conscious experience includes "sensory experience" but is a far broader category. "Sensory experience" or "sensation" or "that which can be known directly through the senses" are themselves rather narrow abstractions, derived from our *direct conscious experience* but not identical with it. For these fundamental categories of empiricism have themselves become so "obviously fundamental" through our unquestioning domination by that same subject-object split. To achieve this split, we conceptually divide "output" from "input," divide our "actions" from the consequent reactions of our "sensory feedback," separating them in a way that, though it seems to give our understanding of our place in our world a wonderful simplicity, leaves out our most fundamental reality, which is the *inseparability in our conscious experiencing of action and response*.

That enlarged and unified worldview eludes nearly all of us nearly all of the time—but can be achieved for moments, I find. When I've thus inverted my perspective (which, in truth, has now been turned *right-side-up!*), Chalmers' *"hard"* problem disappears—or at least becomes another and very different kind of question. From the new perspective we may still be mystified by assumptions of particular correlations between mechanism and subjectivity. But now we can turn the mystery around. We will no longer ask: Why is it that this particular kind of neural mechanism or activity is accompanied by that extra (seemingly unnecessary!) feature, our subjective experience? Rather, we begin to wonder: Why is our subjective experience accompanied by this particular action—e.g., by this postulated neural process? That turns the *"hard"* problem around. For, to repeat my main point again, it is the *experiencing* which is there first, as the primary given, and therefore does not need to be explained. It is prior to all explanations.[3] It is the matrix, the deepest foundation of all explanations.

---

3   As also emphasized recently by Altsmanspacher (1995).

Thus, conscious experience had seemed to us like something "extra" that we had to *add* to our theory only because (as was said at the start) our view of reality was fractured by our subject-object dualism.

A. Toward Theory

As Chalmers (1995) notes, to build a non-reductive theory of consciousness, the next step after giving consciousness its proper place as a "fundamental property" is to introduce fundamental "*bridging* principles" (Chalmers 1995, p. 15) that will connect the fundamental datum of experiencing with something physically describable. These principles will then be the foundation of the theory.

But now in giving my "bridging principle" from an enlarged and unified perspective, my assertion can be, as has already been intimated, something significantly different from the formulation that gives rise to the "*hard*" problem. Rather than saying, "here is this mechanism, and I assert that it is accompanied by conscious experiencing," I will make an inverse statement: "Here is my conscious experiencing, and here are some of its characteristics—I therefore infer that it is accompanied by these cognitive *functions* and their underlying mechanisms." Then, if you want to question my choice of this linking, instead of being able to ask: "Why do you say that this particular function or process happens *with* rather than *without* conscious experiencing?"—you will need to ask: "Why do you say that your conscious experiencing is accompanied by that particular cognitive function or process rather than some other?"

My own task from the enlarged and unified perspective, then, is not to explain to you why I assert that *accommodative self-organization*[4] *is conscious rather than unconscious. If that were my task, I would be up against precisely Chalmers' "hard"* problem. But now my task is a little different—and I think easier: it is to *explain why I have chosen this particular function, process or action rather than some other as the objective background of my experiencing.* And that I can do by examining what the proposed theory predicts about the properties of my conscious experiences.

I will be helped by an appropriate procedure of theory-construction. If I want to work out a theory of consciousness I have a choice of strategies. I will sketch two. The first of them is certainly tempting, as it seems the most simple and direct, but it's the one that also is most vulnerable to challenge by the "*hard*" problem. The second strategy, though not quite so simple and direct, is however less vulnerable.

---

4   See above, **Section 2:** "*Knowing Consciousness*"—especially essays "➜On consciousness: What is the Role of Emergence" (Atkin 1992) and "➜Conscious Beyond Mechanism" (Atkin 1994).

Here's the first way—what seems the simple and direct way: Wanting a *Theory of Consciousness*, I will naturally focus my attention mainly upon my target, which is "consciousness," will note all I can about its functional characteristics—its properties, structure, actions, etc.—and construct my theory to explain these. But then I will have, as Chalmers says (1996, pp. 7-10), a theory of *awareness*—of functional correlates of consciousness. My assertion that my theory explains consciousness may well be met by an objection of the sort expounded by Chalmers— "[Certainly] your theory may account for those features of *awareness*; but you haven't yet explained why should they be accompanied by *experiencing*." That objection could go thus:

> You say that phenomena $A_1 \ldots A_m$ are accompanied by conscious experiencing and that your theory explains those phenomena. Nevertheless, though you give supporting evidence for your explanations of phenomena $A_1 \ldots A_m$, you have not yet explained *why* they are accompanied by conscious experiencing.

Is there a sounder way to ground a theory of consciousness? *There is!* Another strategy that can produce a theory that will be less open to this kind of objection could be sketched thus:

> Look for phenomena $C_1 \ldots C_q$ that sometimes are accompanied by consciousness, sometimes not, with no detectable determinant of this difference among criteria $x_1 \ldots x_r$.

> Then search for differentiating criteria and/or a differentiating function that will predictively distinguish between conscious and unconscious instances of each of those $C_1 \ldots C_q$ phenomena—say, e.g., the criteria $y_1 \ldots y_s$, or some function $f(y_1 \ldots y_s)$ of them.

> Devise a theory to explain the efficacy of these differentiating criteria and/or of this differentiating function. (The resulting theory may or may not be given as explicitly grounded upon a bridging hypothesis.)

At the end of a previous essay ("➜ Further Thoughts on … Atkin 1992"—see above) I put it this way: "What's the difference in brain 'states' and actions (and/or *systems*) between conscious and unconscious cognition?"

Will the resulting *differentiating theory*, which proposes to explain precisely what differentiates conscious from non-conscious cognitive functions, also be vulnerable to the objection that Chalmers (1995) raises as his challenge to the general run of "Theories of Consciousness"—the objection that the correlation between the explained cognitive phenomena and conscious experiencing has not been explained?

I think that it will not be, because—unlike the thrust of theories constructed by the first strategy—the theory generated in accord with the second strategy is exactly directed toward explaining the function-consciousness correlation.

One prominent consciousness researcher, Baars (1988), has presented his theory of consciousness as a product of the second strategy—that is, as a *differentiating* theory. Does this mean that his theory should be less troubled than some others by the *"hard"* problem? I believe that it does. And on the same basis I hold that my own "continual creation" (CC) metatheory,[5] which has been constructed in a way that in most respects parallels Baars' theory, is also a *differentiating* theory and so speaks to the *"hard"* problem.

Yet CC metatheory differs significantly from the theory of consciousness developed by Baars (1988)[6], and the differences centers exactly upon each theory's explanation of the similarly recognized conscious-unconscious differentiations. Baars shows how these differentiations are well explained by his hypothesis of a global workspace (which can be restated as a *"bridging* hypothesis"); arguments for CC metatheory assert that the very same differentiations can be as well explained by using another bridging hypothesis, which will be given in the next section.

B. Fundamental Unexpectedness

I started with the idea that "consciousness is learning"—a linking that seemed deeply consistent with my own experience. Now I find that it is also close to ideas in the careful theory of consciousness elaborated by Baars (1988). He says: "From a theoretical point of view, we expect consciousness to be involved in learning of novel events, or novel connections between known events" (p. 214), noting that his theory "claims that consciousness inherently involves adaptation and learning" and that it "suggests that there is an upward monotonic function between the amount of *information* to be learned and the duration of conscious involvement necessary to learn it" (p. 381).

This implies just when there will be the need for learning. For what catches our attention, always? Something *unexpected*. We are always most acutely aware of that which in our present sensory field is in some way in conflict with our *expectations*. We automatically pay attention to the new and unfamiliar—this is where we *need* to direct our attention so that we can *accommodate* our understandings

---

5   A theory of consciousness described in Atkin, 1992, 1994. See **Section 2** (above), also first essay ("➔ Being, Doing, Knowing") in book's **Summing Up** section, and **Glossary** at back.

6   For discussion of these differences, see the essay "➔ The Primacy of Self-Organizing Structural Transformation: Can Consciousness Theories Converge?" further on in this section.

and actions to demands that we have not met before (at least not in the form and context in which they now confront us).

Conversely, whatever is most closely congruent with our expectations is least noticed, most superficially attended to (if at all). Everybody knows that we run off well-learned skills with little attention to the details of our performance, being aware only of how we must adjust them to present demands. We all take this for granted—we pay attention primarily to the interstices of discrepancy and difficulty, where we don't quite know the way automatically.

II: Consequences

A. Consciousness as the Creating-of-Automatisms

Thus there seems to be some very immediate and pervasive relationship between *newness*, in the sense of *unexpectedness* that evokes some form of *learning*, and the intensity of our experiencing.[7] Given this relationship which appears to be a fundamental feature of all[8] our experiencing, it might reasonably be used as foundation for any theory of consciousness. That is what I have done in the "CC metatheory" described in earlier writings (e.g., Atkin 1992; and see essay "➔ Conscious Beyond Mechanism," above).

The connection of consciousness to *learning evoked by novelty* can be more precisely expressed than before by stating the bridging hypothesis thus: *Consciousness is the **creation** and **revision** of **automatizations.**[9]* For this points directly to the vast and highly dynamic unconscious substructure of all our experiencing, and specifies just what of this enters our consciousness, when, and how.

If, as Chalmers (1995) puts it, *cognitive functions* are to be accounted for by mechanisms, and if (by CC metatheory) *consciousness* is transformation of mechanism, then we might say that our cognitive functioning is continually evolving through our conscious experiencing.

So consciousness is immediately based upon yet somehow beyond cognition. It is, one might say, *meta*cognition—how cognition re-structures itself. The work

---

7   Observational and experimental evidence for such generalizations about an association between novelty and consciousness have been surveyed by Baars (1988).

8   Apparent exceptions are, it can be shown, only apparent. Seeming difficulties raised by these seeming exceptions will be dealt with elsewhere.

9   The word "automatizations," as used here, has very much the same significance as the word "processor" in Baars' (1988) theory, also as the words "agent" and "agency" in the AI framework developed by Marvin Minsky (1986), and is related to ways in which other terms—e.g., "module" or "schema"—are sometimes used (e.g., see Baars 1988, pp. 51-63).

of the cognitivists (e.g., see Gardner 1987) is certainly of the greatest value, but it studies the matrix within which experiencing arises rather than experiencing itself. What it tells us about is *functions* (as Chalmers [1995] emphasized), and it therefore does not account for *consciousness*, leaving the *"hard"* problem untouched. (That is, in CC terms, it is not about *accommodation* but rather about *assimilation*—see foregoing essay "➔ Conscious Beyond Mechanism," and *Glossary*).

Basically, what we're looking for happens with learning. Previous researchers have painted various parts of the picture. Penrose (1989)—like Calvin (1989) and also like Baars (1988), Dreyfus & Dreyfus (1986) and Edelman (1989)—had concluded that (just as CC metatheory asserts) consciousness cannot be mechanical. Thus these authors, though somewhat vague in specifying what consciousness "is," come close CC metatheory in assertions about what it is not. The assertion here is not that mechanistic explanations are wrong, but that they leave something out, and that this *something* is only rediscovered by a paradigm expansion to include, as theoretically legitimate, the self-organizational capacities of dissipative systems. Thus CC metatheory sets the stage for a partial rehabilitation of the algorithmic or computational nature of consciousness, now not as consciousness *itself* but as its necessary matrix, its *substructure*.

The character of this substructure was clearly presented by Baars (1988) in a paragraph entitled "*The development of automaticity with practice*":

> Any highly practiced and automatic skill tends to become "modular"— unconscious, separate from other skills, and free from voluntary control … and any complex skill seems to combine many semiautonomous specialized units.
>
> (Baars 1988, p. 51)

This substructure is crucially important, but not sufficient. The picture here is that the assimilating (unconscious) mechanisms constrain the evolution of conscious experience, but they do not determine it. Further, the complexity of this constraint is enormous.

Automatic skills have become unconscious, but that does not mean that they are simple—their *structure* may be just as complex and their *functioning* just as subtly adaptive as those of any conscious processes. For our system of automatizations is almost endlessly multi-level. It is a hierarchy—a vast Bureaucracy. The situation was well described by Minsky (1986)—myriad "agents" linked into superordinate "agencies."

This means that our statement that **consciousness is the creation and revision of automatizations** is an almost endlessly multi-level proposition. For this statement refers not only to the lowest-level automatizations but on upwards to those of all levels—and there are many. That means many levels of expectation—and if novelty signifies unmet expectations, then many levels of novelty.

B. Conditions for and Contents of Consciousness

Now the characterization of conscious experiencing can be broadened to look not only at conditions which evoke it but also at its *contents*. Our experiencing never repeats exactly. This observation has often been made. Thus we experience that:

> The stream of consciousness, itself ever changing, is attracted to the unknown—more exactly, to whatever is unknown within the known.

Note that novelty thus plays a double role in our characterizations of our stream of consciousness—it enters in describing both the **conditions for consciousness** (it "is attracted to the unknown") and the **contents of consciousness** (it is "ever changing"). If both of these two roles of novelty in consciousness are in fact as they seem, are these two roles two independent "facts"? Or are they related to each other? And if so, how?

Here's a way that a link might be forged. I have suggested that "unexpected-ness" as a *condition* for consciousness be taken as a primary, primitive observation, which leads in a direct manner to our CC metatheory—or something close to it—as an abstract "bridging" principle that directly accounts for this *condition* for our experiencing. But then, once we have begun to develop our theory of consciousness using this bridging principle as its main foundation, the unrepeti-tiveness of our *contents* of consciousness ("the flow of consciousness itself is ever changing, ever new") follows as a necessary inference.

According to the metatheory that is based upon CC metatheory, the *function* of consciousness is the *construction*—and the always-ongoing *renovation*—of mind.[10] But if that is subjective experiencing's *function*, then it is inevitable that its *contents* are ever-changing. Why? Exactly because it is the nature of "experienc-ing" to wreak modifications upon the matrix from which it emerges.

Thus exact repetition of any given accommodative action is in principle impos-sible because the first instance of accommodative action has changed its mind-substrate—the unconscious substructure of consciousness—and any subsequent

---

10 "Mind" here meaning the total complex structure of our automatisms (hierarchies of processors or agencies: Baars 1988; Minsky 1986), most but not all of which remains beneath our conscious awareness. (And see "mind" in **Glossary** at end of book). Thus "mind" includes the contents and structure of our consciousness awareness—but is also its far larger unconscious substructure.

accommodative action upon that "same" unconscious substructure must inevitably find that it actually is *not* the same.

In short, since each action changes the ground of action, each action must itself be a new and different action. Thus, no pattern of conscious *accommodative* activity can return to the same unconscious assimilative substrate twice! And that is exactly *why* the stream of consciousness is always changing, always new.[11]

C. About the Invisibility of Stable Presuppositions

But certainly, there are many determinants and limiters of change that do not themselves change. If what we experience is the self-organizing alteration of our cognitive structure, then it is predictable that the stabilities of our structure are not experienced and remain beneath our conscious awareness.

Both CC metatheory and the GW theory of Baars (1988) predict this. It is why we find it so hard to think about the determinants of our habitual dualistic thinking and of the dominance of abstract over concrete cognition which it enforces. In a previous paper (not included here), I noted the way in which it follows from CC metatheory that unconscious mechanisms constrain conscious freedom, so that *the meshing paradigms that govern my every thought and action* remain almost entirely invisible. Baars put this very well:

> [Our] *stable presuppositions* tend to become unconscious. Whatever we believe with absolute certainty we tend to take for granted. Moreover, we lose sight of the fact that *alternatives to our stable presuppositions can be entertained.* Indeed, scientific-paradigm shifts generally take place when one group of scientists begins to challenge a presupposition that is held to be immutable (and hence is largely unconscious) in the thinking of an older scientific establishment.
>
> (Baars 1988, p. 152)

Certainly, we tend to be dominated in our cognitive framework by our presuppositions concerning the absolute separation between subjective and objective and by the primacy which we automatically give to the objective. We unquestioningly *know* that this is the only stance from which real science can arise. In raising the question here I wish to return those presuppositions to our consciousness so that we can at least begin to talk about them.

---

11 Just this argument is clearly made by Baars (1988), who notes that 'conscious involvement in learning leads to adaptation, which alters *the context of experience*: but we know that a change in context in its turn alters subsequent experience' (p. 214).

> Notice that once we question a presupposed idea, it is no longer pre-
> supposed, but focal and conscious. It is therefore interpreted in its own
> conceptual context. When we *talk* about our conceptual context we can
> make a piece of it conscious.
>
> (Baars 1988, p. 154)

So again, let us remember that in our scientific deliberations about the nature
and grounding of our conscious experiencing, the very experiencing we wish
to explain is prior to all our explanations, being their necessary ground. As we
remember this, can we thereby begin to see another way past this obstacle to
which Chalmers (1995) has called our attention—his *"hard"* problem?

Coda: First Person Present Tense

Rereading, I'm startled. The arguments I am making here aren't always clear to
me. It seems that this crucially depends upon my own "state of consciousness." It's
very interesting!

When my attention is almost entirely focal and my awareness dominated by
abstractions (which is my state more often than not) then I find what I have been
writing here quite difficult to comprehend. It's only when I am able to become
more reflective in a relaxed way and to enlarge the spaciousness of my experiencing to *simultaneously* include my focal, context-stripped abstractions *and* the
experiencing behind and around them that I better know what I have here been
talking about. That is, when I'm fragmented I'm incapable of detecting my fragmentation or of even suspecting that it's a cause of problems. (Thus the "Catch
22" comes home again!)

The idea that consciousness researchers may need to open and enlarge the span
of their own consciousness has occurred to a few of them.[12] I was brought to it at
the end of a previous paper (see "➔ Conscious Beyond Mechanism" in **Section 2**,
above) and again see its importance from my own immediate experience in constructing the discussion presented here.

III. Summary

The purpose here has been to take a new look at Chalmers' *"hard"* problem
(Chalmers 1995); in doing so, I've had thoughts seeming to point toward more
fundamental ways to understand it, as follows:

---

12 E.g.: see Altmanspacher 1995; Varela *et al.* 1991.

(1) First, I ask: Does conscious experiencing need to be added to the other foundation assumptions of our objective science as a new "fundamental property," as Chalmers (1995) suggested? Or alternatively (as I suggest), can we remember that the **experiencing** *is there first* as the primary given, thus is *prior* to all explanations and already *fundamental* **without** *having to be* **added?** That could mean that part of the hardness of his *"hard"* problem is a consequence of our unconsciously dualistic habits of thought.

(2) But another part of the *"hard"* problem depends upon the *strategy of theory-building*. One common way looks immediately for cognitive functions that correlate with consciousness and explains those but cannot explain why these functions are accompanied by experiencing. A second strategy[13] (less common) is to study cognitive functions that sometimes are conscious, sometimes not, seeking to determine what causes that difference. The result may be a theory that is less vulnerable to the *"hard"* problem.

(3) One such cause of that difference between conscious and unconscious functions, which we might reasonably use to derive a "bridging principle" (Chalmers 1995, p. 15) to serve as foundation for a non-reductive theory of consciousness, is the close relationship between *newness* (in the sense of *unexpectedness*) and the intensity of our conscious awareness. This attraction of experiencing to the unknown—more exactly, to whatever is unknown within the known—is grounding for the bridging principle[G] of the continual creation (CC) metatheory.

(4) One form of that bridging principle states: *Consciousness is the creation and revision of automatizations.* This principle points directly to the vast and highly dynamic unconscious substructure of all our experiencing and specifies just what of this substructure enters our consciousness, when it does, and how. We thereby get a deeply meaningful and non-mechanistic *function* for consciousness that explains its *causal efficacy*[14], and are at the same time provided with a clear explanation of *downward causation.*[15]

(5) Then—thus grounded in our direct knowledge of the role of novelty in setting the *conditions* for our conscious awareness—we see how CC metathe-

---

13   Described and advocated by Baars (1988).

G   See *'bridging principle'* (and also *'CC metatheory'*) in **Glossary**.

14   Regarding causal efficacy of consciousness see discussion of it in essay "➔Conscious Beyond Mechanism" in *Section 2*.

15   Regarding this see e.g. the foregoing essay "➔Conscious Beyond Mechanism" in **Section 2** and the later essay "➔Something on Holarchic Structure and Downward Causation" in the **Summing Up** section (also **Glossary**).

ory predicts another datum of our experiencing: The unrepeatability, in the large, of the *contents* of our conscious awareness.

(6)   The invisibility of stable presuppositions is also predicted and is thought to be the reason that presuppositions responsible for the hardness of the *"hard"* problem have usually remained beneath awareness.

(7)   Finally, it is noted how this invisibility of stable presuppositions continues even now to make it difficult for this author to consistently sustain full comprehension of his own arguments.

\|/oOo\|/oOo\|/oOo\|/oOo\|/oOo\|/oOo\|/oOo\|/oOo\|/oOo\|/oOo\|/oOo\|/

→ *Addendum: Relations to Alternative Perspectives*

That last observation—concerning how difficult it is to comprehend our experiencing and to understand the principles by which it arises—is immediately pertinent to some things I've been reading lately, advising us that we should fundamentally shift our perspective. They say: (1) That we should abandon our habitual *individualism* and instead relate to all *intersubjectively* (Ziman 2006); and (2) that we should abandon the usual "supposition that, although an external event and its representation in the brain are causally connected, they are nevertheless separate," and realize that from a process oriented view "there is a unity between the 'external world' and the 'perceived world'" (Manzotti 2006, p. 7).

What are the possibilities for an *intersubjective* rather than *individualistic* framework (Ziman 2006) for my theorizing? Certainly my whole upbringing, cognitive development, and ways of seeking to better my understanding have mostly remained within the individualistic framework—and I believe that all the writings here (and in Atkin 2007) can be so characterized. Is this a flaw? Or is it a convenient way for problem and world-structure simplification—a convenience which may remain useful but needs to be *recognized*. Reading Ziman has helped me to recognize those habitual and convenient simplifications, allowing me to glimpse alternative ways to perceive and cognize. But yet, I am not persuaded that I should abandon the way I've been thinking and expressing myself about consciousness—only that I should remember its limitations. It was noted by Boden (2006—commenting on Ziman 2006) that:

Given the huge complexity of adult human minds (not to mention their capacity for deliberate dissimulation), a large number of our interpretations are questionable in practice, not merely in principle. That's true irrespective of whether we follow Ziman in rejecting methodological individualism.

Boden 2006, p. 60.

Much of my writings (e.g., Atkin 2007) have also focused upon limitations inherent in all the ways we seek for and claim *understanding!* And certainly we need to recognize how the convenient simplicity of staying within an individualistic perspective rather than opening to the complexities of intersubjectivity will continually be imposing certain limits upon our understanding. Can we attain that recognition and stay with it? (Usually we have no awareness of this cause of ignorance—nor of most others.)

Similar considerations are pertinent to the ways my thought patterns relate to Manzotti's (2006) "process oriented" view of the mind—which he presents as a superior alternative to our usual habits of *objectification*. Manzotti gives importance to recognition of our habitual objectification even in regard to brain:

The brain as an object is obviously separate from the environment. The brain activity as a process is much less obviously separate from the events in the environment. Brain and events are the two sides of the same flow of events.

Manzotti 2006, p. 17

Note that this comes close to the view I've been presenting—especially if we interpret Manzotti's use in the foregoing of the word "events" with the meaning given to this word by Abraham Joshua Heschel (1955) who's writings about "process" and "event" had helped to start me on the theoretical path I've been following. Certainly, like Manzotti I too have given some attention to the habitual way we treat our flow of self-world interactions as the doings of separate *objects,* and have seen the pernicious effects of such habitual objectification (Atkin 2007)—so I find Manzotti's arguments concerning non-objectifying relations of brain to environment to be meaningful. I do see (quite happily) how—if we simply replace "process" with "self-organizing transformation" and substitute "mind" for "brain"—Manzotti's viewpoint comes quite close to mine:

If conscious experience is identical with a process that links the world to the brain, the brain must be continuous with the external world by means of the body. Everything the brain is conscious of is an object/

event/state of affairs involved in the brain history. Development, embodiment and situatedness are all crucial aspects for the occurrence of a subject ... Development is needed since the brain is not simply an object, but is the end point of a causal web of interactions with the environment.

Manzotti 2006, p. 37

Note here the close parallels (given those substitutions) with my ways of seeing the role of consciousness in the *evolution*, the *history* and the present *state* of one's *mind*. In Atkin 2007 (towards the end of the essay "➔ Conscious Beyond Mechanism (Shifting a Paradigm)") I said:

My present Anticipating self-world model (A[sw]) would be a complex construction (or virtual machine) that has in this way been evolving over my whole life. I have constructed my reality by being conscious, and am keeping it current now through the accommodations that are my consciousness in the present moment.

Further, there's a related philosophical perspective that also parallels my own in interesting, perhaps important ways—that of the "radical externalism" promoted by Ted Honderich (2006). He also emphasizes the inadequacy of taking consciousness as simply a matter of what's in the brain—e.g., as a correlate of brain states or mechanisms. He says:

... this fact of consciousness necessarily was what it seemed to be, ... a state of affairs outside your head ... More fully, to be perceptually conscious is only for an extra-cranial state of affairs to exist—for there to be a spatio-temporal set of things with a dependence on another extra-cranial state of affairs and also on what is in a particular cranium.

Honderich 2006, p. 6

Now, as I've already written I can subscribe to something quite close to this. In Atkin 2007 (in the essay just cited above) I say of my awareness that "what I know is always and everywhere pointing at that which is beyond my map; thus, what I know is exactly and completely *not* my map (my A[sw]), but rather a *pointing* out toward near parts of boundless territory *beyond* it." Though I have not consistently done so, it is quite easy to take my understanding of my consciousness (as the accommodative actions necessitated by incoherences between my proactive A[sw] and my world's elaborate flow of sensory messages) and to interpret this in a way that's close to the recommendations of Manzotti (2006) and Honderich

(2006). That is, I can take my consciousness to be a single, non-objectified internal-external field of action that extends out from the cranium into the world—a single dynamic field which includes the whole thing simultaneously, thus *includes* the "external" feedback-sources as well as the brain-processes.

Further, I find that my CC metatheory to be better than most other approaches I know of in meeting Honderich's (2006, pp. 11-12) "criteria for a theory of consciousness." I believe CC metatheory corresponds well to "consciousness as we know we have it" (his first criterion) and that it tells the about the *truth* of our awareness (his second criterion). It also specifies clearly the nature of the *subjectivity* of consciousness' (his third criterion) and indeed makes of it an extremely important, indispensable *realty* which is "reducible to the physical" (his fourth criterion). Finally—and I believe of particularly great significance—it give a very clear answer to the question about the causal efficacy of consciousness—about the nature of the "causal interaction between consciousness and the physical" (his fifth criterion). Does it not meet these requirements of this philosopher of consciousness better than most other theories?

➔ MORE ON DOWNWARD CAUSATION AND FREE WILL

Now a shift back to questions and insights concerning downward causation and free will. These topics were first discussed in Section 1 in the essay "➔On Free Will, Holarchic Structure and Downward Causation." There it was shown that what we've named the "Structure-Causality Identity Postulate" makes it obvious that the most basic kind of downward causation is present everywhere as a fundamental characteristic of the holarchic world-model.

This may be the most fundamental, basic kind of downward causation (so-to-speak, the "lowest level" of this kind of effect). But it's not the whole story—for by CC metatheory another sort of downward causation is also of great significance. This is a meta-level of downward causation that comes out of ongoing emergent change in structures. In what follows we will attempt to work out some implications of this duality for our understanding of free will.

I. Tautological *Downward Causation (DC$_t$)* and Meta *Downward Causation (DC$_m$)*

So we need to account for two orders of downward causation, the most basic kind that is present everywhere as a fundamental characteristic of the holarchic world-model, and the meta-level which is also of great significance as an implication of CC metatheory.

Let's call these two important and very different species of downward causation (DC) "Tautological Downward Causation" (DC$_t$) and "Meta Downward Causation" (DC$_m$). Here's what they are:

> The tautological downward causation (DC$_t$) of the "Structure-Causality Identity Postulate"[16] is 1st-order (simple) DC. It is everywhere! Wherever there is more than one order of structure, each higher order will relate to lower orders in this way. It is, so to speak, "static" DC in that it's what's operative when *structure* is remaining *static*—is not changing. That is, *unchanging structure manifests simple (tautological) DC*—here abbreviated as DC$_t$.

> But structures always undergo change, and change of structure—evolution of new structure or devolution that degrades structure—brings 2nd order,

---

16   This was explained in subsection "*V. Downward Details*" of the essay "➔On Free Will, Holarchic Structure and Downward Causation" in **Section 1**, above; see also "Structure-Causality Identity Postulate" in **Glossary**.

meta-DC (for short, label it DC_m). Engineers, builders, mechanics (and playful, experimental children!) are always causing change of structure. And *changing structure makes 2nd order meta-DC*—here abbreviated as DC_m.

Most of this out in the world, of course, is externally mediated change of structure—some agency external to the structure we have in mind is modifying it. But it may be that neuronal systems—such as brains—are expert at self-modifying their own structure. They seem to be specialized for self-organization. Thus, they might actually be world's main locus of DC_m!

The kind of organization that brains have—and have at wonderfully immense levels of connectivity and complexity—has been partially reproduced by simulation techniques to make artificial systems called "neural networks." These constructed systems are almost infinitely simpler than the living systems that inspired them (Globus 1995), yet they show active, organized self-change that is highly reminiscent of the functions of brains; e.g., among other wonderful feats they learn to discriminate between different patterns of "sensory input." So self-organizing pattern recognition changes are seen at amazingly low levels of complexity (amazingly low in comparison with nervous systems).

By self-organizing these parallel networks become virtual machines. They *spontaneously* develop higher orders of structure—higher-level structure that was not put into them by the engineers that built them, but that they *evolved through their own experience*. These higher-order structures, once they have evolved, certainly display the simple tautological type of downward causation (DC_t)—that's a logical necessity! But further, as they self-organize and modify their structure—as they grow new structure—they are also manifesting 2nd-order (meta) downward causation (DC_m).

II. Downward Causation and Non-Algorithmic Causality

Next I will take a look at another aspect of causality—what I'm viewing as a kind of *non-algorithmic causality* that seems related to Koestler's concept of *self.*

As noted in the first two sections of the foregoing essay, we know and relate to ourselves and our world by constructing dynamically predictive maps. The evolution both of a field of scientific study and of an individual's cognitive structure progressively enlarges the dimensionality of the maps they are able to construct, so that higher and higher levels of structure can be represented. But:

> At any given level of theoretical (science) or cognitive (mind) development, there is some highest represented level of structure.

All the predictive algorithms that a theory or mind can develop and apply will of course only predict phenomena of the already represented levels, not those that include downward causal influences from higher (not yet represented) levels.

Yet some regularities that depend upon higher levels may be observed but not "understood"—not *understood* exactly because such regularities cannot be mapped by or predicted with any of the theory's or the mind's algorithms.

So then any downward causation from a higher, still non-represented level is to be categorized as "non-algorithmic causality" because predictive algorithms to account for it are totally unavailable to us.

Given this way of understanding non-algorithmic causality, it becomes immediately apparent that two seemingly different notions about FW—one being the idea that it has to do with *downward* causality, and the other the idea that it has to do with *non-algorithmic* causality—may actually be the same!

Note how all this ties together: Koestler's concept of *self*—as one's "private model of the universe" with unending upwards progression of levels, continuing upwards beyond our possibility of knowing (Koestler 1978, p. 239)—corresponds closely with what I have said and exactly predicts the kind of non-algorithmic causality deriving from downward causation that I have just outlined.

Look at this again: The foregoing implied that different theories or minds can be developed to account for phenomena up to different levels—e.g., A's theory or mind may map higher levels than B's theory or mind. Then what's normally (algorithmically) predictable by A may look "non-algorithmic" to B.

But then this idea *might* simply be saying that "non-algorithmic" means "we haven't found the algorithm yet *but we will!*" And that seems at first look to be merely an extension of the *scientism* perspective—that there are problems we haven't solved yet, but no problems for which our general problem-solving methods are inapplicable.

However, that's certainly not the whole story on non-algorithmic causality. Maybe after all some non-algorithmic causality is really completely incompatible with scientism! Remember that in the preceding subsection we dealt with a differentiation between two kinds of downward causation: *Simple (tautological) downward causation* (DC_t) and 2nd-order (meta) downward causation (DC_m). Let's intersect that dichotomy with the non-algorithmic story just sketched. Then there can correspondingly be two kinds of non-algorithmic causalities. Our story just above about non-algorithmic causality was assuming only the first, the simple tautological kind (DC_t), but lets see what the story might be with the other kind—with 2nd-order (meta) downward causation (DC_m). These would be causal phenomena that are relevant to *consciousness* (that by CC metatheory are the basis for consciousness) because they include *self-organizing transformations of structure*. As I said earlier in this essay, if consciousness and choice are *transformation* of structure, they can be inherently beyond prediction—and thus free. Therefore the non-algorithmic causality of meta downward causation (DC_m) would be inherently beyond prediction and thus really, *inherently* non-algorithmic.

But now, lets look at this last again: The perspective advanced in this essay does not propose that there are specifiable realms of phenomena that must forever remain beyond understanding (though this may well be so)—only that there is no empirical or rationally sustainable basis for terminating the potential upwards-progressing sequence of our mappings of ourselves and our universe. Thus mind and scientific theory—though also capable of development without limit in the direction of including larger and higher levels of structure—must always remain insufficient to complete description and in fact will so far as we know never be describing and predicting more than tiny bits of the whole. These *tiny bits* may be getting larger as mind and science evolve, but will, we presume, nevertheless always remain tiny in relation to the (mostly unknown) whole.

Now, it has been held in what was written above that it is this fundamental incompleteness that distinguishes the perspective being advocated from *scientism*, which tends to arbitrarily (and wishfully) terminate its conceptions of the structural levels needed for adequate mapping right at the level that has already been reached in its theories and empirical methods, or at best not very far above that level. It seems, therefore, that according to this closed belief-system the problems of adequately representing any already observed (or even conceivable) phenomena must be soluble either within the present paradigm of conceptual, methodological and theoretical algorithms, or by some expansions and extensions of these—that can now be envisioned even if they have not yet been accomplished.

But we've been describing how the perspective here advocated does not see our position and potentialities in quite that way. It is, in contrast, a totally open-ended concept of the upwards progression of structural levels—of levels of adequately predictive structural mapping. Within this *topless* paradigm it is *inevitable* that presently observable phenomena are in some way under the influence and control, via downward causation, of still unobserved phenomena of higher structural levels; and further, that some of these downward influences are unknowable and *inconceivable* from within our present paradigm or any elaboration of it that we can presently even imagine. (We might characterize such mysterious happenings with phrases such as "unexplainable intrusions from above...")

But could then such unrepresented downward causal influences really constitute what we've labeled "non-algorithmic causality"? If so, we come to this conjecture:

> A non-algorithmic transformation of structure may simply be a transformation governed by algorithms (laws) of a holarchic level that is above that level within which algorithms are being sought and tested.

III. Another Point of Logic on FW & Consciousness

In seeking to better comprehend the multi-leveled character of reality, and finding most suitable the holarchic paradigm outlined by Koestler (1967, 1978) and further developed by Wilber (1997), I came to insights suggesting some relatively simple logical relationships that I had never thought of before. I am now wondering how I can go further with this—whether these several logical relationships when taken together have some further implications I had not previously noted. In very preliminary sketch, my line of thought goes thus:

> *If* (1) higher levels of structure evolve by *self-organizing transformations*; and
> *if*—given those higher levels—(2) *downward causation* (DC) is *tautologic* (see Structure-Causality Identity Postulate[17]); and
> *if* (3) *free will* (FW) is a manifestation of DC[18];
> *then* (4) the occurrence of *FW* may be *identical with* the occurrence of *self-organizing transformations*.

That is, this line of reasoning suggests that **conscious awareness and FW are identical!**

\|/oOo\|/oOo\|/oOo\|/oOo\|/oOo\|/oOo\|/oOo\|/oOo\|/oOo\|/oOo\|/oOo\|/

---

17 Again, that's explained in the third essay of ***Section 1*** "➔On Free Will, Holarchic Structure and Downward Causation" (in its subsection "***V. Downward Details***"); see also "Structure-Causality Identity Postulate" in the ***Glossary***.

18 Again see ***Section 1***'s third essay "➔On Holarchic Structure, Downward Causation and Free Will."

~~RELATIONS TO TWO OTHER THEORIES

This subsection will compare what I've been saying with some other writings on consciousness. It consists of two essays reflecting upon relations of CC metatheory ideas about consciousness first with those that were put forth by Varela *et al.* (1991), and then with those by Baars (1988).

> First my essay (written 1994-5) regarding Varela, Thompson & Rosch (1991) presents their *ungrounded psychology of enaction,* which I find to be remarkably consistent with CC metatheory (as set forth in *Section 2,* just preceding):

→ WORLDS WITHOUT GROUND

I am at the moment captivated by the sweep and depth of the new book "*The embodied mind: Cognitive science and human experience*" by Varela et al. (1991) and find their main line of argument highly congenial to my own search for understanding. They show how our contemporary intellectual constructs of science and philosophy are inherently inadequate to give us understanding of our ordinary, everyday experience—or understanding of the "common sense" with which we unfold and regulate our lives. My own ongoing attempts to comprehend the relations of consciousness to life, brain, organismic behavior and evolution have brought me to a similar point of view.

I. Confluence

The underlying ideational system that I've been developing and trying to communicate is fundamentally consistent with the *ungrounded* standpoint that Varela et al. (1991) are teaching. I conclude that overall the conceptual systems that we each now espouse are remarkably consistent, though quite differently expressed.

A. Our Respective Ideas on Cognition/Consciousness

Varela et al (1991) emphasize the inseparability of sensory and motor, of perception and action, asserting that "(1) perception consists in perceptually guided action and (2) cognitive structures emerge from the recurrent sensorimotor patterns that enable action to be perceptually guided" (173).[19] Their summariz-

---

19 Page numbers are from Varela, Thompson & Rosch 1991.

ing statement of their position is that "organism and environment are mutually enfolded in multiple ways, and so what constitutes the world of a given organism is enacted by that organism's history of structural coupling" (202).[19]

Now this is very close in overall perspective to the *metatheory* of consciousness that I have developed (see essays in *Section 2*)—though apparently my route to that viewpoint was rather different from theirs. I have earlier (in the 4th essay in Section 2, "➔Conscious Beyond Mechanism") presented some parallel ideas concerning the relations between organism and environment as follows:

> The central idea is this: While both unconscious and conscious actions are the play of mechanisms, consciousness enters when the activated mechanisms are at that moment undergoing essential structural modifications that are altering their laws of operation. It is a notion of consciousness that for brevity has been labeled the "continual creation" (CC) hypothesis.

> …It is next proposed that the inner structure that is thus reorganizing itself is the organism's dynamic (predictive) internal model of itself-in-its-world…[which] has been labeled "*Anticipating self-world model*" (abbreviated 'A[sw]'). My A[sw] is a map or model of my *world*, of my *place within my world*, and of *dynamic regularities* of our actions and interactions—and (by CC metatheory) is changing in structure whenever and wherever I am conscious for my A[sw] needs to be continually *updated*.

> …Based upon studies of motor function (e.g., Atkin 1969), it is proposed that the Anticipating self-world model (A[sw]) anticipates the organism's actions and predictively generates controlling feedback ("virtual feedback"), which is derived from *SIMULATION of the activity and effects of the organism's own action systems* (Atkin 1992)….In *assimilative* updating (or simply, *assimilation*) the "virtual machine" performs actions of which it is capable with its *present* structure, so that its *configuration* changes in accord with the dynamic virtual-machine laws that define it and without change in those laws. Since the function of the model is predictive…, this *change of configuration without change of structure* will occur when the model's actions continue to "fit" (Glaserfeld 1984) the organism's situation accurately.

> But whenever during wakefulness the continuing assimilative prediction is imperfect (as is usual), then fit can be improved by *modifications of A[sw] structure*—modification, that is, of the virtual-machine laws governing the ongoing changes in A[sw] configuration. This structure-

changing component might be termed "*accommodative* updating" (or simply, *accommodation*). CC metatheory…would imply that consciousness has to do with accommodation.

…Both *external* and *internal* discrepancy (incoherence) will evoke accommodation and thus give rise to contents of consciousness: The former, evoked by action, are accommodations that modify A[sw] in directions that lessen discrepancies between the predicted and externally-generated sensory feedback; in contrast, the latter incoherencies, which are intrinsic to the A[sw], may evoke internally-referenced accommodations and thereby generate stimulus-independent thought.

(Atkin 1994)[20]

That was my general picture of how consciousness arises, and its role in the organism's adaptive behaviors. The crucial role that consciousness may play in the history of mind's construction was then noted, followed by remarks on *downward causation:*

So ***consciousness*** means the virtual machine[G] is redesigning itself (1) to accommodate its dynamic structure more fully and accurately to the organism's interactions with its world and (2) to resolve its internal inconsistencies. Presumably, these ongoing accommodations are my experience of every conscious moment. My present Anticipating self-world model (A[sw]) would be a complex construction (or virtual machine) that has in this way been evolving over my whole previous life. I have constructed my reality by being conscious, and am keeping it current now through the accommodations that are my consciousness in the present moment.…

Using CC metatheory, I assume that my A[sw] is structured as a many-layered hierarchy (something like Minsky's [1986] postulated "society of agents")—a hierarchical network of a great many subsystems, many of which may seem to function with partial autonomy, but which are nevertheless closely linked together. A great many of these subsystems are active assimilatively much of the time, but assimilation remains beneath awareness. The linkings of active and accommodating (conscious) subsystems with the active and non-accommodating (unconscious) subsystems

---

20 This is the 4th essay in ***Section 2***, "➜Conscious Beyond Mechanism (Shifting a Paradigm)."

G See "virtual machine" in ***Glossary***.

that surround them are two-way. Therefore, not only do unconscious processes constrain conscious choices..., but reciprocally, conscious choices are at every moment profoundly modulating the directions of the ongoing unconscious processes in which they are embedded. Thus the accommodative changes that effect conscious choosings may be said to "supervene" over the assimilative activities both of the accommodating subsystems and also of non-accommodating subsystems to which they are linked. Such causal influences of consciousness upon "lower-order" unconscious mechanism are *downward causation* in action....

Thus *two nested hypotheses*, independent yet augmenting each other, have been presented: (1) the **continual creation** (CC) hypothesis, stipulating that consciousness is ongoing, emergent change whereby structure is transforming itself (generating new information); and (2) the **pro-active world-model updating** hypothesis, stipulating that the self-transforming structure is a model of organism-in-world (*Anticipating self-world model* or *A[sw]*) that predictively assimilates the organism's actions and their context, responding to external incoherence by accommodatively modifying its structure to maintain accuracy.

(From Atkin 1994)[21]

Then another internal source for accommodative readjustment was proposed to account for awareness unlinked from motor actions. Finally, the causal efficacy of consciousness was addressed, as well as downward causation and the role of the unconscious in mentation.

But in relation to those understandings from CC metatheory, what about the conceptual position that Varela et al. (1991) expounded? When I read it, it feels entirely consistent with my own. Their central tenets included the following main points:

By using the term *action* we mean to emphasize...that sensory and motor processes, perception and action, are fundamentally inseparable in lived cognition. Indeed, the two are not merely contingently linked in individuals; they have also evolved together.

We can now give a preliminary formulation of what we mean by *enaction*. In a nutshell, the enactive approach consists of two points: (1) perception consists in perceptually guided action and (2) cognitive

---

21 Again the essay "➔Conscious Beyond Mechanism (Shifting a Paradigm)," the fourth essay in *Section 2*.

structures emerge from the recurrent sensorimotor patterns that enable action to be perceptually guided. (173)

We are claiming that organism and environment are mutually enfolded in multiple ways, and so what constitutes the world of a given organism is enacted by that organism's history of structural coupling. (202)[22]

Now, in my position as well there is certainly an "inseparability of sensory and motor, of perception and action," and further, "(1) perception consists in perceptually guided action and (2) cognitive structures emerge from the recurrent sensorimotor patterns that enable action to be perceptually guided" (173). Finally, the logic of my position implies (as does theirs) that "organism and environment are mutually enfolded in multiple ways, and so what constitutes the world of a given organism is enacted by that organism's history of structural coupling" (202).

And while nowhere do they explicitly suggest an idea about consciousness that corresponds to our CC metatheory (which says that *consciousness is ongoing, emergent change whereby structure is transforming itself*), I have found one statement of theirs that could be interpreted (i) as relating "cognition" to the *discrepancies* between predicted (i.e. virtual) and actual feedback that we have postulated to evoke accommodative change and thus consciousness, and (ii) as suggesting that the actions of organisms are, as we have postulated, directed by that virtual feedback. It says:

[C]ognition as embodied action is always about or directed toward something that is missing: on the one hand, there is always a next step for the system in its perceptually guided action; and on the other hand, the actions of the system are always directed toward *situations* that have yet to become actual. (205)

As noted, I find this statement of theirs consistent with my perspective on mind and consciousness. In CC metatheory, furthermore, consciousness as emergent change is envisioned in much the way that cognition is in Varela's understanding. Varela et al. (1991) say that "cognition is embodied action…inextricably tied to histories that are lived" (213). Nevertheless, the detailed relation between our viewpoints may be somewhat tenuous as the specifics of my perspective are in no wise explicitly derivable from their statements.

Yet the correspondences that I intuit are of great interest to me, and some of these intuited correspondences will now be spelled out in greater detail.

---

22 As already noted, in this essay these **numbers in parenthesis** (other than those which give publication-year) refer to ***page*-numbers**.

B. Questions About Representation & Realism

Varela et al. (1991) are particularly critical of the way "representation" is used in cognitive psychology—what they call the strong sense of representation in which we "assume that the world is pregiven, that its features can be specified prior to any cognitive activity" (135). The strong sense of representation has an important place in the prevalent worldview, which they describe thus:

> We then have a full-fledged theory that says (1) the world is pregiven; (2) our cognition is of this world—even if only to a partial extent, and (3) the way in which we cognize this pregiven world is to represent its features and then act on the basis of these representations. (135)

This, they say, is metaphorically—

> the idea of a cognitive agent that is parachuted into a pregiven world. This agent will survive only to the extent that it is endowed with a map and learns to act on the basis of this map. (135)

They assert that this assumption of a "pregiven world" is unwarranted—a kind of willful delusion. Why do I see this criticism as inapplicable to my own ideas about cognition and the world, and therefore as a *non-issue?* Is it because I stubbornly blind myself to the full meaning of this delusion? Or is it because the non-representational, non-adaptationist worldview that they strongly advocate is already implicit in the thinking that my CC metatheory has brought me into? I believe that the latter is the reason for my unconcern with their criticism. But despite such qualifications, the *language* in which CC metatheory and (especially) the associated A[sw] idea have been discussed is representational and seems to assume a "pregiven" external world.

This assumption of a "pregiven" external world is the *realist* philosophy. Am I a realist? It would seem so—at least as a starting point. Or is it mainly a linguistic convenience—the conceptual route by which I can make clear what is actually an *ungrounded* epistemology? Certainly, my final understanding seems to me, upon reading Varela et al. (1991), a version of an *ungrounded* worldview (e.g., look at the concluding paragraphs of the *Section 2* essay "➜Conscious Beyond Mechanism").

This can be seen from the ways in which I have been citing the radical constructivist paradigm expounded by Glaserfeld (1984), who speaks about the "fit" of an organism's anticipations with regard to its environment—a non-representational approach that is consistent with the non-realist, "enactive" position of Varela et al. (1991).

Yet I am constrained to speak (and think) in an old, nearly deconstructed conceptual system because my capacities for comprehension are severely limited. The capabilities of my cognitive apparatus are products of my unique yet relatively conventional intellectual history. I can comprehend and convey meanings only by means of the language that I know; how can I understand what I am saying if I move totally beyond my familiar—and seemingly simple—realist framework? (I'm sure that in this way I'm like many others.) It seems I need my realist mode of ideation as my starting point, not only historically but right now, to "make sense" of these otherwise strange and elusive ideas.

My world falls apart if I cannot view my ideas in relation to the old familiar framework. Yet I become increasingly attentive to the limitations of that framework and begin to move beyond it as I attempt to fully grasp this ungrounded view and connect it with the realist conceptual system that I was born into and raised with. Thus, I generate for myself a kind of language bridge between seemingly incommensurate paradigms. So, what I believe I now have is a *connection* between grounded and ungrounded ways of thinking about knowledge, intelligence, consciousness, and the place and process of this being in the world.

I still need such a bridge. The ungrounded, no-self stance seems full of immediate, present-moment complexities. In contrast, a conventionally grounded, realist, self-and-other dualist stance has made existence more easily comprehensible through convenient abstractions that simplify by simply ignoring—or denying—many of these present-moment complexities. *Process*, always changing, always transforming, is simplified into unchanging *object*. If the method involves absurdities, they are absurdities of convenience. Networks of reciprocal causation are simplified into simple unidirectional cause-effect chains by leaving out (ignoring or denying) nearly all causal links—or deferring their recognition and consideration until some later time (see the attentional strategy of *segmentation*, to be discussed later[23]).

What it comes down to then is these two related questions: (i) How can I understand the full complexity of mind-and-world when I cognitively remain within my inherently simplistic framework of abstract theorizing; and (ii) even when my cognitive space is enlarged and can encompass the greater complexity and transformational fluidity of life as lived from an open stance, how can I convey even a beginning of this understanding to another being whose stance has remained more abstract and conventional? Therefore I adopt this "as if" methodology for explaining to myself *(to whom?*[24]) and to another *how it all is.* It's a bridge that can (perhaps) be let go of after the crossing.

23 See the essay "➔Attention and Violence" (last essay in **Section 3**); also look at "Segmenting, high or low" in the **Glossary**.
24 This question explained in next subsection ("*II. Dualities and Self-Groundings*").

So, what I've said is that although I've been writing in the terminology and images of a grounded view that smacks of realism, it *ain't necessarily so!* Consider my use of representational language: Varela et al. (1991) point out that a representational characterization of mind is a symptom of a *realist* metaphysic (see above[25]). But I maintain that my use of representational language does not signify a naive realist philosophy. In the CC metatheory approach the concept of "assimilation"—as an active anticipation of evoked patterns of sensory feedback—is the kind of *weak* representation that Varela et al. (1991) speak of as "the sense of representation as construal" (134). For example, a "map…is about some geographical area; it represents certain features of the terrain and so construes the terrain as being a certain way" (p. 134). This, they emphasize, is distinct from the "much stronger sense of representation" in which we "assume that the world is pregiven, that its features can be specified prior to any cognitive activity" (135).

The ideas of representation that were used to characterize the A[sw] under CC metatheory are entirely consistent with the weaker sense of representation as *construal*, for this "representation"—that under CC metatheory manifests predictive assimilation—does not involve any assumption of a "pregiven world" as does the strong sense of representation. Rather, world-features manifest themselves implicitly in consciousness as "that which predictive mismatch is pointing toward" (Atkin 1994)[26]—a pointing which is inherently constructive (and always tentative).

II. Dualities and Self-Groundings

A. Knowing Selves

The preceding subsection concerned the (at least partial) dissolution of my former unquestioning belief in the grounded "pregiven" world of a realist ontology. But another type of grounding that had also had my unquestioning belief is still harder to let go of. We experience a stable world and feel *centered* in an obviously continuing ego-self out of which we interact with that external world. What is "self?" Is "self" reality or illusion? Varela et al. (1991) opt for the latter:

> We wish to make a sweeping claim: all of the reflective traditions in human history—philosophy, science, psychoanalysis, religion, meditation—have challenged the naive sense of self. (59)

---

25   Subsection entitled "Questions About Representation & Realism" (near beginning of essay).

26   Printed here as 4th essay in **Section 2**, "➔Conscious Beyond Mechanism".

The tension between the ongoing sense of self in ordinary experience and the failure to find that self in reflection is of central importance to Buddhism—the origin of human suffering is just this tendency to grasp onto and build a sense of self, an ego, where there is none. (61)

The authors do refer to a possible way out from this dilemma—one that seems to point in the direction of some of my own notions. But they then reject the idea as unhelpful:

Perhaps the self is an emergent property...?...At this point, however, the idea is of no help. Such a self-organizing or synergistic mechanism is not evident in experience. More important, it is not the abstract idea of an emergent self that we cling to so fiercely as our ego; we cling to a "real" ego-self. (69-70)

Here I feel that both branches of Varela's argument are in error. First, it is a general conclusion of neuropsychology that the mechanisms of our perceptions are *not* themselves evident in our experience. For example, our *experience* tells us almost nothing of the mechanisms by which photons activate retinal receptors, nor the subsequent sequence of two-way neuronal interactions that ultimately affect much higher brain levels, nor the network modulations at those higher levels that presumably have something to do with our visual perceptions. Thus, the observation that "a self-organizing or synergistic mechanism is not evident in experience" (Varela et al. 1991, pp. 69-70) does not constitute evidence that it plays no role in experience.

And the second point—that "it is not the abstract idea of an emergent self that we cling to so fiercely as our ego; we cling to a 'real' ego-self" (Varela et al. 1991, pp. 69-70)—seems tautological. For if some emergence is now actually *happening*, then certainly (by this hypothesis) it is real and not abstract. Furthermore, this applies not only to the process but also to the product of the emergent action; that which emerges (or has emerged)—if such has actually taken place—is thereby real and not an abstraction.

Here's a way in which the experience of self can be understood under CC metatheory: Under that theory I have constructed my reality by being conscious, and am now keeping it current (and internally consistent) through the accommodations that are my consciousness in the present moment. That's what I meant when I said earlier (as a compressed evocation of CC metatheory) that "***Experiencing is self-creation.***" If my Anticipating self-world model (A[sw]) is synonymous with my *mind*[27]—which certainly has been evolving over my whole previous life—then my consciousness is my *change* of mind.

But who am *I*? Am "I" my whole mind? Or am I this moment's change of mind? Is *self* enduring or ephemeral? Certainly, my experience of self in the present moment is wonderfully changeable!

To see this in the context of CC metatheory, I postulate that:

* Self-organization is *experienced* by the self that *self-organizes*.

This says that the experienced "self" is exactly and only that which in each moment is self-organizing. And this in turn suggests a way to define the *experienced* self: If the self-organizing system is conceptually stripped of adventitious features that do not participate in the self-organizing change of structure but merely "go along for the ride," then what is left—all those dimensions and all those parts or components that are essential for the actually observed self-organizing transformation—might be termed the *self* that self-organizes. Notice that this "self" of our immediate experience is not a continuing entity[28] since it is defined by the self-organizing structural transformation going on in the moment—and this will be always changing, always different from moment to moment.

B. Experienced Continuity

How can this relate to the experienced *continuity* of self? Varela et al. (1991) say:

> We are caught in a contradiction. On the one hand, even a cursory attention to experience shows us that our experience is always changing and, furthermore, is always dependent on a particular situation. To be human, indeed to be living, is always to be in a situation, a context, a world. We have no experience of anything that is permanent and independent of these situations. Yet most of us are convinced of our identities: we have a personality, memories and recollections, and plans and anticipations, which seem to come together in a coherent point of view, a center from which we survey the world, the ground on which we stand. How could such a point of view be possible if it were not rooted in a single, independent, truly existing self or ego? (59)

But why must this remain a problem? Without change there is no continuity. Conversely, without some kind of continuity there is no change. It is another

---

27 See "Anticipating self-world model (A[sw])" and "Mind" in **Glossary**.
28 This issue is well addressed in Varela, Thompson & Rosch (1991).

example of the inseparability (the unity?) of seeming opposites. Certainly, that which evolves is changing, but that does not mean there is no continuity. Continuity is not the same as constancy.

Is the structure that is continually changing the *self*? If so, then it also exhibits continuity in change. After all, (i) each new self-structure arises out of an earlier self-structure—that's continuity of ongoing *genesis*. This is self's *extrinsic* history—it is the moment-by-moment story of self described from the outside.

And (ii) everywhere in an evolving structure there may remain traces of earlier stages of its evolution—continuity of structural *constraints*. (It's an idea like the Buddhist idea of "the coherent pattern of dependently originated habits that we recognize as a person."[29]) This—along with the organism's evolving system of historical memories[30]—is self's *intrinsic* history; that is, it is the story of self as experienced in each moment from the inside.

Both of these—(i) continuity of ongoing genesis and (ii) continuity of structural constraints—figure in my direct experience of my life in each moment and in my ordinary experiencing of "self." When I am challenged with some sort of novelty, some new demand, that is when (in response to that novelty, that new demand) I am most likely to be undergoing some personal change and likely also to be sharply aware of those change-evoking challenges. This means that it is my *consciousness* that is tying my "self" of one moment to my changed "self" of the next moment. In fact, that is exactly the point of CC metatheory—that the ongoing evolution of my structure is what is experientially known to me as *my consciousness*. Thus my awareness—which is awareness of *change*—is the thread of my identity. (In another metaphor, it is simultaneously the root and fruit of my story.)

So that's one way in which "self" comes to the fore in each moment's present experiencing; it is what my awareness is always pointing to. Another has to do with my *memory*, always recreating a context that is telling me who I am. My networks of memory are continually constructing and reconstructing a framework, a structure of spatial and temporal reference frames, that is not only giving me a present position in my world but is also telling me right now about the continuity of this position with remembered past and anticipated future positions. This reference frame is permeating my present moment of experienced consciousness through a billion tugs and adjustments that constrain the restructuring in which I'm now actively engaging.

---

29 Varela, Thompson & Rosch (1991), p. 124.

30 See paragraph-after-next (end of this subsection).

III. Dualities and World-Groundings

Yet my automatic, unreflective reaction to the assertion of the groundlessness of my world and self is one of dismay, of mourning or, at the very least, of some anxiety upon confronting a great loss. ("Look—here we face the abyss!")

Certainly, Varela et al. (1991) note this. They write:

> When contemporary traditions of thought discover groundlessness, it is viewed as negative, a breakdown of an ideal for doing science, for establishing philosophical truth with reason, or for living a meaningful life. (233-4)

They then describe a very different attitude toward groundlessness:

> In the Madhyamika tradition, on the other hand, as in all Buddhism, the intimation of egolessness is a great blessing; it opens up the lived world as path, as the locus for realization. (234)

> We think that the denial of an ultimate ground is tantamount to the denial of there being any ultimate truth or goodness about our world and experience. The reason that we almost automatically draw this conclusion is that we have not been able to disentangle ourselves from the extremes of absolutism and nihilism and to take seriously the possibilities inherent in a mindful, open-ended stance toward human experience. (234-5)

That last phrase—"a mindful, open-ended stance toward human experience"—is especially pregnant as it feels to be the essence of the direction along which I now wish to continue.

A. How Large is an Ungrounded Worldview?

One fundamental insight has helped me to know and appreciate this direction. The insight concerns a way in which I can understand and experience "groundlessness" as *adding to* rather than subtracting from my world—a way in which movement toward a groundless stance takes on a positive rather than a negative significance. This welcome reversal of understanding comes out of the notion that *the groundless viewpoint is larger and more inclusive than grounded viewpoints*—i.e., that *grounding is accomplished through cognitive constriction.*

I find an intimation of this idea (though not a direct statement of it) in Varela et al. (1991):

[G]roundlessness is the very condition for the richly textured and inter-dependent world of human experience....The greatest ability of living cognition...consists in being able to pose, within broad constraints, the relevant issues that need to be addressed at each moment. These issues and concerns are not pregiven but are *enacted* from a background of action, where what counts as relevant is contextually determined by our common sense. (144-5)

The last line, expressing the fundamental importance in human experience of "background" and "context," suggests the vastness of the ungrounded worldview.

Here, more pointedly, is a way in which the movement toward an ungrounded awareness can be viewed as an *expansion of consciousness*: "*Ungrounded*" might be interpreted to mean "*infinitely* grounded—therefore wide open and forever unfin-ished (inherently incomplete)." And "*grounded*," in contrast, might be interpreted to mean "*finitely* grounded—therefore closed and *completable* (if not already fin-ished)." Understood thus, **the ungrounded worldview lacks nothing; rather, it is incomparably vaster than the grounded worldview, which attains its illu-sory solidity through subtractions disguised as additions**—that is, by fragmen-tations and denials.

I did not find such a notion expressed explicitly in Varela et al. (1991). It may, however, be implicit in their ideas. For example, they say:

[V]arious forms of groundlessness are really one: organism and envi-ronment enfold into each other and unfold from one another in the fundamental circularity that is life itself.

...The worlds enacted by various histories of structural coupling are amenable to detailed scientific investigation, yet have no fixed, perma-nent substrate or foundation and so are ultimately groundless. (217)

That reciprocal enfoldment is a far larger, more complex conception (and/or experience) of our situation than our familiar dualistic paradigm of *world repre-sented in mind.* I take that just-quoted statement to be an excellent picture of who we are, in each moment, in relation to our world. This understanding remains open, free of any illusion that it can ever capture the totality of the happenings to which it points.

On the other hand the closure implicit in a more conventional theoretical stance is an illusion of *progress toward **complete** understanding.* There the project is to arrive at the full and final answer—to find some mechanism (or system of mechanisms) as (hopefully!) the *complete* explanation for the realm of phenomena with which it deals.

That's the overconfident stance that I've abandoned. Through successive steps of deconstructing my well-conditioned deterministic worldview I have come to be sure that predictive theories of mechanistic lawfulness, though *necessary* to our understanding, can never be *sufficient* to account for all that we wish to understand. That is, my present viewpoint is more open—and, I believe, less arrogant—than the one with which I started.

Nevertheless I know I'm not altogether free of the old conceptual framework. Was there also a lapse of that sort in the well-crafted book by Varela et al. (1991)? Throughout their book they emphasize the human need (both in our everyday patterns of thought and in our dominant scientific paradigm) for just that kind of wondering and context-expanding openness which they advocate, if we are ever to move beyond our present cognitive limitations and ethical crudities and achieve an ungrounded worldview. Do they nevertheless sometimes get caught in the very conceptual net of *absolute mechanism* from which otherwise they want (it seems to me) to free us? That's how I read their appeal to mechanistic understandings, seemingly as the be-all and end-all of possible scientific knowledge, in a couple of sentences at the beginning of their last chapter. There they say:

> The inquisitive scientist then asks, How can we imagine, *embodied in a mechanism*, that relation of codependence between mind and world? *The mechanism that we have created* (the embodied metaphor of groundlessness) is that of enactive cognition, with its image of structural coupling through a history of natural drift. (237-8, emphasis added.)

Perhaps the issue I am raising here is not substantive, but semantic, in that they are using the word "mechanism" in a much looser way than I am, as metaphor perhaps for any rigorous theoretical description. Or have they here actually slipped back (in those two lone sentences of their wide-ranging book) into the modern scientific paradigm that promises an eventual "theory of everything"—the system of *mechanisms* that will totally account for all the phenomena we experience? (I will assume they have not "slipped" in that way, rather that our difference is semantic and inconsequential.)

In summary, here is what was asked: Is our automatic anxiety reaction to intimations of ubiquitous groundlessness based upon an erroneous assumption that in losing our changeless groundings we have lost something substantive? Can we rise to further understanding by intuiting directly how those ideas of groundings rested upon unwarranted simplifications that deleted from our awareness most of our wonder and amazement at our world and our place in it? If so, then—as was just suggested—we come to know that what we had thought was the confining prison of an *ungrounded worldview* is actually a liberation into a vastly larger space.

Now we will briefly look at a way in which that reversal in my understanding of the relation between grounded and ungrounded worldviews can be generalized.

B. Are All Absolutes Constrictive?

Such an inversion of our understandings—such as that about world-expansions and world-contractions implicit in groundless and grounded worldviews (above)—may be appropriate medicine also for our addiction to *absolutes*. Isn't it interesting how we conceive of an absolute as having attained the highest status, the ultimate value? Our assumption seems to be that when we make an absolute of something, we have made it into something more, enlarged it vastly into some powerful agent of reassurance—a solid foundation upon which to erect the strongest structures. Certainly, that has been my automatic notion. But is it correct? It is not beyond questioning! Varela et al. (1991) say:

> By definition, something is…absolute only if it does not depend on anything else; it must have an identity that transcends its relations. (224.)

> These two extremes of absolutism and nihilism both lead us away from the lived world; in the case of absolutism, we try to escape actual experience by invoking foundations to supply our lives with a sense of justification and purpose…(235)

Is the status of absolute an enlargement or a contraction? I suggest now that it is actually a *contraction*. For in giving a property or entity the status of absolute, we have removed from it its capacity for change, for evolution, for self-organization. It is no longer a present participant in ongoing creation.

An absolute may be regarded as the epitome of a static *abstraction*. And (as discussed more extensively elsewhere) abstracting is the action of stripping away and disregarding *context*. As we remove context from our awareness, we constrict it; the span of our consciousness becomes smaller.

Here, then, may be another way in which we are tempted to unreflectively adopt limiting assumptions in the absence of any evidence—assumptions that, by veiling our ignorance, provide us an illusion of increased certainty and therefore control, thus conveniently simplifying our cognitive task. (But at what cost?)

IV. Free Choice

Those thoughts lead me into questions about "freedom." What *is* it? What do I *mean* when I speak of it? The slant I've lately come to on *freedom* is that I've been thinking about it as an absolute, but it is not an absolute. Perhaps to accurately speak of "freedom" we must specify—freedom with respect to what? The idea here is that freedom is not an alternative to determination, nor is it the absence of determination. Rather, freedom and determination are indissoluble aspects of a larger dynamic complex.

A. Complementarity of Freedom and Mechanism

Here's the gist of my present thinking on this problem. Exactly because consciousness means (by CC metatheory: Atkin 1992, 1994)[31] that new order is continually emerging, consciousness is identical with freedom. And this freedom of consciousness means that assimilative actions are entraining a component of freedom exactly to the extent that their mechanisms are undergoing transformation in ways that are not fully definable by the causal principles that are sufficient to specify those mechanisms.

Conscious actions occur within the far larger context of ongoing unconscious activity. Thus, the depth of my possibilities for freedom is directly dependent upon the depth of my consciousness, which in turn rests upon the depth of my A[sw] (which is operating mostly beneath my awareness). This can be a great depth, which I presume to have something like—though perhaps not precisely—a fractal structure. That is, it is a dynamic system comprised of a hierarchical complex of systems and subsystems—nested levels within levels. Correspondingly, there can be many levels of consciousness (and therefore of freedom) exactly because there are many levels of mechanism.

Assume, then, that my A[sw] is so structured as a many-layered hierarchy—a network of subsystems, many of which may seem to function with partial autonomy, but which are, nevertheless, closely linked together. Further, assume that many of these subsystems are active, assimilatively, much of the time. But since assimilation remains beneath awareness, the awareness I am now experiencing must correspond to the accommodative change in structure of some subset of those actively assimilating A[sw] subsystems.

The picture, then, is that there is some subset of A[sw] subsystems that is now performing assimilative actions, and within this assimilating subset is a smaller

---

31 See especially two essays in the preceding section, **Section 2** ("➜On consciousness: What is the Role of Emergence" and "➜Conscious Beyond Mechanism")—see also "CC metatheory" in the **Glossary**.

subset which simultaneously is undergoing accommodative change in structure. Further, since all the subsystems are interconnected, the assimilative activities of these accommodating (conscious) subsystems are embedded in and tightly linked to the assimilative activities of the larger group of non-accommodating (unconscious) systems. In general, it may be those more inclusive but unconscious systems which are the primary sources of *initiatives, motivations, drives* and *purposes* that are experienced as external "givens" by the accommodating (conscious) subsystems.

If, as suggested above, *choice* is the ceaseless redirection, as consequence of a system's ongoing accommodation, of that system's assimilative action, then choice continually accompanies awareness everywhere. What was proposed, that is, is that *active choice is coextensive with awareness.*

Earlier[32] I wrote this:

- In this way I begin to better understand the near invisibility of all the paradigms that govern my every thought and action—not only the paradigms of my science, but those of my habitual movement styles and those governing my interests and aversions, my language habits and my social relationships.

- These dynamic patternings must be the dynamic patternings of ongoing assimilative actions of my A[sw], most of which go on with little or no accommodation and so without awareness, yet which constrain my choices by driving and guiding the assimilative actions of the more restricted A[sw] regions that do accommodate as they move and thus move with awareness.

- Therefore myriad unconscious constraints always surround the choices that accompany my awareness—constraints not only invisible but also durable, as they don't change so long as they do not enter my awareness.

Looking from above downwards, one can appreciate mechanism as the ubiquitous context, the matrix of my awareness. But then, to the extent that one can look from below upwards, one sees the complementary relationship: That emergent creation—the original and ultimate source of mechanism—is also the context and matrix of mechanism. My choosing (my *freedom*), therefore, is embedded in and inseparable from mechanism. Each grows out of the other; each includes the other.

---

32 From subsection "D. Conscious and Unconscious Mind" of the 4th essay in **Section 2** "➜ Conscious Beyond Mechanism."

B. Levels of Coherence

Freedom and coherence are intimately related. Just what this relationship may be is an extremely interesting question. Ordinarily, when we assume that freedom is nothing more than lack of constraint, we may in effect be tying it to deficiencies of coherence, for loss of coherence can lessen constraints.

But lack of coherence can lead to randomness rather than choice—rather than freedom of action. For (from a higher-order perspective) that component of lower-level behavior that is unmodulated by higher-order coherencies may be considered *random* or contingent.

Could this suggest that the contrary of our single-level common-sense assumption is the case—that freedom requires more rather than less coherence? Yet how can we understand that freedom can increase only as coherence increases? This would seem to tie freedom to more rather than less constraint, would it not?

Here's an attempt to reconcile this seeming contradiction. "Freedom" may mainly refer to **lack of constraints that prevent the following of higher-level laws.** So understood, freedom would not simply be a matter of *lack* of constraints in general; rather, it would be the lack of certain sorts of constraints in the presence of others. And the presence of the others is as essential as the lacks. What is then crucial is the *level* of the operative constraints. The tighter but higher, the freer!

To understand this better, first consider the notion of "level":

- The more inclusive is a pattern of order (of coherence), the higher its level. The higher includes the lower but is not included within the lower.

With "level" thus understood, the level of freedom would increase with an increase of some kinds of coherence. More specifically, this would mean that coherent linkages with the most inclusive, largest regularities will yield the greatest freedoms. It could work like this:

- The *freedom* of phenomena at one level is to be connected with the *coherence* of a higher and more inclusive level.

Consequently, the greatest freedom accompanies coherencies (regularities) of the greatest inclusiveness. In brief:

- The greater the inclusiveness of the coherencies, the larger the freedom they can give to the phenomena they entrain at lower levels.

This is very interesting! But it may not go far enough. Consider Sperry's image of downward causation (e.g., Sperry 1980) as entrainment, or *supervenient* control, of the lower-level regularities by higher-level (more inclusive) orders; this super-venience imparts freedoms to those lower level happenings (processes) that they would not otherwise have. I find I can best understand this as a matter of coherence—as the coherence of many part-processes that, if their coherence were less, would tend to "cancel each other out," but to the extent that they are coherent, rather build together some larger integrated process. For example, remembering Sperry's "wheel" image, the structural coherencies in which the individual atomic and molecular processes are participating guide their participation in the overland progressions of that larger device, and thus their still higher-level participation in various rapid and purposive transports of a motor vehicle. The possibility for such purposive transports opens the possibility for many sorts of choices that otherwise would be unavailable.

C. Dissolution of Absolutes

Yet does that actually bring us more freedom? How exactly does *freedom* arise out of such downward causation? Certainly I'd very much like to know—but have my doubts about ever getting an answer, since I begin to suspect that this is a mis-guiding question. For upon reflecting upon my own thought processes right here and now, I get a glimpse of the possible problem. It's this:

- There I go, puzzling at highly abstract ideas, hunting for a highly elusive *absolute*. I want to pin down the *essence* of freedom. I'm grasping for a secure grounding, asking: What is it *really?*

- Is this not the proverbial wild goose chase—a misguided search for a quarry that lives elsewhere?

Having come this far, I am driven to the conclusion that this first attempt at reconciling the seeming contradiction between coherence and freedom has in fact been a wild goose chase. Something new will have to be added—and this new element will be exactly the central element of CC metatheory. For this image (of the large wheel-structure supervening over the level of molecules and their immediate interactions) makes it perfectly apparent that such structural participation of parts in an already established order that constitute a larger, encompassing whole will be obligatory and not free, no matter how elevated the encompassing order. Then, I will further suggest, the freedom that I'm looking is to be found in the *arising of new order*. That, as was just noted, is CC metatheory.

Yet such ongoing creation of new kinds of coherence may totally escape any abstract characterization. If so, then what I have been hunting for—an abstract characterization of the "inner dynamic structure" of freedom—will never be found. I will have been looking in the wrong place—looking where I thought the light was best, not where the quarry actually lived. Here, in an attempt to clarify this, I will insert a brief diversion. First I recall an earlier thought, expressed elsewhere, that A[sw] (the organism's dynamic predictive internal model of itself-in-its-world)[33] is identical with *mind*. Then I further suggest the following definitions and derivations:

(1)   All that is undergoing assimilative change is active **mind**.[34]

(2)   Ordinarily, most of active mind is unconscious, but some is **conscious;** active but non-accommodating mind is unconscious mind, while active mind that is accommodating is conscious mind.

(3)   These correspond to two totally different types of downward causation: In the first, older, more mechanical type, unchanging higher laws of larger wholes "supervene" over the lower-level laws of their separate parts[35] (Sperry 1980). This is the downward causation of unconscious mind—i.e., of mind that is active but not accommodating. In contrast, mind that is both active and accommodating has a second and more momentous kind of downward causation, which is the effect of ongoing transformation. By this ongoing transformation the lawfulness of larger wholes is being created anew in each moment. This second and commonly unrecognized kind is (by CC metatheory) the downward causation of conscious mind (Atkin 1992, 1994).[36]

The viewpoint presented here is that the label "freedom" points exactly to the *difference* between these two very different types of downward causation. They differ in that the downward causation of conscious mind is experienced from within, subjectively, and may be experienced as "free," while the downward cau-

---

33   My "**Anticipating self-world model,**" abbreviated 'A[sw]' (see *Glossary*) is a map or model of my **world**, of my **place within my world**, and of **dynamic regularities** of our actions and interactions (e.g., see 4th essay in *Section 2*, "➜Conscious Beyond Mechanism").

34   See just-previous footnote (and in *Glossary* see "mind").

35   As explained in the *Section 3* essay "➜More on Downward Causation and Free Will" this is "*Tautological* Downward Causation (DC$_t$)"; also see "Structure-Causality Identity Postulate" in *Section 1*'s third essay "➜Holarchic Structure, Downward Causation and Free Will" and also in *Glossary*.

36   As explained in the *Section 3* essay "➜More on Downward Causation and Free Will" this is "*Meta* Downward Causation (DC$_m$)"; also see two essays in the preceding section, *Section 2* ("➜On consciousness: What is the Role of Emergence" and "➜Conscious Beyond Mechanism")—see also "Downward Causation (DC)" in the *Glossary*.

sation of unconscious mind is not—rather, the latter can be known primarily as constraint upon the former.

Here, then, is the direction I will now pursue in attempting to resolve this puzzle. It is to assert that *there is no meaningful reality to "freedom" in the abstract.* This "freedom" that we commonly speak of—an idea about some kind of absolute essence—is useful only as a tag, directing attention to a certain fundamental but entirely non-separable aspect of every unique situation.

What thus comes to be known is that in truth this generalized idea of "freedom" is *empty*—empty of any reality as a foundation for our understanding. As an abstract absolute, freedom is a myth! And correspondingly, "choice" as an abstraction is equally non-existent. There can be no entity or *mechanism*, no uniform reproducible *process* of *choosing*. Thus understood, the idea of "choice" as some particular reproducible process or mechanism is also empty.

For if this were not so, then to make a free choice would be to do something old, to do *again* something that has been done before. But if, on the contrary, every free choice is a new action that in some essential way(s) is unlike any action done before, then the only adequate characterization of a free choice must be completely *particular* and concrete, describing that event as a unique happening imbedded in a vast context, and comprehensible only to the extent that this context can be known. This, then, is the epitome of *concrete thinking* (Ruddick 1989).

==<<((([]||[]))>>==((([^]/\[^]))==<<((([^]|_|[^])))>>==((([^]/\[^]))==<<((([]||[]))>>==

/~*~\/~*~\/~*~\/~*~\/~*~\/~*~\/~*~\/~*~\/~*~\/~*~\/~*~\/~*~\/~*~\/~*~\/~*~\/~*~\/~*~\/

Now an essay from 1997-99 regarding the book *A Cognitive Theory of Consciousness* published in 1988 by Bernard Baars.[37] Again two theories of consciousness will be compared and contrasted: Bernard Baars' "global workspace" (GW) theory and A. Atkin's "continual creation" (CC) metatheory[G] (the central topic of *Section 2* of this book). It will be concluded that there are fundamental similarities. Both theories are based in the notion that consciousness arises out of a complex, dynamic and hierarchically-structured matrix of unconscious automatisms. However, I suggest that this essay be read not as a final analysis of relations between his and my theoretical stance, but rather as the story of my progression—after initial difficulty over differences that at first seemed substantial—toward seeing how the deeper meanings and implications of the two theories are actually very close if not identical. Here's the essay:

→ THE PRIMACY OF SELF-ORGANIZING STRUCTURAL TRANSFORMATION: CAN CONSCIOUSNESS THEORIES CONVERGE?

I. Introduction

This paper will discuss parallels between the "global workspace" (GW) consciousness theory of Bernard Baars and my "continual creation" (CC) metatheory. I did not discover and read the deep and meticulously supported theory of consciousness elaborated by Baars in his book *A Cognitive Theory of Consciousness* (1988) until after I had formulated my own CC metatheory of consciousness and had worked out some of its implications in several papers. Thus my theory was developed independently. But when I read of Baars theory, I was immediately interested in the relations between the two. Now, finally in this paper I attempt to look at them more carefully than I had before.

When I read Baars I intuited that the two theories were very close, though expressed in different metaphorical and terminological systems—and that in fact they might be very nearly equivalent in basic structure. My closer examination of Baars' theory supports this, and it is a conclusion I find highly significant since it means that much of the experimental research data that Baars cites in support of his GW theory should equally well give support to main ideas of CC metathe-

---

37 Cambridge Univ. Press.

ory. Baars has been meticulous in studying experimental data on consciousness and relating them to his theoretical proposals. Further, the neurophysiological correlates that he and Jim Newman have inferred for GW theory (e.g., Baars & Newman 1994; Newman, Baars & Cho 1997; Baars, Newman & Taylor 1998) should serve also as underpinnings for CC metatheory.

II. Conscious Accommodation in GW & CC

In expounding his theory, Baars places primary emphasis upon his idea of a "global workspace" (GW) and contends that consciousness is best accounted for in terms of that idea. In contrast, I start with a primary idea that appears to be quite different—the idea of an ongoing process of *emergence*, of self-organization, which I label "continual creation" (CC)—and then propose that *this* is the way to explain consciousness.

But perhaps the difference is only apparent. Though it is not given as a postulate or first principle of his theory (as it is of mine), Bernard Baars says further on that "an informative conscious event translates into a demand for adaptation" (1988, p. 184)—and expresses that same general idea in various ways in many other places.

Here is how he sums up the thrust of his theory of consciousness in his 1988 and 1997 books:

> ...From a theoretical point of view, we expect consciousness to be involved in learning of novel events, or novel connections between known events.
>
> (Baars 1988, p. 213)

> Consciousness appears to be the major adaptive faculty of the brain. Our personal experience of the world is the subjective aspect of that adaptive activity.
>
> (Baars 1997, p. 166)

That, I believe, is the heart of the matter. It is also exactly the central thrust of the "CC metatheory" of consciousness that I arrived at through quite another route. This may be summarized as follows:

• The idea offered here is that while both unconscious and conscious actions are the play of mechanisms, consciousness enters when the activated mechanisms are at that moment undergoing essential structural modifications that are altering their laws of operation (Atkin 1992). This idea will be referred to as the continual creation (CC) hypothesis.

- It is further proposed that the inner structure that is thus re-organizing itself is the organism's dynamic (predictive) internal model of itself-in-its-world (Atkin 1992; Craik 1943; Kawato, Furukawa, and Suzuki 1987)—an evolving virtual machine (Dennett 1991) that is the ongoing product of the brain's neural networks (Edelman 1989; Flohr 1991; Hebb 1949; Kawato, Furukawa, and Suzuki 1987). This dynamic map—to be labeled the organism's self-world *model* or self-world *anticipator*, A[sw]—anticipates the organism's actions and predictively generates controlling feedback ("virtual feedback"), which is derived from **simulation of the activity and effects of the organism's own action systems.**

- The model's predictions are continually being tested, and the model readjusts, modifying its structure to compensate for discrepancies so that its subsequent predictions will be more accurate. That is, it "accommodates" by actively incorporating these adaptive structural modifications—as well as other modifications to resolve internal A[sw] inconsistencies. It is the ongoing accommodative changes in the organism's *self-world anticipator* that generate conscious awareness (Atkin 1992). In this way *downward causation* and the causal efficacy of consciousness can be understood anew, as can the relations of conscious to unconscious process.[38]

Now in the light of these ideas, consider what is going on according to GW theory. The "global workspace" (GW) is "a central information exchange that allows many different specialized processors to interact" (Baars 1988, p. 43). What we are *experiencing* is the communicative interaction within the "global workspace" of these "processor" experts. Yet what Baars then postulates to be actually happening there is remarkably similar to the fundamental idea about consciousness in CC metatheory:

> From the adaptation point of view, *an informative conscious event translates into a demand for adaptation.* This is of course the claim stated in the chapter title: that conscious experience is informative—it always demands some degree of adaptation.
>
> (Baars 1988, p. 184, emphasis added)

I read that statement as formally equivalent in meaning (with one possible caveat, to be dealt with below in *Subsection IV. A.*—"Adaptation and Accommodation")

---

38 Based mainly—but with some modifications—upon **Section 2** essay "➔ Conscious Beyond Mechanism" (my presentation at the first Arizona "Towards a Science of Consciousness" conference in 1994).

to the statement at the start of this section that presented the main postulate of my CC metatheory.

And where, more exactly, is this adaptation taking place? In the Baars theory the unconscious matrix of processor activity is called the "context" of consciousness.

> ...context consists of those things to which the nervous system has *already* adapted; it is the ground against which new information is defined.
>
> (Baars 1988, p. 182—author's italics)

Baars considers an event *informative* when it departs from—cannot be fully reconciled with—the information content of unconscious context; when there is a difference, then the event is carrying non-redundant information, whereas if there is no difference, there is only redundancy.[39]

But this is very similar (though presented in different terms) to the notion in CC metatheory that the accommodative restructuring of the module matrix is evoked by departures of actual sensory feedback from that predicted by the unconscious assimilatory activities of the A[sw] modular matrix of anticipatory automatisms.

So in Baars' theory the "informativeness of an event" (Baars 1988, p. 180) may be identical with what in my theory is *incoherence* (i.e., non-redundancy) between unconscious prediction and event. It seems to me, then, that this "informativeness of an event" is an exact measure of how much "a distributed system of intelligent information processors" (Baars 1988, p. 86) will need to undergo accommodative reorganization. Baars does not make much use of the word "accommodation," but it seems to convey just what he means by "adaptive processes" (e.g., Baars 1988, pp. 189, 213, 221).

III. Mind's Structure—Consciousness and Context

There is a general parallel, I believe, between what Baars refers to as *context hierarchies* and *goal hierarchies* and what I have labeled my self-world *model*—or more recently *self-world anticipator*, abbreviated *A[sw]*.

Let's look at the overall pattern of equivalences between the two theoretical frames:

---

39 See first part of Sect. V, below—"Mind's Structure"—for more about *context*.

—*traditional jargon*—	*Baars: GW Theory terms:*	*AA: CC metatheory terms:*
"Mind"	GW + context hierarchies	Self-world *anticipator*=A[sw]
"Unconscious mind"	Context hierarchies	Assimilating A[sw]
"Conscious mind"	Global workspace=GW	Accommodating A[sw]

Both theories are based in the notion that consciousness arises out of a complex, dynamic matrix of unconscious automatisms, which Baars refers to as "a distributed system of intelligent information processors" (1988, p. 86). According to CC metatheory there are vast and complex dynamic interactions between processors going on all the time, unconsciously; in the Baars theory this unconscious matrix of processor activity is called the "context" of consciousness.

"Contexts are organized knowledge structures" (Baars 1988, p. 164). They are the matrix within which consciousness arises and are always constraining conscious experience—but at the same time are formed and modified by conscious experiences: "*A major function of conscious experience is to elicit, modify, and create new contexts—which in turn set the stage for later conscious experiences*" (Baars 1988, p. 167—author's italics). And these contextual changes will generally be adaptive, for (as already quoted): "Conscious experience is informative—it always demands some degree of adaptation" (Baars 1988, p. 177). But what is the structure that—with the help of consciousness—is adapting?

As explained throughout **Section 2** (above), the business of my A[sw] is *anticipation*, and my awareness is the continual self-remodeling by which it carries out its business.

> Using CC metatheory, I assume that my A[sw] is structured as a many-layered hierarchy (something like Minsky's [1986] postulated "society of agents")—a hierarchical network of a great many subsystems, many of which may seem to function with partial autonomy, but which are nevertheless closely linked together. A great many of these subsystems are active assimilatively much of the time, but assimilation remains beneath awareness.

The linkings of active and accommodating (conscious) subsystems with the active and non-accommodating (unconscious) subsystems that surround them are two-way. Therefore, not only do unconscious processes constrain conscious choices…, but reciprocally, conscious choices are at every moment profoundly modulating the directions of the ongoing unconscious processes in which they are embedded. Thus the accommodative changes that effect conscious choosings will redirect the assimilative activities both of the accommodating subsystems themselves and also of non-accommodating subsystems to which they are linked. Such causal influences of consciousness upon "lower-order" unconscious mechanism is *downward causation* in action. It seems therefore that downward causation may be easier to comprehend as a direct implication of CC metatheory than it has been when consciousness was explained as a "past-tense" emergent—as it was by Sperry (1980).

…

Comprehension of the relation of conscious to unconscious mind, so emphasized in dynamic psychology, may also thereby be made easier. Certainly, conscious actions occur within the far larger context of ongoing unconscious activity. The awareness I am now experiencing is therefore presumed to be the accommodative change in structure of only certain subsystems within my more widely active A[sw]. If the ongoing assimilative activities of these conscious (accommodating) subsystems are embedded in and tightly linked to the assimilative activities of larger unconscious (non-accommodating) systems, then it may be those more inclusive but unconscious systems that are the ultimate sources of my *initiatives, motivations, drives* and *purposes*.

In this way I begin to better understand the near invisibility of all the paradigms that govern my every thought and action—not only the paradigms of my science, but those of my habitual movement styles and those governing my interests and aversions, my language habits and my social relationships. These dynamic patternings would be the dynamic patternings of ongoing assimilative actions of my A[sw], most of which go on with little or no accommodation and so without awareness, yet which constrain my choices by driving and guiding the assimilative actions of the more restricted A[sw]-regions that do accommodate as they move and thus move with awareness. Therefore myriad unconscious constraints always surround the choices which accompany my awareness—constraints not only invisible, but also durable, as they don't change so long as they do not enter my awareness.

(Atkin 1994)[40]

These ideas from CC metatheory correspond very well, I believe—at least in the large, if not in details—with those put forth by Baars in his book's *Part III* (entitled *"The fundamental role of context"*—Baars 1988, pp. 135-221). He has based it widely in psychological research from many sources, therefore giving it an empirical solidity from which I am delighted to borrow.

For what does he say is happening in a "global workspace?" He says that it's a "central information exchange that allows many different specialized processors to interact" (Baars 1988, p. 43). And these interactions are new, evolving patterns of cooperation that are self-organizing—for if not, then what was happening would simply be unconscious "context," which is stereotyped, redundant. Remember that "context consists of those things to which the nervous system has *already* adapted; it is the ground against which new information is defined" (Baars 1988, p. 182—author's italics).

Further: "Contexts are organized knowledge structures" (Baars 1988, p. 164) which are the matrix within which consciousness arises. When it does, these contextual changes will generally be adaptive, for (as already noted): "Conscious experience is informative—it always demands some degree of adaptation" (Baars 1988, p. 177).

And Baars notes that contexts are always constraining conscious experience, but that at the same time they are formed and modified by conscious experiences. To quote him again on this: *"A major function of conscious experience is to elicit, modify, and create new contexts—which in turn set the stage for later conscious experiences"* (Baars 1988, p. 167—author's italics).

Now, this is almost exactly what I have said about *mind*, which I've defined so that it includes *both* the contexts and workspace of the GW theory. *Contexts* then correspond to *unconscious* mind.[41] Given that correspondence,

• …Mind—the "matrix" out of which consciousness arises—**"assimilates"** moment-to-moment world-structure by anticipating it…Consciousness—arising by accommodative changes of mind—is Meta-Mind…

• We see, then, that each is the source of the other—we have what might be termed a "paradox of reciprocal priority": [Unconscious] Mind is the necessary matrix of consciousness, for consciousness appears when mind requires correction.

40   This is from the fourth *Section 2* essay "➔Conscious Beyond Mechanism."
41   See table of *overall pattern of equivalences* at the beginning of this subsection.

• Yet, though consciousness thereby arises within mind, it at the same time is prior to mind. For it is consciousness that creates and changes mind; mind's evolution is consciousness. Thus they are different but inseparable—two aspects of a single dynamic of evolutionary unfoldment[42]

Thus we see that the two theories seem very similar—if not identical—not only in some of their details, but also in large perspective and implications.

The big difference between theories may be in language rather than mean-ing—especially in the metaphor by which the *conscious cooperation of processors* is described. For GW theory this image is of an open problem-solving committee of experts—or a "board meeting" attended by myriad experts who can get together by posting all about their task/problem of the moment on the "blackboard" vis-ible to all.[43]

The CC metaphor is a bit different—it is a neural network, of many layers and tremendously high connectivity. But most of this network is the unconscious "distributed system of intelligent information processors" (Baars 1988, p. 86) which are functioning automatically without the *plasticity* of the neural network that self-organizes. The part that corresponds to the GW has, in contrast, been in some manner "opened" to self-organization. How this might happen may be found by looking into the complex flow of processes coordinated by ERTAS,[44] according to the work of Newman & Baars (and their collaborators).[45]

Here are just a few bits from a much larger structure of ideas:

The Context of Imagery…over the past decade very interesting findings have emerged, suggesting constraints on visual imagery of which we are generally unconscious.

…*The Context of Conceptual Thought*…Anyone who has tried to think very clearly about some topic must know from experience that our *sta-ble presuppositions* tend to become unconscious. Whatever we believe with absolute certainty we tend to take for granted. Moreover, we lose

---

42 These three paragraphs were abstracted from the first essay in the **Summing Up** sec-tion, below (essay entitled "➔Being, Doing, Knowing—A Theoretical Perspective on Consciousness").

43 Nowadays an even better metaphor might be an internet newsgroup such as *Psyche*, where a question or comment from one or another participant is frequently posted with the expectation of responses from others.

44 Extended Reticular-Thalamic Activating System.

45 Here, see especially Baars & Newman 1994; Newman, Baars, & Cho 1997; and Baars, Newman & Taylor 1998.

sight of the fact that *alternatives to our stable presuppositions can be entertained.*

(Baars 1988, p. 152.)

Why is it so difficult for committed scientists to change paradigms? From our model, it would seem that change is hard, at least in part because at any single moment the bulk of a paradigm is unconscious. In our terms, paradigms are conceptual contexts. If one tried to make a paradigm conscious, one could only make one aspect of it conscious at any one time because of the limited capacity of consciousness. But typically paradigm-differences between two groups of scientists involve not just one, but many different aspects of the mental framework simultaneously. This may also be why conversion phenomena in science (as elsewhere) tend to be relatively rapid, all-or-none events that seem to have a not quite rational component.

(Baars 1988, p. 156.)

...*The current Dominant Context imposes unconscious constraints on what can become conscious*...The Dominant Context at any time is a coherent mix of perceptual-imaginal, conceptual, and goal contexts. Our experience at any time is controlled by numerous mutually consistent contexts.

(Baars 1988, p. 163.)

In a sense, context consists of those things to which the nervous system has *already* adapted; it is the ground against which new information is defined...

The case of conceptual presuppositions: Conscious contents can turn into new contexts

(Baars 1988, p. 197.)

I found all those thoughts interesting and important. They follow also from the framework of CC metatheory—there's virtual identity between what Baars terms the system of "contexts" and what I've termed the dynamic, self-organizing structure of the "self-world anticipator."

I have found study of Baars' consciousness theory highly rewarding, as I find in it—especially in his work on contexts—the beginning of an answer to my wish for better understanding of mind's structure (of its functional properties and also of its specific developmental constraints). I wish to thank him especially for this aspect of his work—as well as for the ways in which he gives theory such a firm grounding in careful, controlled observations.

IV. What's the Difference?

So the two theories seem in many ways to be saying the same thing. The phrase in GW that "conscious experience is informative" seems to carry the same meaning (or very nearly so) as the assertion in CC metatheory that "conscious experience is accommodation." That, certainly, seems a strong—perhaps a fundamental—similarity between the theories. But we also find differences. Here are several (we'll try to see if they are merely superficial):

A. Adaptation and Accommodation

Noting that in his GW writing a "major concept...is *adaptation*," Baars then says he "will use it in a narrow sense, as the process of learning to represent some input, to know it to the point of automatic predictability" (1988, p. 183). And it is right here that he relates this concept to Piaget's idea of "accommodation" in a way that suggest to me that my own use of this term may need some revision. He says:

> We can borrow Piagetian terms here to represent different ends of the adaptation continuum (Piaget 1952). When confronted with a situation that is new and strange, people need to find new contexts for experiencing the input; the result resembles Piagetian accommodation. In other words, accommodation has to do with the discovery of usable contexts. On the other end of the continuum, when input is highly familiar and predictable, minimal adaptation is required to assimilate it into readily available contexts....
>
> Conscious experience of an event seems to occur midway between the outer poles of assimilation and accommodation. If we can automatically predict something completely, we are not conscious of it. But if the input requires a deep revision of our current contexts, we do not experience it either—it is too confusing or disorganized to experience *as such*, though we may experience fragments and tentative interpretations of the input. Somewhere between these two extremes, between the assimilation and accommodation poles of the continuum, we may have an accurate conscious experience of the event.
>
> (Baars 1988, pp. 183-4)

This differs from my use of "accommodation" in CC metatheory,[G] for it's been my understanding that it could refer to a broader range of contextual change than that.

Clearly, I must check this—perhaps I should not be using that Piagetian term in the way I have been; because here Baars is saying that Piagetian "accommodation" is *not* what he means by the term "adaptation." Yet I've been using "accommodation" to mean just about what Baars does mean by "adaptation."

Let me then define my use of "accommodation" in CC metatheory to mean *adaptation* in the way that Baars uses that term, which I take to be in the sense of adaptive *transformation* (adaptive *self-organizing* transformation).

B. Questions on Multiplicity of Mind

But now with regard to the entity I've been referring to as *the* "self-world anticipator" (A[sw]), do I make a mistake in using the singular form of this term, as if referring to it as *a single thing?* Baars talks about his "context hierarchies" in the *plural*—they are a *multiplicity* of apparently unknown and perhaps indeterminate and/or highly fluid extent. At any given moment there may be a *dominant* context hierarchy, and we may observe after some time interval its replacement in dominance by another one, so that there is a progression through many different dominant context hierarchies. But is there any particular entity that constitutes all of them in a single *dynamic structure?* Maybe not! However, that kind of singleness is what I imply with my concept concerning each higher organism's "self-world anticipator" (A[sw]).

Of course, I might be absolved from this "sin of *thinging*" (and of "*single*-thinging") if we remember my postulation that self-world anticipator (A[sw]) has an open holarchic structure and thus a potentially unlimited upward development, by which—even if divided into relatively separate parts at lower holarchic levels—it becomes more and more unitarily inclusive at higher levels. In that way it's multiplicity can become progressively less and less its controlling character.

So that's very interesting! Perhaps I need to learn from Bernard Baars a better way to speak about these ever-present processes of anticipating, recognizing more explicitly their multiplicity.

But I also note that there seems perhaps to be a reverse situation with regard to his most central concept, the "global workspace"—for he speaks about this as a "thing," a single entity—whereas that which most closely corresponds to it in CC metatheory is the ongoing and highly fluid, ever-changing process that I call

---

G   See Glossary.

"accommodation" and he calls "adaptation"—and this is not made single, not spoke of as any kind of entity.

C. Necessary Conditions for CONSCIOUS Events

In the *summary* chapter (Chapter 11) of *A Cognitive Theory of Consciousness*, Baars first asks "[what] are the necessary conditions of conscious experience?" (Baars 1988, p. 362), and then concludes:

> In sum, we find again that surprising simplicity emerges from the apparent complexity. The evidence…seems to converge on only five necessary conditions for conscious events: global broadcasting, internal consistency, informativeness, access by a self-system, and perceptual or quasi-perceptual coding.
>
> (Baars 1988, p. 364)

So we will now look at four[46] of these "necessary conditions" (leaving global broadcasting for last) to see if each can be as well accounted for using differently-stated principles of CC metatheory as it was by Baars using his GW theory. The second of the "five necessary conditions for conscious events" is "internal consistency" (Baars 1988, p. 364).

Internal Consistency: Baars derived this "necessary condition" from GW theory through its notion of "contexts." In the following paragraph entitled "*Internal consistency and the role of organization in contexts*" he says:

> Contexts are organized knowledge structures. This implies that they are internally consistent; they tend to resist changes that are inconsistent with them, and resist more strongly the greater the inconsistency; there is a tendency to complete partial input, and when one component changes, another one may have to compensate. All these phenomena are observable about contexts.
>
> (Baars 1988, p. 164)

As should become more apparent later, since CC metatheory has in most respects a similar conceptual structure, with a "self-world anticipator" taking the role of GW theory's "contexts," most implications of the two theories are also very similar. Specifically, in both theories there is an intimate connection between consciousness and internal consistency.

---

46 All except "access by a self-system."

But there is also an interesting difference: Whereas in GW theory internal consistency is a **condition for** consciousness, in CC metatheory it is, rather, a **consequence of** consciousness—because a fundamental postulate of CC metatheory is that the accommodative activity that is our *conscious experience* is evoked by incoherencies and *moves in the direction of resolving incoherencies.*

And if that's true—if *consciousness is the accommodative resolution of incoherence*—then it would follow that rather than being a "necessary condition for conscious events," internal consistency is an *effect* of conscious events. But whichever way it works, both theories quite tightly connect internal consistency with consciousness.

Now, there's another facet of this that I hadn't thought about before. I just read that "other features, like limited capacity and seriality, follow from the internal consistency constraint" (Baars 1988, p. 362). Well, that sounds right! I hadn't given much attention to those features of consciousness, but know they're there and that a theory needs to account for them. This seems the way to do it—in CC metatheory as well as in GW theory.

Informativeness: Both theories give what Baars calls "informativeness" a central and essential role in consciousness—but with a difference.

In both, *consciousness* should occur when *accommodation* occurs, but one theory (GW) connects consciousness to *that which evokes* accommodation while the other (CC) connects it with *the accommodative change* that is thereby evoked. If "informative stimulation" (Baars 1988, p. 178) does in fact reliably evoke accommodative restructuring of the "distributed system [of] numerous intelligent specialists [that] cooperate or compete in an effort to solve some common problems" (Baars 1988, p. 87), then there should not be much difference in what the two theories predict.

Perceptual or Quasi-Perceptual Coding: Baars (1988) says that—

> Perception, imagery, bodily feelings, and inner speech seem to be involved in the conscious components of thought and action, not merely in input processes...Even abstract conscious concepts may involve rapid quasi-perceptual events. This suggests that perception may be closer to mind's lingua franca than other codes. The evidence is good that images become automatic with practice, and thus fade from consciousness, though they continue to serve as a processing code...
>
> (Baars 1988, p. 363)

I find that this observable *property* of consciousness can also be understood in CC metatheory by examining the role in our consciousness of our "world model"—our "A[sw]."

Global Broadcasting: In this "global broadcasting" area are statements that highlight both the similarity of the two theories of consciousness and what seems to be the greatest divergence between them:

> ...From a theoretical point of view, we expect consciousness to be involved in learning of novel events, or novel connections between known events. The rational is that novel connections require unpredictable interactions between specialized processors. Hence global communication from "any" specialist to "any other" is necessary...Widespread broadcasting serves to make this any-any connection.

> ...[What] is the evidence for this claim? Perhaps the most obvious is the radical simplicity of the act of learning. To learn anything new we merely pay attention to it. Learning occurs "magically"—we merely allow ourselves to interact consciously...and somehow, without detailed conscious intervention, we acquire the relevant knowledge and skill.
>
> (Baars 1988, p. 213-14)

These last passages—beginning with the mutually-shared idea that "we expect consciousness to be involved in learning of novel events, or novel connections between known events"—seem then to pinpoint an apparent difference between theories. For Baars says (in the first of the paragraphs) that "global communication from 'any' specialist to 'any other' is necessary...Widespread broadcasting serves to make this any-any connection" (Baars 1988, p. 214). Now, my CC metatheory approach to this same problem seems slightly different in that I employ a neural network framework within which the level of connectivity between processors is very high. Then for the need to achieve "unpredictable interactions between specialized processors," such a network may do that not by means of some kind of "Widespread broadcasting" but rather by the capability of neural network systems to self-organize, to generate new and unprecedented transfer functions between their inputs and outputs, in a kind of pattern-recognition function (Hebb 1949; Rumelhart et al. 1986; Caudill & Butler 1990; Flohr 1991; Jantsch 1980).

Well, but it's not altogether sure that this is a real rather than an apparent difference. Perhaps Baars' ideas on what can actually be going on in his "global workspace" during consciousness are really equivalent—though put into quite different descriptive (metaphorical) terms—to my neural network conception of an accommodative transformation of patterns of interconnectivity. A little further on Baars says the following:

> Model 3...serves to put a conscious experience in a temporal context, described as the "adaptive cycle." All conscious experience, it is argued,

involve a stage of adaptation in which a defining context has been accessed, so that the conscious information can be understood; but not all degrees of freedom have been determined....

Information that fades from consciousness does not disappear; rather, it serves to constrain later conscious experiences. It may become part of a new unconscious context, within which later experiences are defined. One implication is that every event is experienced with respect to prior conscious events...

Thus we are compelled to view even a single conscious experience as part of a dynamic developmental process of learning and adaptation. Increasingly it seems that the system underlying conscious experience is our primary organ of adaptation.

(Baars 1988, p. 221)

Is this a description of "global broadcasting"? To me, it sounds more like the self-organizing transformations of a neural network![47]

So it looks very much as if even here the two theories are largely equivalent, in basic ideational architecture. They seem, at least, to *point in the same direction.*

D. More on What's Broadcast

But if, as GW theory seems to maintain, *global broadcasting* does play a fundamental role in our consciousness, then what is it actually that's broadcast? Is it really complex and sensory-inflow-specific "messages" that form the contents of consciousness? Or is it rather *feedback signals* to activate and control the distribution and depth of adaptation ("accommodation") processes? My metatheory says it's probably more the latter than the former—i.e., it's a swing-by of the proverbial "searchlight beam" of attention.

After all, the reticular activating system *(RAS)* is crucial for consciousness—and it's an *activating* system. It's a central component of Baars' "Extended Reticular-Thalamic Activating System" or *ERTAS*, which is postulated to *be* the global workspace. Of course ERTAS is a far larger and more complex system than RAS and therefore must have flows of information within it that are much more complex than the kind that were attributed to the latter. But do ERTAS information-flows actually have the richness in kinds of information that's attributed to them in GW theory? I wonder...

---

47   More on this a little later in this essay, in the subsection below entitled "Is Workspace a Network?"

Let's consider some of the cited evidence—e.g., that cited from Roy John's "Event-Related Potential" studies: "John's major finding of interest to us was that electrical activity due to the visual flashes can initially be found everywhere in the brain, far beyond the specialized visual pathways" (Baars 1988, p. 102). But then, with repetition and habituation, the distribution becomes "more and more localized—until finally it is limited only to the classical visual pathways" (p. 102). Baars relates this change to *habituation* phenomena of consciousness, noting that such change in evoked-potential distributions is just what would be expected from GW theory.

But what does such experimentation say about the *kinds* of information that are so globally distributed? After all, the kinds of stimuli used in evoked-potential studies severely limit the conclusions that can be drawn from them. *Clicks* and *light-flashes* are maximally-simplified sensory inputs; so the distribution of the responses temporally-linked to their occurrence cannot be used as evidence for such a distribution of responses to the more normal sorts of sensory inputs commonly associated with the extremely complex (fractal!) contents of consciousness. However, if those response-signals were, rather, *activation* regulators involved in control of *adaptation* processes, then we would expect the same kinds of temporal linkings and wide-spread distributions that were found in the Roy John experiments.

This shortcoming of evidence from evoked-potential studies applies also to the implications that Baars draws from them concerning *Orienting Responses* (p. 103). Certainly, as he says (e.g., p. 103), the brain's ERTAS system is closely associated with consciousness, and the distribution of its inputs and outputs fits with his GW hypothesis. He concludes that "it can broadcast information to the cortex" (p. 103). But again, this says nothing about the *kinds, variety* or *complexity* of information so broadcast.

Neural network (NN) ideas may also be helpful here. What's receiving current sensory inputs? Is it a *context hierarchy* that is a hierarchically-interconnected set of *pattern-recognizing neural networks*? For those "intelligent processors" may be exactly that—*pattern-recognizing neural networks*. Certainly this would be quite consistent with the evidence Baars cites from neuroanatomy and neurophysiology (see, e.g. Baars 1988, pp. 121-2).

It's also a plausible idea for me right now but nevertheless suggests a possible difference between the GW and CC perspectives—that between *recognizing* and *anticipating*. As noted above in the table at the beginning of subsection *III,*[48] I've put Baars' *context hierarchy* as equivalent to *unconscious mind*. For that kind of a *context hierarchy* would seem to be essentially a passive system that *responds* but does not otherwise act. However I lean toward the idea of a more active system

---

48   I.e., at the start of the "Mind's Structure—Consciousness and Context" subsection.

that's to be understood as a proactive pattern-*anticipator,* not a passive pattern-*recognizer.*[49]

So is there a way in which pattern-*recognition* and pattern-*generation* can be a single process? I found nothing very explicit in Baars' book concerning this, but there are some provocative suggestions—e.g., concerning the prevalence of feedback arrangements. He says: "Most sensory systems allow for a flow of information 'top down' as well as 'bottom up'" (p. 130). May it perhaps be that *recognition* at *lower* levels in some way shades into *generation* at *higher* levels? For example, let's say that low-level recognizers activate high-level generators. Could that work? Does it make sense?

Isn't the living organism fundamentally an *active* being? What is living feeds and grows. If it is an animal life, it feeds, grows and *moves about.* Certainly, to survive and flourish it needs to know where it is and what is happening around it. Thus it needs to be continually recognizing and internally responding to the patterns of energy that impinge upon its exteroceptors. But at the same time it is busy modifying those patterns through its own externally-directed activities. That of course is just elementary biology.

So with regard to such basic biological activities there seemed at first to be a difference between this GW theory and CC metatheory. In the latter, my self-world anticipator (A[sw]) is intrinsically *dynamic.* Its actions flow onward, unfolding automatically except as certain components of this unfolding are guided by conscious adaptation.

According to both theories there are vast and complex dynamic interactions between processors going on unconsciously all the time. (As we've noted, in the Baars theory this unconscious matrix of processor activity is called the "context" of consciousness.) But in CC metatheory consciousness arises not simply out of their *intercommunication,* as some GW statements suggest, but rather out of the *accommodative (adaptive) restructuring* both of individual active modules and of their automatized patterns of interaction.

Nevertheless, though not stated as a first principle in GW theory as it is in CC metatheory, *adaptation* seems to play the same sort of fundamental role in GW theory that *accommodation* plays in CC metatheory—and to designate the same kinds of structural transformation.

But there remain some questions about the equivalence across theories both of the unconscious and of the conscious components in this picture. With regard to mostly-unconscious dynamism of mind portrayed in CC metatheory, I'm not

---

49 It seems however that Baars, Newman & Taylor (1998) have also given this alternative favorable consideration from the way they cite the work of Gray (1995) defining and supporting it. (See reference to Gray [1995] in **Glossary** entry for "Anticipating self-world model".)

sure (as already noted in subsection *"Questions on Multiplicity of Mind,"* above) how fully this characterization applies to the largely equivalent unconscious *context hierarchy* of GW theory.

And with regard to the conscious adaptive component, I just noted above that for me the term "accommodation" is synonymous with "adaptation" as used by Baars. (But as remarked earlier in the part on "Adaptation and Accommodation" of the *"What's the Difference"* subsection of this essay, my use of the term "accommodation" differs slightly from that of Baars.)

E. Is a Workspace a Network?

As already said several times, in the GW theory the adaptive changes take place in a "global workspace" which is, first of all, "a central information exchange that allows many different specialized processors to interact" (Baars 1988, p. 43). Thus, what is explicit in this theory about *consciousness* is that what we are *experiencing* is the communicative interaction within the "global workspace" (GW) of these "processor" experts.

CC metatheory seems to be saying something different about the nature of this underlying matrix of consciousness: In CC metatheory "the inner structure that is…re-organizing itself is…an evolving virtual machine…that is the ongoing product of the brain's neural networks."[50]

But perhaps the difference between them is more apparent than real. After all, we have already seen that in Baars GW theory we become *aware* when the intercommunicating system of processor experts in the global workspace gets an *informative demand for adaptation*. And further, it seems that major features of the brain's neural processing that Baars refers to *functionally* as the "GW"—including its plasticity, its pattern recognition capabilities, and how it is organized largely in terms of interconnected modular processors—can be *structurally* understood in terms of neural networks of extremely high connectivity.[51]

Thus, a functional architecture that is characterized as a "global workspace" is probably to be realized as particular functional modes of those neural network systems. At least, this seems to me a plausible implication of Baars' reasoning that

> novel connections require unpredictable interactions between specialized processors. Hence global communication from "any" specialist to

---

50   This point was made and explained in two essays of **Section 2**, above: "➔ On consciousness: What is the Role of Emergence" and "➔ Conscious Beyond Mechanism."

51   It seems that since 1988 the GW theorists may have been moving in that direction too, judging from the discussion of neural networks in Baars, Newman & Taylor (1998) in relation to GW activities.

"any other" is necessary…Widespread broadcasting serves to make this any-any connection.

(Baars 1988, p. 214)

In a sense, it's as if there is simply a difference in priorities: The GW priority places the plasticity of the interactive complex of intelligent processors first, then moves to the adaptive function served by this plasticity; while the CC priority places the adaptive function first, but needs of course to postulate the plasticity necessary for it to occur.

F. When is a Global Workspace system useful?

About exactly *when* a global workspace is useful, Baars says this:

The main use of a GW system is to solve problems that any single expert cannot solve by itself—problems whose solutions are *underdetermined*.

(Baars 1988, p. 92)

But as I read this neat idea, I can see it in another way—set it into another theoretical framework closer to that of cybernetics (also of Hebb's brain-model) and now of newer work with neural networks (e.g., see Kawato *et al.* 1987; Tani 1998). Then I see the problem-solving process that Baars sketches in another light—as the *self-organizing transformation of a complex neural network system*.

Yes, those specialized processors are indeed highly interconnected. This is so not just when they "communicate with each other through a global workspace" and thus participate in conscious experiencing—it is so (I postulate) *all* the time. That is, specialized processors are also working closely together while the problem-solving is going on *automatically*, without a hitch, and while therefore it all remains beneath consciousness. They are then running their automatic algorithms to *solve* the problems of each moment (thus not needing to alter them) and cooperating tightly with each other to do that.

But when those automatic algorithms are not quite working—when the predictions thus generated don't quite jibe with what actually happens (i.e., when predicted sensory feedback does not match actual sensory feedback)—then those discrepancies (incoherencies) are used to generate *new* ways of cooperating, *new* patterns of response, *new* transfer functions.

The point is that these adaptive changes (what I've referred to as *accommodation*) may well be taking place while the *connectivity* of the participating sets of specialized processors does not undergo major change—and especially, does not become much greater than before, as GW theory suggests that it should.

That is, "I assume that my A[sw] is structured as a many-layered hierarchy (something like Minsky's [1986] postulated 'society of agents')—a hierarchical network of a great many subsystems,…which are…closely linked together."[52] So, in effect, they're always in a "global workspace"—all working together.

What I can do, then, is to shift my own perspective—to open up my own idea of the meaning of "workspace." Certainly the "global workspace" idea (as it has come across to me in Baars 1988) at first did not quite fit with my own way of seeing the relation of consciousness to the whole dynamic structure of mind. But consider: What's the *work* that's going on in the workspace? Just interpret that *work* not only as "doing a job," "solving practical problems," etc., but as *self-organizing, transformative change in the dynamic structure of mind.* (That, after all, has been a meaning for the word "work" in some of the spiritual traditions, where teachers may speak of "working on oneself," etc.)

G. Mind Unconscious and Conscious?

There's also another way in which I find an interesting difference in the architecture of the two theoretical structures. It concerns something about the relation of conscious mind to the whole of mind. In GW theory, when conscious content arises and the intelligent processors that are involved in it undertake some involvement in the GW, it seems that they thereby leave the context in which they were participating till then. I don't find in GW theory the expression of a perspective on the whole structure mind that includes *both* the intelligent processors responsible at any moment for consciousness because they are operating in the global workspace and *also* all those intelligent but unconscious processors that are participating in context hierarchies but not in the GW, thus remaining out of consciousness. The impression is that though there's considerable discussion of ways in which conscious mind and unconscious mind interact, nevertheless they seem to be portrayed as quite separate regions—entities in contact but clearly separate and differing profoundly in structure.

In seeming contrast, in CC metatheory *consciousness is totally continuous with and intimately part of the total mind-structure.* Baars does at certain points seem to say something like this. But in CC metatheory this continuity is more centrally explicit.

---

52 From 4th essay in ***Section 2***, "➔Conscious Beyond Mechanism."

H. The Discrepancy or Its Resolution?

There's also the appearance of another difference. It concerns a stimulus-or-response kind of question: In GW theory an event that is conscious is informative, meaning that it is "a *demand for* adaptation" (Baars 1988, p. 184; my emphasis); in CC metatheory an event that is conscious is one in which accommodation—which is the means of adaptation—*is taking place*. That difference can be brought out by a question to Baars (and to me):

- Does consciousness (which is identical with adaptive change) *respond to* information or does it *create* information?

- It seems to me that in Baars' perspective it is the former whereas in mine it is the latter.

It can't be *both*, can it? But if not then *which* is it? Nevertheless as already noted above in subsection *IV* of this essay (*"Necessary Conditions for Conscious Events: Informativeness"*) in practical outcome it's not much of a difference. Here's what was said there:

> In both, *consciousness* should occur when *accommodation* occurs—but one theory (GW) connects consciousness to *that which evokes* accommodation while the other (CC) connects it with *the accommodative change* that is thereby evoked. If "informative stimulation" (Baars 1988, p. 178) does in fact reliably evoke accommodative restructuring of the "distributed system [of] numerous intelligent specialists [that] cooperate or compete in an effort to solve some common problems" (Baars 1988, p. 87), then there should not be much difference in what the two theories predict.

V. Not Much Difference After All

And this interpretation is confirmed by Baars' further statements:

> One explanation of the fleetingness of conscious events is that adaptive processes are continually learning from conscious events, reducing *their* alternatives, and nibbling away at the information provided. If that is true, then most conscious events lose most of their information value very quickly, as uncertainty is reduced by adaptive mechanisms. The evanescence of conscious contents is consistent with the notion of informativeness as a demand for adaptation.

> (Baars 1988, p. 189)

Redundancy implies a perfect match of input with expectation....In the Piagetian dimension of assimilation and accommodation, redundancy corresponds to the extreme pole of assimilation.

(Baars 1988, p. 190)

Further, here's a quote from his new book (Baars 1997) that also seem relevant to my questions about similarities and differences of theoretical approach. With regard to the central idea of CC metatheory, Baars (as already noted at the very start of this discussion) again gives it striking support, saying that:

Consciousness appears to be the major adaptive faculty of the brain. Our personal experience of the world is the subjective aspect of that adaptive activity.

(Baars 1997, p. 166)

Not only is this fundamental relationship between consciousness and informativeness-as-call-to-adaptation very similar to the fundamental relationship between consciousness and accommodation posited in CC metatheory, but also, if we look at some of the further implications and predicted correlations which Baars draws from his theory, they correspond quite closely with the implications and predictions of CC metatheory.

Therefore I find real comfort in what I take to be this implicit support of such a thorough and eminent researcher. And I believe the evidence that Baars uses to support his theory should likewise give support to mine. Here, for example, are some observations about consciousness that he says are well supported by data and previous studies and that he finds consistent with and/or supportive of his GW theory:

If we are unconscious of these routine, cooperating systems, what are we conscious of? Our previous discussion...suggests that the most informative aspects of action should be conscious: that is, those that are unpredictable and significant. It is the underdetermined choice points in the flow of action that should be conscious most often.

(Baars 1988, p. 259)

[Two] countervailing tendencies: the search for information and adaptation to information. The first leads to more conscious access, and the second reduces conscious access: Obviously our model should reflect both of these countervailing tendencies, as they balance each other out...

...The more predictable the input becomes, the more redundant it is with respect to its mental representation, and the less will it be conscious.

(Baars 1988, p. 203)

To summarize: Repeated signals may not fade from consciousness if they are incompletely known so that each repetition allows more information to be learned; if the signals are variable; if they are ambiguous, so that they can be re-interpreted; if they serve a larger purpose that is not redundant; or if the context drifts, so that the same input signal remains informative....So far, we have suggested that all conscious experience must be informative—that true redundancy leads to a loss of consciousness of a message. The evidence for this is quite pervasive.... Although more research is clearly needed..., the position that informativeness is a necessary condition for conscious experience seems to be quite defensible.

...

If consciousness always involves adaptation, there should be an intimate connection between conscious experience and all kinds of adaptive processes, including comprehension, learning, and problem solving....

(Baars 1988, p. 213)

These generalizations concerning verifiable observations about properties, occasions and correlations of consciousness that he finds supportive of GW theory are also altogether consistent with CC metatheory and therefore support it as well.

When I reread Chapter 2 of *A Cognitive Theory of Consciousness* (Baars 1988) in which the author contrasts "capabilities of comparable conscious and unconscious processes" (Baars 1988, Table 2.1) and then proposes his "basic model: A global workspace (blackboard) in a distributed system of intelligent information processors" (Baars 1988, p. 86), I understand him to be saying that the function of the conscious GW is the *creation*—by invention, learning, habituation or some other way—of new and more adequate unconscious "intelligent information processors." That is, as the experts cooperate in answering the call for help that some of them have posted on the GW blackboard, somehow a *new* expert is formed so that the GW is no longer needed for that particular challenge. This is neatly summarized in Baars' description of "the development of new human skills":

When people start learning some new task, doing it takes a great deal of conscious processing. Apparently many functionally separate processors need to cooperate in new ways in order to perform the task. Over time, however, simpler means are found for reaching the same goal, and control over the task is relegated more and more to a single specialized processor (which may take components from existing processors). Thus the distributed "committee system" should be surpassed in the normal course of events by the development of a new expert system.

(Baars 1988, p. 90)

That's really also the essence of my CC metatheory.

Now note below that Baars also speaks about "adaptation" in a way that gives further support to this idea about the possible equivalence of the theories.

The key step in deliberate learning is to become conscious of precisely what is to be learned. Doing this is sufficient for learning to take place...Thus consciousness seems to facilitate learning....

Finally, we are driven by our theory to a rather radical position about most learning. Very often, conscious involvement in learning leads to adaptation, which alters *the context of experience*; but we know that a change in context in its turn alters subsequent experience. It follows that learning alters the conscious experience of the learned material.

(Baars 1988, p. 214—author's italics)

5.5.2 Learning alters the experience of the material learned

If it is true that learning involves the generation of new contexts, and if contexts shape and bound new conscious experiences, it follows that we experience the same materials in a different way after learning.

(Baars 1988, p. 215)

We have argued that all conscious contents must be informative in that they trigger widespread adaptive processes. Receiving specialists must feed back their interest in the conscious content, so that they join the coalition of systems that support it. This is Model 3. It serves to put a conscious experience in a temporal context, described as the "adaptive cycle." All conscious experience, it is argued, involves a stage of adaptation in which a defining context has been accessed, so that the conscious information can be understood; but not all degrees of freedom have been determined. Consciousness occurs during the stage where the remaining uncertainty in the defining context is being reduced. After that point, adaptation has taken place, and repetition of the same input will not result in a conscious experience. There is thus an intimate connection between consciousness, adaptation, information, reduction of uncertainty, redundancy, and context.

Information that fades from consciousness does not disappear; rather, it serves to constrain later conscious experiences. It may become part of a new unconscious context, within which later experiences are defined. One implication is that every event is experienced with respect to prior conscious events...

The more information we must adapt to, the longer we need to be conscious of the material in order to create new contexts for dealing with it; and the more new contexts we create, the more our subsequent experiences will be reshaped. This suggests an unconventional view of learning and development. Namely, learning becomes a matter of developing contexts that cause us to experience the same reality in new and different ways....

Thus we are compelled to view even a single conscious experience as part of a dynamic developmental process of learning and adaptation. Increasingly it seems that the system underlying conscious experience is our primary organ of adaptation.

(Baars 1988, p. 221)

So it looks very much as if the two theories are largely equivalent in basic ideational architecture. They seem, at least, to clearly point in the same direction.

VI. On Span of Consciousness

My key question, as I probe into the implications of this theory of consciousness more deeply, will concern just how the "global workspace" situation works with regard to my "segmentation" idea. If processors are kept apart, divided into subgroups that do not interact with each other, how does this affect the possibilities for problem solutions? The *size* of the cabal—the *simultaneity* of interactions—should be crucial. But is it? And if so, exactly how and why?

Perhaps this parallel is simple and obvious—so obvious that I didn't see it before! For if (as already noted) "conscious experience involves a *global workspace*, a central information exchange that allows many different specialized processors to interact" (Baars 1988, p. 43), then the *inclusiveness* of this information exchange may be crucial. If "[together], several specialists may perform better than any single processor can" (Baars 1988, p. 87); if such cooperation among specialists is especially useful when the problem "does not have a known algorithm for its solution" (Baars 1988, p. 89); and if "[the] global workspace architecture is designed precisely to allow resolution of ambiguity by unpredictable knowledge sources" (Baars 1988, pp. 92-3), then affirmation is thereby given to the importance—for arriving at more optimal resolutions that may require the generation of new algorithms—of keeping consciousness most open to multiple problem dimensions, and also open to knowledge sources the relevance of which could not previously have been predicted.

VII. Summary and Conclusions

1. Comparison of Baars' (1988) "global workspace (GW) theory" of consciousness with the independently constructed "continual creation (CC) metatheory" (Atkin 1992) shows them to be very similar in principle and implications—perhaps equivalent. The terminological differences between them, though considerable, may be of little or no real significance. (But this needs further study.)

2. In both theories, *adaptive modifications* in the dynamic structure of a matrix (or network) of intercommunicating processors (modular automatisms, schemata, etc.) is the fundamental correlate of consciousness. In GW theory "conscious experience is *informative*—it always demands some degree of adaptation" (Baars 1988, p. 184). CC metatheory says that "consciousness enters when the activated mechanisms are at that moment undergoing essential structural modifications that are altering their laws of operation..." and that "the inner structure that is thus re-organizing itself is the organism's dynamic (predictive) internal model of itself-in-its-world."[53]

3. From the evidence on consciousness Baars derives "only five necessary conditions for conscious events: global broadcasting, internal consistency, informativeness, access by a self-system, and perceptual or quasi-perceptual coding" (1988, p. 364). These conditions are generally consistent with the implications of CC metatheory on how the whole system of A[sw] (equivalent to the GW system of contexts) develops (*evolves*) through the individual's conscious experience.

---

53 From 4th essay in *Section 2*, "➔Conscious Beyond Mechanism (Shifting a Paradigm)."

4.   The theories seem to differ mainly as follows:

(a) In GW theory the adaptive changes take place in a "global workspace" that is, first of all, "a central information exchange that allows many different specialized processors to interact" (Baars 1988, p. 43) so that what we are *experiencing* is the communicative interaction within the "global workspace" of these "processor" experts; however, in CC metatheory what we are experiencing is an "inner structure that is...re-organizing itself" and that is "an evolving virtual machine...that is the ongoing product of the brain's neural networks."[54]

(b) In GW theory an event that is conscious is informative, meaning that it is "a *demand* for adaptation" (Baars 1988, p. 184; my emphasis); while in CC metatheory an event that is conscious is one in which accommodation—which is the means of adaptation—*is taking place*.

5.   I conclude that the two theories are very close though expressed in different metaphorical and terminological systems, and in fact might be very nearly equivalent in basic structure—a conclusion I find highly significant since it means (i) that much of the experimental research data that Baars cites in support of his GW theory should equally well give support to main ideas of CC metatheory; and (ii) that the neurophysiological correlates that he and Jim Newman have inferred for GW theory (e.g., Baars & Newman 1994; Newman, Baars & Cho 1997; Baars, Newman & Taylor 1998) should serve also as underpinnings for CC metatheory.

What is now most important for me to realize, however, is that the direction to pursue need not involve a decision *between CC metatheory and GW theory* but rather will be further exploration of ways to combine the *best* (most pertinent) of each into some new, still more inclusive way to account for our awareness. Note that this may be understood as work toward attaining a *new and higher holarchic level for understanding of consciousness.*

==<<((([]||[]))>>==(((\[^]/\[^]))==<<(((\[^]|_|[^]))>>==(((\[^]/\[^]))==<<((([]||[]))>>==

---

54   Again, from 4th essay in *Section 2*, "➔ Conscious Beyond Mechanism."

And the following short essay came to me shortly after the preceding:

→ IMAGINATION AND ANTICIPATION

I. Day and Night Experiencing: The Mind's Eye (Looking Into It)

I have been consciously observing and playing around with my *inner model of self and world*—my dynamic anticipator, which (by CC metatheory) I am always forming and modifying.

- I look at the scene before me, then close my eyes. I still *see* it—though less vividly and certainly.

- Now I'm walking along. I look at that tree-trunk I'll be passing on my left after a few more steps—then close my eyes as I keep walking. Look! With eyes closed I still see that tree-trunk, approaching me as I walk. And now, in this moment, it's come very close—is just to my left. I *see* it (with my eyes still closed) moving past over at my extreme left. I open my eyes. Yes! That's just about where it actually is!

And this experience is remarkably vivid. I can repeat it with many other objects—closing my eyes yet continuing to see each one and following how it changes its relation to me—its position in my inward visual world—as I move along. I even *see* it from a changing perspective, and its shape shifts as my viewpoint shifts. Remarkable! It's just about how I observe the same scene when I keep watching with eyes open.

- Also, when I look attentively at some such inward visual memory—at this dynamic inside-image of what's around me in the moment—I can attend to some particular bit of it and get a real (though a bit dim!) *qualia*, can *see* the blue color of that bit of a poster I had seen with my eyes a short while before.

So, qualia is *here now*, even though a bit dim, while I'm awake with eyes closed. But what about in sleep, during dreaming? Then—all I've heard and my own experience (including one episode of lucid dreaming) tell me—sensory experiencing is just the way it is in waking life. Then qualia are not faint or dim. Certainly, that presents a problem!

In a moment, though, I recall my thought about the perhaps crucial importance of *relative* intensities of input. Now, during the day, though I close my eyes my waking consciousness is impinged upon by many sources of sensory inflow other than my eyes (and even they are providing some sensation, for light goes through closed lids, and after-image stimuli also are still seen). Sounds bombard me, kinesthetic and skin sensation continues undiminished. There's taste and smell too, though I'm not attending to them. Compared to this barrage of sensation the "self-world predictor" (A[sw]) images and qualia are very faint, therefore (perhaps) hard to give much feeling of "reality" to. But in dreaming this is all changed, as in REM sleep all those other sources of sensation are also shut off—not just those from eyes.

Then—recently remembering another feature of dreaming—I wondered about the eye movements of REM sleep.

• I found that in waking with eyes closed I could easily shift attention to different parts of my "imaginary" visual world and "look around." So I made eye movements—it was very like doing the same with eyes open.

• Now (with eyes closed) I put my hand before me and move it. I clearly *see* its position and changing form!

Imagination? Or is this manifestation of movements of my "self-world predictor" (A[sw])—certainly that's a major component of my *imagination*).

How does an artist "see" that a dab of a certain clearly visualized *red* in just *this* spot on her canvas will change it in a way that she wants?

• I can look now at this monochrome screen and *imagine* a spot of yellow just above the cursor, covering some of the words. At moments, its color is really pretty bright (though I can't sustain that). Well (continuing to *imagine*), I think I'll get rid of the yellow smudge and put some green there with a red rim around it. And put a shining white spot in the middle—looks like a bull's-eye. Interesting! That red and green clash. And this is not just by language or symbolism—I do *see* it!

Certainly, I can see color in my mind's eye. Can't you?

In fact, looking up now, I can *see* what this wall in front of me would look like if I painted it blue! Is that not a *real* blue qualia? It's certainly much fainter than the one I'll see after I've actually painted the wall, but is it not, nevertheless, really an experience of *blue*? That seems like *qualia* to me—just a little down in intensity because it's almost drowned out by other more intense qualia evoked by my sense organs.

And anyone in design or engineering knows how one can and does build virtual structures, virtual machines—doing it all the time: Visualizing them; constructing them "in one's head." Now, are these *visions* bereft of any qualia? Certainly, the same structures or machines, if "seen" in a dream, would be vividly visual with *lots* of qualia. But while waking? Again, I postulate that it's mainly a matter of *relative intensity*. Ordinarily, when I'm up and around, my delicate, fluid *inside* imagery will be almost totally overwhelmed by my strong, vivid, insistent *out-side* impressions...(And in relation to this, I know that—though I haven't hunted them down—one can find reports of dream-like and other imaginal phenomena during perceptual deprivation experiments, including those of the "Ganzfeld" type.)

II. Further Exploration

But now, how does the "creation" part of CC metatheory fit in with these thoughts?

- World and self are ever changing—each nested within the other.

- Got to keep making up my mind. That's what I'm doing every moment as I live—at least if I'm awake. Do it also when I sleep, at least during the REM episodes.

- Where am I going? Can't tell, if I don't know where I am! And if I didn't know where I was in previous moments, I'm not very likely to know where I am now. So it's all very simple—just keep right on mapping! Is there a sensory inflow now? Well—***map it***!

Fully-detailed anticipation of my *next* moment's total web of momentary relationships can only be as full and detailed as my A[sw] is in *this* moment. Therefore, to be continually anticipating with accuracy I must be always bring as much detail as I can into my A[sw]. So that's what I'm doing right now—and in every moment: I'm using all sensory inflows (in combination with motoric re-afference and inflow from all ongoing action-choice processes) to elaborate all those regions of my A[sw] that are directly relevant to my presently ongoing action-choice processes. (This is, I believe, another way of talking about those processes that in the past have been labeled short-term memory or working memory.)

- How can I process what I will be seeing in coming moments? Through anticipations based upon what I am seeing in this moment.

- Therefore: The more I see *now*, the more I will see *next*. Build up the *truth* of this moment's details—to gain access to more of the next moment's. To anticipate what will happen I must see what's happening! Build the map, make it more adequate—*improve it every moment.* Then it will help me better to know *where* and *how* to go. See where you **are!** How can you know where you're going if you don't know where you are?

• Thus "be present in the moment" is very good advice. Be mindful!

• Mind is always asking "Where am I?" Mind wants to know "What's happening?" Because the better its answers to those "now" questions, the better it can anticipate "What's coming next?"—and the better it can come to decisions on just "What action to take next?"

O.K.—maybe that's the story on how I experience my ongoing story of being-in-the-world while doing, sensing and perceiving in wakefulness. It's the CC metatheory idea of accommodative modification of my A[sw] to resolve *external* incoherencies. But what of the stories I experience—apparently with equal vividness—while dreaming? Here in REM sleep, with sensory inflow almost entirely blocked, the story cannot be driven by external incoherencies.

So my dreaming during the night must—like my day-dreaming and other "thinking"—be driven by *internal* incoherencies. Why then the apparent difference between night dreaming and waking thought, if both are so similar in their evoking sources? For now in waking a great deal of my thought processes are concerned with planning, problem-solving—with asking and answering questions concerning those plans and problems. But in dreaming, isn't the main thing some ongoing experienced story?

Well, maybe. But all those kinds of thinking are also often important during dreaming. It's just that they are imbedded in a stream of doing-experiencing that is very like the "day-dreaming" I may accomplish during waking with the difference that now, in the absence of any *competing* sensory or motor signals from a different flow of happenings, this dreaming is experienced as "real."

```
==<<(([]||[]))>>==((([^]/\[^]))==<<((([^]|_|[^]))>>==((([^]/\[^]))==<<(([]||[]))>>==
```

➜ *Brief note on pertinent robot research*

Can the sorts of phenomena I've been writing about be modeled in an engineering laboratory? I came across a report (Tani 1998) on robot-learning experiments suggesting ways to account for properties of conscious and unconscious mind through neural network modeling. The described cognitive robot seems a significant advance toward biologically-relevant neural network (NN) systems to simulate research data on consciousness (e.g., see Baars 1998, 1997)—and also explain our own subjective experiences functioning as *acting* and (sometimes) *aware* selves. I am particularly captivated by Tani's modeling because in the late '60s I had developed schemes (on paper only) for systems with some very similar architectural features to those of Tani's model. The impetus for my modeling had come out of my eye-movement research, the results of which pushed my ideas about brain function in a direction very close to the one Tani has taken in his own very fascinating work.

I. Tani's Neural Network Findings

The results of Tani's (1998) robot learning experiments were summed up thus:

> A neural network model consisting of multiple modules is proposed, in which the interactive dynamics between the bottom-up perception and the top-down prediction are investigated. Our experiments with a real mobile robot showed that the incremental learning of the robot switches spontaneously between steady and unsteady phases. In the steady phase, the top-down prediction for the bottom-up perception works well when coherence is achieved between the internal and the environmental dynamics. In the unsteady phase, conflicts arise between the bottom-up perception and the top-down prediction; the coherence is lost, and a chaotic attractor is observed in the internal neural dynamics....we draw the conclusion that (1) the structure of the 'self' corresponds to the 'open dynamic structure' which is characterized by co-existence of stability in terms of goal-directedness and instability caused by embodiment; (2) the open dynamic structure causes the system's spontaneous transition to the unsteady phase where the 'self' becomes aware.
>
> Tani 1998, p. 516 (from abstract)

Note how this is remarkably similar to what I proposed in **Section 2** on my general metatheory of consciousness. Though the terminologies and some aspects of the conceptual structures differ considerably, the overall picture has remarkable parallels. And this picture is generally close also to that projected by Baars (1988— see above essay "➔The Primacy of Self-Organizing Structural Transformation").

II. An Elaboration of Tani's Predictability Measure

So, I'm particularly interested in Tani's postulation (and use in his architecture) of a *"predictability measure"* or *PM* (p. 328) that may guide the organism in its moment-to-moment choice of its strategy of attending. But I suggest a further elaboration of his proposal. To attain greater precision I would modify Tani's proposal of guidance by a continually-updated PM to a more complex idea of two PMs—one a *"local* PM," and the other a *"global* PM." The immediate purpose of a particular action I am taking will be to modify and/or control some particular, relatively small set of variables—and the "local PM" will refer to (measure) the actual success of that relatively simple anticipation. But there are also far larger, long-range effects of my action that may relate to a much wider set of variables. Have I succeeded in predicting much of this—of these larger long-range effects? My failure to do that could be indicated by a relatively low value of a "global PM."

That last kind of short-sightedness is clearly a world-wide epidemic; principle source of world's problems—as well as of our individual sufferings. So the modified concept (*"global* PM") I find to be a very good one—one that may be worth developing, generalizing and applying far beyond the modeling project in which Tani (1998) cogently presented it. Specifically I hope that the *"predictability mea-sure"* will become even more important and useful when refined as I've suggested with the local and global differentiation.

==<<(((\[\]||\[\]))>>==(((\[^\]/\\[^\]))==<<(((\[^\]|_|\[^\]))>>==(((\[^\]/\\[^\]))==<<(((\[\]||\[\]))>>==

~~On some Social and Ethical Implications

And now, what can all this mean for possibilities of moving towards world peace? Clearly inferences about consciousness can not only be pertinent to depth psychology but also can lead us to glimpse ways we can address some of the world's more intractable social problems. Implicitly obvious in the above-described CC metatheory of consciousness (**Section 2**) are some very fundamental hints to help us move in that direction.

> The following discussion was a conference presentation (given at the 2nd conference "*Toward a Science of Consciousness*," in Tucson, AZ, April 1996) on—

→ Attention and Violence: How Each Moment of Consciousness Matters

Here I will attempt to develop, based on the "Continual Creation" (CC) metatheory[G] (Atkin 1992, 1994)[55], a view of mind and consciousness that may begin to better illuminate our daunting problems with violence and evil.

A Glimpse Ahead

The argument to be presented will be straightforward, saying in effect that what we don't look at, we will not see—and what we don't see, we can harm without knowing it. That is, it's about **dangers of unappreciated blindness**. It runs like this:

> **Consciousness is the adaptive evolution of mind**—the ongoing self-organizing reconstruction of mind's predictive abilities (Atkin 1992, 1994).[45] At another level, **the function of consciousness is to reduce disorder (entropy) by resolving incoherencies.**

> **There are different levels of order, different *structural levels*.** (A reasonable null hypothesis is that there is no upper limit to structural levels).

G   As already noted, this symbol after a technical term means it may be looked up in the *Glossary* at the end of the book.

55   See two essays of the preceding section, **Section 2** ("→On consciousness: What is the Role of Emergence" and "→Conscious Beyond Mechanism")—see also "CC metatheory" in the *Glossary*.

Each higher level *includes* and *supervenes over* those beneath (Sperry 1980, Cooper 1995).

Mind's theory of world-dynamics is a multi-level structure. Thus it predicts phenomena at various structural levels, but it cannot predict phenomena at structural levels above the highest level that its multi-level theory maps. This limitation affects every kind of cognitive construction, whether it's the social construction of scientific theory or the individual construction of mind.

A **cognitive enterprise** will not rise to a structural level that is higher than that implicit in the set of observed variables by which its construction is being guided. The lower the dimensionality of that set of variables, the lower the structural level that can be mapped by the resulting theory.

Thus any "**simplification strategy**"—one that restricts the dimensionality of the attended variables in order to simplify the task of problem solving—will necessarily exclude higher structural levels from the theory and from mind's comprehension. The unavoidable consequence is that predictive abilities—though perhaps sharpened and speeded for phenomena at lower structural levels—are degraded for those at higher levels. The resulting increased incoherence between predictive theory and phenomena is a source of entropy.

Violence can be one symptom of this cognitive deficit. Violence is breakdown of order—an increase of entropy. But violence is specific to level—it is relative to structural level: Actions not guided by structure of level n may disrupt structure at that level. Thus, in relation to level n they may be "violent."

However, destruction of n-level structure will also disrupt higher-level structure. So, n-level violence destroys order at and above level n but not below. A "low-level" violence (e.g., murder or war) can destroy all levels of structure, while a higher-level violence (e.g., emotional cruelty or subservience to experts) will leave lower levels intact. Thus, the higher the structural level of violence, the less order is destroyed—so *we can lessen the destruction by opening our attention to higher orders of structure.*

Therefore how we habitually *pay attention* has great consequences. The Cartesian strategy for raising the speed and efficiency of problem solving cuts the problem up into successive segments, each of lower dimensionality. This gives us great power to control a few focal variables—but at the same time (though we may not notice!) we lose sight of much higher-order structure and thus bring on vast epidemics of unanticipated *side effects* (or "negative externalities"). Raised levels of violence can be one of those unfortunate results. Should we not protect ourselves from such surprises by **broadening the habitual span of our attention**?

That was a preview of what will now be presented in greater detail, starting first with important implications of CC metatheory of consciousness:

I. Levels of Order (Nested Realities)

A. Consciousness Creates and Integrates Mind

(1) **Consciousness is Meta-Mind**
Mind's automatisms are created by consciousness. Mind is a deterministic web of dynamic automatisms—a great web of *functions* (or of *schemas* [Neisser 1976]; *agents* and *agencies* [Minsky 1986]; *modules* or *processors* [Baars 1988]; etc.)—that can be described and explained by reductionistic methods. But in relation to the mind-level, consciousness is a meta-level.

(2) **Each is the Source of the Other**
Mind is the necessary matrix of consciousness; for *consciousness* appears when mind requires correction. Thus we have what might be termed a "paradox of reciprocal priority": Though consciousness arises within mind, it at the same time is prior to mind. For it is consciousness that creates and changes mind; mind's *evolution* **is** consciousness.

(3) **Opposite Effects upon Systemic Entropy**
It is proposed that predictive incoherencies of mind are a component of systemic *entropy*, so that an increase in mind's predictive incoherencies is an increase in entropy. But conscious *accommodation*[G] (Atkin 1994)[56] heals mind's structural rifts—modifies the *structure*[G] of its mechanisms so that their incoherent actions become coherent.[57] Thereby *consciousness creates negentropy* (or "syntropy," Szent-Gyoergyi 1974), reducing incoherence by modifying the unconscious web of predictive mechanisms to give a more ordered relationship between parts of the larger system.

(4) **Mind Metaphor—*Unconscious Mind* is to *Consciousness* as *Technician* is to *Scientist***
From the perspective of CC metatheory there is a close analogy between *unconscious* mind and a "finished" science—finished in the sense that its

---

56 This is 4th essay in **Section 2**, "➔Conscious Beyond Mechanism (Shifting a Paradigm)."

57 See 4th essay in **Section 2**, "➔Conscious Beyond Mechanism (Shifting a Paradigm)"; also last essay in that section, "➔Reflections on Order and Disorder"—especially its subsection "V. How Consciousness Might Create Order."

theoretical foundations are not at present undergoing any important modification. Main functions of both unconscious mind and science are to make predictions, and the continuing test of each is the accuracy of its predictions. That predictive accuracy of either will determine whether its operating principles can remain as they are. Creative restructuring—either of scientific theory or of mind's mechanisms—may only be needed when predictions are in error. Thus we might say that if we take the brain to be a vast, highly active and usually effective research organization, then *unconscious mind* is the whole roster of *technicians* (who industriously *apply* scientific theory but do not generate or modify it) together with their instruments, equipment and supporting administrative bureaucracy. *Conscious experiencing*—much more limited in scope but nevertheless crucially important for the mission of the research organization—is the group of directing *scientists* who are *creating* and improving the theoretical structures, *reconstructing* predictive theories to better their predictive adequacy.

B. Higher-Order Structure

(1)　Levels—*Inclusion* and *Supervenience*
The most efficient, economical way to describe our experience and to map our knowledge of *reality* will be a nested sequence of maps—an upwards progression of more complex and more inclusive levels. We see *causality* in the regularities of phenomena within and between levels. Of particular interest are downward causal links—the causal influences of *higher-level structures* upon their lower-level component parts. Here the primary relationships are those of *inclusion* and of *supervenience*—each higher level *includes* and *supervenes over* those beneath.

(2)　Orders of Structure—*Dimensionality*
Different "*orders of structure*"[G] can be defined in terms of their dimensionality—i.e., in terms of the size of the set of variables required to specify them. Thus, at the simplest level will be those structural characteristics that can be fully revealed by relations between the fewest numbers of variables. These will define a relatively simple, locally definable level of structure. Other structural characteristics will be revealed only in relations between a larger number of variables and therefore remain concealed if our data-set is of too small dimensionality. The idea is that *it takes more variables to reveal higher-order structure*, for it is structure of higher *dimensionality*.

(3) Higher-Order Variables
Of course, it gets a little more complex. When a particular set of variables is thought to be predictively useful, some function of those variables will commonly be used to define a new *higher-order* variable. Then relations between (a smaller number of) such higher-order variables will define the higher-order structure of this new level and will be used to describe and predict the phenomena of this level.

(4) Role of Higher-Order Structure in Prediction
These generalizations apply equally well to scientific theory-construction and to the activities of conscious mind as the functional analogy between them[58] is so close. But something more is also required: For both of them, if we are to more fully predict the behavior of a particular local structure x, we need to understand more than that structure itself—we need also to know and understand the encompassing higher-order structure Z of which that particular structure x is a part.[59] (That is a consequence of the supervenient control that the encompassing structure Z has over structure x.)

(5) Invisibility of Causes
The implication of supervenience therefore is that I can't understand very much of what's going on—what's happening to me, around me, and within me—if I don't recognize the effects of higher-order structure. And it is certain that I don't, for we cannot know how much structure lies beyond our awareness—how much beyond our present awareness and how much, perhaps, forever beyond our awareness.

II. Costs of Cartesian Strategies

A. Why Constrict Attention?

(1) Segmenting[G] Reduces Dimensionality
When I segment my problem the data-set relevant to each segment is smaller than that of the problem taken as a whole. In effect, segmenting allows me to contract the dimensionality of the problems I must tackle. Thus I can tackle each segment of my larger problem with a simpler (lower-order) theory than I would need for the problem taken as a whole.

---

58 See subsect. *I. A.(4)*, above.

59 Small x indicates the particular local structure; large (capital) X then symbolizes the larger encompassing higher-order structure of which small x is part.

G See my usage of this term in ***Glossary*** (back of book).

(2) Segmenting Degrades Predictive Power

But this simplification has a cost: When I've segmented my problem, it will mean that my solution cannot take into account any orders of structure above those accessible in the individual segments. So this is the central point: If I segment my process of problem-solution, then I inevitably degrade the quality of the predictions I will be able to make. I may reach a solution more rapidly and more easily—but it will be, over all, a less powerful solution.

(3) Invisibility of Most Segmenting Effects

By segmenting the problem—dividing it into subproblems of lower dimensionality—I unavoidably lose access to much higher-order structure. This "blindness" to the particularities of higher-dimensional structure is ordinarily accompanied by an inability to even conceive of its existence—by obliviousness to its possibilities.

B. Other Aspects of Constriction

(1) Segmenting Speeds Theory-Making but Impoverishes Theories

The loss of access to higher-order structure that results from segmenting will be reflected in the theory-apparatus that I use for making predictions. Since my theory does not need to account for any levels of structure that are beyond those I can see in the data against which I am testing it, the structural level of my theory need not be higher than that. That is, the inclusiveness and complexity of the theory need not be greater than that of the data set.

(2) Segmenting Constricts Freedom (Free Will)

The freest choice will be the choice that is least dominated by lower-level influences. And the more globally inclusive the determinants of my choice, the greater the freedom with which that choice is made. Since segmenting strategies of attention lower the level of structure that can be accessed by perceptual/cognitive processes, they correspondingly lower the level of freedom with which choices can be made.

III. Violence and Power

A. How Constriction Hurts

(1) Inattention to "Negative Externalities"

If attention is focal, and awareness of the (predicted and actual) effects of an act is restricted to a very small set of attended criterion variables (say, one or two), then there will be no constraints from unwanted effects on other criterion variables—there will be no such constraints because no other criterion variables are being monitored. It is exactly this that makes it possible to satisfy the few criterion variables with seeming ease and rapidity. Thus sustained but very narrow attention can be powerful in finding a problem solution that is highly effective in lowering *local* entropy, but that is also powerfully effective in regions *outside those that were attended to* in ways that can be extremely effective in raising entropy. Those latter effects are the solution's *"negative externalities."*

(2)   Violence as Contracted Consciousness
It will be assumed now that *unconscious mind is necessarily without conscience.* Why? Conscience requires *empathy*, and empathy must be conscious. Thus unconscious mind will stop at nothing so long as some mechanical sequence—e.g., some set of *algorithmic* rules of procedure—is effectively evoked by the circumstances. Empathy is a deep and open-ended exploration of consequences. Only consciousness can fully explore consequences and then direct actions in accord with foundational values. Thus it is smallness of consciousness—and gaps in consciousness—that make violence possible. *Mind-closure*^{G} *generates the fragmentation of consciousness that provides fertile soil for violence and therefore for "evil."*

B. Exclusion & Temptation

(1)   An Extension
Here is one direction that may lead toward that increase in precision. Using a *multi-dimensional space* metaphor for *mind* and *consciousness*, two "fundamental questions" (**question #1** & **question #2**) might be stated thus: **Question #1** asks *"what is mind's (or worldview's) dimensionality?"* And **question #2** asks *"what are the usual dimensionalities of conscious experience?"*

Up till now, the mind-closure about which I've been speaking has been **global** (that is it has eliminated *all outside* of some defined boundary). But mind-closure can also be **local** (eliminating only specific fields or algorithms).[60] So to those two questions that focus *generally* and *globally* on what **can** occur, a third (**question #3**) can be added to focus upon what *specifically* and *locally* **can't** occur. That is, this **question #3** asks *"are there any dimensional subsets that are always excluded from consciousness?"* Any affirmative answers to this question will be telling us about certain *particular characteristics* of mind or

---

60   See *"Closure* and *non-closure"* in **Glossary**.

consciousness and will in general be relevant to study of fixed ideas, of unexamined presuppositions—of *ideologies*.

(2) Unchanging Invisibilities

What we're really talking about here is *kinds of blindness*: At the *mind-structure* level (that of **question #1**), the patterns of exclusion referred to in answers to **question #3** are *preserving my presuppositions*. Those unexamined presuppositions that get built into my worldview have powerful effects on the way I live—my motivations, my likes and dislikes, values and ethics, the skills I develop, etc. But the *exclusions* referred to in **question #3** are also reflexively disabling—they are keeping me from becoming conscious of them. So all those presuppositions remain unexamined and therefore unchanging. But since it is the frozen assumptions and unchanging presuppositions that are preventing any growth in the connectivity and coherence of my whole mind,[61] the local areas of mind-closure for which the third "fundamental question" is probing can also generate *"the fragmentation of consciousness that provides fertile soil for violence and therefore for 'evil'."*[62] So though local power may be local increase in order, the global cost is increased disorder.

(3) Entropic Cost of Local Power

We'd like to slow that decay. Thus it is natural to ask: If consciously created but almost entirely unconscious mind-mechanisms undergo inescapable entropic degradation, can the consequences of this disordering tendency be minimized? Bringing the degrading mechanisms into the field of conscious awareness should, by hypothesis, modify and/or transform them in an entropy-reducing way. But if the degrading mechanisms are of great expanse *in toto*, and only a small region of this expanse is brought into conscious awareness, then only a correspondingly small reduction of entropic degradation will thereby be achieved.

The more expansive and broadly inclusive the strategy of attention, the better the control of entropic degradation. A global and maximally receptive, responsive consciousness is the means for constructing a more unified, highly-ordered mind; that is, for maximizing both the generation of negentropy in the present moment and the dynamic coherence of the resulting structure. But (driven by our culture via our closest relationships) we have developed a *structure of closures* that effectively blocks such motion toward greater unity.

---

61 See above subsection **I.A. Consciousness Creates and Integrates Mind**—especially its part *(3) Opposite Effects upon Systemic Entropy.*

62 This is again I'd said just above in subsection *III.A.(2)* "Violence as Contracted Consciousness."

IV. In the Grip of the Vortex

A. Societal Disease, Individual Prescription

(1) Comprehending Self and Other

This is all tremendously complicated by those close connections between violence and *power*—and further, by how all stays frozen in the absence of consciousness. Exactly because negative externalities in general and violent actions in particular are the product of unconscious mechanisms *unmodulated by conscious experiencing*, the perpetrator truly does not know what s/he has done. Thus *the lives of "victims" become externalities.* This situation, of primary drives by unconscious automatisms, thereby makes for great complications in situations of social conflict.

Now, should I not say that I lack self-knowledge exactly to the degree that I unconsciously remain under the control of unexamined presuppositions and remain almost totally unaware of my fixed ideas, my ideologies? So mostly I don't know myself—and it's highly unlikely I'll be able to know any other person any better than I know myself. But the problem is not just that I don't know myself and therefore don't know the other. *The terrible difficulties arise primarily because I don't know that I don't know.* Therefore—with total incomprehension of my lack of access both to the other's motivations and to the other's perceptions—it is inevitable that I will completely misinterpret the other's actions. And of course the other, being in exactly the same pickle, is bound to similarly misinterpret my actions. Such mutual misinterpretation is a positive feedback situation with disastrous potentialities. Thus, *wars may be the necessary endpoints of societal domination by unconscious automatisms insufficiently modulated by conscious accommodation.* The explosions thus generated can be understood in terms of a positive-feedback escalation of map-territory incoherence—the new entropy variable suggested by CC metatheory.

(2) Violence and Responsibility

This story has clear implications for questions about *personal* responsibility. It says that the responsibility of the person who commits an evil act does not lie in their having made that choice—there was **not** such a *choice*. One who commits a violent act will, in general, have neglected both to anticipate and to experience the full range of consequences of the act. Rather, the person's responsibility is for the prior and present *retreats from choosing* that have predetermined the choicelessness of the evil act in question. For those retreats must have been—over time, if not in the instant of acting—subject to particular choices. If evil is an outcome of continuing choices to **avoid** choosing, then *a violent act is more an act of omission than of commission.* It follows that **to reduce violence, increase consciousness.**

B. Personal Implications

(1) Awareness

This issue of personal responsibility applies directly to me. For the single implication of CC metatheory that can most penetrate and transform every moment of my awareness is this: *Right now, and in every moment, I am constructing myself.* It is an understanding that requires that I take responsibility for who I am, and for all that I understand and do not understand. Of course, it works both ways: *My awareness now is largely determined by who I am; but who I am is the product of the history of my past moments of conscious awareness.* Nevertheless because every moment of awareness is creative and unpredictably new, not only is the course of my mind's evolution continually constrained by its structural history, but also it is wide open to conscious choices which permit continual and free shifts in the direction of its evolution.

(2) Responsibility

This is a vast increase in my *awareness of responsibility.* Once I have begun to be aware of the deep consequences of my attention-strategies and therefore to understand the implications of my real though limited conscious control over their moment-by-moment implementation, then my responsibility for exerting or not exerting this control—and for *how* I exert it—expands correspondingly. In the same way, *the responsibility of those who educate, inform and entertain is amplified since they exert their talents and energies to affect and shape many moments of their audience's attention, and thus are instrumental in channeling, at least to some degree, the way many attentive minds are evolving—and to what they will evolve.*

V. Postview of Attention and Violence

There are three implications of CC metatheory's fundamental axiom[63] that seem especially pertinent to the arguments that have been presented:

(1) *Mind,* which is postulated to be identical with the intricate dynamic network of our (mostly unconscious) behavior patterns, is the product of ongoing creation by consciousness.

---

63 See **Glossary,** "**Continual creation (CC) metatheory.**"

(2) The prerequisite for conscious access to higher-order structure is the simultaneous conscious awareness of the full set of variables/dimensions that are needed to generate structure at that level.

(3) Consciousness-contraction (e.g., by the Cartesian attention-strategy of *segmentation*) means that the dimensionality of conscious awareness is reduced. This in turn means (by point 2 above) that access to some levels of higher-order structure will be lost.

These implications derivable from CC metatheory lead directly to further generalizations concerning consciousness and violence: That *wars may be the necessary endpoints of societal domination by unconscious automatisms insufficiently modulated by conscious accommodation;* that therefore **to reduce violence, increase consciousness**; and finally that once I have begun to be aware of the deep consequences of my attention-strategies and therefore to understand the implications of my real though limited conscious control over their moment-by-moment implementation, then my responsibility for exerting or not exerting this control—and for *how* I exert it—expands correspondingly. (These last implications were summarized from the immediately preceding subsection *IV—"In the Grip of the Vortex"*).

I believe the aforementioned generalizations I derived from CC metatheory would not have followed from other theories or philosophies of consciousness. That's because a critical element in their derivation was the contention of CC metatheory that unconscious mechanisms of mind enter our awareness just when their structure is being transformed. This *transformative* requirement for consciousness is what's lacking from most other theories I've examined.[64] So if this unconventional CC metatheory of consciousness has such social and ethical consequences that could lead towards better ways for dealing with urgent human dilemmas, then this nascent exploration of its implications should be continued.

/~*~\/~*~\/~*~\/~*~\/~*~\/~*~\/~*~\/~*~\/~*~\/~*~\/~*~\/~*~\/~*~\/~*~\/~*~\/~*~\/

---

64 Regarding this lack in several other theories—those of Jaynes 1976, Klopf 1982, Bittista 1982, Dennett 1991, Johnson-Laird 1988, Calvin 1990 and Minsky 1988—see subsection IV.A. ("Has Something been Left out?") of the **Section 2** essay "➔ Further Thoughts About...(Atkin 1992)." However their were strong anticipations of this idea by Sperry (1980, 1991), and Baars also went far towards it—see the preceding essay "➔ The Primacy of Self-Organizing Structural Transformation: Can Consciousness Theories Converge?" on Baars' GW theory (which was found in many respects to closely parallel CC metatheory).

/~*~\/~*~\/~*~\/~*~\/~*~\/~*~\/~*~\/~*~\/~*~\/~*~\/~*~\/~*~\/~*~\/~*~\/~*~\/~*~\/

>>PREVIEW OF "SUMMING UP"

The initial essay (presented at "Toward a Science of Consciousness" conference in 1998) is entitled "→ **Being, Doing, Knowing—A Theoretical Perspective on Consciousness.**" It again goes over main themes dealt with in previous sections, showing how our understanding of consciousness is key to a larger paradigm of knowledge. Laying out an over-all framework for my present understanding it comes to the following tentative conclusions:

(I) To understand *world's over-all structure* I need the related concepts of *structural levels* and *downward causation*, and I need to look at the ways these concepts are used to map our world. World's basic structure then maps as a holarchy of multiple nested levels (Koestler 1978), each a holon constructed out of (and including) the holons of the level beneath in a way that yields downward causation as tautological necessity.

(II) My *mind* is a holarchic system of dynamic maps that anticipate my actions and their consequences. Thus, mind is predictive process, analogous to a predictive scientific theory.

(III) The *function of my consciousness* is postulated to be the reconstruction of my anticipatory maps, and the present structure of these maps (of my mind) is product of the total history of my consciousness.

(IV) *Freedom* (i.e., "free will") arises out of downward causation when my choice is determined from a higher level (thus by something *larger*) than the ordinary compulsions that are predictively modeled by my unconscious anticipatory automatisms. My choice may also be freed by non-algorithmic components in the accommodative^G restructuring that characterizes conscious volitional actions—a freedom far thinner than I know because (by my situation's logical structure) my awareness has no immediate access to its own depth. Finally, it is postulated that mind's action-choosing is inseparable from its effect-predicting.

(V) What can be known is relatively tiny; my *ignorance is inevitably vast yet invisible*. The complexity—the dimensionality—of my maps is necessarily limited because human cognitive capacities are limited. But if (as postulated) there is no upward limit to the dimensionality that would be required to exhaustively map all the world's levels of order, then the existence of levels higher than any we can know or imagine is *undeniable* and the human generation of complete predictions is in principle beyond reach. This perspective can reconcile free will with determinism. Conflict between the advocate of *free will* and that of *determinism* is unnecessary because each is correct even though their thoughts, problems, intentions and interests occupy different universes. *We can best enlarge our paradigm, opening it to further evolution and inclusion of seeming opposites, by probing and questioning our unconscious presuppositions.*

But where can that big picture point? First a very brief diversion ("**➔A couple of thoughts on Skinner**") suggesting how Skinner's mental laws could be modified through inversion to better help us in dealing with questions of *free will*.

This is followed by the final essay called "**➔Can that Big Picture Help with Mind and Violence?**" It's a short recapitulation exploring again what I feel to be important social and ethical implications of all the foregoing. First it tells again something of matters presented in the essay "**➔Reflections on Order and Disorder**" at the end of Section 2, then it repeats and carries a little further the thoughts of the essay at the end of *Section 3* (the 1996 conference presentation "**➔Attention and Violence: How Each Moment of Consciousness Matters**").

This last essay will present the following arguments:

According to CC metatheory[G], mind is a vast web of predictive mechanisms, and it is consciousness that forms and reforms this web. As described in the 5th essay of *Section 2* ("**➔Reflections on Order and Disorder**"), conscious accommodation is modifying mechanisms so that their incoherent actions become coherent, thus generating more ordered relationships between parts of the larger system and thereby *creating syntropy*. But further (as put forth at end of the preceding section in the earlier essay "**➔Attention and Violence**") violence is a manifestation of decaying order—of the rise in entropy to which all mechanical systems are subject. Unconscious mind—a vast network of automatisms—cannot escape such degradation. Specifically, *disorder and violence can arise where there are gaps in consciousness*. The smaller the conscious mind, the less protection it provides against the disordering violence so easily generated by automatic mechanisms.

Thus fragmentation of consciousness provides fertile soil for violence. Certainly, sustained but very narrow attention can be powerful in finding a problem solution that is highly effective in lowering *local* entropy; however, this local lowering will ordinarily be accompanied by *global* increases. For the more constricted the frame of problem solution, the greater the likelihood that entropy will be raised—through *negative externalities*—in regions outside those that were attended to. However because these are kept outside the field of consciousness they continue unnoticed and therefore unabated. The responsibility of the person who commits an evil act does not lie in his/her having made that choice—there

---

G   See this term in *Glossary*.

was *not* a *choice!* Rather, the person's responsibility is for the prior and present **retreats** *from* **choosing**.

Counter-movement, by which higher and more integrated levels of order can arise, comes only through the emergence of new and different automatisms. CC metatheory says that this negentropy-generating emergence of new structure *is con-sciousness*. So again, it follows that **to reduce violence, increase consciousness**.

How? Greater precision in understanding the vicissitudes of consciousness should help us answer that question.

And at the very end comes "→**Finally—Main Points in Short**" listing nine summarizing statements from preceding parts of the book.

==<<((([]||[]))>>==((([^]/\[^]))==<<((([^]|_|[^]))>>==((([^]/\[^]))==<<((([]||[]))>>==

SUMMING UP

Finally this last section will present one longer and two short essays that recapitulate the main thoughts of the preceding three sections.

First is another conference presentation ("Toward a Science of Consciousness," Tucson 1998) in which now I'm truly trying to see the biggest picture. (As befits a *Summing Up*, some thoughtful passages from earlier writings appear again here.)

→ *BEING, DOING, KNOWING—*
A THEORETICAL PERSPECTIVE ON CONSCIOUSNESS

>==((([^]/\[^])) (([^]/\[^]))==<

Introduction

Without ever going very deeply into academic philosophy, I've spent a long time probing the underpinnings of my own moment-by-moment subjective experience—thus bumping up against some of those "ultimate questions"—and now have a few thoughts that I can share. These are working papers. It is a personal perspective—gropings toward a more adequate and satisfying paradigm.

Originally I had entitled the paper "A Perspective on Known and Unknown Structure: Intuitions of a Worldview Framework." Its stance, while strongly questioning many tenets of Modernity, does not quite correspond with what has been labeled "Post-modernism." Rather, it might perhaps be referred to as "Meta-modern" in that it includes all the positive assertions and contributions of Modernism, but by questioning and doubting many of that powerful paradigm's *negative* assertions—limiting beliefs that have made it a closed system—it opens up the Modern viewpoint and goes beyond it.

For me a main result of these explorations has been to strengthen and give further support to my understanding that our habitual attention-distribution strategies have serious consequences both for our own individual lives and for our effects upon others—right up to our effects upon our planet's prospects and the survival-options of all humanity. I see ever more urgently how constricted consciousness is the source of many kinds of violence and destruction. Striving to open, expand, deepen one's awareness in each moment is, metaphorically speaking, trying to *wake up!* I have found the necessary unawareness of being partially asleep to be a tremendous challenge—and this insight is now a driving force for me, a main incentive for my attempts to 'get this all together' in my understanding and to put it down in some sort of communicable written form.

So here's an over-all perspective—a framework of understanding—that I've arrived at. It is best introduced through *four primary questions* it attempts to answer.

QUESTIONS

I. What is world's over-all structure?

As we shall see, I've begun to think about this **ontological** question in terms of the concepts of levels of *structural order* and of *dimensionality*—as well as to give a fundamental place to the notion of *downward causation*.

II. How can I know world's structure?

The **epistemological** question then asks: "How can my *understanding* of the ontological question arise, and what supports it?" I've begun to look into this through the lens of a metatheory of consciousness that places the arising of awareness in the active restructuring of mind's mechanisms—the *transforming* of the mechanisms by which my mind anticipates the course and outcome of my actions and of my interactions with my world.

III. Can I relate causality to "free will"?

Does the wonderfully successful scientific disclosure of world's lawful predetermination allow place for any real freedom of choice? If it does, then how? Here (as with **Question I**) the idea of *levels* is again of fundamental importance as my understanding of downward causation assumes a central role—as does also the idea of algorithmic and non-algorithmic causation. Both of these are ideas that concern the reality and meaning of freedom. In addition, however, there is the question of scale: Even if freedom is *real*, is it big or small? (And in comparison with what?)

IV. Is limitless ignorance inevitable? And if so, why?

In dealing with this question I've begun to look toward a worldview that is totally open to the unknown and thus vastly larger than the one that I've left behind (which had rested confidently in the limiting presuppositions of modern *scientism*).

I believe that those four questions are a natural sequence of study. They are, in a sense, bivariate—i.e., they fit naturally into a two-by-two contingency table in which one dichotomy asks about *the structure of acting* vs. *the structure of knowing*, and the other dichotomy compares *what is possible with regard to predetermination and prediction* with *what is not possible with regard to predetermination and prediction*. In relation to our four questions, these two dichotomies interact as follows:

	With regard to *PREDETERMINATION & PREDICTION:* **What is** possible?	With regard to *PREDETERMINATION & PREDICTION:* **What is not** possible?
What is the *STRUCTURE* of **ACTING?**	I. What **is** world's over-all structure?	III. Can I relate **causality** to **free will?**
What is the *STRUCTURE* of **KNOWING?**	II. How can I **know** world's structure?	IV. Is **limitless** ignorance **inevitable?**—if so, why?

What are the two rows? The first line ("What is the structure of *acting*") deals with a perspective about doing, about causality, about the control of happenings, especially in the objective world of "externalities." This is the realm, in Ken Wilber's knowledge-map, of his **right-side** regions of *objective* knowledge (Wilber 1997). The second line ("What is the structure of *knowing*") deals with a perspective about the generation of understandings (e.g., how we can come to understand patterns of causality) that take place in the subjective world of "internalities." This is the realm, in Ken Wilber's knowledge-map, of his **left-side** regions of *subjective* knowledge (Wilber 1997).

And now the two columns? The left column ("With regard to predetermi-nation/prediction, what *is possible?*") is about how happenings can be predicted, about what predetermines them. The right column ("With regard to predetermination/prediction, what is **not** *possible?*") is about what in the world must remain fundamentally unpredictable, beyond full determination. In the sphere of our *volition* that question is central with regard to the meaning of freedom, of free will. And in relation to our *knowing* that right-column question about "what is not possi-ble?" points straight at its fundamental incompleteness—at what must remain beyond our knowledge.

So that shows a little about how those four questions relate to each other. But now can I actually move in the direction of answering? Here's a start:

ASSERTIONS

My attempts to sketch out a line of thought that yields some answers to these four questions involves the following assertions:

1— World's structure is multi-level—a **"holarchy"** in which each higher level includes and orders/coordinates those beneath. A reasonable null hypothesis is that there is no upper limit to structural levels.

2— **"Mind"** is a complex mapping—an automatic system of dynamic representa-tions—that models all that has been found to be predictable in the actions of the organism and its environment (its "world"). *Mind* may be analogized to a multi-level scientific theory that predicts phenomena at various structural levels.

3— **Consciousness** is the adaptive evolution of mind—is the ongoing self-orga-nizing reconstruction of mind's predictive abilities (Atkin 1992, 1994).[1] Awareness of world's higher-order structure is the emerging of higher-order mind-structure.

4— If this is an accurate picture of world-structure, the reality of **downward causation** becomes a logical necessity. Freedom then enters, as follows:

5— Freedom is a cognitive perspective. The freedom I feel and speak about as my "free will" ("FW") is free from the perspective of this presently-inhabited choice-level ("the action level") *in relation* to lower levels of order, in that it

---

1   See two essays in **Section 2** ("➔On consciousness: What is the Role of Emergence" and "➔Conscious Beyond Mechanism")—see also "CC metatheory" in the **Glossary**.

is not reductionistically determined by phenomena at or causal links from those lower levels.

6— But mind cannot predict phenomena at structural levels above the highest level that its multi-level theory maps. A cognitive enterprise will not rise to a structural level higher than that implicit in the set of observed variables by which the cognitive construction is guided.

7— This limitation affects every kind of cognitive construction, whether it's the social construction of scientific theory or the individual construction of mind. The lower the dimensionality of that set of variables, the lower the structural level that can be mapped by the resulting theory.

Now, some responses to the first of those four questions.

I. What Is World's Over-All Structure?

First of all, let us look at ways of understanding "levels" and "downward causation" so that we may then go on to use these concepts to better comprehend ourselves and our world. The following principles seem (to me) to be self-evident:

A. Higher-Order Structure

(1) *Levels—Inclusion and Coordinative Ordering*
The most efficient, economical way to describe our experience and to map our knowledge of *reality* will be a nested sequence of maps—an upwards progression of more complex and more inclusive levels. We see causality in the regularities of phenomena within and between levels. Of particular interest are downward causal links—the causal influences of higher-level structures upon their lower-level component parts. Here the primary relationships are those of *inclusion* and of *coordinative ordering*—each higher level includes and orders/coordinates those beneath.[2]

(2) *Orders of Structure—Dimensionality*
Different *orders of structure* can be defined in terms of their dimensionality— i.e., in terms of the size of the set of variables required to specify them. Thus, at the simplest level will be those structural characteristics that can be fully revealed by relations between the fewest numbers of variables. These will define a relatively simple, locally definable level of structure. Other structural

---

2   Here "ordering" and "coordinating" refer to downward causation—the causal influences of higher-level structure upon its lower-level components.

characteristics will be revealed only in relations between a larger number of variables, and therefore *remain concealed if our data set is of too small dimensionality.* The idea is that it takes more variables to reveal *higher-order structure[3] because higher-order structure is of higher dimensionality.*

(3)   *Higher-Order Variables*

Of course, it gets a little more complex. When a particular set of variables is thought to be predictively useful, some function of those variables will commonly be used to define a new *higher-order* variable. Then relations between (a smaller number of) such higher-order variables will define the higher-order structure of this new level and will be used to describe and predict the phenomena of this level. (Nevertheless, because of the high dimensionality of each single higher-order variable, the dimensionality of a level that is defined by only a few higher-order variables can be very large.)

B. Levels and Maps

But perhaps the situation is a bit more complex. Where exactly are these "levels" we've been speaking about? Are they out there in the world that we want to describe and understand? Or are they perhaps located in our systems of description—in the ways in which we attempt to understand our world.

With this latter possibility in mind, and wanting to briefly characterize the world-system, I first briefly consider how the concept of "levels" may be related to the concept of "mappings." Here is how I now see it:

(1)   *Levels are perspectives on one unitary world-system*

A *level* is not a thing. Therefore, different levels are not different things. Rather, they are in a sense different *aspects*—or *visions*, images, maps—of *one* "thing." This **one thing** is the total system.

(2)   *Levels belong to maps*

It is the *mappings* of this one indissoluble system that can be accomplished at different levels by focusing upon its different subsystems[4] and thus accounting only for specific subsets of variables. By using distinct mapping techniques and parameters we generate different map-levels. This means that the levels we

---

3   Note that when we here speak about the different orders or levels of structure we are really characterizing features of our maps—for when we define structural characteristics by relations between variables, we are speaking about a *mapping* of the studied system. See subsections B(1) and B(2), below.

4   "Subsystems" also are creations of the mapping process—but for convenience in communication they are here spoken of as given 'parts of the mapped territory.'

observe do not characterize the system, they characterize our *mappings* of the system; we ascribe levels to particular subsystems of the mapped system's structure[G] in accordance with the map-level that describes those particular subsystems.

(3) *World's high connectivity necessitates downward causality*

Thus, our *experience* is that different ways of mapping reveal different levels of structure. But since the mapped system is one indivisible structure of a depth surpassing our comprehension,[5] it is the singleness and interconnectedness of this unitary structure that instantiates all the observed paths of causality—every particular observable causal path is simply one tiny causal *linkage* abstracted from this dense mesh of interconnectedness.

(4) *Downward causality may be simpler than it has seemed*

If this is an accurate picture of world-structure, then the reality of downward causation becomes a logical necessity. By the *Structure-Causality Identity Postulate*[6] the observed (n+1)-level structure is identical with dynamic coherencies at level (n), and these dynamic coherencies are identical with "downward causation" from level (n+1) onto level (n).

Thus world is most comprehensively represented by a holarchic mapping (Koestler 1978; Wilber 1997) and to comprehend its behavior we need to use a concept of downward causality as a property of our mappings.

II. How Can We Know World's Structure?

But how can we come to know all this? How does the structure of mind relate to and reveal world structure? I am beginning to understand that this question brings us to whole new realms of complexities. After all, what is "*knowing*"? Obviously, it has to do with awareness, with consciousness. So what is that all about?

This question is not only about "knowing" in the present moment; it is also a developmental question about how we have come to know what we now know. Here's how I see it:

G Again, for the specific way in which this term is being used, see **Glossary** at the end of the book.

5 Is the structure infinitely 'deep'? There is no empirical basis for assuming that its depth is finite. So if some limit is not to be arbitrarily assumed, the null hypothesis is that it is infinite. See "Fundamental Holarchic assumption" and "No-End assumption" (in essay "➜Minimalist Basis for Expanding Understanding" in **Section 1**).

6 See 2nd essay in **Summing Up** section, "➜Something on Holarchic Structure and Downward Causation" (subsection "Downward Details; The Structure-Causality Identity Postulate").

A. Mind and Consciousness

First I'll give a very brief sketch of the perspective on mind and knowing that I have called the "continual creation (CC) metatheory of consciousness." It was so named because it rests upon the continual creation hypothesis that consciousness is ongoing emergent change whereby mind's predictive structure is transforming itself.[7]

In my usage *consciousness* corresponds with only a small subset of *mind*; most of mind remains beneath awareness—i.e., is unconscious. In CC metatheory I've related the terms "mind" and "consciousness" to each other in the following way:

- *Mind*, developed as an active web of anticipatory mechanisms, is the predicting process.

- *Consciousness* is the mind-modifying process of reorganizing/resetting the predicting structures so that their predictive actions are altered.

I have called these predictive structures of mind—this web of anticipatory mechanisms—the "self-world anticipator," to be abbreviated A[sw].[8]

- This perspective on mind and consciousness, though long neglected, is not entirely new.[9] Erwin Schrödinger, by a line of reasoning very like mine, arrived at essentially the same idea more than 30 years before. He wrote that "consciousness is associated with the learning of the living substance; its knowing

---

7   Originally, I came to this hypothesis after reading Abraham Joshua Heschel's theory of history (Heschel 1955, p. 210), in which he distinguishes lawful and basically repetitive *"processes"* from *"events"* which alter those laws and are new, unique transformative occurrences.

8   Formerly named (in my earlier writings) the 'self-world *model*' (or s-Wm). But the term is here shifted to emphasize the presumed central function of predicting or *anticipating*.

9   As previously noted (Atkin 1992; and see essay above in **Section 2**, "➔ On consciousness: What is the Role of Emergence") this alternative to the search for mechanisms was anticipated nearly a century ago by William James (1905), and more recently by D. M. MacKay (1982), Jean Piaget (1976), Karl Pribram (1976), Hans Flohr (1991), Israel Rosenfield (1992), and Allan Combs (1994)all of whom have published remarks implying that consciousness is meta-change, that it is not structure or mechanism but rather structural *change* and *modification* of mechanism that is fundamental for the development of consciousness. Further, the broad framework of this idea seems generally consonant with recent thinking about 'dissipative structures' (Prigogine & Stengers 1984) and *self-organizing systems* (Jantsch 1980; Maturana & Varela 1988). (There have been other anticipations of this idea about consciousness-but for reasons of brevity they will be cited elsewhere.)

how…is unconscious" (Schrödinger 1958, p. 105). Further, Jaynes (1976, pp. 6-8) recalls that this was a common idea[10] among psychologists at one time.

Now, for better understanding of this view on mind and consciousness, here's an illustration straight from my own professional concerns with education and research:

• **Mind metaphor**—*Mind is to Consciousness as Technician is to Scientist:*[11] From the perspective of CC metatheory there is a close analogy between *unconscious* mind and a "finished" science—finished in the sense that its theoretical foundations are not at present undergoing any important modification. Main functions of both unconscious mind and science are to make predictions, and the continuing test of each is the accuracy of its predictions. That predictive accuracy of either will determine whether its operating principles can remain as they are. Creative restructuring—either of scientific theory or of mind's mechanisms—may only be needed when predictions are in error. Thus we might say that if we take the brain to be a vast, highly active and usually effective research organization, then *unconscious mind* is the whole roster of *technicians* (who industriously *apply* scientific theory but do not generate or modify it) together with their instruments, equipment and supporting administrative bureaucracy. *Conscious experiencing*—much more limited in scope but crucially important for the mission of the research organization—is the group of directing *scientists* who are *creating* and improving the theoretical structures, *reconstructing* predictive theories to better their predictive adequacy.

So, from this perspective, my mind is busy generating and testing predictions concerning my relations with my world—how they are unfolding, what's going to occur next (what feedback I can expect), and also what the longer-range consequences of my actions are likely to be. It is proposed that mismatch between prediction and actual occurrence causes consciousness by causing restructurings of the predictive mind-mechanisms.

---

10 Jaynes himself rejects the idea as "Ridiculous!" Certainly, as Jaynes points out, many kinds of behavioral modification—which he puts under the headings of "the learning of signals, skills, and solutions" (p. 32)—take place in the absence of consciousness. But acquisition of such behaviorally-defined automatisms does not exhaust the meanings of "learning," or the ways that "predictable process may undergo a nonpredictable modification."

11 This paragraph was originally written for **Section 3** essay "→ Attention and Violence: How Each Moment of Consciousness Matters" presented at the "Toward a Science of Consciousness" conference two years before in 1996.

B. Consciousness Creates and Integrates Mind

Now I will introduce a few more terms and ideas that can help in discussing this view of mind and consciousness and will then consider further the relationship between them. First, the relevance of the Piagetian notions of "assimilation" and "accommodation":

(1) ***Mind***—*the "matrix" out of which consciousness arises*—***assimilates*** *moment-to-moment world-structure by actively anticipating it.*[12]
Mind is a deterministic web of dynamic automatisms—a great and highly active web of functions (or of schemas [Neisser 1976]; agents and agencies [Minsky 1988]; modules or processors [Baars 1988]; etc.)—that can be described and explained by reductionistic methods. It is hierarchically-ordered structure that acts to *anticipate* sensory information and other information fed back from actual event occurrences.

(2) ***Consciousness***—*arising by* ***accommodative*** *changes of mind*—is ***Meta-Mind.***
When actual feedback *differs* from mind's assimilatory predictions, the discrepancy (or "incoherence") between anticipation and actuality evokes *accommodative* modification of mind's structure, and that modifying is what we *experience.* That is, it is this accommodative creation and/or change of structure that (by CC metatheory) **is** *consciousness.* Thus, in relation to the *mind*-level, *consciousness* is a meta-level.

In short, consciousness is accommodation, and over time mind's automatisms are created by consciousness.

We see, then, that each is the source of the other—we have what might be termed a *paradox of reciprocal priority:* Mind is the necessary matrix of consciousness, for *consciousness appears when mind requires correction.* Yet, though consciousness thereby arises within mind, it at the same time is prior to mind, for it is consciousness that creates and changes mind; i.e., *mind's evolution is consciousness.*

Thus they are different but inseparable—two aspects of a single dynamic of evolutionary unfoldment.[13] And further, the relation between conscious and unconscious mind concerns their respective relations to time's arrow.

(3) *Opposite effects upon* ***systemic entropy***
Conscious accommodation heals mind's structural rifts (see Section 2 above, especially essay "➔Conscious Beyond Mechanism: Shifting a Paradigm")—modifies the structure of its mechanisms so that their incoherent actions

---

12　This usage of "assimilation" is in general accord with Piaget's; that by actively *anticipating* events, mind "*assimilates*" them.

13　Or—aspects of a single complex "process," in one common usage of that term.

become coherent. It is proposed that predictive incoherencies are a component of systemic entropy so that an increase in incoherencies is an increase in entropy. Thus consciousness creates syntropy,[14] reducing incoherence by modifying the unconscious web of predictive mechanisms to give a more ordered relationship between parts of the larger system.

1. How Might Brain Work This Way?

What kind of brain substrate could be matrix of such continual creation? This is *self-organization*, and self-organizing systems are everywhere (Jantsch 1980). They are non-linear systems, far from equilibrium—they are dissipative systems (Prigogine & Stengers 1984). They eat available energy, and in degrading it at the same time generate new kinds of order—generate negentropy. It seems, however, that such capabilities have evolved to a very high level—still mostly beyond our present comprehension—in the ultra-high connectivity networks of brain.

Certainly the brain has little in common with a digital computer (e.g., see Globus 1995). Emergent self-organization is a kind of change that is far more characteristic of parallel, high-connectivity *neural network* systems than of sequential digital computer systems (Caudill and Butler 1990; Edelman 1989; Globus 1995; Hebb 1949; Kawato, Furukawa and Suzuki 1987; Rumelhart et al. 1986). Thus neural networks seem capable of mediating the proposed assimilative and accommodative activities of an A[sw]. Adaptive *self-organization* by neural networks has been demonstrated in many computer simulation experiments that have already demonstrated self-organizing abilities that not long ago had seemed beyond the capabilities of any machine (Rumelhart et al. 1986; Caudill & Butler 1990). Thus "emergence" has been given reality in the positivistic sense—it has been demonstrated in the laboratory!

All this suggests that the neural network aspects of an organism's structure are crucial for its adaptive behavior and thus for its biological survival as a living system. A neural network learns patterns; given transducers for interacting with a "world," it incorporates that world's patterns—generates a "world-model." This internalized world-model is the system's chief adaptational tool, giving it powers of anticipation, direction-setting and compensatory adjustment that preserve the system as it learns the world and maneuvers itself.

This corresponds quite closely to the theory presented by Hans Flohr (1991) who notes the "activity-dependent self-organization of neural nets, i.e. changes in synaptic connections that are induced by synaptic activation and dependent on the degree of activation" (p. 251). He then proposes a "speculative hypothesis claiming that the occurrence of phenomenal states depends critically on the presence of [these self-organization] processes" (p. 251)—and specifically, that "the

14 Szent-Gyoergyi 1974—and see **Glossary**.

occurrence of phenomenal states depends on the rate at which activity-dependent synaptic changes occur and neural assemblies are formed" (p. 251).

2. Two Other Related Theories

Finally, I wish here to call attention to close parallels between this "CC" perspective on consciousness and that of Bernard Baars (1988).[15] Both theories are based in the notion that consciousness arises out of a complex, dynamic matrix of unconscious automatisms, which Baars refers to as "a distributed system of intelligent information processors" (Baars 1988, p. 86). According to CC metatheory there are vast and complex dynamic interactions between processors going on all the time unconsciously—in the Baars theory this unconscious matrix of processor activity is called the "context" of consciousness: "Contexts are organized knowledge structures" (Baars 1988, p. 164). They are the matrix within which consciousness arises and are always constraining conscious experience, but at the same time are formed and modified by conscious experiences: "A major function of conscious experience is to elicit, modify, and create new contexts—which in turn set the stage for later conscious experiences" (Baars 1988, p. 167). And these contextual changes will generally be adaptive, for "[c]onscious experience is informative—it always demands some degree of adaptation" (Baars 1988, p. 177).

But what is the structure that—with the help of consciousness—is adapting? There is a general parallel, I believe, between what Baars refers to as context hierarchies and goal hierarchies and what I have labeled my *"Anticipating self-world model"* (or A[sw]). As already noted, the business of my A[sw] is anticipation, and my awareness is the continual self-remodeling by which it carries out its business.

So the ideas of CC metatheory correspond very well, I believe—at least in the large, if not in details—with the theoretical perspective put forth by Baars (1988) in his book's *Part III* (called *"The fundamental role of context"*—pp. 135-221). And since he has based that theoretical perspective widely in psychological research from many sources, this gives it a kind of empirical solidity from which I am delighted to borrow.

Comparison with Edelman's work is also interesting. Though Edelman's more recent writings (e.g., Edelman 1989) are not so close to our CC metatheory, some of his earlier theorizing (Edelman & Mountcastle 1978) shows closer parallels. There he says that "consciousness is considered to be a form of associative recollection with updating, based on present reentrant input, that continually confirms or alters a 'world model' or 'self theory' by means of parallel motor or sensory outputs" (Edelman & Mountcastle 1978, p. 95). Though the vocabularies and

---

15 Of course these parallels were gone into in greater detail above in my 1999 essay "➔The Primacy of Self-Organizing Structural Transformation: Can Consciousness Theories Converge?" (**Section 3**).

conceptual backgrounds of our two proposals differ considerably, there are nevertheless major kinds of overlap. The most crucial overlaps may be (i) in ideas of the historical emergence of unpredictable change, and (ii) in the notion that consciousness has something to do with "updating...a world-model" (Edelman & Mountcastle 1978, p. 95).

3. Limitations to Our Cognitive (Predictive) Abilities

Now, how might these notions about mind and consciousness relate to what was said earlier concerning levels of world-structure? What can levels have to do with the efficacy of mind's predictive occupations? I think it may go like this:[16]

(1) **Role of higher-order structure in prediction**
Generalizations about structural levels and predictive efficacy should apply equally well to scientific theory-construction and to the activities of conscious mind—as the functional analogy between them is so close. But something more is also required: For both of them, if we are to more fully predict the behavior of a particular structure x, we need to understand more than that structure itself—we need also to know and understand the encompassing higher-order structure Z of which that particular structure x is a part. That is a consequence of the ordering/coordinative control that the encompassing structure Z has over structure x—that is, of "downward determination" or "downward causation."[17]

(2) **Invisibility of causes**
The implication of downward causation, therefore, is that I can't understand very much of what's going on—what's happening to me, around me, and within me—if I don't recognize the effects of higher-order structure. And it is certain that (beyond very narrow limits) I don't. For we cannot know how much structure lies beyond our awareness—how much beyond our *present* awareness; and how much, perhaps, *forever* beyond our awareness.

(3) **Simplification limits prediction**
Any *simplification strategy*—one which restricts the dimensionality of the attended variables in order to simplify the task of problem-solving—will necessarily exclude higher structural levels from the theory and from mind's comprehension. The unavoidable consequence is that predictive abilities—though perhaps sharpened and speeded for phenomena at lower structural levels—are degraded for those at higher levels. The resulting increased inco-

---

16 Note the first two of the following points were taken almost verbatim from the just preceding 1996 essay (end of the *Section 3*) "➔ Attention and Violence."

17 For more on *downward causation* see 2nd essay in *Summing Up* section, "➔ Something on Holarchic Structure and Downward Causation".

herence between predictive theory and phenomena is a source of entropy—an egregious source, everywhere,[18] of "unanticipated side-effects."

(4) *Widen attention to more fully know world*
Consequently, constriction or dilation of attention is important because a constricted tactic reveals (that is, *maps*) only lower levels of structure, while a more dilated tactic can also reveal (map) *higher* structural levels.

I believe that the points just made are of crucial importance! My habits of simplification blind me to most of "reality," and I remain conveniently unaware of almost all of my mistakes (unintended negative consequences of my actions) and of my inevitably vast ignorance. (The last section of this essay—Sect. IV, below—will go into this more deeply.) Wisdom is in the direction of expanding, opening my attention to include more. To decide wisely—to make choices that more fully anticipate consequences—I should attempt to *enlarge the span of my consciousness*.

4. How Deep?

Such an admonition may sound wonderful, but what good is it? After all, I can sometimes get a glint of where I am—sunk into a rut deeper than I can ever imagine! But mostly I haven't a clue—literally. When all I'm experiencing is the same old stuff, then—if consciousness is transformation—how can I reconcile my continuing consciousness with my stereotypical, seemingly unchanging experiences? So I'm mystified: "Seems like there can be no 'CC' anywhere in my boring life—yet I know I'm *conscious!*"

Looking around yesterday, I was struck by the flood of immediate, real *image*—by the powerful flow of "all-here-there/where-I-am/everything-around-telling-me-my-place." That was immersion in cityscape, and in floods of infinitely variegated persons passing. Yet I was just slightly interested, almost bored—hardly seeing anyone. All was being taken in as nearly empty *signs* orienting me to my *path* and to avoidances of contact or conflict. Then, I asked: "What do I see?" I remembered my new questions about *consciousness, familiarity,* and *inner change.*

Yesterday I asked again how all that dramatic, gripping yet stereotypical, nothing-new perception could have anything to do with inner transformation. How could CC metatheory square with my total lack of awareness of anything new coming to me, and my lack of any feeling that I myself was changing? Could I really be undergoing any significant *restructuring?*

---

18 That is, everywhere outside of the very limited areas in which prediction has been sharpened by the simplification strategy—and since what's outside is vast beyond measure, that means, certainly, very close to everywhere.

Now looking out this window, seeing the bright golden maple leaves in intricate fractal forms waving—what am I "seeing"?

But now (as I look at an object on my desk) this inflow seems to bring me only an awareness of total familiarity. I look at this yellow notebook-cover—and as I keep looking at it, it is still there, unchanged. My awareness also seems unchanging. It seems that my awareness continues only because I am awake, the object is there, and my eyes are open and directed in that direction. It is all a static situation, lacking any kind of novelty, innovation, or creative action. Remembering again my insights on consciousness as *transformation*, I'm again mystified.

But then a sudden new thought: What I now need to remember is exactly that former insight that the depth of my consciousness will almost never enter my awareness—because by the logical structure of my situation, its own depth is a datum to which generally my awareness has no access. Remembering that now, why not shift from my ordinary frame of reference to the one suggested by this insight—so that I will now assume that my present awareness (in this instant) is of gossamer weight even though it necessarily *seems* to have all possible depth?

Look—what if my consciousness *is* exactly that thin? What if most of my mind is now closed to accommodative change? Then in fact very little "novelty, innovation, or creative action"[19] will be occurring there, but I will be oblivious of this poverty; it can only become apparent to me as I remember to look for something more—to seek out some more open connection with that which faces me. What is *there*? Is there more *there* than I'm now aware of?

Asking this question in this moment brings to my conscious awareness a movement of opening that demonstrates how closed I have been. This becomes apparent only with that question. It seems that the asking itself results in the shift.

For the question is itself a realization of *possibility*—a realization that ordinarily is not part of my awareness. This realization brings a shift of attention, so that some bit of attention now can scan for the previously unnoticed. And as something is thereby revealed—no matter how small—the possibility that awareness can expand is confirmed. This confirmation then evokes further questioning, pointing toward unlimited possibilities for expansion.

So:

- There is an inner gesture of opening. More sensation floods in, not only from where I am looking, from what I hear—but also from my intensified feelings of "self" and "body" (sensation that before had been minimal because disregarded). My awareness had been narrowly focused—I attended very strongly to only a very limited region of my predictive mappings—but further, it had been focused in a way that completely excluded from attention nearly everything that was

---

19 What I'd asked about four paragraphs before!

outside its focus. Thus there had been a "point" of awareness, with only a very modest penumbra.

• Now (after that question) the awareness is nearly the same, yet somehow stronger. I am surprised by both its expansion and its intensification. The *point* focus becomes more *global*, and at the same time more vivid. Feelings become vibrant parts of the whole.

And that is opening myself to inner change! I can feel it thus: The difference from the preceding flatness is that now there is *flame;* the paper now is *burning.* (The feeling has some touch of *fire;* certainly, much more is "going on"…)

Thus, **remembering** that opening is possible makes opening possible! (**Attention** is our most intimate means of adaptation.)

C. Emotion and the Biology of Information

And if I do open up my consciousness more—does that matter? What are our adaptational strategies? What are our strategies, individual and collective, for dealing with *information?* These questions are not to be divorced from *emotion.*

With regard to information flow the big question about emotion is how fully I open myself to the implications (the meanings) of each action or happening that vitally concerns me. Will my awareness open to include, so far as possible, all that is relevant? Or will "inconvenient" inputs be excluded?

Pribram's theory of emotion speaks directly to such a question: When disturbing inputs are pushing an open system out of balance, the system can actively maintain its integrity and move back toward better balance through either of two contrasting strategies—or a combination of them:

> Two…mechanisms have been identified: one achieves stability by mobilizing the already available subsystems to exclude input; the other reorganizes the system to include input.
>
> (Pribram 1967, p. 4.)

A preparatory process is one that prepares the organism for further interaction by repairing its perturbed system to its previous stability. A participatory process utilizes perturbation to adapt the system to the current input.…Preparatory operations are conservative and even defensive; they serve to deal with input by de-emphasis and elimination. Participatory operations enhance the effect of input and so serve to increase the likelihood that the system itself will be changed.

...Preparatory processes re-establish continuity at the cost of simplification. Participatory processes tolerate transience for the gain of flexibility through a more complex organization.

In terms of information measurement theory, these emotional processes effect a subtle balance between maximum redundancy, through preparation, and maximum information density, through participation...

(Pribram & Melges 1969, p. 325.)

Anxiety is closely associated with resort to preparatory strategies. Fear tends to narrow consciousness; while love, appreciation, compassion, joy tend to widen it. In general, what are considered "positive" emotions are *participatory* and therefore *broaden* consciousness; while what are considered "negative" emotions are *preparatory* and therefore *constrict* consciousness.

These two emotional operating principles seem orthogonal, leading to vastly different strategies of living. A total commitment to the outer-directed preparatory strategy of simplification is constrictive—promotes helplessness, immaturity, dependence, lack of fulfillment, blaming self-justification, domineering or passive demandingness, and frequently also violence. In contrast, the inner-directed participatory strategy of inclusive elaboration is expansive—promotes self-actualization, or in more ordinary terms, responsible maturation and fulfillment.

Could mental illness have anything to do with the balance between these strategies—perhaps through strong tendencies to favor the constrictive preparatory mode of adaptation, especially in the face of emotional stress? If many of the mentally ill are so guiding their thought and behavior,[20] then that could be where their pervasive patterns of avoidance, denial, and uncooperativeness come from. Commonly, they avoid the admission that there is any way in which they should change, deny that they have any responsibility for their troubles—and therefore remain unwilling to cooperate in changing their situation if that will mean in some way taking such responsibility.

Could this therefore be labeled pathogenesis through life-style *choice?* There exactly is our next big question. For it's not clear how much our emotional response strategy is subject to our volition.

Yet, although by far the greater part of our life-style may not be deliberately chosen, remaining beneath awareness, it can nevertheless with effort and intention sometimes be brought into awareness so that it can be either continued or altered by conscious choice. But for such choice to be meaningful we must have

---

20 From this perspective, refusals to open to the resolution of incoherencies are at the base of the maintained disorder, and therefore are at the root of the "illness."

knowledge of consequences; until we know the costs of our life-style choice, they are likely to remain more accidental than deliberate.

How can these reflections about life-style volition apply to mental illness? Might it be that at some stage of life the mentally ill individual *deliberately* refused to exercise various coping skills—and then that refusal, though once in some degree deliberate, has eventually become *habitual* (that is, mechanical, automatic) so that subsequently it remains entirely beneath awareness?[21]

Such habituated awareness-narrowing (or "attachment") is caricatured by the effects of various central nervous system lesions—these are destructive simplifications that remove brain inputs at a stage earlier than that of preparatory rebalancing.[22]

Certainly, such trained unconcern has pervasive effects seen everywhere in myriad brutalities—for this unconcern allows and generates *violence*. Violence is a short-cut, a reflexive reaction aimed at quickly altering some undesired situation by an invasive plunge into the core of a perceived threat, forcibly altering or destroying it. As consciousness constricts, not only may alternatives to focused force disappear, but further, as the costs of violence fade from awareness, its temptation loses all constraints.[23]

The question, then, is whether over-reliance upon preparatory strategies—which exclude information in order to defend the status quo within the excluding system—is responsible in the long run not only for much personal pain (for this strategy can be taken as the basis for addictive styles of adaptation) but also for vast social evils. Of these, the most savage is war.

However, though those ideas about consequences of alternative life-style strategies may be interesting, they have a lesser significance if I do not in fact have some way to choose freely. If all choosing—all volition—is illusory in that the "choice" I've made has resulted inevitably from previous conditions that may be beneath my awareness, then is there any real meaning to the idea of "wise choice"? What

---

21 Then we would have another instance of life-style pathogenesis where this time the pathology is maladaptive cognitive and behavioral patterns. Mental illness may thus combine accidental with deliberate pathogenesis.

22 For example, after certain cerebral lesions of visual areas there can be an awareness-constriction in which half the world seems not to exist—called "hemi-spatial neglect"—and generally it is difficult to persuade the patient that that they are missing anything. There seems at least a functional analogy with a trained and later self-maintained "brain damage"—in both situations there is loss of responsiveness to categories of information, accompanied by little or no awareness of or concern about those categories.

23 As a Dostoevsky character said "if there is no God, then everything is allowed." This can be understood non-theistically, as referring to loss of consciousness both of broader consequences and of values.

exactly is the reality of choice—what might be the source and meaning of its freedom? That is, how do I have "free will"?

In the next section I will address this question and give what to me now is a highly meaningful understanding of the way in which I am in fact free to choose.

III. Can We Relate Causality to Free Will?

If causal links tie everything together, how can we be *free?* In my first thrust at dealing with this question I can really say nothing about what my freedom is—except that it's a word, an idea, that almost always characterizes my ongoing experience (when I remember to ask about it).

Nevertheless, I can quite clearly and positively see how it is irrational to deny the reality of this experience (reasons why have already been sketched in several places[24]).

A. Size and Significance: Uniqueness

But in giving weight to the reality of free will, I must counter this by asking about its *size* in relation to the vast expanses of determinism that scientists have been exploring, first in the world we perceive to be outside of our minds and brains and more recently in what happens within those *inner* realms. As I look more carefully, I come to understand that though freedom is real, it is also, in an important sense, very small!

Certainly if the field of my volition or *free will* (FW) is my whole field of consciousness, then this *feels* like a vast expanse of freedom. Yet it may be far smaller than it seems; my ordinary frame of reference may be in error since *the depth of my consciousness will almost never enter my awareness.* As noted above, by the logical structure of my situation, a datum to which my awareness generally has no access is its own depth. It may be, therefore, that my present awareness (in this instant) is actually of gossamer weight even though it necessarily *seems* to have all possible heaviness and depth.

So bearing this relative *smallness* of my free will in mind, we can now turn again to its *reality*. For it may be very small yet of the highest significance. Can we give further support to our conviction that "free will" is real? Scientism attempts to reduce all phenomena to deterministic mechanism or (more recently) probabilis-

---

24   First see beginning of essay "➜On Free Will, Holarchic Structure and Downward Causation" in **Section 1**; then also see essays "➜On consciousness: What is the Role of Emergence" and "➜Conscious Beyond Mechanism" in **Section 2** and "➜More on Downward Causation and Free Will" in **Section 3**.

tic mechanism. But there have been increasingly convincing hints that this reductionistic project has inherent limitations—e.g., remember Gödel's theorem...

CC metatheory of consciousness (Atkin 1992, 1994)[25] says this: If consciousness and volitional choice are transformation of structure, then they can be inherently beyond predictionand thus free.

Unlike mechanistic frames of reference, the CC frame requires that the full uniqueness of each instance be recognized and unfolded, and thereby encourages pointed discussions of *particular* free choices. This suggests a more rigorous way to define the meaning of "free": It may precisely correspond with the depth of each conscious action's *uniqueness*. Then the *free* aspect of a free choice is exactly the aspect that cannot be pinned down. This, I propose, is why the idea of freedom cannot be comprehended in our customary way. It is beyond our ordinary analytic approaches to understanding.

B. Consciousness PERCEIVING and Consciousness ACTING

What am I doing and why? Before getting back to probing relations between causality and freedom, I'll try to unravel meanings of choosing, and will look at connections between perception and volition.

Trying to look still more closely at the nature of volitional action, I will first suggest the following:

- A *volitional action* is performed within a certain dimensional framework of consciousness, and is a self-organizing transformation of my A[sw] that serves to resolve some *internal incoherence* of that dimensional A[sw] subsystem.

Taking this notion together with those previously put forth in CC metatheory, we now have not one but two different varieties of self-organizing transformation, both of which are associated with conscious experiencing but in different ways. That is, in addition to the sort of A[sw] transformation that is consequent upon A[sw]'s *predictive* imperfections as a voluntary act unfolds (the kind of transformation labeled "accommodation" that we've discussed at length before), we are now recognizing another sort—this is the A[sw] transformation that *evokes* the voluntary action. These two kinds of A[sw] transformation occur in a cycle, each the product and origin of the other.

A "need" is a symptom of such an internal incoherence. I *need* to resolve inconsistencies (i.e., to "reduce tensions"), and *need* evokes volitional action. The volitional action (or *volition*) that then unfolds will be guided by A[sw] predictions, and any resulting external incoherence (inaccuracy of prediction) will evoke

---

25　See two essays in **Section 2** ("➜On consciousness: What is the Role of Emergence" and "➜Conscious Beyond Mechanism")—see also "CC metatheory" in the **Glossary**.

accommodation. Thus *volition precedes accommodation.* But accommodation also precedes volition, as it is accommodation that (together with volition) has been constructing the structure that acts. Therefore the relationship between them is *intrinsically and continually cyclical*—each is the product and origin of the other. Baars, who writes about it in terms of the *construction of and constraint by contexts* (e.g., Baars 1988, p. 163.), has quite clearly seen this.

Up to this point, we've pictured volition and perception as two interdependent, closely interacting processes. Yet maybe that's not quite right. Could it be, rather, that they are completely inseparable—one process rather than two?

How do we act? Look further at all this. What exactly is the relation between the *action* itself and the *prediction* that is simultaneously generated—and how do both of these relate to the *perception* that characterizes the voluntary act? That is:

- Can A[sw] be not only a consequence-predicting theory, but also a system both of action possibilities and of action-choice mechanisms?

- Then mind would be continually choosing its paths, every moment in every active part—but only where these action-choice mechanisms were undergoing adaptive modification would the choosings be conscious and volitional.

That's my present view. I now strongly suspect that predicting effects of action is *not* separable from action. My older idea that I'd been putting forth before was that prediction was used to *regulate* an action (by providing "virtual feedback") but not to *initiate* it. Initiation, via activation of action-driving automatisms, was assumed to arise elsewhere. Now, however, I'm proposing that it may be exactly the generation of action-predictions that drives action. In that way, action becomes inseparable from prediction. (And if so, then separating them conceptually may be a great cause of problems!) Here's more specifically how this could work:

- Actions are accomplished by the generation of **goal-images** (e.g., see Baars 1988). Generation of goal-image may be functionally identical, in almost all respects, to generation of predictive image (i.e., to generation of "virtual feedback").

- If true, this would mean that voluntary action and perception are "done" in almost exactly the same way—and further, this could mean that they are always being done at the same time.

Are they not, then, a single unified process? Right now, I make my next perceptual instant by a shift into a new body-position and body/environment-configuration. That volition and its perception are a single action—not an "either-or"; not even a "both-and," for it's one unified process: Perception-action, one and the same! Perception is the accommodating aspect of the change-process; volition is its doing aspect.

Mind-transformation (both perceptual and volitional) is not only change of predictive dynamics and algorithms but also (as integral part of this) of incentives, values, motivational context hierarchy, etc. Thus mind-transformation alters not only predictive transfer functions concerning consequences of an action-impulse but also the action impulse itself. Both are components in resolving an incoherency.

C. What are the Constraints of Choice?

Implicitly, volition means *choosing*. That's the locus of my experience of *freedom*—it's inseparable from my experience of volition. And of course the ability to choose implies having *free will*. Here then is something more on free will.

There seem to be two fundamental aspects to my experience of freedom: One having to do with downward causation, the other with non-algorithmic causation. Both concern the intuited absence of certain kinds of constraints.

1. Freedom—Downwardly Caused (FW$_{dd}$)

First, I can feel free of lower-order constraints on my *choosings* (of action, attention, or thought-progression)—can "know" that my choice is determined by something larger than the ordinary compulsions that are predictively modeled by my unconscious anticipatory automatisms. That's the mode of "freedom experience" in which downward causation plays an essential role. It is a negative characterization—what I "know" is various ways in which my decision has not been forced because I know that its determinants originated elsewhere. They originated in the whole that constitutes a higher level of structure. The choice-determinants have not been the parts of this whole—they've been all of it (the whole itself). That is, the choice was downwardly, not upwardly caused. So this aspect of free will (FW) I will label "FW$_{dd}$," for downwardly directed choice.

Here, more specifically, is how *downward causation* ("DC") may relate to our experience that our choices are volitional—to our experience of *free will*. We start with:

(1) ***The action level***

Every choice between alternative actions has a structural level. This is the level at which each of the alternative actions being considered can be fully described and defined. If—as will often be the case—*determinants* of choice between alternative actions come from structural levels *above*[26] the action

---

26 Note that the downward-determining structural levels here referred to are levels of mind's A[sw] structure. Thus, they are levels of mind's *map*, not of the map's *target* (see point I.B(2): "Levels Belong to Maps").

level, then from the perspective of this level (the level of the set of alternative actions that were considered) the choice has been free—i.e., was not strongly determined by structure beneath or at the action level. Therefore

(2) **FW is relative**
The freedom we feel and speak about as "FW" is free from the perspective of this presently inhabited choice-level ('the action level') *in relation* to lower levels of order in that it is not reductionistically determined by phenomena at or causal links from those lower levels. However, this does not mean it is acausal, but rather that it is determined from higher structural levels and thus (paradoxically) is product of those special constraints. In consequence:

(3) **The depth of freedom comes from the height of choice-determinants**
The higher the level of the determinants of my choice, the freer the choice. Since a higher level is inclusive of all levels beneath, this means: The more globally inclusive the determinants of my choice, the greater the freedom with which that choice is made.

This monist way of understanding FW differs from the purely reductionistic way and is more like the dualistic way in that it refers to control of action from above rather than (only) from below. However for the dualist the controlling region is absolutely separated from the controlled region by an ontological chasm; in the proposed monist answer the controlling regions are continuous with—though above and inclusive of—the controlled choice-region.

So again, as in the previous section on mind's predictive abilities, I conclude that:

• Wisdom is in the direction of expanding, opening my attention to include more. To decide wisely—to make choices that more fully anticipate consequences—I should attempt to enlarge the span of my consciousness.[27]

And now I find that this is exactly the direction in which I attain greater freedom. The wiser choice is the freer choice! It seems to me that here my logic and my intuition converge.

2. Freedom—Non-Algorithmic (FW$_{na}$)
The other aspect of my experience of freedom is also about kinds of constraint that are *not* controlling my choice, but now it's that I know that the determinants arose in a manner that can be described as "non-algorithmic." That is, I deduce that the choice was made in a way that cannot be fully characterized by an obedi-

---

27 From end of foregoing subsection entitled "3. Limitations to Our Cognitive (Predictive) Abilities."

ence to rules or to specifiable principles of procedure. This other aspect of FW I will label "FW$_{na}$" for non-algorithmic choice.

From this perspective choosing is made possible by the non-algorithmic component in volitional actions—according to CC metatheory (see previous section) the accommodative restructuring that generates awareness is that non-algorithmic component. Earlier it was put thus: "*Choosing* is the non-algorithmic component in volitional actions—is the accommodative restructuring that generates conscious awareness through the non-algorithmic transformation or creation of algorithmic structure" (from the **Section 1** essay "➔On Free Will, Holarchic Structure and Downward Causation").

A voluntary action is deliberate. In "deliberating" one thinks before acting—thoughts that include "imagining what will happen." One "looks ahead" to anticipate the consequences of the action one is "considering." These are all imaginal thought-processes—in terms of CC metatheory sketched in **Section 2**, they are anticipatory assimilative-accommodative processes unhooked from direct and immediate comparison with present sensory feedback.

This source of freedom in choice can be thought of as play. After all, play can be, in part at least, algorithmic, but its playfulness is beyond algorithm—is the non-algorithmic transformation or creation of algorithmic structure. Our free will is a direct consequence of our ability to play with our maps.

IV. Is Limitless Ignorance Inevitable?—If So, Why?

So I postulate an unending holarchic structure of *world* and see what I need to do to achieve greater unity of *mind*, to enable transitions to higher levels of structure. However, most of the world-levels (that *logic tells me must be there*) remain totally outside of my day-to-day experiencing. The possibilities I sometimes glimpse for improving the wisdom and freedom of my choices (by opening my consciousness to apprehend higher levels of world-structure) remain mostly fantasies—verbal fantasies stimulated by an abstract idea that has no content, no reality of true knowing for me. There is a certain elevation of understanding that I can sometimes rise to—a level of complexity and subtlety above my usual, which I sometimes attain in flashes—and above that: Nothing! Yet as already sketched, my logic tells me that levels should rise endlessly—or at least that there is no evidence that supports the notion of any terminal top-level.

This section will attempt to explore that—it is about stymied understanding. Here I attempt to sketch why we are (usually) unable to experience anything above our present level of understanding.

A. Infinitude of *World's* Structural Levels

(1) New levels of world-complexity are continually being discovered, yet a usual presupposition of "scientism" is that a grand "Theory of Everything" is immanent—a *T.O.E.* by which every phenomenon and every kind of order in the world will be reductionistically accounted for by a relatively simple set of comprehensive laws. (It's what has been called "promissory science.") However, although this dogmatically reductive science assumes that all the levels of order in the world are conceivable now or soon will be, and that they rise only to some knowable, finite limit—in actuality there is no evidence whatsoever of any upper limit to levels of order. Therefore to presuppose the likelihood—let alone the inevitability—of any such final accounting is unparsimonious (e.g., see book's first section, *Section 1*—"Closed and Open Worldviews").

(2) Certainly, any workable human *theory* of the world's phenomena will be based upon a finite set of propositions and will at best account for the phenomena of a finite set of levels of order. But we have no experiential basis for limiting the *world's* levels of order to a finite set of levels (e.g., see essay "➔Minimalist Basis for Expanding Understanding" near the beginning of *Section 1*, above). How then can our theories ever exhaustively portray all the world's levels of order? It is arrogant to assume that we have this capability when there is no evidence for it—and when, further, it could not be demonstrated by any conceivable form of evidence.

(3) A more parsimonious stance does not rest upon the assumption of an ultimate cap to the world's levels of order (again, see essay "➔Minimalist Basis for Expanding Understanding"). Therefore it is reasonable to keep one's worldview totally open with regard to the levels of organization that may ultimately be discoverable in ourselves and our universe, leaving us with the "null hypothesis" that world's levels of order extend upwards without end—infinitely. (E.g., see "No End assumption" in the **Section 1** essay "➔Minimalist Basis for Expanding Understanding.")

That's what I can intuit—and what my reason tells me—about world-structure. But what they tell me about mind-structure is significantly different.

B. Finitude of Mind's Structural Levels

(1) By the continual creation (CC) metatheory, *all the order that we know* is incorporated in our predictive, representational mind—our "Self/World

anticipator" (A[sw]). As already noted above (sections *II.A.* and *II.B.* of this essay), our A[sw] is a proactively predictive network of automatisms; its predictions are continually being tested, and it responds to predictive discrepancies with accommodative alterations of its structure.[28]

(2) Thus (as already noted) our A[sw] is continually transforming itself to improve the adequacy of its predictions. It evolves through the ongoing accommodative transformations of its structure—transformations that are continually being evoked by the inevitable predictive discrepancies or incoherencies. The central hypothesis of CC metatheory is that *consciousness* is the action of this ongoing *accommodation* of A[sw].

(3) It's a story about mind's evolution—where each mind is assumed to be identical to that organism's A[sw]. So a mind is a deterministic apparatus that is continually evolving by non-deterministic accommodative transformation, becoming more and more complex yet (if all goes well) better integrated.

(4) However, though mind thereby becomes an apparatus of tremendous complexity, it is forever finite and therefore is forever limited in the levels of order that it can include. Thus, although world's succession of structural levels may be endless, their accessibility by minds is necessarily limited.

1. Evolution of Mind Must be Sequential

(5) This limitation of mind's access to world's levels of order results not only from the finitude of mind's structural levels but also from the necessity that each individual mind can only develop sequentially (e.g., Wilber 1997).

(6) This in turn is a necessary result of the way in which every mind-level is founded upon and emerges from the level beneath. Thus the order of a given world-level can be incorporated in A[sw] only after the order of preceding world-level is adequately represented.

---

28 What kind of neural substrate could be matrix of *continual creation*? The proposed assimilative and accommodative activities of an A[sw] may be mediated by neural networks (Caudill and Butler 1990; Edelman 1989; Hebb 1949; Kawato, Furukawa and Suzuki 1987; Rumelhart et al. 1986). Hans Flohr (1991) notes the "activity-dependent self-organization of neural nets" (p. 251), and then proposes the "speculative hypothesis claiming that the occurrence of phenomenal states depends critically on the presence of [these self-organization] processes" (p. 251). This of course merits further discussion, which it will receive elsewhere.

2. *"Completeness" in Developmental Progression*

(7) This last requirement is quite stringent. The order of a given level includes all the order in levels beneath.[29] Not only must lower levels of order be adequately represented in A[sw] before the next A[sw]-level can begin to evolve, but this required adequacy of representation must come close to being complete representation. That is, it is a *developmental*[30] process, and before the next level of A[sw] structure can form, the structure of previous levels must be sufficiently developed.

(8) However, by CC metatheory mind-structure consciously evolves by continuing accommodative transformation of A[sw]. Therefore this full development of a level can take place only if the accommodative transformations occurring on that level are—at least some of the time—fully and simultaneously inclusive of all that level's kinds of ordering.

While many kinds of order in mind-structure can be attained through accommodative transformation restricted to relatively small parts of the total A[sw] system, other kinds of order will arise only through accommodative transformation of much larger parts and ultimately of the whole. Thus the structure of a given level develops fully, to encompass all the order present at that level, only when accommodative inclusiveness spans all of that level's order.

Therefore one's attentiveness and consciousness will need to open widely, expanding maximally within the level of understanding that one has achieved so far, before one's consciousness can begin to include content of a higher level. What may be especially crucial here is that this consciousness-expansion should include attaining an awareness of one's previously unquestioned presuppositions. One thereby open's oneself to being "broken open"—to the profoundest kind of inner structural reorganization.

C. How, Therefore, *Understanding* is "Capped"

Looking now at one great *negative* consequence of the above sequence of points, we can perhaps begin to see more clearly why we are (usually) unable to experience anything above our present level of understanding.

• Although world's levels of order continue upwards (see first two essays in **Section 1**, above), world's levels of order are *known to us* through their for-

---

29 Koestler 1978, Wilber 1997.

30 Concerning the necessity for full elaboration of the present level of development before the next level can start to form, more study than I've done so far is need. (But clues might be found in the works of Piaget, Erikson, Koestler, Wilber, etc.)

mative effects on our A[sw]'s evolution—so that we can only know the levels of order that have come to be implicit in its structure.

- Our A[sw]'s structure must evolve sequentially, and the next level of A[sw] order can only begin to form after its preceding levels of order have been completed.

- Further, I hypothesize that for this transition to be possible, the span of our consciousness must be inclusive enough to complete the ordering of our A[sw]'s structure at its present level. And such complete ordering, which must be both encompassing and unitary, will (I believe) require that we bring our unconscious presuppositions into our awareness.

What all this says, then, is that because few of us have come close to accomplishing such a complete[31] ordering of our present level of understanding, we do not yet have the means to even begin to bring into the structure of our A[sw] any order of a higher level, and thus *have no means to experience any order beyond that of our present level.*

However the consequence is deeper than our inability to experience any higher level—for it usually extends also to *inability to even suspect the possibility of the existence of a higher level.*[32] That is why I'm grateful to have discovered a line of reasoning that drives me toward recognizing this possibility, even though my direct experience remains sparse or nil.

I thus begin to see a main conclusion of my essay—the *undeniability* of the existence of "higher powers." The foregoing argument (which can be supplemented and strengthened by others based upon Gödel's Theorem) explains the inevitable invisibility of levels of order beyond those that the individual has already attained. An understanding of this argument may, therefore, provide a rational and, I believe, persuasive basis for believing that most of the world's order must inevitably remain profoundly unknowable and therefore that we are inherently incapable of ever escaping from the deepest kind of ignorance. (From a theistic perspective, such persuasion can undergird a position either of *agnosticism* or of *faith*.)

---

31 The meaning of "*complete*" here includes attributes of being unified, yet fully open to flexible change.

32 If we accept the arguments or the authority of those who tell us of such existence, then we may tentatively or fanatically accept the *idea* of higher levels, even totally in the absence of experiential validation. But otherwise, we must await our own transition to a higher level of consciousness (e.g., see Wilber 1997).

The bottom line of this wide-open worldview is that the existence of levels of order higher than any we can know or even conceive of is **undeniable**.[33]

V. End Thoughts: Free Yet Imprisoned

Finally, a few words on why all this needs to be said. If it's so simple, why has it not always been obvious to everyone? And what's for this writer even more to the point: Why has it been until very recently completely hidden from me? Well—that too is very simple! In fact, it's all (as we shall see) a *tautology* about consciousness. This whole finishing section is about a very fundamental logical limit to insight—i.e., about why it's inevitable that most of us are not so smart as we think we are! (I wonder—does an understanding of this idea help one to wake up?)

It has been suggested (in writings that purport to be based on ancient traditional knowledge) that I become *free* only to the extent that I become *conscious*. But this is inconsistent with most modern psychology that's based upon deterministic assumptions—e.g., "psychic determinism"—because the perennial thought that locates freedom in consciousness seems to predict a great deal of freedom and insufficient determinism.

But does it? What are the relative sizes of "free" consciousness and "determined" non-conscious processes? I will argue (as has also been asserted in some of those aforementioned writings) that our consciousness is far more restricted in its range and depth than we are able to appreciate or acknowledge—and that this blindness to its smallness is unavoidable.

A. Big Without Limit (Unknown Boundaries)

The following is based more upon deductive reasoning than upon any of my direct experience. It's about my surprise at realizing how by logical necessity my conscious experience *must* mislead me *about itself* in a fundamental way.

How do I experience this moment of my world? What do I see? The experienced world is vivid: I am struck by its drama and complexity, its constant surprise—and at the same time by its "ordinariness." So much is going on here! All this grips me! I look at the vast complexity, the overwhelming intricacy of what I am now experiencing—details and subtleties beyond numbering![34]

---

33 Please note that **undeniable** means exactly that and no more. It does not mean that those levels exist, only that it is unreasonable to deny their existence.

34 E.g., see the **Section 2** essay "➔Addendum: Amazing Complexity and Vivid Creativeness of Visual Awareness."

But what is beyond the miraculous, mind-boggling *present experience*—what can lie behind it? Can I have any real feeling for its underpinnings?

I cannot. Though I know a little of the richness of the world and the richness of myself (and of myself in relation to the world), ordinarily (here always behind my dense veil of *familiarity*) I am blind to nearly all of their vastness. Therefore I cannot even suspect what a *tiny* part of the totality of these (potential) riches I am experiencing.

So that's how the space of my worldview is terribly constricted—and it's why (I now begin to deduce) my consciousness must be correspondingly tiny!

- But this in itself is not what causes the problem of my unknowing "sleep"— it is my *total **lack of awareness** of this constriction*. And it seems that exactly this defect in experiential understanding is the logical necessity.

- For is it not in fact a truism that my field of consciousness exactly fills my whole field of consciousness, so that I am not conscious of what is not in my field of consciousness? (Buddhists say that "the eye cannot see itself.")

- That is, I am aware of nothing outside of the field of my awareness. Consequently, I do not *experience* that my consciousness is bounded, for I can know a boundary only by my awareness of something beyond it. Here I cannot have that awareness.

And I therefore cannot directly experience the smallness of my consciousness. Lacking awareness of its boundaries, I therefore lack awareness of the realms outside of its boundaries—i.e., of that with which it is to be compared if we are to actually know its smallness. That is, all the constraints upon my freedom from the vast array of my unconscious automatisms necessarily remain invisible to me.

Of course, if I open myself, I may gain insights—may begin to understand something that before had been entirely beyond my awareness. I may bring something into my field of consciousness that had been beyond the boundary—may, for example, begin to consciously experience some previously unconscious automatism.

So then, the boundary will shift an iota, and the infinitely vast field of unknown happenings will be diminished a tiny bit. But though the size of my field of knowledge may thereby increase significantly, the size of my ignorance is not correspondingly reduced. After all, $\infty - n = \infty$. Thus my general unawareness both of the boundary and of the infinitesimal smallness of my consciousness remains, even though I may have momentarily *seen* a bit of it and thus shifted it a little (—a very little!).

B. The Resulting Assumption and An Alternative

In each moment the field of my awareness is filling up the whole of my known experienced world. Obviously, that which completely fills an unbounded container must be pretty big! That, it now seems to me, has always been my automatic and unchallenged inference. For if my consciousness is experienced as unbounded, then I have no experiential hint that there is any way in which it could be any larger! To have a finite, quantifiable size, a field has to be *bounded*.

The result of this natural inference from my direct experience—that my consciousness is large—is the assumption that my field of *freedom* is likewise large. For I assume the ego-syntonic stance that I am free in regard to all that in the present moment concerns me.

What I will assert, however (like the aforementioned writings that purport to be based on ancient traditional knowledge) is that both my consciousness and freedom are very small—perhaps vanishingly small—most of the time. (I've described just above how the contrary illusion that I usually suffer from is simply a natural consequence of mind's topology.)

* This, then, is my grand limitation—this is my "sleep": I am "asleep" to most of what concerns me; that is, **I am not aware** of it, and **I have no control** over it.

But understanding this I need not conclude—as do behaviorists, logical positivists, and other reductionists—that my consciousness of *freedom of choice*, of *action*, of *will* is merely illusion; perhaps what I consciously experience is quite veridical! What is illusion is the *importance* that I tend to attribute to it. Because this minuscule field of my free choice is all I see, I easily believe that it is all there is, thus large; and while a psychologist can persuade me with arguments that some of my thoughts, feelings, actions are determined in ways of which I am not aware, I am incapable of appreciating the relative dimensions of these two realms.

Thus I now see the following way to a resolution of the philosophical conflict between the acolyte of "free will" and the acolyte of "determinism": They seem to present contradictory worldviews—and they really do in their respective *strong forms* that press their respective points to the limit. But each of them can retreat slightly while continuing to observe from almost the same perspective and continuing to assert most of her/his own original contentions. The person believing in and concerned with "free will" will continue as before to focus upon and to appeal to my *conscious* processes of freely choosing, while the person believing in and concerned with "determinism" will continue to focus upon and to inform me about my *unconscious* determinants.

That is, the first speaks to my consciousness about my consciousness; while the second, likewise speaking to my consciousness but talking about my unconsciousness, describes the vast but dark terrain that *surrounds* my consciousness.

•   The *free will* advocate asks me to use my consciousness in certain ways—and by my "free will" assumption I have freedom to do so, within constraints set by the surrounding terrain.

•   The *determinist* tells me of those constraints, for that is his/her primary focus of interest. And if I listen and understand, then I may better be able to conform my use of consciousness to those enormous unseen constraints by bringing them also into my awareness so that they too become regions of choosing.

Thus each is correct—but their thoughts, problems, intentions and interests occupy different universes. For this real freedom can be tremendously smaller than my perception of it, because of the way I frame my questions about it and the way I structure the space of possibility within which this freedom may have its place.

C. Nature of Imprisonment: Freedom Is Real but Minute

And now I wonder at the persistence and difficulty of this "free-will versus determinism" controversy. Both are right, and each is talking past the other. How can something so simple and obvious have remained so hidden from me? But then, how have I finally managed to uncover something that logic seems to keep hidden?

So there we are: Consciousness and freedom are very small![35] They are almost nothing in comparison with the vast dimensions and complexity of our automatic unconscious mechanisms. Our actions, thoughts, memories, emotions are ever-so-slightly free, under our volitional control—mostly they are pre-programmed in ways that are entirely beneath our awareness. Thus, it is as if we are unknowing prisoners of our own mechanisms with very little actual freedom to choose, yet always entertaining wonderful dreams of our powers to make choices—*dreams* that we ourselves are always and fully able to choose the path we will take in the next moment.

Is that all illusion, or can we in fact actually make free choices? I'm sure we can—but only within strong and complex constraints that are mostly hidden

---

35   This has been gone over before in this essay—at the start of *Sect III* (above) on "Free Will."

from us. So, by this diagnosis, our freedom is real but very small—almost vanishingly small.

That's in the perspective of a moment—a very short-term view. There's another and longer-term perspective—that of a life-history—from which the role of this tiny consciousness and highly constrained freedom is seen as far more central. For (by CC metatheory) the whole structure of mind—of that vast and complex (hierarchically-organized) network of adaptive automatisms—is continually being constructed and reconstructed in the accommodative self-organizing transformations that *are* consciousness.

Thus the whole *imprisoning* network of mechanical constraint, that was spoken of as so vast in comparison with a relatively tiny conscious freedom of choice, has actually been totally constructed by its history of conscious accommodative transformations. (We might say, therefore, that *in the realm of mind "that which is small is creator of all!"*)

Nevertheless, the key idea for me right now is the minuteness of my space of choice in *this* moment, for usually I will have trapped myself within a single dimension. In decision-making, I traffic in dualities. That is, when I direct my actions in a deliberate way—attending to the path I will take, deciding what to change—then ordinarily I see a *choice* between this way or that way, this movement or that movement, between making *either* this change *or* making that change (which might be no change). Thus my consciousness is usually occupied with ('identified" with) a succession of dualities, dealing with them one at a time.

Sometimes though my consciousness and my choice process may be broader—as when I speak or write. Does the breadth of my consciousness, the complexity of my choice-process, rise to the dimensional level indicated by George Miller's (2003) "seven plus or minus two"? This is certainly a far larger scale of freedom, is it not! But in comparison with the myriad possibilities for response that a wider consciousness could offer to me (so my theorizing tells me!) it's tiny too.

So here's the famous prison that I ordinarily do not perceive. Is this not analogous to real imprisonment? The prisoner moves about, takes actions, looks after her/his needs—but only within severely restricted limits. The prisoner has some freedoms, but they are kept within narrow boundaries. I know the boundaries of my prison only as I begin to suspect that something exists outside—that there may be some "outside world." So long as I remain entirely unaware of the existence or possibility of anything else, then what I have here is all and everything, and my freedom therefore appears to me to be very nearly total. After all, within the whole of possible or existing space that I know of, I can go anywhere or—over time—everywhere! That is:

- I wish to deny limitations, to deny that the "outside" exists or is a potentiality, do I not? *How much better to remain comfortable here!*

It's all obvious—yet it hasn't been so obvious to me! *Now* it seems obvious. I *seem* to be proposing and attempting to clarify ideas. But what am I *really* trying to do? I am trying to break something open within myself—to scrape off an invisible enchantment that protects me from the terrors of plunging more completely into my life.

VI. Summary

Here's the over-all perspective—the framework of understanding—that I've arrived at:

I. World's Over-all Structure

Taken together, the related concepts of structural levels and of downward causation may aid us greatly in our desire to understand our world. It is suggested, however, that these are not really ideas about that given world but rather about the ways in which we map it. It is further suggested that world's actual connectivity is so vast as to be beyond full portrayal in any humanly achievable map.

Our map of a higher-order structure is a map of the interdependencies (the linkings) of the components of that structure. For components functionally connected into a coherent interrelationship generate a higher level of order; and it is just that coherent interrelationship between components that is the downward causation "exerted" by the higher level upon the level beneath—the level of those components. Thus a map of world's structure will give me the means to predict the actions of components at a certain level only if it maps not only that level but also levels above that of the components with which I am directly concerned.

II. Knowing World's Structure

My mind is a system of such dynamic maps by which it anticipates my actions and their consequences. Thus, mind is predictive process analogous to a scientific theory used to predict outcomes of known happenings. As my brain reconstructs its processes of anticipation, I am aware of those map-structures—my awareness is postulated to be the process of revising them. That is, the function of my consciousness is the reconstruction of my anticipatory maps. The present structure of these maps, therefore, is the product of the total history of my consciousness.

Yet my ordinary frame of reference may be in error since the *depth* of my consciousness will almost never enter my awareness. By the logical structure of my situation, its own depth is a datum to which, generally, my awareness has no access. It may be, therefore, that my present awareness (in this instant) is of gossamer weight even though it necessarily seems to have all possible depth.

III. Causality and Free Will

I am free to choose but simultaneously am enslaved by causal necessity. My brain is a great complex of deterministic mechanism. Precise causal sequences are everywhere—are parts of tremendously elaborate *networks* of causal sequences. Yet here and there are wisps of patternings that are now in process of self-generating—that are building new transformations of existent mechanism. These are transformations that cannot be accounted for by the mechanical laws that are able (at least *in principle*) to account for nearly everything else—for the occurrence of the *self-organization* is *volition* (and that which self-organizes is the *self*, the agent).

One aspect of volition is the role of *downward causation* in the making of conscious choices. The experiencing of free choice is, of course, experiencing a *lack of compulsion*. Specifically, I can feel *free of lower-order constraints* on my choosings (of action, attention, or thought-progression)—that is, can *know* that my choice in this moment is determined by something larger than the ordinary compulsions that are predictively modeled by my unconscious anticipatory automatisms. This is a freedom that depends for its magnitude upon the inclusiveness of the maps by which I guide my actions—it depends, therefore, upon the contracted or expanded span of my consciousness in each moment during choice-making.

Another aspect (which may not be independent of the first) has to do with the presence of a non-algorithmic component in the accommodative restructuring that characterizes conscious choices.

IV. Known and Unknown—Dimensions of Ignorance

This whole perspective implies that both my wisdom and my freedom, though real and important, are severely limited—in fact, that they must remain far smaller than I can ever realize. For the upwards mapping process upon which my wisdom and freedom depend can never go far enough; the complexity—the dimensionality—of my maps is necessarily limited because human cognitive capacities are limited. Yet (it is hypothesized) there is no upward limit to the dimensionality that would be required to exhaustively map *all* the world's levels of order—these must (for lack of any contrary evidence) be presumed to be infinite. Therefore, if this is true, then the existence of levels of order higher than any we can know or even conceive of is *undeniable*, and the human generation of complete predictions is in principle beyond our reach.

V. End Thoughts—Free Yet Imprisoned

The conclusion, then, is that (1) free will is *real*, yet (2) deterministic mechanisms may account for *nearly* all that happens not only in our world but also in ourselves. This perspective provides a way in which free will can be reconciled with determinism. It's a way that ordinarily I do not see because (though I have *some* vision) the space of my worldview is terribly constricted and my consciousness is correspondingly tiny. Further, my unknowing "sleep" is my total lack of awareness of this constriction. It is asserted that this defect in experiential understanding is a logical necessity, for it follows from the truism: *I am aware of nothing outside of the field of my awareness.* This means I cannot experience how my consciousness is bounded, for I can know a boundary only by my awareness of something beyond it. Yet with my consciousness I don't have that awareness and therefore cannot directly experience the smallness of my consciousness.

That insight enables resolution of the philosophical conflict between the acolyte of "free will" and the acolyte of "determinism" even though in their respective strong forms they present deeply contradictory worldviews. For in actuality *each is correct*, but their thoughts, problems, intentions and interests occupy different universes. The person believing in and concerned with "free will" speaks to my consciousness about my *consciousness*; in contrast, the person believing in and concerned with "determinism" talks about my *unconsciousness*, describing the vast but dark terrain that surrounds my consciousness. Thus the first speaks about how I can use my volitional consciousness in certain ways within constraints set by the surrounding terrain while the second tells me of those constraints and focuses all interest upon them. So both are right, and each is talking past the other. (Amazing how something so simple and obvious had long remained so hidden from me!)

\|/oOo\|/oOo\|/oOo\|/oOo\|/oOo\|/oOo\|/oOo\|/oOo\|/oOo\|/oOo\|/oOo\|/

==<<(([]||[]))>>==((\[^]/\\[^]))==<<((\[^]|_|[^]))>>==((\[^]/\\[^]))==<<(([]||[]))>>==

Now another very short essay written at about the same time as the preceding, in which I recall a traditional facet of scientism—its ancient history in the area of psychological understanding/research—then briefly suggest a new way to fit it all together!

→ *A COUPLE OF THOUGHTS ON SKINNER*

Certainly, our scientific and philosophical frames of reference have for decades been quite different (see Baars 2003). But is this old-new conflict beyond repair? Perhaps not.

I. "Yes! But..."

In Skinnerian Behaviorism (Baars 2003) all behavior is assumed to be exhaustively determined by systems of *upward* causation. (That's the old.) How might I relate this to CC metatheory? (Which I'm now presenting as new.)

Here's how.

Skinnerian Behaviorism is a totally reductionist system of explanation. The reductionists claim (as obvious, indisputable truth) that only upward causation has any scientific explanatory value. Thus all their explanations reduce to effects coming upward from lower holarchic levels. I can accept that such reductionist explanatory systems can be of real value and can help us to greatly increase our understanding of behavior. For certainly there is an enormous portion of our behavior that is in fact determined by systems of upward causation.

So reductionist explanatory systems have great value. It's just the *"nothing but"* that I dispute. I maintain not that the reductionists are wrong, but only that such explanatory methodology cannot be exhaustive.

So here again, in the conflict of reductionists against nonreductionists, is an excellent example of what I was discussing earlier in **Section 1** of this book when I said

> I've come to the following notion: That in fact the proponents of those warring perspectives are all saying valuable truths in what they *assert* positively and specifically (concretely) about our being, the world and our relations to it. But they are making errors primarily in what they each *deny*—more specifically, in their denials of the truths pointed to by the other paradigms.[36]

---

36 In the 1998 essay entitled "→Thoughts on the Progression of Paradigms" (the first essay in **Section 1**).

There I noted that the fundamental hallmark of *scientism* is its dogmatic focus upon negative assertions that extend far beyond the evidence (in fact, beyond any possible evidence). Certainly, that describes exactly how Skinnerian Behaviorism was a kind of *scientism*. It claimed to provide a properly deterministic route to the *only* scientifically possible realm of psychological understanding and dreamt confidently of arriving sooner or later at the messianic "theory of everything"—endgame of the religion of "*nothing but!*"

Therefore, we should acknowledge that this system had value in what it affirmed—it was an adequate explanatory paradigm for ubiquitous processes that are of enormous importance. It's just that they are *not* the whole story—this system therefore was quite wrong in what it so dogmatically *denied!*

The larger picture viewed through CC metatheory may be sketched as follows: Certainly, the upward-causation mechanisms are at work in almost every detail of our life-processes, of our interactions with our environment, and in the neural processes by which we generate and guide our actions. They are at work there and everywhere else in realms of process too numerous to exhaustively mention. However, there's also something else going on that—though it may be small in extent compared to those deterministic mechanisms—is of enormous importance because it is central in how those deterministic mechanisms have *evolved*. It is *accommodation* accomplishing the evolution of mechanical (paradigmatic) systems. (A preceding section, **Section 2**, was all about that.) And that something else—accommodation—is also of enormous importance because it is the source of our possibilities for some real freedom in making choices—therefore it is the source of any capabilities we may have for meaningful rational discourse.

Free choice and rational discourse are vastly important possibilities that are not realized so often as we like to imagine. Nevertheless, they occur, and it is of great importance that our paradigm be capable of recognizing them. That, of course, is where standard Behaviorism, with its addiction to dogmatic denials, has been sorely deficient!

II. Therefore Invert It!

But why deny Behaviorism? We've already observed how there's lots of truth to it! Let's simply add a new component to it, that will be like Skinner's life-work—his "radical Behaviorism"—turned on its head!

In standard Behaviorism, reward and "reinforcement" were (I believe) entirely upwards-causative agents. That's what made Behaviorism completely reductionistic. All behavior was determined by mechanisms from simpler and therefore fully specifiable levels.

But can't we use our "freedom as downward causation" story to generate a less reductionistic Behaviorism by simply adding a new, downwards-oriented component to supplement the standard upwards-only version? For certainly, we experience that decisions and choices guided from above (rather than only from below) can be highly *rewarding!*

In fact, isn't that why I make choices guided from above? In my own conscious experience when I've just made a free choice (but note that such words are forbidden to the strict behaviorist!) I may immediately come to the rewarding conviction that—taking all in all, to the very best of my understanding, guided by the very deepest of my anticipations of consequences—the choice I've made is *best.* If I do, that *conviction* is itself my immediate *reward.* (Of course, such a conclusion may not make any sense to a *true* behaviorist for whom "convictions," "ideas," "thoughts," "mind," "consciousness" are all non-scientific fictions…)

But there is perhaps another slant on guidance of choices by downward causation: If in fact my anticipations were accurate, so that the consequences of my choice are satisfying, *that* is my reward—my "reinforcement. Of course, the expected behavioral effect is that I will tend therefore to seek more such reinforcement again. Given the accuracy of our proposition that this reinforcement was the consequence of choices guided in some way by *knowing* downward causal links, won't such reinforcement then increase my tendencies to continue deliberating from the highest, most open stance of which I am capable?

I hope so!

\|/oOo\|/oOo\|/oOo\|/oOo\|/oOo\|/oOo\|/oOo\|/oOo\|/oOo\|/oOo\|/oOo\|/

I'm ending, finally, with a last glance at the social implications for our world predicament of an open holarchic worldview and CC metatheory of consciousness. Therefore the following will deal with themes already discussed at the ends of the preceding two sections. So what follows draws most of its substance (in its first subsection entitled *"Order and Disorder"*) from the last essay of **Section 2** entitled "➔Reflections on Order and Disorder: Is Consciousness Inherently Negentropic?", and then (in its second subsection entitled *"Violence and Power"*) continues with further development of themes that had been explored above at the end of **Section 3** (in the paper "➔Attention and Violence: How Each Moment of Consciousness Matters" which was presented in Tucson in 1996).

➔ CAN THAT BIG PICTURE HELP WITH MIND AND VIOLENCE?

Understanding what's been discussed till now and what's to follow rests upon my vision of the exact reciprocal relationship between consciousness and mind. If consciousness in fact forms the structure of mind, then it is the detailed history of consciousness that determines the present structure of mind. But reciprocally, the forms which consciousness can now take are restricted by the present structure of mind.

I. Order and Disorder

A. Quick Rise, Long Fall

What about order and disorder, negentropy and entropy? I have suggested that the accommodative transformations that *are* consciousness introduce new coherence to mind's structure, and reduce its discords, both internal and external. It is held that this is equivalent to a reduction of entropy—i.e., to the generation of *syntropy*. But if consciousness is anti-entropic (as suggested here) and is also the construction and improvement of mechanisms, it follows, then, that such construction and improvement of mechanisms must be anti-entropic.

So that's very interesting! It seems that the unconscious mechanisms are entropy-sources while subjective experiencing is an entropy-sink. Unconscious mechanisms—like all mechanisms—can only increase in entropy as their structures decay with use and with *aging*, while conscious experiencing counters this disordering decay by bringing greater order; that is, by generating *syntropy*.

Yet (as was noted earlier[37]) experiencing does this precisely by constructing those very structures that will then run down. It seems that this principal source of negentropy is thereby the source of new fountains of entropy. Is it not a little strange to conclude that the operation of constructing (and improving) mechanisms that are themselves generators of entropy is anti-entropic?

Perhaps that's not so paradoxical as it may at first seem. We might take a metaphor from transformations of state—from phase changes and boundaries between phases—and consider that the regions of self-organizing transformation constitute a moving interface between states, or a "phase transition." We could visualize a "wave front" of creative transformation—a "syntropy wave front." Whatever order now exists is either still in this wave front or is already behind it.[38] While the wave front of active self-organization is now busy creating new order where it is, everywhere else the order that it has created in the past is gradually or rapidly decaying.[39]

B. How Consciousness Might Create Order[40]

Let's try to see a little more precisely how consciousness generates syntropy.[G] Consider the order and disorder of a *mapping* relationship—the more accurately predictive the map, the higher the level of order of the map-territory system. Conversely, defects in predictiveness are elements of disorder—of entropy.

Since CC metatheory specifies that consciousness is the accommodative response to predictive discrepancies,[41] it further predicts that *consciousness creates syntropy* and that the end result of accommodative responses is the overall reduction of the predictive discrepancies that evoke them.

---

37 See especially subsection "Consciousness as Negentropy-Generator" in **Section 2** essay "➔ Reflections on Order and Disorder: Is Consciousness Inherently Negentropic?"

38 Note however that when we're examining mind, any region which is ahead of the wave front (i.e., due to enter it eventually) is at the same time behind it, since at an earlier stage the wave front was its origin.

39 Where it is decaying rapidly, we have acute sickness; where the decay is only gradual, we may have stable and well-functioning mechanisms somewhat degraded, perhaps, by 'aging' and/or chronic illness.

40 This whole subsection is a condensed version of a subsection by the same name near the end of the earlier essay "➔ Reflections on Order and Disorder: Is Consciousness Inherently Negentropic?" (last essay in **Section 2**).

G For meaning of this term here, see **Glossary** at the end of the book.

41 E.g., see **Glossary** entries for "Assimilation and accommodation," and "Virtual feedback."

Let the map be an *inner virtual machine* defined by the virtual-machine laws that specify its behavior. Consciousness is *repair of incoherencies between map and territory* by modifying the mapping process—by modifying the latter's virtual-machine laws in ways that will lessen the incoherence between its predictions and what actually occurs. This resolution of inner-outer incoherence is mind's most intimate and significant response to what is actually occurring. We may consider such responsiveness the most fundamental meaning of mind's *receptivity*.

Inflows to the "A[sw] constructor" initiate and guide the creation and revision of A[sw]. The pre-existing receptive structure—the A[sw]—is tuned to receive experiences that do not differ too widely from those that constructed it. For only then does A[sw] have means to generate predictions. Thus, what it is most easily responsive to can be called "the known." Here the incoherencies that generate consciousness are of modest magnitude. What happens when there cannot be prediction?

Certainly, one needs to be receptive to the "known," but it is just as necessary to be receptive to the "unknown," for it is always impinging as if from everywhere. Thus, not all accommodative updating of A[sw] will respond to discrepancy between assimilative prediction and actual response—some (perhaps much) will respond to inflows that A[sw] in no way attempted to anticipate, or anticipated only very partially.

These are two distinguishable varieties of incoherence. In one instance, we have incoherence between configurations that are at approximately the same level of specificity and detail—though some of the particular specifications and details of the prediction differ from the corresponding specifications and details in the actual occurrence. In the other, the incoherence derives from the *lacks* of specificity and detail in the predictive mapping configuration; the occurrence provides specificity and detail *that had not been anticipated at all*. In the first instance, therefore, there is accommodative *revision* of assimilatory mechanism; in the second instance, *creation* of *new* assimilatory mechanism. (This distinction is important, for it is important to include both kinds of "continual creation" (CC) in our model of consciousness.)

Thus, incoherence is reduced either by *fixing something old* or by *creating something new*. Both result in a more ordered relationship between parts of the larger system, thus in a higher level of order of the system as a whole. Both result in lessened disorder, lessened randomness—and in this sense can be said to have generated syntropy.

In summary: The dynamic, *predictive* coherence of the mapping system with the mapped system is a high level of order that might be specified in terms of a measure like *negentropy* or *syntropy*. Thus consciousness, in continually creating the capacity to sustain this coherence, is thereby in effect creating *syntropy*.

II. Violence and Power

A. Violence as Contracted Consciousness

Now a most difficult question may be tackled. How is it that destructive, disintegrative processes seem to be growing and expanding in hegemony even though human knowledge and wisdom appear to become more and more subtle? Is the syntropic effect of our consciousness insufficient to counterbalance these vast sources of entropy? How is it that love and peaceful connectedness appear to be such weak forces in our world, always trampled over by violence and evil?

What follows will be based upon the idea that ***unconscious mind is necessarily without conscience***. Consciousness requires *empathy*, and empathy must be conscious. Thus unconscious mind will stop at nothing so long as some mechanical sequence—e.g., some set of *algorithmic* rules of procedure—is effectively evoked by the circumstances. Empathy is a deep and open-ended exploration of consequences. Only consciousness can fully explore consequences and then direct actions in accord with foundational values. That is:

1. Unconscious mind is capable of every evil; consciousness is the only real protection.

2. Therefore each gap in consciousness[42] is a gap in protection, and when consciousness is small, protection will be correspondingly small.

Specifically, it is smallness of consciousness—and gaps in consciousness—that make violence possible. The smaller the conscious mind, the less protection from the violence so easily generated by automatic mechanisms—especially when they are operating coherently only locally but are globally in conflict. The hypothesis advanced here is that every gap in consciousness gives permission to some form of violence.

It's interesting how these insights might be connected with those from much earlier times. Why did early monotheists consider idolatry such an abomination? Perhaps because it opened the way to practices that could be labeled "evil" and that entailed violence and even sadism in much the way that, as we've been attempting to describe, Cartesian strategies of consciousness-segmentation seem to generate "negative externalities," many of which have elements of violence and/or "evil." If this is a valid parallel, then the situation that we've been describing might well be tagged "the idolatry of closed and fragmented mind." The idolater says "I know all the answers!"

---

42 Gaps in consciousness are greater when consciousness is more segmented—see "*Segmenting*, **high or low**" in Glossary.

In contrast, the non-idolater says "I know a little…" All is questions—accompanied by awareness of the inescapable operations of our necessary and constrictive rules of attention.

The implication of connecting violence to consciousness-contractions (the contractions of consciousness that we can tag as "idolatry") is that serious evils result from presuppositions that some limited *part* of a situation is its totality—i.e., from taking some part of reality and asserting that it is the whole. We have seen our familiar segmenting strategies of consciousness do exactly that, and we have seen how they set the stage for violence. These strategies generate externalities and ensure that the externalities remain almost entirely beneath awareness. The externalities are ejected from the attended image of reality, not permitted to emerge from the unconscious background.

Again it's my understanding that mistaking a part for the whole is the essence of idolatry. The idolater's world-closure terminates reality in very much the same way that the closures of scientism and other "-isms" do, for (as noted just above) the idolater knows answers beyond the shadow of a doubt. But even more important, the idolater knows all the important questions! That's the essence of "closure."

In contrast the non-idolater remains open to the unknown possibility of vast unplumbed realms of still-unasked questions. This is exactly what I mean by "non-closure." Mind-closure generates the fragmentation of mind and of consciousness which provides the fertile soil for violence, and therefore for "evil."

B. Cost of Local Power

That fragmentation is the entropic deterioration of our mind—the unavoidable decay of every mechanistic system. We'd like to slow that decay. Wishing for peace, love, and tranquility, we greatly favor the generation of syntropy and dislike the opposite entropic movement towards conflict and disorder, aging and dissolution. Thus it is natural to ask: If the mechanisms that are consciously created undergo inescapable entropic degradation, can the consequences of this disordering tendency be minimized?

It has already been indicated how this can be done. Bringing the degrading mechanisms into the field of conscious awareness should, by hypothesis, modify and/or transform them in an entropy-reducing way. But if the degrading mechanisms are of great expanse *in toto* and only a small region of this expanse is brought into conscious awareness, then only a correspondingly small reduction of entropic degradation will thereby be achieved. The more expansive and broadly inclusive the strategy of attention, the better the control of entropic degradation. A global and maximally receptive, responsive consciousness[43] is the means for constructing a more unified, highly-ordered mind; that is, for maximizing both the generation of negentropy in the present moment and the dynamic coherence of the resulting structure.

This broadly inclusive strategy of attention may be a natural human capacity that tends to be submerged by trainings intended to improve competitive strengths. As small children, we originally were totally **open**; then (driven by our culture via our closest relationships) we began to develop a *structure of closures*. As we matured, we became more and more skillful at elaborating this structure while remaining totally unconscious of its existence.

This amounts to constructing a tiny world, enclosing it impermeably through our exclusions. Our "tiny world" is safe—any move to breach its walls is felt as highly dangerous. However within that tiny-world one may not only feel relatively secure but may experience great power, for one does in fact have some remarkable powers *within* it—it is only that from the vaster perspective of the great world, they are indeed hardly significant. But so long as the great world remains entirely beyond one's awareness, one remains blind to this fearsome smallness—one only knows one's exhilarating power within one's tiny world. That's so comforting!

In **real play** (as described by O. Fred Donaldson [1995]) the original openness of childhood can be regained. Original play, he says, is a "practice…of changing our own relationship with the world just as it is" (p. 30). However, "[to] knowingly play with the world as it is, with love and fearlessness, certainly is liberating and exhilarating, but it is also devastating and terrifying" (p. 30).

With this we are brought face to face with the over-arching problem of *"negative externalities."* We see everywhere around us (sometimes within us also) how good intentions lead to bad consequences. What was intended may often bear small similarity to what comes about. We see this in the effects of legislation: What the legislators and those who supported them wished to achieve may sometimes be brought about, but whether it is or not, it is often followed by other results, sometimes far larger than the intended effects, that cause new and more severe problems that then call forth attempts at further corrective legislation. And so on…

Negative externalities can be both overwhelming and never-ending. The same goes for all kinds of "technological fixes"—the unanticipated consequences are often very large, and very troubling. Our environmental disasters bear witness to this.

Now look at this again in terms of *entropy* gains and losses. A general characterization of problem-solutions is that they are attempts to reduce entropy, most

---

43 What Pribram has referred to as a *participatory* strategy of emotional response to a stressor (Pribram and Melges, 1969).

often through creating or modifying mechanisms. We know that the mechanisms created to reduce entropy can be powerful in their effects. But mechanisms that have been produced to *reduce* entropy *locally* can *generate* it *globally*, and the smaller the region of entropy-reduction, the larger the region that is left to entropy generation.

Put in more familiar terms of conscious *problem-solving*, the smaller the region attended to, the simpler the problem that is apprehended. And simplification of the problem gives more possibilities for simple solutions—which is the virtue of focal simplification, and its danger. Certainly a simple solution to a simple problem can often have a very large and rapid effect. However, the magnification of intended local effects will commonly be accompanied by a corresponding—and often even greater and more lasting—magnification of unintended global effects. These magnifications arise because: (i) The limitation of the search for a solution to few variables and few criteria of "success" enables actions that can wreak great shifts in those variables and satisfy those criteria with seeming ease and rapidity; but (ii) the large changes within the field attended to will unavoidably be accompanied by correspondingly large effects in other regions outside that field.

Thus, sustained but very narrow attention can be powerful in finding a problem solution that is highly effective in *lowering* local entropy, but that is also invisibly effective in regions outside of those attended to in ways that can be extremely effective in *raising* global entropy. Those latter effects are the solution's *negative externalities*. Until the problem-solver's attention broadens and opens so that it can enter those initially non-attended regions, the "negative externalities" will continue unnoticed and therefore unabated.

In short:

1. Cartesian (abstractive) techniques for control of attention generate *externalities*.

2. Predictive neglect of externalities allows the local magnification of control—i.e., of "*local power.*"

3. But predictive neglect of externalities also allows choices with tremendously negative consequences—*negative externalities* which are systematically neglected by the abstractive strategy of attention, thus remaining beneath notice.

Local power is not itself illusory; the illusion is the invisibility of its tiny magnitude in relation to larger, globally-encompassing systems. But fuller knowledge of effects requires evaluative procedures that include many more dimensions than the few usually attended to by those focused upon local power. For power may be enormous locally, yet globally insignificant. To remain ignorant of this can be highly gratifying. This is one of the most seductive of all illusions. It supports willful ignorance of "externalities."

I will end this subsection with a paragraph from the essay "→Consciousness, Holarchy, Negentropy" (in the ***Introduction***):

> What needs to be recognized is that Cartesian compartmentalization nevertheless intrudes everywhere because it generates, both individually and in society, an *addictive illusion of power*. We are all victims of conditioned cognitive strategies that fragment our consciousness. We close off our queries by *willful* neglect of contextual questions, thus simplifying our awareness. We thereby gain both security and dreams of power. That is, we achieve apparent power through inattention (the *addictive illusion of power*).

That's why it's very important to gain clearer awareness and understanding of the close connections between violence and power—of their character and their consequences. The gaps in consciousness that permit violence *seem* to magnify personal power. The lives of "victims" can become externalities.

III. To Exit Violence Expand Consciousness

This picture shows how "evil" is, in a deep sense, choicelessness. Not only violent acts themselves, but also the exclusions from experiencing that open the way to violence, are *habitual*—are mostly determined by unconscious automatisms. And exactly because negative externalities in general, and violent actions in particular, are the product of unconscious mechanisms unmodulated by conscious experiencing, the perpetrator truly does not know what s/he has done. This has tremendous consequences. It is the crux of our present pickle!

This situation, of primary drives by unconscious automatisms, makes for great complications in situations of social conflict. But the terrible difficulties arise primarily because *I don't know that I don't know.*

This analysis may give the essence of our violent social confrontations—the main reason they escalate so explosively. Thus, wars may be the necessary endpoints of societal domination by unconscious automatisms insufficiently modulated by conscious accommodation. For the explosion can then be understood also in terms of a positive-feedback escalation of map-territory incoherence—the new entropy variable suggested by CC metatheory.

This story has clear implications for questions about personal responsibility. It says that the responsibility of the person who commits an evil act does not lie in her/his having made that choice, for there was not such a choice. One who commits a violent act will, in general, have neglected both to anticipate and to experience the full range of consequences of the act.

Rather, the person's responsibility is for the prior and present **retreats from choosing** that have predetermined the choicelessness of the evil act in question. For those retreats must have been—over time, if not in the instant of acting—subject to particular choices. In short:

1. Evil is an outcome of continuing choices to avoid choosing.

2. Thus, a violent act is more an act of omission than of commission.

So—as Buddha said—suffering results from *ignorance*. But can one be held responsible for one's ignorance? Our thesis is that one can—that remaining in ignorance may be an irresponsible act.

All this fits right in with our understanding (discussed in subsection at the start of this essay entitled "*Order and Disorder*") that entropy-generation is inherently unconscious, while syntropy is produced by our conscious experiencing. If that's so, then our conscious experiencing is the world's great peacemaker—now pervasive, ubiquitous, and essential to our continued existence. It's just that it's too small, fragmented, everywhere cut into bits. That's how the syntropic trend towards peace is everywhere aborted. Essential—but still insufficient. (Remember again what Buddhists say—that *the main source of our suffering is our ignorance*.)

A first step toward an end to this continuing self-sabotage is to simply *recognize* that conscious experiencing is syntropic and is potentially the doorway to peace. Then we can begin to know the danger that inheres in every stratagem that keeps our consciousness contracted, fragmented. Until we know that, why should we begin any movement towards opening up?

For violence is a manifestation of decaying order—of the rise in entropy to which all mechanical systems are subject. Unconscious mind—a vast network of automatisms—cannot escape such degradation. Counter-movement, by which higher and more integrated levels of order can arise, comes only through the emergence of new and different automatisms. CC metatheory says that this negentropy-generating emergence of new structure **is** *consciousness*. It follows that **to reduce violence, increase consciousness**. How? Greater precision in understanding the vicissitudes of consciousness should help us in knowing how best to do this.

\|/oOo\|/oOo\|/oOo\|/oOo\|/oOo\|/oOo\|/oOo\|/oOo\|/oOo\|/oOo\|/oOo\|/

<\^_^/> <\-_^/> <\^_^/> <*_*/> <\^_^/> <\^_-/> <\^_^/>

Now finally what are central thoughts of the whole book? This very last little essay will attempt to recall some of them—*Summing Up*'s last summary:

➜ *Finally—Main Points in Short*

(1) World's basic structure maps as a holarchy[G] of multiple nested levels (Koestler 1978), each a holon constructed out of (and including) the holons of the level beneath, in a way that yields downward causation as tautological necessity.

(2) My *ignorance is inevitably vast yet invisible.* The dimensionality of my maps is necessarily limited because human cognitive capacities are limited. But if (as postulated) there is no upward limit to the dimensionality that would be required to exhaustively map the world's levels of order, then the existence of levels higher than any we can know or imagine is *undeniable*, and human generation of complete predictions is in principle beyond reach. This perspective can reconcile free will with determinism.

(3) My *mind*[G] is a holarchic system of dynamic maps that anticipate my actions and their consequences. Thus, mind is predictive process, analogous to a predictive scientific theory. Its overall structure is determined in large part by its *belief system*, that is shaped largely by systems of *presuppositions*.

(4) CC metatheory postulates that *consciousness* is the accommodative *reconstruction* of these anticipatory maps, and therefore that the present structure of these maps (i.e., of my *mind*) is the product of the total history of my consciousness. Further, conscious accommodation is continually increasing the dynamic predictive coherence of the mapping system with the mapped system, thereby producing higher levels of order—which means *consciousness is creating syntropy*.

(5) My *freedom* (i.e., *free will*) has two aspects—it arises from the self-organizing transformations that (by CC metatheory) **are** my consciousness and is further amplified when (through downward causation) my choice is determined from a higher level than the ordinary compulsions that are predictively modeled by my unconscious anticipatory automatisms.

(6) Though mind's overall structure is determined by its belief system shaped largely by systems of *presuppositions*, yet unconscious mind's many substructures (or *context hierarchies*: Baars 1988) are almost always almost entirely

inaccessible to our awareness—which knows almost nothing explicitly about our systems of presuppositions.

(7) The *open* person (or culture) is parsimonious of *simplifications* and *maximizes* attention to *context* (Hall 1976); therefore those people form the group of "context-maximizers." In contrast the *closed* person (or culture) is parsimonious of *complications*—tending to *simplify* by narrow localized attention—and *minimizes* attention to *context*; such people can be thought of as forming the group of "context-minimizers."

(8) But mind-closure's local simplifications lessen the unity of overall cognitive structure. And exactly because attention is always under the control of present mind-structure, the overall patterning of that structure tends to perpetuate itself. In particular, a *closed*, disunified, fragmented cognitive structure tends to perpetuate the disunified, fragmented strategies of attention by which this kind of mind-architecture originally arises and is sustained.

(9) Cartesian compartmentalization nevertheless intrudes everywhere because it generates, both individually and in society, an *addictive illusion of power*. It goes thus: I achieve some local control—control that may actually be tiny since enormous surrounding regions escape or even negate that control. Yet exactly because in this moment those non-controlled regions are almost entirely excluded from my attention, the tiny region of control that now fills my awareness is experienced as very large—an illusion I love and wish to preserve! Organizations and societies similarly treasure illusions of power.

(10) From an entropic perspective, *violence* is the rising entropy to which all mechanical systems (including unconscious mind) are subject; since the self-organizing change-of-mind that's postulated to be identical with consciousness tends to raise the overall coherence of the mind-world system, thereby lowering entropy, it follows that **to reduce violence, expand consciousness.**

/\/\/\/\/\/\END\/\/\/\/\/\/\/\/\/\END/\/\/\/\/\/\/\/\/\END/\/\/\/\/\/\/\/

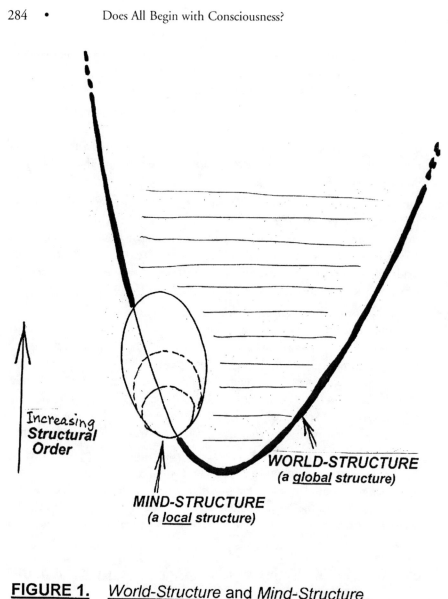

FIGURE 1. _World-Structure_ and _Mind-Structure_
(An Unimaginable 'Size' Disparity):

GLOSSARY

ABBREVIATIONS

CC—*continual creation*

A[sw]—Anticipating self-world model

FW—free will

nNW—neural network

NOTE: In each section below, terms that are defined or discussed in other **Glossary** sections are **bold-italics**.

Anticipating self-world model (A[sw]) (See also ***Mind***)*:* The organism's dynamic (predictive) internal model of itself-in-its-world (Atkin 1992; Craik 1943; Kawato, Furukawa, and Suzuki 1987)—an evolving virtual machine (Dennett 1991) that is the ongoing product of the brain's neural networks (Edelman 1989; Flohr 1991; Hebb 1949; Kawato, Furukawa, and Suzuki 1987). Gray (1995) cites many sorts of data showing that the contents of consciousness "correspond to the outputs of a comparator that, on a moment-by-moment basis, compares the current state of the organism's perceptual world with a predicted state."[1] Originally, I named this concept the "self/world model (sW-m)" (and before that "World-Model")—but have changed to ***Anticipating self-world model, A[sw]***, in order to emphasize the active, predictive motoric function in which *simulation of the activity and effects of the organism's own action systems* is the central source of controlling feedback. Since this is *predicted* feedback, generated by the ***assimilative*** action of the model, it has been referred to as ***virtual feedback***.

The ***A[sw]*** model's predictions are continually being tested, and the ***A[sw]*** model readjusts (that is, it ***accommodates***), modifying its structure to compensate for discrepancies so that its subsequent predictions will be more accurate. It is the ongoing accommodative changes in the organism's ***A[sw]*** that (by ***CC metatheory***) generate conscious awareness (Atkin 1992).

In ***CC metatheory***, the term *"**mind**"* is generally equivalent to A[sw].

---

1   From the paper's abstract.

Assimilation and accommodation: I have used the term **assimilation** to refer to the lawful actions of mind's network of automatisms (or *agents* and *agencies* [Minsky 1986]; modules or *processors* [Baars 1988]; or *schemas* [Neisser 1976]; etc.). Then I use the term **accommodation** to refer to *adaptive changes* in those laws of assimilation—to this adaptive modification of **mind's** network of unconscious automatisms.

Assimilative updating of the **Anticipating self-world model (A[sw])** generates predictive **virtual feedback**. To do this, the A[sw] "virtual machine" performs actions of which it is capable with its *present* **structure**, so that its *configuration* changes in accord with the dynamic virtual-machine laws that define it, and without change in those laws. Why **assimilation**? Because the mind-system that has accurately predicted an event has, in a way, made that event "part of itself" (in the sense, at least, of precisely *mapping* it)—has "assimilated" it. Since the function of the model is predictive, this *change of configuration without change of structure* is all the **A[sw]** updating that is needed when the model's predictions are confirmed.

But mismatches of predicted **virtual feedback** with actually-occurring feedback generate *modifications of A[sw]* **structure**—modification, that is, of the virtual-machine laws governing the ongoing **assimilative** changes in **A[sw]** configuration. This **structure**-changing component will be termed "**accommodative** updating" (or simply, **accommodation**). CC metatheory implies that when we *do* something, much **assimilative** activity is going on, but what we are *experiencing* is the **accommodation**, not the assimilation.

Thus, **assimilation is unconscious and without memory.** It is without memory because, if there is no accommodation, the assimilatory mechanisms remain unchanged. But by **CC metatheory, accommodation is conscious—** and further, is **always making memory,** because ongoing accommodation means that the assimilatory mechanisms are continually changing. That is, by CC metatheory it is this transformation of mechanisms that generates conscious experiencing and is postulated to be required for the generation of memory. (This usage of "**accommodation**" and "**assimilation**" is generally consistent with Piaget's.)

Bridging principle: As Chalmers (1995) notes, to build a non-reductive theory of consciousness the next step after giving consciousness its proper place as a "fundamental property" is to introduce fundamental "*bridging* principles" (Chalmers 1995, p. 15) that will connect the fundamental datum of *experiencing* with something *physically* describable. These principles will then be the foundation of the theory.

But now in giving my own ***bridging principle***, my assertion is different from the formulation that gives rise to the *"hard"* problem. Rather than saying "here is this mechanism, and I assert that it is accompanied by conscious experiencing," I make an inverse statement: "Here is my conscious experiencing, and here are some of its characteristics—I therefore infer that it is accompanied by these *cognitive functions and their underlying mechanisms."* Then our bridge is simply from those cognitive functions to their mechanisms—both of these operationally-definable. Then I have, as Chalmers (1996, pp. 7-10) says, a theory of *awareness*—of functional correlates of consciousness.

Now my task is to *explain why I have chosen this particular function, process, or action*—specifically, *why I have chosen* **accommodative** *self-organization*—as *the objective background of my experiencing rather than something other.* And that I can do by examining what the proposed theory predicts about the properties of my conscious experiences. (See discussion of this question in essay above: "➔Finding the Beginning: Consciousness Precedes Theories," in ***Section 2***.)

Closure **and** ***non-closure:*** In this usage, "mind-closure" (more briefly "***closure***") is a fundamental characteristic of *my presuppositions concerning my maps* of "reality." I attain *mind-closure* by firmly believing that my present map can, through extension and elaboration of details but without other fundamental change, be adequate to *completely* describe the real system that it maps. So ***closure*** *signifies that I view my world-maps either as complete or—at least in principle—completable (and moving toward completion).* Thus attaining closure is *establishing unquestioned* (and unquestionable) *bounds to what I will question.* Then **non-closure** will signify *knowing that my maps must remain forever incomplete*—not just incomplete in detail, but radically incomplete in basic structure.

Note here the intersection of ***closure*** **and** ***non-closure*** with ***local*** vs. ***global*** (which see below). Our discussion and definitions have mostly implied kinds of closure or non-closure that are global: E.g., if as just stated "**non-closure** will signify *knowing that my maps must remain forever incomplete*—not just incomplete in detail but radically incomplete in basic structure"—then this admission of ignorance is *global*, extending out to the "all" and beyond! Then global ***closure*** is simply the obverse—the total denial of that global ignorance. ***Local closures*** would be much smaller—localized denials of particular modes or systems or methodologies—thus ***global non-closure*** is entirely compatible with ***local closures***.

Note that we've also spoken in many places about *mind-**closure*** in contrast with *mind-**non-closure***—i.e., about ***closed mind*** in contrast with ***open mind***.

Continual creation (CC) metatheory (in some earlier writings I'd used the equivalent terms *"CC prototheory"* or *"CC metahypothesis"*—and in certain places also had said that *"CC"* stood for *"consciousness is creation"*): ***CC metatheory*** rests upon an axiom that asserts the identity of consciousness with processes of continual creation—*that consciousness is ongoing emergent change.* The basic idea is that *consciousness occurs when active neural systems self-organize, undergoing essential structural modifications that alter their laws of operation* (see ***Structure***, below). This may be taken as what Chalmers (1995) calls a ***bridging principle*** (see above)—but I feel it's highly significant to take its *directionality* opposite to that implied by him.

CC metatheory proposes that in our consciousness (and that of other higher animals), the main inner structure that is thus re-organizing itself is the organism's dynamic (predictive) internal model of itself-in-its-world, its ***Anticipating self-world model*** or ***A[sw]*** (see above; and see *"**mind**"* below), which anticipates the organism's actions and predictively generates controlling feedback (***virtual* feedback**) derived from SIMULATION *of the activity and effects of the organism's own action systems.*

Downward Causation (DC): *Causative actions of holarchically higher-level structures upon lower-level structures.* Above in ***Section 3*** ("➔ More on Downward Causation and Free Will") the distinction is made between *meta* DC, referring to the effects of self-organizing transformation, that is, to lower-order effects of structural change at higher levels; and *tautological* DC, when the unchanging structural laws of a higher holarchic level causally affect structure and entities at lower levels—this is *tautological* DC.

Here in brief is how the latter works: From the multi-level holarchic world-model (see *Holarchy*, above) it follows that an (n+1)-level structure is *identical* with dynamic coherencies at level (n); and these dynamic coherencies are *identical* with "downward causation" from level (n+1) onto level (n); therefore the *(n+1)-level structure of (n)-level components is identical with downward causation from level (n+1) onto level (n).* This is the *Structure-Causality Identity Postulate* (see below).

Also important is the relation between downward causation and non-algorithmic causality. The evolution both of a field of scientific study and of an individual's cognitive structure progressively enlarges the dimensionality of the maps they are able to construct so that higher and higher levels of structure can be represented. But at any given level of theoretical (science) or cognitive (mind) development, there is some highest represented level of structure. Then any downward causation from a higher, still non-represented level will be "non-algorithmic causality."

External and Internal Incoherence: When the "stimulus" for accommodative adjustment is discrepancy between predicted (virtual) and actual (sensory) feedback from the outer world, this is ***external incoherence***—a concept derived through studies of how animals move, and the means by which they *adaptively* regulate their movements. But what of *thoughts* and *feelings* that may be linked very loosely or not at all with immediate awareness of motor actions? To account for these, we find need for another kind of incoherence, to be called ***internal incoherence***. It originates from inevitable internal inconsistencies between the assimilative actions of different A[sw] subsystems.[2]

Both *external* and *internal* discrepancies (incoherence) will evoke accommodation and thus give rise to contents of consciousness: (1) The former (**external**) incoherences, generated through action, evoke accommodations that modify A[sw] in directions that lessen discrepancies between the predicted and *externally*-generated sensory feedback; in contrast, (2) the latter (**internal**) incoherencies, which are intrinsic to the A[sw], may evoke *internally*-referenced accommodations and thereby generate stimulus-independent thought.

So, ***consciousness*** means the virtual machine[3] is redesigning itself (1) to accommodate its dynamic structure more fully and accurately to the organism's interactions with its world, and (2) to resolve its internal inconsistencies. Presumably, these ongoing accommodations are my experience of every conscious moment. My present Anticipating self-world model would be a complex construction (or virtual machine) that has, in this way, been evolving over my whole previous life. I have constructed my reality by being conscious, and am keeping it current now through the accommodations that are my consciousness in the present moment.

---

2   Subsystems which might correspond to Minsky's (1986) idea of "agents"—or perhaps more precisely, what he calls "agencies" (pp. 23, 25).

3   What kind of neural substrate could be matrix of *continual creation*? The proposed assimilative and accommodative activities of an A[sw] may be mediated by neural networks (Caudill and Butler 1990; Edelman 1989; Hebb 1949; Kawato, Furukawa, and Suzuki 1987; Rumelhart 1986). Hans Flohr (1991) notes the "activity-dependent self-organization of neural nets" (p. 251), and then proposes the "speculative hypothesis claiming that the occurrence of phenomenal states depends critically on the presence of [these self-organization] processes" (p. 251). This of course merits further discussion, which it will receive elsewhere.

Holarchy: World's basic structure maps as a holarchy of multiple nested levels (Koestler 1978; Wilber 1997), each a holon constructed out of (and including) the holons of the level beneath, in a way that yields downward causation as tautological necessity. It means that there are always levels above levels of structure, rising as an endless progression, with each higher level larger than and inclusive of all levels below.

Local* vs. *Global: In general, a local action will have a closed, constricted field, and a global action an open, extended field. If I am characterizing or modifying some extensive system, I may do it either locally by confining my characterization or modification to some relatively small part of the total system, or globally by extending my characterization or modification to the whole system.

In the way I used these terms, they are closely related to another dichotomy, *Segmenting,* high and low (see below). Local vs. global is a dichotomy applicable to the field of power-attributes. Also it may relate conceptually to some present-day use in economics of the terms "micro" and "macro" (e.g., discussions of microeconomics and macroeconomics—of "micro efficiency" and "macro efficiency" of stock market rules and procedures, etc.).

Mind: In CC metatheory this term is given a special, narrower meaning, generally equivalent to that given to *"Anticipating self-world model" (A[sw])*—see above. In this sense, then, "*Mind"* is a complex mapping—an automatic system of dynamic representations—that models all that has been found to be predictable in the actions of the organism and its environment ("world"). It may be analogized to a multi-level scientific theory, which predicts phenomena at various structural levels. "*Mind"* is here meaning the total complex structure of our automatisms (hierarchies of processors or agencies: Baars 1988; Minsky 1986), most but not all of which remains beneath our conscious awareness. So this "*mind"* includes the contents and structure of our consciousness awareness—but is also its far larger unconscious substructure.

***Segmenting,* high or low:** This concerns whether in my moment-by-moment consciousness *segmentation of questions* is a universal strategy and maximized, or is merely occasional and minimized.[4]

---

4   This dichotomy also relates to the *closed* or *open* dichotomy spoken of in **Section 1** in the essay "➔ The Restriction of Ignorance: Inverting the Principle of Parsimony": "The *closed* person (or culture) *minimizes* attention to context (Hall 1976) and is parsimonious of *complications;* such people can be thought of forming the group of 'context-minimizers.' While the *open* person (or culture) *maximizes* attention to context and is parsimonious of *simplifications;* and those people would then form the group of 'context-maximizers.'"

An attention-strategy of *high segmenting* (a strategy of **local** attention) is a narrowly focal strategy that breaks a complex problem into many simpler segments. (Abstract thinking, which largely disregards context, is one form of segmented thinking employing **local** attention—but is *not* the only one.) When one segments one's problem, the data-set relevant to each segment is smaller than that of the problem taken as a whole. Further, the high segmenting attention strategy is likely to leave many mind-regions totally untouched by accommodation—thus to leave many *gaps* in one's fields of consciousness.

In contrast, an attention-strategy of *low segmenting* is a broadly global strategy that attends to the broadest perspective on the whole problem, its setting and implications. With such an attention-strategy of consciousness-expansion (a strategy of global attention), one becomes aware of more of the consequences of one's actions. The amount of segmenting (e.g., high or low) can be considered a *dimension* of attention.

In short, the question of whether my strategy of attention is one of *high* or of *low segmenting* asks whether I usually keep only a small portion of the total situation in my awareness and ignore nearly all else (a local view)—or rather attempt always to see the largest possible view of the situation (a more global view). Note that when I've segmented my problem this will mean that my solution cannot take into account any orders of structure above those accessible in the individual segments. So this is the central point: If I segment my process of problem-solution, then I inevitably degrade the quality of the predictions I will be able to make. I may reach a solution more rapidly and more easily—but it will be, over all, a less powerful solution.

Structure: Here "structure" is used in the following sense: The "set of rules or functions that relate the variables of a system to one another" and provides "'information about the particular way a system is organized...is known as the structure of the system" (Battista 1977, p. 67—emphasis added). "[The] elements of a structure are subordinated to laws, and it is in terms of these laws that the structure qua whole or system is defined." (Piaget 1970, p. 7.) Since structure, then, has to do with predictable pattern of change, consciousness is thereby identified with change in this pattern of change; that is, with meta-change (Watzlawick et al. 1974).

Structure-Causality Identity Postulate: In the multi-level holarchic world-model (see ***Holarchy***, above) the key idea is this: An (n+1) structural level refers to systems of coherence between structures of level (n). These systems of coherence are cooperative dynamic interrelations of those n-level structures. Thus (n+1) structure is a particular way in which "things" at level (n) "work together." So downward causation from the n+1 level—whereby (n+1)-level structures have causal effects upon (n)-level structures—is implicit in the very existence of that (n+1) level. That's because these downward causal effects are the coherence of interactions at level (n)—the very coherencies that define the (n+1) structure. Thus understood, downward causation becomes a kind of tautology, for it simply says in two different ways that "an (n)-level coherence exists." The first time it calls this (n)-level coherence an (n+1)-level structure; and the second time it calls this (n)-level coherence the "downward causation that this (n+1)-level structure exerts upon (n)-level structure." Note that the (n)-level coherence is **not** an *effect* of the (n+1)-level structure—rather, it *is* that (n+1)-level structure.

Also, however, there is a meta-level of downward causation that comes out of ongoing emergent change in structures. We thus define two important and very different species of downward causation (DC), "Tautological Downward Causation" (DC_t) and "Meta Downward Causation" (DC_m). The tautological downward causation (DC_t) of the **Structure-Causality Identity Postulate** is 1st-order (simple) DC—the DC when **structure** is not changing. Wherever there is more than one order of structure, each higher order will relate to lower orders in this way. But structures always undergo change, and change of structure—evolution of new structure, or devolution that degrades structure—brings 2nd order, meta-DC (DC_m). Neuronal systems—brains—seem to be specialized for self-organization (see ***Continual creation (CC) metatheory***, above), so might be world's main locus of DC_m. Higher-order structures will display the simple tautological type of downward causation—that's a logical necessity. But also, as they self-organize and modify their structure—as they grow new structure—they are also manifesting 2nd-order (meta) downward causation.

Syntropy: Convenient abbreviation (see Szent-Gyoergyi 1974) for "negentropy"—or *negative entropy*. Therefore, increasing syntropy in a system means increasing its orderliness. A central implication of CC metatheory is that while mind as complex structure of automatisms is, like any mechanical system, subject to continually increasing entropy, consciousness is reversing that entropic decline and is therefore a principal source of syntropy.

Virtual feedback: The ***Anticipating self-world model, A[sw]*** (see above) anticipates the organism's actions and predictively generates controlling feedback (***virtual feedback***), which is derived from *simulation* of the activity and effects of the organism's own action systems (Atkin 1992). This "pro-active" control-mode has adaptive advantages. Regulation of movements by virtual feedback can increase the rapidity and flexibility of complex yet precise actions since a feedback control strategy is retained, while the feedback time-lags that would be inescapable with control through external feedback loops are effectively eliminated.

The organism that uses reactive updating to keep track of where it is and what it's doing can accomplish this with a world-model and body-image (body schema) that primarily represents geometric information (relative positions and velocities, etc.). But the organism that uses pro-active updating to control its own actions by means of virtual feedback needs this and much more—along with the world-model and body image, a functional representation of the whole motor control loop must be integrated with them, and a wide range of its dynamic capabilities must be functionally represented.

\|/oOo\|/oOo\|/oOo\|/oOo\|/oOo\|/oOo\|/oOo\|/oOo\|/oOo\|/oOo\|/oOo\|/

REFERENCES

Altmanspacher, H. (1995). Complexity and meaning as a bridge across the Cartesian Cut. *Journal of Consciousness Studies*, **1** (2), pp. 168-181.

Anderson, Walter Truett (1990). *Reality isn't what it used to be.* Harper & Row.

Armstrong, D.M. (1981). *The nature of mind.* NY: Cornell University Pr.

Atkin, A. (1967). Selection of sensory information in control of pursuit eye movements. *Psychonomic Science*, **8**:133-134.

Atkin, A. (1969). Shifting fixation to another pursuit target: Selective and anticipating control of ocular pursuit initiation. *Exp. Neurol.*, **23**:157-173.

Atkin, A. (1991). *Alarms and mirrors* (poems). New York: Sea Tree Press.

Atkin, A. (1992). On consciousness: What is the role of emergence? *Medical Hypotheses*, **38**:311-314. <This whole essay is reprinted above, in **Section 2**>

Atkin, A. (1994). Conscious beyond mechanism: Shifting a paradigm. Presented at the 1st conference "*Toward a Science of Consciousness Toward a Scientific Theory of Consciousness*" (Tucson, Arizona). <This whole essay is reprinted above, in **Section 2**>

Atkin, A. (1996). Attention and violence: How each moment of consciousness matters. Presented at the 2nd conference "*Toward a Science of Consciousness Toward a Scientific Theory of Consciousness*" (Tucson, Arizona). <This whole essay is reprinted above, at end of **Section 3** >

Atkin, A. (1998). Being, doing, knowing—A theoretical perspective on consciousness. Presented at the 3rd conference "*Toward a Science of Consciousness Toward a Scientific Theory of Consciousness*" (Tucson, Arizona). <This whole essay is reprinted above, in **Summing Up**>

Baars, B. (1988). *A cognitive theory of consciousness.* Cambridge Univ. Press.

Baars, B. (1997). *In the theater of consciousness: The workspace of the mind.* NY: Oxford Univ. Pr.

Baars, B. (2003). The double life of B.F.Skinner: Inner conflict, dissociation and the scientific taboo against consciousness. *J. Consciousness Studies*, **10**(1): 5-25.

Baars, B. & Newman, J. (1994). A neurobiological interpretation of Global Workspace Theory. In: A. Revonsuo & M. Camppinen (Eds.), *Consciousness in philosophy and cognitive neuroscience*. Hillsdale, NJ: Erlbaum.

Baars, B., Newman, J., & Taylor, J.G. (1998). Neural mechanisms of consciousness: A relational global workspace framework. IN: S. Hameroff, A. Kaszniak, J. Laukes (Eds.), *Toward a Science of Consciousness II: The second Tucson discussions and debates* (pp. 269-278). Cambridge, MA: MIT Press.

Baars, Bernard J., Newman, James B. and Banks, William P., editors (2003). *Essential sources in the scientific study of consciousness*. Cambridge, MA: MIT Press.

Bartlett, F.C. (1932). *Remembering*. London: Cambridge University Press.

Bateson, G. (1972). *Steps to an ecology of mind*. NY: Ballantine Books.

Battista, J.R. (1977). The holistic paradigm and general system theory. *General Systems*, **22:** 65-71.

Battista, J.R. (1978). The science of consciousness. IN: Pope, K.S. & Singer, J.L., (Eds.); *The Stream of consciousness: Scientific investigations into the flow of human experience* (pp. 55-87). New York: Plenum Press.

Battista, J.R. (1982). The holographic model, holistic paradigm, information theory and consciousness. IN: Wilber, K. (Ed.); *The holographic paradigm and other paradoxes* (pp. 143-155). Boston: New Science Library/Shambhala.

Berman, M. (1984). *The Reenchantment of the World*. NY: Bantam (Cornell Univ. Pr., 1981).

Bisiach, E. (1988). The (haunted) brain and consciousness. IN: Marcel, A.J. & Bisiach, E. (Eds.); *Consciousness in contemporary science* (Pp. 101-120). Oxford: Clarendon Press.

Boden, Margaret A. (2006). Of islands and interactions. *Journal of Consciousness Studies*, **13**(No.5): pp. 53-63.

Bohm, D. (1983). *Wholeness and the implicate order*. London & New York: Ark/ Routledge & Kegan Paul, Ltd. <1980>.

Bridgman, P. W. (1927). *The logic of modern physics*. NY: MacMillan.

Bridgman, P. W. (1950). *Reflections of a physicist*. NY: Philosophical Library.

Bronowski, J. (1966). The logic of the mind. *American Scientist*, **54**(1): 1-13.

Buber, Martin (1970). *I and Thou*. New York: Charles Scribner's Sons.

Bunge, M. (1977). Emergence and the mind. *Neuroscience,* **2:**501-509.

Bunge, M. (1980). *The mind-body problem: A psychobiological approach.* New York: Pergamon Press.

Calvin, Wm. H. (1989, *The cerebral symphony: Seashore reflections on the structure of consciousness* (New York: Bantam).

Caudill, M. & Butler, C. (1990). *Naturally intelligent systems.* Cambridge, MA: MIT Press.

Chalmers, David (1995), 'Facing up to the problem of consciousness,' *Journal of Consciousness Studies,* **2**(3): 200-219.

Churchland, P.S. (1986). *Neurophilosophy: Toward a unified science of the mind/ brain.* Cambridge, MA: MIT Press/A Bradford Book.

Clynes, M. (1969). "Precision of essentic form in living communication," in *Information Processing in the Nervous System,* edited by K.N. Leibovic and J.C. Eccles, (Springer, New York), pp. 177-206.

Cohn, C. (1990). "Clean bombs" and clean language. IN: Elshtain, J.B. & Tobias S. (Eds.). *Women, militarism, and war: Essays in history, politics, and social theory.* Rowman & Littlefield.

Combs, A. (1994). Psychology, chaos, and the process nature of consciousness. IN: Abraham, F. and Gilgen, A., *Chaos theory in psychology.* Westport, CT: Greenwood.

Cooper, Ellis (1995)., <Personal communication.>

Craik, K.J.W. (1943). *The nature of explanation.* Cambridge, GB: Cambridge University Press.

Dennett, D.C. (1991). *Consciousness explained.* Boston: Little, Brown & Company.

Donaldson, O.F. (1995). Belonging: That bargain struck in child's play. *Revision,* **17**(4), pp. 25-34.

Dreyfus, H.L. and Dreyfus, S.E. (1986). *Mind over machine: The power of human intuition and expertise in the era of the computer.* New York: Macmillan, The Free Press.

Edelman, G.M. & Mountcastle, V.B. (1978). *The mindful brain: Cortical organization and the group-selective theory of higher brain function.* Cambridge, MA: MIT Press.

Edelman, Gerald M. (1987). *Neural Darwinism: The theory of neuronal group selection*. NY: Basic Books.

Edelman, G.M. (1989). *The remembered present: A biological theory of consciousness*. New York: Basic Books.

Elitzur, A.C. (1989). Consciousness and the incompleteness of the physical explanation of behavior. *J. of Mind and Behavior*, 10(1):1-20.

Emmeche, C., Køppe, S. & Stjernfelt, F. (2000). Levels, emergence, and three versions of downward causation. IN: P. B. Andersen, C. Emmeche, N. O. Finnemann & P. Voetmann Christiansen (Eds.): *Downward Causation. Minds, Bodies and Matter*. (pp. 13-34) Århus: Aarhus University Press.

Flohr, H. (1991). Brain processes and phenomenal consciousness: A new and specific hypothesis. *Theory and Psychology*, 1(2):245-262.

Freeman, W.J. (1990). Consciousness as physiological self-organizing process. *Behavioral and Brain Sciences*, 13(4):604-5.

Gardner, H. (1987). *The Mind's New Science: A History of the Cognitive Revolution*. New York: Basic Books.

Getting, P.A. (1989). Emerging principles governing the operation of neural networks. *Annual Rev. Neurosc.*, 12:185-204.

Glaserfeld, E. von (1984). An introduction to radical constructivism. IN: Watzlawick, P. (ed.); *The invented reality: How do we know what we believe we know?* (pp. 17-40). New York: W.W.Norton.

Globus, Gordon G. (1995). *The postmodern brain*. Amsterdam/Philadelphia: John Benjamins Pub. Co.

Gray, J.A.. (1995). The contents of consciousness: A neuropsychological conjecture. *Behavioral and Brain Sciences*, 18:4, 659-722.

Hall, Edward T. (1976). *Beyond culture*. NY: Anchor Books/Doubleday.

Hebb, D.O. (1949). *The organization of behavior: A neuropsychological theory*. New York: Wiley.

Heschel, A.J. (1955). *God in search of man*. New York: Farrar, Straus & Cudahy.

Hodgson, D. (1995). Why Searle has not rediscovered the mind. *Journal of Consciousness Studies*, 1 (2), pp. 264-74.

Honderich, Ted (2006). Radical externalism. *Journal of Consciousness Studies*, 13(No.7-8): pp. 3-13.

Hooper, J. & Teresi, D. (1986). *The three-pound universe.* New York: Macmillan.

James, William . (1905). The stream of consciousness. *Psychology: The briefer course.* (Chapter XI, pp. 151-175) Henry Holt & Co. (published originally in 1892.)

Jantsch, Erich (1980). *The self-organizing universe.* New York: Pergamon Press.

Jaynes, Julian (1976). *The origin of consciousness in the breakdown of the bicameral mind.* (Boston: Houghton Mifflin).

Johnson-Laird, Philip N. (1988). *The computer and the mind.* Cambridge: Harvard Univ. Press.

Kaplan M.L. & Kaplan N.R. (1991). The self-organization of human psychological functioning. *Behavioral Science* **36:**161-178.

Kawato, M., Furukawa, K., and Suzuki, R. (1987). A hierarchical neural-network model for control and learning of voluntary movement. *Biological Cybernetics,* **57**(3):169-185.

Klopf, A.H. (1982). *The hedonistic neuron: A theory of memory, learning and intelligence.* New York: Hemisphere.

Koestler, A. (1967). *The ghost in the machine.* New York: Macmillan.

Koestler, A. (1978). *Janus.* London: Hutchinson.

Korzybski, Alfred (1941). *Science and Sanity.* NY: Science Press.

Kuhn, T.S. (1970). *The structure of scientific revolutions* (2nd edition). Chicago: University of Chicago Press.

Laszlo, E. (1987). *Evolution: The grand synthesis.* Boston: Shambhala (New Science Library).

Laughlin, C.D., McManus, J. and d'Aquili, E.G. (1990). *Brain, symbol and experience: Toward a neurophenomenology of human consciousness.* New York: New Science Library/Shambhala.

Lucas, C. (2005). Evolving an integral ecology of mind. *Cortex,* **41**(5):709-726.

MacKay, D.M. (1982). Ourselves and our brains: Duality without dualism. *Psychoneuro-endocrinology,* 7(4): 285-294.

Manzotti, Riccardo (2006). A process oriented view of conscious perception. *Journal of Consciousness Studies,* 13(No.6): pp. 7-41.

Marcel, A.J. (1988). Phenomenal experience and functionalism. IN: Marcel, A.J. & Bisiach, E. (Eds.); *Consciousness in contemporary science* (pp. 121-158). Oxford: Clarendon Press.

Maturana, H.R. & Varela, F.J. (1988). *The tree of knowledge.* Boston: New Science Library.

Miller, G.A. (2003). The magical number seven, plus or minus two: Some limits on our capacity for processing information. IN: Baars, Bernard J., Newman, James B. and Banks, William P., editors. *Essential Sources in the Scientific Study of Consciousness* (pp. 357-372). Cambridge, MA: MIT Press.

Miller, G.A., Galanter, E., & Pribram, K.H. (1960). *Plans and the structure of behavior.* New York: Holt, Rinehart & Winston.

Minsky, M. (1988). *The society of mind.* New York: Touchstone/Simon & Schuster.

Mountcastle, V.B. (1978). An organizing principle for cerebral function: The unit module and the distributed system. IN: G.M. Edelman & V.B. Mountcastle (Eds.), *The mindful brain: Cortical organization and the group-selective theory of higher brain function.* Cambridge, MA: MIT Press.

Neisser, U. (1976). *Cognition and reality: Principles and implications of cognitive psychology.* NY: W. H. Freeman & Company).

Newman, J., Baars, B., & Cho, S. (1997). A neural global workspace model for conscious attention. *Neural Networks,* **10**(7): 1195-1206.

Noë, A. & O'Regan, J.K. (2002). On the brain-basis of visual consciousness: A sensorimotor account. IN: A. Noë and E. Thompson (Eds.) *Vision and Mind: Selected Readings in the Philosophy of Perception* (pp. 567-597). Cambridge, MA: MIT Press.

Oatley, K. (1988). On changing one's mind: A possible function of consciousness. IN: Marcel, A.J. & Bisiach, E. (eds.); *Consciousness in contemporary science.* Oxford: Clarendon Press. Pp. 369-389.

Ornstein, R.E. (1977). *The psychology of consciousness.* (2nd edition.) New York: Harcourt Brace Jovanovich.

Pagels, H.R. (1988). *The dreams of reason: The computer and the rise of the sciences of complexity.* New York: Simon & Schuster.

Penrose, R. (1989). *The emperor's new mind: Concerning computers, minds, and the laws of physics.* New York: Oxford Univ. Press.

Piaget, J. (1952). *The origins of intelligence in children.* New York: International Universities Press.

Piaget, J. (1970). *Structuralism.* New York: Basic Books.

Piaget, J. (1976). *The grasp of consciousness.* Cambridge, MA: Harvard Univ. Press.

Pribram, K.H. (1967). Emotion: Steps toward a neuropsychological theory. IN: Glass, D.C. (Ed.). *Neurophysiology and emotion* (pp. 3-39). New York: Rockefeller University Press—Russell Sage Foundation.

Pribram, K.H. (1976). Problems concerning the structure of consciousness. IN: Globus, G.G., Maxwell, G., and Savodnik, I. (Eds.). *Consciousness and the brain* (pp. 297-313). New York: Plenum.

Pribram, K.H. (1986). The cognitive revolution and mind/brain issues. *Amer. Psychologist* 41(5),507-520.

Pribram, K. (1991). *Brain and perception.* Hillsdale, NJ: Erlbaum Associates.

Pribram, Karl H. & Melges, F.T. (1969). Psychophysiological basis of emotion. IN: Vinken, P.J. & Bruyn, G.W. (eds.); *Disorders of higher nervous activity (Handbook of clinical neurology—Vol. 3*: pp. 316-342). New York: Wiley.

Prigogine I, Stengers I. (1984). *Order out of chaos: Man's new dialogue with nature.* New York: Bantam.

Rosenfield, Israel. (1992). *The strange, familiar, and forgotten: An anatomy of consciousness.* New York: Knopf.

Ruddick, S. (1989). *Maternal thinking: Toward a politics of peace.* Boston, MA: Beacon Press.

Rumelhart, D.E., McClelland, J.L., and the PDP Research Group. (1986). *Parallel distributed processing: Explorations in the microstructure of cognition. Vol. 1: Foundations.* Cambridge, MA: MIT Press.

Sacks, O. (1984). *A leg to stand on.* New York: HarperPerennial (HarperCollins).

Schmitt, F.O. (1984). Molecular regulation of brain function: a new view. *Neuroscience,* **13:**991-1001.

Schrödinger, E. (1958). *Mind and matter.* In: combined reprint (1967). *What is Life? & Mind and Matter* (pp. 99-178). (Cambridge: Cambridge University Press).

Seager, William (2006). Emergence, epiphenomenalism and consciousness. *Journal of Consciousness Studies*, **13**(1-2): pp. 21-38.

Searle, John R. (1992). *The rediscovery of the mind*. Cambridge, MA: Bradford/ MIT Press.

Searle, John (1993). The problem of consciousness. *Social Research*, **60**(1):3-16.

Sloman, Aaron & Chrisley, Ron (2003). Virtual machines and consciousness. *Journal of Consciousness Studies*, 10(4-5).

Smith, H. (1976). *Forgotten truth*. NY: Harpers.

Smith, Huston (1989). *Beyond the post-modern mind*. Wheaton, IL: Theosophical Publishing House.

Sokolowski, Robert (1992). Parallelism in conscious experience. *Daedalus*, Winter 1992, pp. 87-103.

Sperry, R.W. (1952). Neurology and the mind-brain problem. *Amer. Scientist*, **40**(2):291-322.

Sperry, R.W. (1980). Mind-brain interaction: mentalism, yes; dualism, no. *Neuroscience*, **5**:195-206.

Sperry, R.W. (1985). *Science & moral priority: Merging mind, brain, and human values*. New York, NY: Praeger Publishers.

Sperry, R.W. (1991). In defense of mentalism and emergent interaction. *Journal of Mind and Behavior*, **12** (2): 221-246.

Strawson (2006). Realistic monism: Why physicalism entails panpsychism. *Journal of Consciousness Studies*, **13** (No.10-11): pp. 3-31.

Szentágothai, J. & Arbib, M.A. (1974). Conceptual models of neural organization (A report based on an NRP Work Session held October 1-3, 1972). *Neuroscience Research Prog. Bull.*, **12**:313-510.

Szentágothai, J. (1984). Downward causation? *Annual Review of Neuroscience*, **7**:1-11.

Szentágothai, J. (1987). The 'brain-mind' relation: A pseudoproblem? IN: Blakemore, C. & Greenfield, S., eds. *Mindwaves: Thoughts on Intelligence, Identity, and Consciousness*. New York: Blackwell. (Pp. 323-336.)

Szent-Gyoergyi, Albert (1974). Drive in living matter to perfect itself. *Synthesis*, Spring 1974, pp. 12-24.

Tani, Jun (1998). An interpretation of the 'self' from the dynamical systems perspective: A constructivist approach. *Journal of Consciousness Studies*, **5** (No. 4-6): pp. 516-542.

Tart, C.T. (1986). *Waking up: Overcoming the obstacles to human potential.* Boston: Shambhala.

Varela, F., Thompson, E. & Rosch, E. (1991). *The embodied mind: Cognitive science and human experience.* Cambridge, MA: MIT Press.

Watzlawick, P., Weakland, Ch.E., & Fisch, R. (1974). *Change: Principles of problem formation and problem resolution.* New York: W.W. Norton & Co.

Weber, R. (1990). *Dialogues with scientists and sages: The search for unity.* London: Arkana (NY: Routledge & Kegan Paul, 1986.)

Wilber, K. (1983). *Eye to eye, the quest for the new paradigm.* Garden City, NY: Anchor Bks., Anchor Press/Doubleday.

Wilber, Ken (1997). *The eye of spirit: An integral vision for a world gone slightly mad.* Boston: Shambhala.

Yates, J. (1985). The contents of awareness is a model of the world. *Psychological Review*, **92**(2):249-284.

Ziman, John (2006). No man is an island. *Journal of Consciousness Studies*, **13** (No.5): pp. 17-42.

\|/\:/\|/\:/\|/\:/\|/\:/\|/\:/\|/\:/\|/\:/\|/\:/\|/\:/\|/\:/\|/\:/\|/

/\/\/\/\/\/\/\/\END\/\/\/\/\/\/\/\/\/\END/\/\/\/\/\/\/\/\/\END/\/\/\/\/\/\/\/

<\^_^/> <\-_^/> <\^_^/> <*_*/> <\^_^/> <\^_-/> <\^_^/>

INDEX

978-0-595-41529-8
0-595-41529-6

Printed in the United States
77935LV00002BA/253-345

9 780595 415298